THE EMERGENCE OF SIN

THE EMERGENCE OF SIN

The Cosmic Tyrant in Romans

Matthew Croasmun

OXFORD
UNIVERSITY PRESS

OXFORD
UNIVERSITY PRESS

Oxford University Press is a department of the University of Oxford. It furthers
the University's objective of excellence in research, scholarship, and education
by publishing worldwide. Oxford is a registered trade mark of Oxford University
Press in the UK and certain other countries.

Published in the United States of America by Oxford University Press
198 Madison Avenue, New York, NY 10016, United States of America.

© Oxford University Press 2017

Library of Congress Cataloging-in-Publication Data
Names: Croasmun, Matthew, 1979– author.
Title: The emergence of sin : the cosmic tyrant in Romans / Matthew Croasmun.
Description: New York, NY : Oxford University Press, 2017. |
Includes bibliographical references and index.
Identifiers: LCCN 2016034114| ISBN 9780190277987 (hardcover : alk. paper) |
ISBN 9780190665272 (epub)
Subjects: LCSH: Sin—Biblical teaching. | Bible. Romans, V-VIII—Socio-rhetorical criticism. |
Personification in the Bible.
Classification: LCC BS2655.S54 C66 2017 | DDC 227/.106—dc23
LC record available at https://lccn.loc.gov/2016034114

For Junia.

May you indeed be counted

ἐν τοῖς ἀποστόλοις.

CONTENTS

ACKNOWLEDGMENTS

This project is as old as my daughter (six years). I submitted the prospectus for the dissertation from which this book is derived just days before she was born; I defended that dissertation days later. In retrospect, so many people have been so important to this project—largely by recognizing the larger vision of what is offered here and not allowing me to get lost in the details.

Yale has been an extraordinary intellectual home for me for many years. Harry Attridge and Adela Collins first introduced me to the joys of biblical exegesis as an undergraduate some fifteen years ago. Each of them has profoundly shaped both my scholarly outlook and the shape of this project, offering penetrating critiques and helpful encouragements along the way. Dale Martin, my doctoral advisor, deserves thanks for having allowed a project like this to take shape in a New Testament program. Dale caught the vision for this project very early on and regularly drew me back to the core insights. Jeremy Hultin provided excellent feedback on drafts and invaluable advice on how to execute a project of this scale. Diana Swancutt's Yale Divinity School (YDS) course on Romans in many ways launched this project.

I must also thank David Kelsey for taking me seriously as a theological thinker, and for several very significant conversations in which the core insight of this project came together. Scott Dolff, too, dared to call me a theologian without snickering. His passion for the theological possibilities latent in this project was eye-opening. Presenting the central idea of an emergent account of Sin to one of his YDS classes was one of the first chances I had to see how this idea might "play" to a theological, even churchly, crowd. (Scott should be credited as the first—though certainly not the last—to introduce me as "an expert in sin.") Steve Davis's seminar on collective memory first got me thinking about collective cognition, which plays a substantial role in the final product here. The ways in which I make use of Judith Butler's work as a valuable source for Christian theology owe much to Luke Grote's thoughts on the same. John Pittard helped me think through some of the larger philosophical issues on which this project touches; the many philosophical infelicities that no doubt remain are due entirely to my stubborn resistance to his wise counsel. My New Testament colleagues in the Yale doctoral program deserve much thanks. Christina Harker, Tyler Smith, Olivia Stewart, Matthew Larsen, and Sonja Anderson: it has been such a joy to work together, to cheer for one another, to genuinely seek one another's best. May we do so for decades to come.

The process of revisions would not have been possible without the dedicated assistance of Brad Gable, who diligently worked through the manuscript, sharpening language, rooting out stubborn errors, and encouraging me to press on. Of course, whatever errors remain are my responsibility entirely. (One such error is my neglecting to note that the translation of 1QS I quote in Chapter 4 came from The Dead Sea Scrolls: A New English Translation, edited by Michael O. Wise, Martin G. Abegg, Jr. and Edward M. Cook [New York: HarperCollins Publishers, revised 2005].) Brad's work would not have been possible without the support of the Yale Center for Faith and Culture, my current intellectual home. Miroslav Volf and Skip Masback have made the Center an extraordinary place to work hard and do theological scholarship for the sake of the common good.

I have to give special thanks to the staff, elders, and community at the Elm City Vineyard Church for their support and encouragement—and for allowing me the privilege of serving this church we've built together. Josh Williams has been the best colleague in ministry a scholar could ask for: patient, inquisitive, and supportive. Gideon Mausner has regularly forced me to keep in the front of my mind the real material consequences of Sin and its dominion in the lives of the poor and powerless.

The various members of the Mory's lunch gathering over the years have provided sharpening, both intellectual and spiritual: Mark Jonas, Caleb Maskell, Todd Kennedy, Ryan McAnnally-Linz, and Ryan Darr. Special thanks in particular go to Ryan McAnnally-Linz for comments on various drafts, checking my translations of theological Spanish, and especially for a late night in a YDS classroom charting out the prospectus, the arc of which remains largely unchanged.

Dave Bruner has been an important colleague and friend from afar, providing input on the large-scale vision of the project. Steve Hamilton has provided thoughtful and enthusiastic feedback on the entire manuscript—the rare bird who asks to read over your shoulder and then does so, voraciously.

One could hardly imagine an environment more conducive to writing than Gary and Joy Best's place in New Brunswick, Canada. The fourth and fifth chapters, in particular, largely came together during an interval that involved two feet of snow, a roaring wood stove, and nightly suppers with my two lovely hosts. Your friendship means so much to me. I will miss Dominion Hill.

My parents deserve thanks not only for fostering a love of learning—and a love of scripture—from a young age, but also for caring so well for their granddaughter during this season, which has made it possible for me to complete my work.

Finally, I am more blessed than any could know to have a wife, Hannah, who loves me, supports me, and believes in what God is doing in and through my work. She has read almost every word I have ever written, heard every sermon (most of them, twice), and, astonishingly, she still loves me. She is this project's number-one fan. Thank you so much.

Matt Croasmun
New Haven, July 2016

INTRODUCTION

This is the network. It's more than advanced technology. It's a living, breathing intelligence . . . It's teaching inventory to learn, allowing content to run faster and helping co-workers work better together . . . Machines have a voice . . . Money works smarter . . . Medical history is brought to life.

—AT&T MARKETING COPY

A recent advertising campaign by the telecommunications conglomerate AT&T (quoted above) employs a remarkable number of personifications.[1] In the mode of persuasive speech, the personifications follow on a thesis statement which provides precisely the kind of framework needed to take these "personifications" as (a certain kind of) ontological claim: the Network is "a living, breathing intelligence." Once this thesis statement is accepted, the cast of mythological characters grows almost without bounds: inventory, machines, money, and medical history. What are we to say about this way of talking? Are these characters *real*?

This manner of thinking about complex systems in our world extends beyond Madison Avenue, and at least as far as Wall Street. Not unlike "the Network," we have "the Market," which is regularly personified in our everyday ways of talking about it: "the Market will correct itself," we say; after all, it is guided by an "invisible hand," which is really just a function of its own constitutive forces. The personification of the Market, like that of the Network, makes for fertile soil for further metaphors (if, indeed, that's all they are). It may seem reasonable enough to dismiss this language as "mere metaphor," but observers from economists to comedians to theologians resist doing so; spiritual or even theological language may be required to describe accurately our disposition toward this Being.[2] Each of these complex systems, which together form the machinery of globalization, are regularly personified, and even divinized or demonized (depending on one's position at either the margins or the center of the emerging globalized world). But our question remains: how are we to think about these entities? Most crucially, we might ask: are they actually *persons*?

Our natural instinct may be to excuse ourselves by claiming we were merely indulging in some lighthearted *personification*—a subspecies of metaphor that involves ascribing personhood to that which manifestly is not a person. Of course, applying this criterion requires a previously established certainty about membership in the category known as "persons." Markets are not persons, we suppose; neither are networks. But what if we come across this discourse while simultaneously entertaining questions about the requirements of "personhood"? What if membership in this category is disputed? It would then be impossible to distinguish between "personification" (of that which is assumed not to be a person) and more straightforward "person-identification" (of that which is, in fact, a person).

These are precisely the challenges the scholar of Paul faces when considering s/Sin in Romans 5–8.³ Scholarship on Sin in Romans is plagued by these questions of how to understand the vivid personal language Paul employs: are we to conceive of Sin as a "real," "personal," power that menaces the human agent; as a social reality, a complex system of human sins; or simply as a literary device that describes to us a feature of individual human agency? Such questions are not going to be answered exegetically. That is the case made in chapter 1. Rather, the questions with which this project is concerned require that we step boldly across disciplinary lines. At minimum, our exegetical concerns will drive us to ask philosophical questions about ontology: What counts as real? How do we decide? By and large, for modern Westerners, these answers have everything to do with a (largely unexamined) scientific world view. So, beginning with philosophy of science, we will find ourselves quickly afloat (but not adrift) on a vast sea of recent scientific reflection on personhood—the body, the mind, and the self.

The vision of Sin offered here is at once scientific *and* theological, social *and* individual, corporeal *and for that reason* mythological. I argue, in good emergentist fashion, *both* that the cosmic power Sin is nothing more than an emergent feature of a vast human network *and* that this power is nevertheless real, personal, and one whom we had better be ready to resist. Ultimately, what is on offer here is an account of the mythological—that is, the world re-mythologized at the hands of chemists, evolutionary biologists, sociologists, anthropologists, and entomologists. In this world, Paul's text is not a relic of a forgotten mythical past, but rather, a field manual for modern living.

1

s/SIN

THE GENEALOGY OF A PERSON(IFICATION)

Unde malum, et quare?

—TERTULLIAN

In Romans 5–8, Sin struts on the stage of the text like a personal being.[1] The "data" are clear on this point. The noun ἁμαρτία (sin) is used as the subject of an active verb no fewer than eleven times in this brief passage.[2] To summarize the familiar language, in these chapters, ἁμαρτία exercises dominion (5:21, 6:12), seizes opportunities to produce covetousness and kill (7:8, 11), revives (7:9), and acts in place of the human agent in whom it dwells (7:17, 20). The noun ἁμαρτία is deployed in personal terms in these chapters. This is not disputed. The question is, rather, whether this constitutes literary "personification," or whether we have instead what we might describe as "person identification."

Literary theorists working on personification agree on one criterion for this distinction: there is an element of self-conscious fiction in "real" personification in the literary sense. Of course, as the need for the qualifier "real" indicates, the term is not universally used with nearly such precision. This drives Jon Whitman to demarcate two different uses of the term "personification":

> One refers to the practice of giving an *actual* personality to an abstraction. This practice has its origins in animism and ancient religion, and is called "personification" by modern theorists of religion and anthropology ... The other meaning of "personification," the one used throughout this study, is the historical sense of *prosopopoeia*. This refers to the practice of giving a consciously *fictional* personality to an abstraction, "impersonating" it. This rhetorical practice requires a separation between the literary pretense of a personality, and the actual state of affairs. ... it is only when the "personality" is a literary fiction separate from the actual condition that we have literary "personification."[3]

Whitman goes on to argue that the literary history of the Roman goddess Fortuna bears this out. Ancient descriptions of Fortuna are not to be understood as personification; one has to wait until the goddess no longer has "a basis in fact" to describe the language this way.[4]

The problem for the interpreter of Paul is that whether Sin as a cosmic agent had "a basis in fact" for Paul is precisely what is disputed. Argument along the lines that Whitman describes quickly becomes circular—and, indeed, holding open the question of Fortuna's status in the minds of various authors both ancient and medieval, one might wonder whether Whitman or his expert on Fortuna, Howard Patch, might be going in precisely such circles.[5] For better or worse, this has not deterred scholars of Paul from arguing one side or the other of this debate. Indeed, the debate goes back at least to a disagreement between figures no less august than Rudolf Bultmann and his doctoral student, Ernst Käsemann. And, indeed, it is with this disagreement that an investigation of the modern debate regarding the person(ification) of s/Sin must begin.

Sin Came Through Sinning: Bultmannian Reduction

In many ways, the argument within the New Testament guild and beyond about the nature of ἁμαρτία in Romans 5–8 constitutes one very long footnote to the work of Rudolf Bultmann. The question for Bultmann is not whether there is a mythological structure to Paul's thought. Indeed, the great demythologizer vividly describes the mythological structure not just of Paul, but of the entire New Testament: "The world picture of the New Testament is a mythical world picture . . . History does not run its own steady, lawful course but is moved and guided by supernatural powers. This age stands under the power of Satan, sin, and death (which are precisely 'powers')." The mythical stage means that the narrative arc of the gospel proclamation is mythological in structure and content. "The proclamation," Bultmann complains, "talks in mythological language; 'when the time had fully come' God sent His Son . . . the demonic powers of the world have lost their power . . . finally, sin, death, and all suffering will be done away."[6]

"All of this is mythological talk," according to Bultmann; there is no denying this. The question, however, is whether *we* ought to understand this language as "figurative" or "realistic"—whether it has a *basis in fact*, as it were. And on this point Bultmann could not be more clear: "Insofar as it is mythological talk it is incredible to men and women today because for them the mythical world picture is a thing of the past." This language may at some point have had some basis in fact in the minds of its writer or hearers, but those days are gone. If for Paul, this was the Fortuna of the ancients, for us it can only be the Fortuna of latter days. We have crossed the great chasm; there is no going back.[7] Bultmann's project of demythologization, then, is in many senses an evangelistic, apologetic project.

He is trying to recover, from the hopelessly mythological New Testament text, a version of the *kerygma* acceptable to the modern reader.

But it is not simply that the Enlightenment has ruined for us a text that was perfectly acceptable in an age gone by. Rather, this mythological text exhibits certain internal inconsistencies. These inconsistencies function for Bultmann much like certain textual *aporiae* function for Origen, encouraging the subtle reader to look for allegory where the "literal" sense of the text simply fails.[8] And, of course, in the work of Whitman as noted above, we've already observed how allegory and personification go hand and hand. Chief among these internal inconsistencies is the contradiction between the account of human beings living under these cosmic rulers, and the account of human agents responsible for their actions:

> Criticism is especially called for, however, by a peculiar contradiction that runs throughout the New Testament: on the one hand, human beings are cosmically determined, and, on the other hand, they are summoned to decision; on the one hand, sin is fate, and, on the other hand, it is guilt; alongside of the Pauline indicative there is the imperative, and so on. In short, human beings are understood, on the one hand, as cosmic beings and, on the other hand, as independent persons who can win or lose themselves by their own decisions.[9]

For Bultmann, this contradiction constitutes nothing less than the contradiction between the mythological significance of the text (the human as cosmically determined), and its existential significance (the human as summoned to decision), which is the central contradiction that the New Testament theologian must adjudicate. And Bultmann has a prescription for this process: namely, demythologizing, which consists precisely in doing away with this cosmic determinism in order to bring the reader to the point of decision. Hence Bultmann's assertion that demythologizing, in its positive sense, *is* existential interpretation.[10]

One witnesses here a trajectory in Bultmann's thought. While pronouncing upon this contradiction *in the text itself* in his essay on "The New Testament and Mythology," Bultmann invokes his apologetic project: "Hence the fact that many words in the New Testament directly speak to us today, while yet others are unintelligible and remain closed to us today."[11] Yet, in the later *Theology of the New Testament*, it is clear that this is no simple matter of what is or is not possible for the modern reader to accept; now, Bultmann attempts to rescue Paul himself from the meaning of his own words:

> The fact that "*flesh*," and through it also "*sin*," *can become powers* to which man falls slave finds especially clear expression in the circumstance that

Paul can speak of both as personal beings as if they were demonic rulers—
but in such a way that we do not have the right actually to ascribe to him
a mythological concept of "flesh" and "sin."[12]

The issue is no longer that Paul is proposing something that modern readers simply cannot stomach. Rather, even for Paul, this language constitutes an "as if." It
is "figurative, rhetorical language," or as he later calls it, "personification," which
we can only assume he means in Whitman's second sense.[13] For all its vividness,
this language nevertheless does not give us a right to ascribe to Paul himself any
mythological concept; this personification cannot have any basis in fact.

So much for the mythology. The related theological concern about human
responsibility, however, is harder for Bultmann to resolve.

> Little as all this constitutes realistic mythology—it is not that, but figu-
> rative, rhetorical language—it is, nevertheless, clear that this language
> stamps flesh and sin as powers to which man has fallen victim and against
> which he is powerless. The personification of these powers expresses the
> fact that man has lost to them the capacity to be the subject of his own
> actions.[14]

The loss of this fundamental human capacity to choose takes control of the
discourse from this point forward. The concept of original sin is the culprit.
Original sin, or at least "inherited sin" (*Erbsünde*), appears, according to
Bultmann, in 5:12–19. Bultmann attributes this idea to a (pre-Pauline) Gnostic
myth. But, Bultmann argues, Paul does better than the Gnostics by insisting
"that sin came into the world by sinning." This, in some sense, is the Bultmannian
slogan against any who would want to find in Paul a "realistic" mythological
entity called Sin. The personification of ἁμαρτία is mere "figurative, rhetorical"
language. Whatever is meant by this personification—whatever truth is to be
unlocked from its mythological casing—can be worked out, for Bultmann, in
terms of transgressions committed by human agents.[15]

Nevertheless, Bultmann is concerned that the language of sin inherited from
Adam makes a viable account of human culpability impossible. "At the most, men
sinning under the curse of Adam's sin could be regarded as guilty only in a legal
sense, inasmuch as law deals only with the guilty deed; but then we would have
no right to speak of guilt in the ethical sense."[16] In order to recover this sense of
guilt—the other side of the coin of existential decision, as it were—Bultmann
suggests we understand this inherited sin in *social* terms:

> At the base of the idea of inherited sin lies the experience that every man
> is born into a humanity that is and always has been guided by a false

striking. The so-derived understanding of existence applies as a matter of course to every man; and every man brings himself explicitly under it by his concrete "transgression," thereby becoming jointly responsible for it. Since human life is a life with others, mutual trust is destroyed by a *single* lie, and mistrust—and thereby sin—is established; by a *single* deed of violence defensive violence is called forth and law as organized violence is made to serve the interests of individuals, etc.—ideas at least hinted at by I Cor. 5:6: "do you not know that a little leaven ferments the whole lump of dough?" So everyone exists in a world in which each looks out for himself, each insists upon his rights, each fights for his existence, and life becomes a struggle of all against all even when the battle is involuntarily fought. So sin is always already here.[17]

Bultmann readily admits that this is not an argument fully fleshed out by Paul himself, but he asserts that later interpreters have a "right" to do so as a way of making plain all that is contained in the Pauline conception of "world," which he defines as the "anti-divine power that controls men . . . the domain of demonic powers."[18]

However, at this point, the demythologizing program resumes, and Bultmann is quick to note that "the 'existence' of these powers has significance only for those who let it be an existence 'for us.'" The ultimate meaning of these "powers" is "unmythological." He summarizes:

> Paul may indeed speak in naive mythology of the battle of the spirit powers against Christ or of his battle against them (I Cor. 2:6–8; 15:24–26). In reality, he is thereby only expressing a certain understanding of existence: The spirit powers represent the reality into which man is placed as one full of conflicts and struggle, a reality which threatens and tempts. Thus, through these mythological conceptions the insight is indirectly expressed that man does not have his life in his hand as if he were his own lord but that he is constantly confronted with the decision of choosing his lord.[19]

In the final analysis, the (only-apparent) realism of Paul's mythology melts away, and we're left with the quintessential Bultmannian existential decision. Indeed, the mythology *has* to take second place, precisely so that this existential decision can take its rightful, primary place in the center. Crucially, Bultmann argues, "the mythological notions of the spirit powers and Satan do not . . . relieve men of responsibility and guilt."[20] This, after all, would render the existential decision meaningless.

From his earlier methodological work to the later theology, Bultmann exhibits a persistent concern with this paradox regarding "man's situation as an enslavement to powers for whose dominion he nevertheless is himself responsible." This is a contradiction which, as insistently as he describes its presence in Paul's text, Bultmann ultimately must resolve in favor of the existential responsibility of the human before the Divine subject. Bultmann has two theological concerns that are driving this interpretation. First, he is concerned that we must preserve some sense of human culpability and ethical responsibility. The greatest fear is that all this mythological talk might "relieve men of responsibility and guilt."[21] This is an especially strong concern for Bultmann, because it pertains to the very heart of his existential program.

The second driving concern is apologetic: if the *kerygma* is inextricably entangled with its mythological packaging, then the gospel can no longer have relevance for modern people. Of this, Bultmann is absolutely certain: "we" can no longer believe this sort of premodern fairytale. As he writes, "We cannot use electric lights and radios and, in the event of illness, avail ourselves of modern medical and clinical means and at the same time believe in the spirit and wonder world of the New Testament."[22] Such strident claims about what is and is not possible for "us" have hardly disappeared. One might compare the much more recent opinion of Troels Engberg-Pedersen: "By far most of Paul's basic world-view, in other words, the basic apocalyptic and cosmological outlook that was his, does not constitute a real option for us now—in the way in which it was understood by Paul."[23]

Nevertheless, as we've seen, even if Bultmann's presenting concern is focused on the modern palatability of the text, his positivist hermeneutic leads him to claim that *even Paul* didn't intend what is apparent on the surface of his text. Ultimately, what is driving Bultmann's interpretation of Paul's own meaning is not Paul's language itself, but Bultmann's sense of what is possible within *his* own modern worldview. That is, to put it in Whitman's terms, Butmann's claim that ἁμαρτία is merely personified in the strict literary sense is justified not on the grounds that Sin did not have a "basis in fact" for Paul, but rather on Bultmann's assumption that Sin as a cosmic power does not correspond to "the actual state of affairs." Because these various mythological characters do not correspond to "the actual state of affairs"—indeed, the entire "world picture" to which they belong has no such correspondence—what we have in the New Testament is instance after instance of mere personification in the literary sense. The emic and the etic are blurred to the point that they can no longer be disentangled. As E. P. Sanders insists: "The seriousness of the position must be realized. Bultmann did not argue that the best we can now do in appropriating what Paul wrote is to translate it into existentialist categories, but that they represent what Paul really meant."[24] On the analogy to the example of the goddess Fortuna discussed earlier, it is as if the later medieval authors' sensibilities have actually changed the character of the original, ancient, "animist" personification.[25]

The language of "animism" is an important nexus here. Indeed, a basic antinomy between "animist" and "Christian" runs throughout much of the theoretical work on personification. Whitman describes "the practice of giving an *actual* personality to an abstraction"—personification in his first sense—as typical of animism; personification in the second sense is typical of more advanced religiosities. We can see the power of this schema when literary theorist Jim Paxson concludes that Whitman's distinction "forecloses the need to look at pre-Christian literary texts that contain fantastic characters and embodiments that are most likely animistic entities."[26] These two senses of personification obtain in two different realms of religiosity: animism or paganism, on the one hand; and Christianity, on the other. One is primitive, the other is advanced; the first is "theirs," the second "ours."

Leaving aside for a moment the historical question of whether Christianity actually marks the turning point between these two different types of personification, it is worthwhile to note that this use of the language of "animism" to marginalize certain religiosities and to foreclose upon certain ways of thinking about Christianity is hardly new. The 1910 World Missionary Conference in Edinburgh, convened when Bultmann was receiving his doctorate in Marburg, described animism as "the religious beliefs of more or less backward and degraded peoples all over the world."[27] In contrast, the Western missionary movement was bringing a more advanced, civilized Christianity to "primitive" peoples and cultures. Bultmann can be seen trading in the same language of primitivity in a footnote to his comment about the incompatibility of modern technology and "mythological" beliefs:

> Certainly, one can say that there are persons today whose confidence in the traditional scientific world picture has been shaken, as well as others whose *primitiveness* qualifies them for an age of mythological thinking. Certainly, there is *superstition* on every hand. But a faith in spirits and wonders that has sunk to the level of *superstition* is something completely different from what it once was as a faith. The question is not what ideas and speculations are present here and there in *unstable minds* nor even to what extent an anti-scientific attitude has become prevalent under the domination of slogans.[28]

Bultmann is aware of the existence of those whose worldview could, indeed, accommodate Paul's mythological narratives as is. But he is absolutely confident that such people are fundamentally backward and essentially marginal. On this point, he is quite in step with the thinking of his day.

The sloppiness of this language—and its embeddedness in an ethically troubling evolutionary paradigm—was exposed by Evans-Pritchard in 1965:

> In these theories it was assumed, taken for granted, that we were at one end of the scale of human progress and the so-called savages were at the

other end, and that, because primitive men were on a rather low techno-
logical level, their thought and custom must in all respects be the antithesis of ours. We are rational, primitive people prelogical, living in a world
of dreams and make-believe, of mystery and awe; we are capitalists, they
communists; we are monogamous, they promiscuous; we are monotheists,
they fetishists, animists, pre-animists or what have you, and so on ... All
this fitted in very well with colonialist and other interests, and some were
prepared to admit that some of the discredit must go to the American eth-
nologists who wanted an excuse for slavery, and some also to those who
desired to find a missing link between men and monkeys.[29]

Indeed, we can see the impact of this evolutionary framework of religious development in Bultmann's language above, describing those outsiders whom he could
imagine thinking differently than "we" do—"we," who couldn't possibly stomach
a "realistic mythology." We have already seen how Bultmann's convictions about
what "we" can take seriously run over into his conclusions about the meaning of
Paul's language—even on its own terms.

But this unbridgeable chasm between "myth" and "metaphor," between animism and monotheism, simply does not exist. Indeed, as certain cultural blind-
ers have gradually been removed, a different relationship has been suggested
between so-called primal religions and Christianity.[30] Gillian Bediako describes
this result "of a new estimation of primal religion ... based on greater empathy
and accuracy of observation" as consisting in large part in "the discernment of
positive affinities between primal religion and Christian faith."[31] The "Christian
faith" of which these scholars write is not the modern European Christianity
of the missionaries, but rather the earliest days of the Jesus movement, in its
encounter with Greco-Roman paganism.[32] And the affinities they find have
much to do with questions of spiritual realism and personification of abstract
concepts.[33]

All this should give us great pause when we see the antitheses of animism and
Christianity deployed once again in the work of Whitman and Paxson, and, even
more so, in the continued use of their theories by contemporary biblical scholars.[34] After all, Bultmann, perhaps, could not have known that his prediction of
a relentless movement of demythologization of necessity going hand in hand
with the propagation of modern technology would be demonstrated as false in
the proliferation of "multiple modernities" in the globalized world of the late
twentieth and early twenty-first centuries.[35] But, reading, as we are—and for that
matter, as someone like Engberg-Pedersen is—from a vantage point when the
prophecy of the death of religion at the hands of an advancing modern hegemony
has been proven false, it is important that the question be asked of Bultmann and

Engberg-Pedersen, when they insist again and again on what "we" can and cannot fathom: "What do you mean . . . WE?"[36]

Nevertheless, in his own cultural context, Bultmann is confident that he can make his point simply by describing, as vividly as possible, Paul's own mythological framework. After all, its implausibility is plain enough. Perhaps Bultmann's description of the mythological language in Paul was, however, in the end, *too* vivid, *too* powerful. Even though he insists that it is no longer plausible for modern man, Bultmann's simple, vivid exposition of the mythological narrative ultimately brings to life the mythological narrative structure of Paul's thought for his readers. One such reader, it seems, was his doctoral student, Ernst Käsemann.

Standing Under Definite Lordship: Käsemannian Dualism

Käsemann, it seems, is quite taken by the "mythological" Paul whom Bultmann described so vividly. Having seen the mythological language in Paul, he is unimpressed with Bultmann's ability nevertheless to produce an account of human individuals existentially responsible for their personal moral choices. Rather, Käsemann is convinced that Paul's mythological language can't be explained away.

> Because the world is not finally a neutral place but the field of contending powers, mankind both individually and socially becomes an object in the struggle and an exponent of the power that rules it . . . Concretely he falls under sin and death. This approach must not be rationalized either moralistically by forcing it into the framework of individual responsibility, guilt, and expiation or causally by associating guilt with lineal descent and making death a natural phenomenon . . . After Adam's fall mankind always finds itself in the power of sin and death.[37]

This is not just metaphorical language. Paul is describing the world as it actually is. To be human is to be the site of contestation for various powers. To be human is to be a node in a network, both social and cosmic. Within the cosmic frame, which Käsemann takes to be primary in Paul's understanding, humanity stands in relation and reaction to the powers of Sin and Death. Against Bultmann, Käsemann insists that for Paul, "the person is not seen primarily as the subject of his history; he is its object and projection. He is in the grip of forces which seize his existence and determine his will and responsibility at least to the extent that he cannot choose freely but can only grasp what is already there."[38] This is the fundamental characteristic of these cosmic powers: namely, that they constrain—or perhaps even eliminate entirely—the freedom of the human "agents" under their control.

Indeed, the conflict between Käsemann and Bultmann is not fundamentally about the character of ἁμαρτία, but rather about theological anthropology, about the character of embodiment. Martinus de Boer explains:

> In short, Käsemann criticized Bultmann for interpreting Paul's notion of σῶμα through the eyes of the modern, essentially Kantian, notion that "the self" can be isolated from the world and is therefore "under its own control, at its own disposal." The Pauline understanding of σῶμα, Käsemann argued, signifies that the human being cannot isolate himself from the world to which he in corporeal solidarity belongs and that a human being is subject to the "rule of outside forces" that determine his existence, identity, and destiny. It is impossible to stand outside such forces, to distance one's self from them, as the Bultmannian interpretation implies. "Corporeality," Käsemann writes in his commentary on Romans, "is standing in a world for which different forces contend and in whose conflict each individual is caught up, belonging to one lord or the other and representing this lord both actively and passively . . . we are never autonomous, but always participate in a definite world and stand under lordship."[39]

Bultmann's existentialist, modern, individualistic concept of self, of σῶμα, will not suffice as a basis for a Pauline theological anthropology. On the contrary, we must recognize that, for Paul, "Anthropology is the projection of cosmology."[40] To be human is to participate in a cosmic struggle, and to be the object of that struggle.

In constraining the real freedom of the human agent, Sin, for Käsemann, is a very literal demonic power.[41] In invoking the language of demons, Käsemann follows in the footsteps of Martin Dibelius. However, for Dibelius, the demonic character of Sin is precisely what makes it *unlike* Death, which Dibelius understands to be a cosmic power.[42] Sin is demonic in the sense that it exercises control over an individual person. Dibelius invokes the analogy of the various possessions in the Gospels, precisely in contrast to the more expansive reign of Death:

> Sin is therefore presented in Rom 6 and 7 as a personal power. It has already been pointed out that the nature of the dominion of Sin cannot be compared to the dominion of Death. Sin has its seat in man; "posession," as described in the Gospels, offers an analogy. So we will be able to describe Sin as a demon that enters into man.[43]

In contrast, for Käsemann, Sin is both: "sin is a power . . . it has a demonic character."[44] When he speaks of s/Sin, Paul "is not speaking primarily of [individual] act and punishment but of ruling powers which implicate all people individually and everywhere determine reality as destiny."[45] Käsemann, as we will see, does at least pause to worry about human culpability for sin. But, his words are largely targeted at a refutation of Bultmann's interpretation, which, as we've seen, was in many senses controlled by an obsession with personal responsibility. Therefore, Käsemann is largely content to describe Sin's cosmic dominion in the strongest terms possible.

These were—and to a great extent in the biblical guild still are—the terms of the argument about the meaning of ἁμαρτία in Romans 5–8. As David J. Southall describes the situation, there are still two poles.[46] On the one extreme, there are those who insist that ἁμαρτία is "merely personified" in the literary sense. Southall describes this position as "The Concrete Action View," in which sin is understood "as specific sinful Actions"; with the nuances noted in the discussion above, we are justified in placing Bultmann at this pole.[47] At the other extreme, there are those who take ἁμαρτία to be personified in Whitman's first, "animistic" sense. Southall describes this position as "The Demonic Entity View," in which ἁμαρτία is understood "as a superhuman being."[48] As I've shown, Dibelius and Käsemann would go on this end of the spectrum, though Käsemann's view of the dominion of Sin is more expansive and more typical of those on the far end of the spectrum. In the middle, Southall puts a majority of scholars who simply talk about "personified sin" without very much precision.[49] This last group is of least interest to me—because my sense is that the way forward in this matter is not through forging a "middle way," but rather through adopting a framework in which both extremes can be occupied simultaneously, because both extremes recognize important features of the Pauline text.

After all, there is much that both Bultmann's and Käsemann's positions have going for them. Bultmann, for his part, is certainly correct that ἁμαρτία for Paul—even in Romans 5–8—still has to do with individual acts. The evidence of Romans 5:12–21 (with which Käsemann struggles considerably) makes it clear that Bultmann's basic slogan has to be accepted: ἁμαρτία—whatever it is—"came into the world by sinning." "Sin came into the world through one man" (v. 12) because of his *deed* in "transgression" of Divine mandate (vv. 14, 15, 17). Sin's consequence, Death, has "spread to all because all have sinned." Even Käsemann can't construe the text other than to decide that there is, in the last part of verse 12, an "undeniable individualizing." Käsemann, for his part, tries to understand this the other way around: that is, that the individual human agent's experience of guilt through his or her own sinful actions "gives depth to what is said about the scope of the [cosmic] disaster."[50] The cosmic disaster—the enslavement to the powers—is fundamental for Käsemann. The individual human agent's acts of sin are only a consequence of this enslavement. I take it that this makes good sense of the subject's experience of an inability to accomplish what the will intends in Romans 7, but not of the apparent causal power of Adam's transgression in 5:12–21. Bultmann's slogan has to be admitted.

But Käsemann and the scholars who have followed him also must be right: ἁμαρτία is much more than just sinful actions, especially in Romans 5–8. To read against this mythology is to invent a "real Paul" who can argue against *the words of Paul*. Bultmann as much as admits this, but he has his reasons, and they are theological. Some of those theological concerns turn on antiquated ideas of evolutionary religious development, as I have shown. But others of those theological concerns are worth taking quite seriously, even simply at the level of critical exegesis—because some of Bultmann's theological concerns turn on something like the "internal consistency" of Paul's own language. These, I take it, belong to the theological species of a general type of check that we often employ in order to see if we've understood a text rightly: Does it cohere? Does it make sense?

Primary among this type of theological concern in Bultmann is the concern with *culpability*. Again, Romans 5:12 is the key text: "Therefore, just as through one man Sin came into the world and through Sin came death, and so death spread to all people, because all sinned." There is an apparent contradiction here, and Bultmann is not wrong to point it out, and not wrong to insist that we have not understood Paul until we have some understanding of how this apparent contradiction operates—even if it cannot be resolved. All to say, Bultmann is right in his identification of a problem to be solved in Paul's conception of ἁμαρτία here. Are human beings guilty of sins, as 5:12d suggests ("death spread to all because all have sinned"), or helpless against the cosmic tyrant Sin, as Paul indeed seems to describe the situation, and as Käsemann insists?

What won't do is simply to decide one way or the other, as Bultmann does. For Bultmann, the language of man's apparent subjection to cosmic powers has itself to be subjected to a dominant motif of individual responsibility and culpability for sin. Käsemann rightly takes Bultmann to task for this. After all, Käsemann points out, if one had to take one or the other side, as it were, within Romans the weight of the evidence is quite clear: Paul's emphasis is on the cosmic determination of the powers of Sin and Death. But Käsemann's account leaves Paul's contradictory picture of human culpability more or less as we found it: "Paul's concern unites what seems to us to be a logical contradiction and what does in fact become antithetical in Judaism: No one commences his own history and no one can be exonerated." [51] The problem is that Käsemann never makes it clear how it is that this merely "seems to us" to be a logical contradiction. Käsemann's reading leaves us, instead, with the suspicion that this *is* a logical contradiction in Paul—a contradiction of the type which, I suggested above, ought to give us pause not just in the constructive theological mode, but in the exegetical mode as well. Granted, it is possible that Paul is simply at odds with himself here. But we would have to prefer a reading that can make sense of all of Paul's language here— not just one "side" of it or the other. We would prefer a reading that can hold together both sides of the contradiction, about which Bultmann and Käsemann more or less choose sides: that is, that human agents are subject to a power, Sin, that constrains their freedom to act; *and* that they are nevertheless responsible for their sin. Liberationist readers move us in the direction of being able to hold these two "sides" of the debate in tension, though not without introducing their own difficulties and limitations.

Sinful Institutions: Liberationist Emergence?

Latin American liberationist perspectives have largely been ignored by scholars studying the debate about the nature of ἁμαρτία in Paul within the biblical guild. The majority of the Latin American output of liberation theology has not been biblical interpretation, at least not of a variety easily recognized as such by the Global North and, by and large, it has been outside of the "mainstream" of Western biblical scholarship.[52] Furthermore, the biblical interpretation that has been produced by the liberationist school has, for the most part, been focused on the Gospels—Paul having been understood quite often as part of the political problem, rather than as a fruitful source for resistance material.[53] But the liberationists are an important source for this study because, in enthusiastically pursuing an understanding of sin as manifested within social structures, they have set off a Catholic debate around the central theological question lurking in the debate between Bultmann and Käsemann: namely, the issue of individual culpability. The Catholic debate is less about the human agent constrained by cosmic powers than it is about the culpability of the human agent constrained by social forces, by institutional structures that embody sin, but the theological argument nevertheless raises nearly identical questions.

The explosion of liberation theology in Latin America in the 1970s prompted a sustained argument between Latin American liberationists and the Vatican (especially Joseph Ratzinger) regarding the nature of social sin.[54] While some insist that Gutiérrez himself never described social institutions as agents of sin, other liberationists were quite eager to do so. For example, Óscar Romero writes, with Romans 6:21–23 clearly in mind, "It is not a matter of sheer routine that I insist once again on the existence in our country of structures of sin. They are sin because they produce the fruits of sin: the deaths of Salvadorans—the swift death brought by repression or the long, drawn out, but no less real, death from structural oppression."[55] These structures manifestly "are sin," because they produce the characteristic fruits of sin (Rom 6:21–22): namely, death.[56] Here, the second kind of oppression is most important for the argument, because while one might be able to personalize guilt in the case of the political executions (say, in the executioner), it would be much more difficult to do so in the case of the "slow death" brought about by those same structures of oppression. Who is personally at fault for death by malnutrition or preventable disease? Here, Romero argues, we see the culpability of sinful structures, which, while they no doubt involve the concrete sinful acts of individual human agents, also seem to rest on a remainder of guilt which is more reasonably assigned to the system as a whole. This is evidence of ἁμαρτία not just as a specific personal act, but not quite as a cosmic power, either. Rather, it is evidence of Sin as a social entity—or at the very least, of sin at the social level.

What Romero identifies theologically (and only by somewhat oblique reference to Romans), Elsa Tamez finds firmly grounded in the text of Romans 7. For Tamez, ἁμαρτία is *primarily* a social concept and, used in the singular, this is precisely what ἁμαρτία refers to: "sin, the sinful system of society."[57] In much the same way that Romero identifies sin in this social sense in the operation of large social systems, Tamez's argument about Romans 7 is to show that the law—understood here not primarily as "Torah," but rather standing for all kinds of legal systems—functions as a legitimizing agent for ἁμαρτία. Human beings live under the power of Sin as slaves, and yet "sin needs the law to hide its wickedness with legitimacy."[58] It is in this way that structural Sin produces deaths of both of the kinds that Romero described. Indeed, Tamez argues, this is how Sin worked to bring about the death of Jesus.[59] What is perhaps most striking about Tamez's language (language that is typical, as we will see, of liberationist authors) is the way she is equally comfortable describing ἁμαρτία as "a personified and enslaving power" and asserting that "it is structural sin *constructed by unjust practices of human beings*."[60] Perhaps, for Tamez, the apparent demonic realism of "enslaving power" is intended to be tempered by the insistence that it is merely "personified" this way, but Tamez's willingness to talk about ἁμαρτία at both the personal and the social levels exemplifies the liberationist innovation. Sin operates at the social level, constraining the moral freedom of human agents, and yet those same sinful, social institutions are themselves constructed by the unjust practices of individual human agents.

This comfort with apparently circular causation is typical of certain strains of liberation theology, and it may be that we have to learn to share their comfort if we are to embrace the fundamental tension in Paul's text. José Ignacio González-Faus, for example, writes, "Sin is not just something done by each individual but is also committed in these sinful structures, which are created by human beings . . . When human beings sin, they create structures of sin, which, in their turn, *make human beings sin*."[61] This attribution of agency to social structures of sin—specifically, their ability to force an individual to sin—is one of the primary sources of the sustained theological disagreement with the Vatican, because it gets at some of the same central theological concerns we've already seen raised by Bultmann regarding human freedom and responsibility for sin. In response to the liberationist insistence upon the sinful agency of social systems, the Vatican struggled in 1977 to make clear what ought and ought not be said about such agency:

> We may dispute how legitimate it is to speak of "institutional sin" or of "sinful structures," since the Bible speaks of sin in the first instance in terms of an explicit, personal decision that stems from human freedom. But it is unquestionable that by the power of sin injury and injustice can penetrate social and political institutions. This is why, as we have pointed out, even situations and structures that are unjust have to be reformed.[62]

While the unjust nature of structures is an important fact of reality that must be accounted for theologically, sin is primarily something that has to do with persons; therefore, structures cannot be described as legitimately "sinful." In 1984, Ratzinger further clarified the Vatican's opinion: "Structures, whether they are good or bad, are the result of human actions, and so are consequences more than causes. The root of evil, then, lies in free and responsible persons."[63] Ratzinger is unwilling to entertain González-Faus's circular causation; structures therefore must be consequences, not causes.[64]

But for many liberationist thinkers, social s/Sin is precisely a *cause* of individual sin. Understanding ἁμαρτία in Paul as something that fundamentally shapes "the structures of our social being," a force that "tyrannizes humanity as a whole," Juan Luis Segundo argues that "sin is a condition that subdues and enslaves me against my own will," and that it "takes over my actions." As a result, Segundo, like Dibelius, can describe Pauline ἁμαρτία in terms of the demonic, precisely on analogy to what we have in the Gospels.[65] Segundo here is interpreting Romans 7, and indeed his language is not far from Paul's. The response from the Vatican, then, is not all that surprising. We saw it above in Bultmann's own response to Paul: the theological concern has to do with exculpation.[66] One ought not take too seriously the agency of social systems, lest the guilt of human individuals be obscured. Nevertheless, Segundo insists that this demonic, deterministic power is embodied in structures both social, and interior to the human subject. The simple fact of existing in these structures necessarily brings about sins.[67]

As in the case of Käsemann's disagreement with Bultmann, so too with the liberationists: this distinct approach to ἁμαρτία corresponds to a distinct understanding of the human person. On this point, Brazilian theologian Leonardo Boff is most instructive. In emphasizing the social dimension of sin (and therefore, of grace), Boff coordinately prioritizes the "social dimension of the human being," stating that it

> is ontologically rooted in the very core of the human being as person. It does not arise after the individual dimension. It is not merely the sum of various juxtaposed individuals who happen to form a community or society. It is not a mere byproduct that is reducible to a more basic reality . . . the social dimension is a web of relationships that constitute the very being of a person.[68]

So, for Boff, the fundamental nature of the social dimension of sin corresponds to an ontology of the human person that sees the social as primary, and the "individual" appearing first of all within that web of relationships.[69] It is in this sense that, for Boff, "the individual is always an abstraction," such that the human being understood "on the psychological level" is dethroned from its presumed primacy.[70] This is not far removed from Käsemann's position, though for Boff the fundamental "level" is the social, whereas for Käsemann it is the "cosmic." In both cases, the decentering of the individual causes substantial problems for the modern Western reader.

These problems perhaps reach their peak in the work of Jerome Murphy-O'Connor, who writes at the nexus of the liberationist debate and the debate within the biblical guild. Murphy-O'Connor understands Sin as a symbol of "the collective thrust of a multitude of individual decisions spread over centuries."[71] Sin is the force of a world full of sins—here he sounds like a liberationist. We can see him struggle, however, to describe the working of this force while ascribing agency and personhood within his operational ontology of persons and commitment to ontological individualism:

> Who is doing the manipulating? No answer can be given, for no one cause or even complex of causes can be singled out to bear the responsibility. There is no dictator who can be blamed. The sensation is that of being caught in a tightly packed crowd swept by a motion of panic. It moves blindly and all are carried along in the grip of irresponsible forces. It is easy to see how this sense of being swayed by a force beyond human control could be transmuted in the mind of simple people into a belief in a supernatural evil power. It is an explanation which alleviates the burden of bewilderment and hopelessness. Paul, as we have seen, refuses this option. The intelligence that seems to be directing humankind on the path of evil is simply the collective thrust of a multitude of individual decisions spread over centuries.[72]

The thesis of my entire project in this book, in many ways, is that Murphy-O'Connor is tantalizingly, maddeningly *wrong.* His analysis is tantalizing in that he attempts to bring a synthesis to all three of the levels of analysis of ἁμαρτία which we see in the scholarship: the individual (Bultmann, Ratzinger); the social (liberationist); and the cosmic or mythological (Käsemann et al.). What is maddening is that, because he lacks an ontology that can hold all of these levels of analysis together, Murphy-O'Connor ultimately has to sacrifice the mythological, and even his account of the social—at least here—seems very much in danger of being reduced to the individual.

The theological interests driving him to do so are by now familiar. Murphy-O'Connor also shares Ratzinger's concern regarding exculpation. Three times in the short paragraph quoted above, Murphy-O'Connor brings up the issue of moral culpability. In the massive, rushing crowd, "no one cause . . . can be singled out to *bear the responsibility* . . . no dictator who can *be blamed* . . . all are carried along in the grip of *irresponsible forces*" (emphasis mine). Murphy-O'Connor has to fight against his own language in order to execute his demythologizing project. On the analogy of a crowd "swept by a motion of panic" (note that the "motion of panic" is the agent of the sweeping), Murphy-O'Connor finds himself talking about an "intelligence" at work in the system, so he must then emphasize that this intelligence only "*seems to be* directing humankind on the path of evil." Ultimately, when Murphy-O'Connor addresses questions of culpability directly, he places much more emphasis on a "real" sense of social or even "world" (cosmic?) constraint on the human agent; that is, he sounds much more in line with certain liberationist strains of thought.[73] Indeed, Murphy-O'Connor admits that on this question, "Paul wants to have his cake and eat it."[74] But Murphy-O'Connor's inability to work out the mechanisms in the passage above betrays the insufficiency of his operational ontology. He simply can't hold together the being of all the relevant characters in Paul's narrative all at once.

Derek Nelson, the curator of much of my account of the liberationist debate, comes up short at precisely the same point. Critiquing the appropriation of liberationist thought by the feminist theologian Rebecca Chopp, who wants to discuss the issue of the poor, the tortured, and the homeless carrying "the special burden of the world's sin,"[75] Nelson worries that

> As haunting and, frankly, as *true* as this perspective is, we flirt with calamity to embrace it uncritically. In the context of a rhetorical flourish, the world can sin, a structure can sin, a system can sin. But this cannot blind us to the incontestable fact that on the everyday level on which we all lead our lives, sin also comes to us in less grandiose ways. We see the wickedness of real people—*individual people*—doing wickedness, ranging from the

spectacularly evil to the pathetically trivial, and everything in between . . .
We are fools to think that our sin could ever be ours alone—that it does
not harm, implicate and stem from others—and therefore we simply must
assert the strongly social character of sin. On this the Latin American liberationists teach us much. But we can also learn from their excesses and
remind ourselves that if social sin is to be properly conceived and theologically explicated, it is nonetheless the social sin of *social individual
sinners*.[76]

Nelson, like Murphy-O'Connor, struggles with what I take to be an inadequate
ontology of social entities. He wants very much to affirm a "true" insight of the
liberationists: "the strongly social character of sin." His proposed program seems
right: we need to find a way of affirming this social character of sin while also
talking about the "less grandiose" embodiments of sin. However, Nelson's ontology of social entities, revealed in his apparent gloss of "real people" as "individual
people," will not suffice for this program.

Conclusions

So, we have not two, but three different "levels" of analysis competing for supremacy: the individual or psychological (Bultmann); the social (the liberationists); and
the cosmic or mythological (Käsemann, et al.). Any attempt to take Paul seriously
at one of the two "higher" levels of analysis is subject to critique for introducing
problems in trying to understand causation.[77] As we will see in the next chapter,
these problems of causation typically arise when analyzing very complex systems.
But at this point, we will do well to note that the problem of causation has been
raised in each attempt to conceptualize ἁμαρτία in Romans 5–8—and, of course,
causation and culpability, or "responsibility," are not far apart. What is the cause of
sins-as-concrete-actions in Romans 5–8? Who or what is responsible? Individual
human agents? A cosmic power—that is, Sin? Social systems? Which of these
can be said rightly to exercise agency? Only human individuals? We are back to
the question of personification, as agency is typically reserved only for persons.[78]
And so these questions of agency rest on interpreters' ontologies of persons—and,
indeed, ontologies of social or cosmic entities as well. These ontologies determine
for readers which candidate entities have an "actual basis in fact"—which personifications are of Whitman's first type and which are of the second. In Paul's vivid
personification, ἁμαρτία in fact exercises agency. Could this agency have an "actual
basis in fact"? Unable to peer into Paul's own mind, interpreters from Bultmann
to Käsemann to Tamez to Ratzinger to Nelson supply the answer from their own
world views, their own senses of "the actual state of affairs."[79]

This may be basic to devices like personification. Hans-Georg Gadamer, describing the interpretation of "writing that is presenting something in disguise, e.g., a *roman à clef*," states,

> This exceptional hermeneutical case is of special significance, in that it goes beyond interpretation of meaning in the same way as when historical source criticism goes back behind the tradition. Although the task here is not a historical, but a hermeneutical one, it can be performed only by using *understanding of the subject matter* as a key to discover what is behind the disguise—just as in conversation we understand irony to the extent to which we are in agreement with the other person on the subject matter.[80]

What we've seen in the genealogy of s/Sin suggests that personification functions much this way. Unmarked as this personification is, the interpreter must use his or her own "understanding of the subject matter"—in this case, an ontology of persons or, more precisely, of agents—in order to discover what, if anything, is behind the disguise. If one can entertain the being and agency of mythological powers (or if one is inclined to suspend one's own disbelief), then Paul's "personification" of Sin is personification in Whitman's first, "animistic," sense. If one can only entertain the being and agency of human persons, then Paul's "personification" of sin is clearly personification in Whitman's second, "literary," sense. If one is writing from a social context in which the force and agency of social structures is only too evident, one would be inclined to adopt an ontology that admits social structures to the category of "agents," and read ἁμαρτία in Paul in light of these structures; and then of course we have witnessed the struggle to square this social ontology and conception of the agency of social structures with prevailing accounts of the freedom of human agents.

I would suggest that Romans 5–8 is patient of each of these readings; presumably, the genealogy just outlined makes this apparent. That is, descriptively, we can see that the text has been read in each of these ways. What I want to suggest is that, in fact, each of these descriptions can coexist—if and only if we come armed with an appropriate ontology. Sin in Romans is a matter of concrete action and also a matter of social structures, and *also* a cosmic tyrant. Uppercase-Sin causes lowercase-sin (Rom 7:8). But so, too, do individual human agents (Rom 5:12). What is needed is not a new middle ground constructed between these two (or three) poles. What we need is a both-and solution, an ontology that permits us to conceive the "actual state of affairs" in a rich enough way to hold the various entities and various agents in Paul's language together, all at once.

2 EMERGENCE

I think the next [21st] century will be the century of complexity.

—STEPHEN HAWKING

In reviewing scholarship on s/Sin in Romans 5–8, we have come to find that ἁμαρτία is a concept that operates at three different "levels" of structure: the personal, the social, and the cosmic. Each of these levels has a different corresponding discipline: psychology, sociology, and what we may call "mythology."[1] The difficulty is that each discipline comes with its own methodology, including, crucially, its own discipline-specific *ontology*, by which I simply mean that each discipline has its own way of deciding what it is useful to talk about as "real."[2] For example, an economic class might seem like a useful unit of concern within Marxist social analysis, but would seem like a horrible oversimplification to a feminist historian interested in the fates of women within and across those classes. Or, an intention might be a hopelessly abstract or even dangerous idea to bring into a conversation in biology, while it might be impossible to do behavioral psychology without invoking such a concept.[3] Similarly, a generic hydrogen atom might very understandably be something which molecular biologists or organic chemists might concern themselves with, but it would be a horribly inexact concept for a nuclear physicist, who would conceive of such an atom only as an abstract representation of a very complex system of subatomic particles.

In each case, the various disciplinary ontologies have different approaches to what they consider "wholes" and what they take to be "parts." That is, each discipline has its own *mereology*. To pick one final example quite relevant to the question of personification, an individual human person might be an "atom" (in the sense of being the indivisible unit of analysis) for a sociologist, whereas such a concept would be the most complex of wholes to a cognitive neuroscientist. Inter- and intra-disciplinary arguments rage over such distinctions: What levels of abstractions "count" as real? Where does real, causal, explanatory power lie?[4] The argument between the Vatican and the liberationists seems to be very much this kind of argument. The way we answer these questions is shaped by what philosophers of science call our *trans-ordinal* theory—that is, a system for relating causal explanations rendered at various different levels of analysis.[5]

As we saw in the last chapter, the philosophical presuppositions of the reader are impossible to set aside in adjudicating whether Paul's description of ἁμαρτία in personal terms is literal, or, rather, an instance of unmarked metaphor. Here, on the contrary, textual interpretation requires that we engage *more* fully with our readerly presuppositions. One way of posing our "exegetical" problem, then, is to ask whether there exists a trans-ordinal theory that permits us to conceive of the "actual state of affairs" in a rich enough way to hold the various entities and various agents in Paul's language together all at once. Philosophers of science have produced a number of trans-ordinal theories that provide frameworks for thinking about the relationship between causal explanations rendered at various levels of analysis. This chapter will argue that emergentism provides the framework we need to hold together the multilevel picture of Sin which Paul paints for us.[6] To that end, I begin with a preliminary discussion of the basic contours of emergence in its most modest form: namely, emergent properties. With this simple picture of property emergence in tow, I will then offer a brief history of trans-ordinal theory, beginning with dualisms and reductionisms of various kinds and, in the context of these two poles, I then describe emergence in more ambitious terms as a third way, with special attention to the generative dialectic of emergence: that is, the tension between supervenience and downward causation.[7] Along the way, we will engage with the testimony of contemporary researchers in fields ranging from physical chemistry to ornithology to civil engineering.[8]

Emergent Properties

Even avid emergentist Timothy O'Connor has called "emergence" "a *notorious* philosophical term of art."[9] Indeed, the concept of emergence is today extraordinarily widely used: in philosophy of mind, philosophy of science, evolutionary biology, psychology, social theory, complexity studies, and theology, among other fields.[10] Nevertheless, across each of these fields, the concept retains a certain contour: that is, emergence is concerned with the appearance of higher-order properties at coordinating higher levels of complexity. The central claim is that these emergent entities, properties, or processes arise from more fundamental entities, properties, or processes and yet are irreducible to them. As the old adage goes, "the whole is more than the sum of its parts."

The most modest way of describing this is simply to talk about the "emergent properties" that wholes have, and that their constituent parts do not. To take a classic example, we might think about the wetness of water. It doesn't make sense to talk about the wetness of individual water molecules, even though water in a glass is composed of such molecules, and that water is certainly wet. It only makes sense to talk about the wetness of a large collection of water molecules in a particular environment (e.g., at atmospheric pressure and room temperature). In this sense, the wetness of the water is an *emergent property* of the large collection of water molecules and their environment. Or we might consider something like the fragility of a vase.[11] Again, the individual molecules that compose the vase are not "fragile" in any sense. Some of their bonds with one another may even be quite strong. "Fragility" is only a concept that makes sense when we talk about the whole (the vase) and is therefore an emergent property of the whole system. Examples may be given in the field of biology as well. Certain blue bird feathers, as it turns out, are not colored with pigments, but rather through constructive interference patterns of light scattering off of intricate nano-structures on the feathers.[12] The blue color, then, is an emergent property of the structure of the feather and the light in its environment. Or one might think of bees. It is common knowledge these days that bee hives as collectives exhibit important behaviors that individual bees do not.[13] These behaviors are emergent properties of the social system of the hive and may, in fact, be indispensable to any account of evolutionary selection in bee populations.[14]

Pressing further into complex biological systems, we might take the act of "remembering" in the case of the human person. It may or may not make sense to talk about the person's brain "remembering" (it depends on how one approaches the mind-body problem and a host of other issues), but regardless it would not make any sense to talk about individual neurons in the brain "remembering," even though they may as a group encode memories.[15] Finally, at the social level, we might note that the concept—and value—of money is strictly an emergent property of a complex social (in this case economic) system, in which a piece of paper with certain markings is taken to have a specific value of exchange.[16] The twenty-dollar bill's value is not a result of its constituent parts. Indeed, that value is not even found in its structure—that is, in the way it is constituted internally. Rather, the bill's value is an emergent property of both the bill *and* the larger socioeconomic system in which it functions as a symbol for a certain amount of value.

The starting point, then, for our discussion of emergence is this: even when restricting ourselves to the simpler examples above, we find that our standard ways of describing and interacting with the world involve regularly talking about simple properties like "wetness" or "fragility" or "blue"—abstract ideas that obtain in the physical world, but are not themselves physical entities and are, in fact, impossible to ascribe to physical particles on the most fundamental (or at any rate, very small) scale. They are, rather, properties of structured wholes, and can be invoked only when talking about these structured wholes. But they *are* appropriately understood as "real," even "literal" or "physical" properties *at that level of analysis*—namely, the analysis of the larger structured whole: whether a puddle in the case of wetness; a vase in the case of fragility; or the blueness of the bird feather. There's nothing "spooky" here; it is simply a different frame of reference—a different level of analysis—that makes one describe a puddle alternatively as "wet" or as a collection of H_2O molecules. And my argument—and the argument of most emergentists—is that things are no more "spooky" in the case of memory or money or any other psychological or social phenomenon.

Problems arise only when one needs to give a description of both the parts *and* the whole—when more than one level of analysis is involved. Necessarily, then, what counts as "real" in the conversation becomes confused. Is it a matter of what would typically be admitted at the "lower," more fundamental level of analysis, or at the "higher," more abstract level? Am I foolish to talk about the wetness of water, given that I know that it is "really" just a heap of H_2O molecules? In the case of the puddle, this seems like a bizarre question; in the case of mental processes like memory or social entities like institutions (as we saw in the last chapter), there are those who are asking precisely such questions and insisting upon certain "reductionist" answers, privileging the lower level of analysis.

One begins to get a sense of the flexibility and expansiveness of the emergentist line of thinking, even when we restrict ourselves simply to thinking about basic intuitions which we have about parts and wholes, and about the world as we describe it. We do operate with various level-specific ontologies which function at different levels of abstraction. The fact that we understand these different kinds of analyses—of the part and of the whole—to be integrally related through the part–whole relationship does nothing to dull this. More systematic reflection, then, on this feature of emergence—the way it exposes certain intuitions that we have about the ways different levels of analysis operate at corresponding levels of abstraction and complexity—has meant that, from the very beginning, emergentism has also had less modest ambitions as a trans-ordinal theory of scientific knowledge.

In this more ambitious mode, emergence is not a scientific theory itself, but rather describes the relationships between sciences that operate at "neighboring" levels of scale and complexity.[17] Emergentism has had tremendous success as this broader kind of explanatory framework: not merely as a technical philosophical term for describing modest problems of attributing properties to wholes that don't appear in their parts, but as a way of understanding the integration of all human knowledge and the world as a complex whole.[18] In this sense, as we will see, emergentism is a rival theory to various kinds of reductionism (ontological, methodological, or epistemic) on the one hand, or various kinds of substance dualisms (mental or vital) on the other. So, to understand emergentism in this more expansive sense, it is best first to lay out the basics of two competing sets of trans-ordinal theories.

Dualisms, Mental, and Vital

Dualism proposes that the proper way to understand apparent discontinuities in the world as we know it—for example, the discontinuity between nonliving and living things, or the discontinuity between conscious and unconscious things—comes through the addition of novel substances that distinguish entities on one side of the discontinuity from entities on the other side. Traditionally, there have been two substance-dualisms that emergentists have resisted: mentalism and vitalism. Mentalism in the modern age is traditionally traced back to Descartes's mind-body dualism, which carves out separate spaces for physical and mental entities, properties, and forces, and postulates a separate mental substance that makes thinking things think, and of which thoughts and ideas and so forth consist. This assures a protected realm for mental properties and causation against the ever-increasing explanatory power of the natural sciences. It also provides natural scientists with a protected realm (non-mental objects) in which causal closure can be reasonably assumed—that is, one need not worry about the unpredictable influence of mental causes in establishing universal laws of gravitation, thermodynamics, and inorganic chemistry. For centuries, the strategy was successful; these were the terms of the uneasy peace that made possible many of the early triumphs of the Enlightenment in the natural sciences. While increasing skepticism about metaphysics generally may have inclined certain thinkers to doubt the necessity of holding mind-body dualism, modern neuroscience was not yet a twinkle in Camillo Golgi's eye, and so the terms of the truce were maintained—indeed, for dualist philosophers of mind, this truce remains workable today.[19]

The first dualism to show substantial cracks was vitalism, which postulated a vital substance that made living things alive, similar to the mental substance that Descartes assumed for mental properties. It was theorized that the presence of this vital substance in compounds resident in living systems (organic materials) was what made them fundamentally different from other (inorganic) compounds. However, advances in chemistry in the nineteenth century began to erode the chasm that vitalism had fixed between inorganic and organic chemistry. While it certainly did not decide the matter instantaneously, Friedrich Wöhler's 1828 synthesis of the organic compound urea from inorganic materials dealt a substantial blow to the vitalist theory.[20] If organic compounds could be synthesized using inorganic materials exclusively, without the addition of any "vital substance," then the case for such a substance's existence was difficult to maintain. Increasingly, chemists came to recognize that findings like Wöhler's had essentially *reduced* organic chemistry to inorganic chemistry, revealing the fundamental unity of chemistry, organic and inorganic. That is, the laws of organic chemistry had been shown to be explainable as a subset of a more general body of knowledge: inorganic chemistry. While some would point out that certain vitalistic attitudes persist to this day (for example, in the minds of those who prefer nutritional supplements isolated from organic sources over those synthesized artificially, despite their chemical identity), vitalism as a scientific theory has more or less disappeared.[21]

Indeed, today, ontological monism—the belief that the universe consists of only one kind of substance—is scientific (and, to a lesser degree, philosophical) orthodoxy.[22] And so substance dualisms of either the mental or the vital variety are decidedly to be avoided. Largely, this is a result of the success of the strategy of reduction in the natural sciences (with Wöhler's findings serving as one important example of such success). Neuroscience has yet to succeed in reducing psychology to neurobiology, but the early results are analogous enough to Wöhler's to suggest that there must be *some* significant continuity between the mental and the biological, rather than a stark, dualist disjunction.

Reduction

Reduction, like emergence, comes in many flavors, ranging from the more modest to the more ambitious. At its most modest, reduction describes a characteristic of scientific discoveries, like Wöhler's, that bring unification to one or more scientific disciplines. Before the synthesis of organic compounds from inorganic components, there were fundamentally two chemistries: organic and inorganic. After such syntheses became commonplace and well-understood, there was a unification of chemistry, and the rules of inorganic chemistry were found to be more universal, and more fundamental. Organic chemistry had been *reduced* to inorganic chemistry. The subsequent reduction of chemistry to physics through the discoveries of physical chemistry in the early twentieth century is often put forward as a important second example of the same principle.[23]

Reductionism takes from such modest successes the grounds for a unifying trans-ordinal theory of scientific knowledge. By calling reductionism a unifying trans-ordinal theory, I mean to emphasize reduction's distinct character in opposition to dualism which, in emphasizing the great discontinuities between different fields of human knowledge and their corresponding levels of abstraction and complexity—and, furthermore, in locating these discontinuities in the introduction of novel *substances*—ultimately works *against* a unified scientific body of knowledge and, in some sense, against a unified human experience of the world as it actually is.[24] This is why, outside of certain philosophical (not scientific) conversations in philosophy of mind, reductionism is emergentism's more or less exclusive rival.

And the two theories, reductionism and emergentism, have much in common. For example, both conceive of the domains of knowledge that make sense of the world as fundamentally stratified, and the order of the strata are more or less identical for both theories:

> Sociology
> Psychology
> Biology
> Chemistry
> Physics[25]

Going "up" the chain, the strata have the following relation: Lower levels are understood to be more fundamental in the sense of applying more universally, while "higher" levels are understood to apply only to a special subsection of the lower field, though at a greater level of complexity and a higher level of abstraction. So, only a certain subset of chemicals are significant biologically, only a certain subset of biological structures seem to have psychological significance, and so on. At any rate, psychologists don't spend much time worrying about the quantum mechanical goings-on in the brains of their subject—even if they would understand all the material in that brain as subject to the standard laws of quantum mechanics that apply to all physical material everywhere. This last concession is an expression of the idea that reductionism holds to ontological monism. That is, reductionism holds, contrary to substance dualisms of any kind, that there is only one kind of stuff in the universe; there are no special "mental" or "vital" substances. (On this point, emergentism and reductionism agree.) The fact that physics is understood to be the most "fundamental" and "lowest"-level science that describes most universally the behavior of this single substance is why reductionism is often called—and amounts to—"physical reductionism."

Reductionism proposes that the relationship between the fields of knowledge at these various different levels is one where the lower level always explains the higher. That is, in terms of trans-ordinal causation—or, synchronic causation between the levels—the arrow always points *up*.[26] In this way, all knowledge is unified. Indeed, the world is unified. There is only one kind of stuff in the world that requires just one kind of explanation (ontological monism), and the (only-) apparently different kinds of explanations that we offer at various different levels of abstraction and complexity can ultimately be reduced to physical causes and physical explanations.

So, if we want to ask about mental or psychological phenomena, we will find ourselves asking for explanations "down" the chain. When asking the question, "What's *really* going on in the case of mental phenomena?" a physical reductionist would answer that mental phenomena are reducible to neurobiological processes—something like the firing of neurons. And how ought we describe the firing of these neurons? There are basic chemical processes happening inside the neurons themselves that create voltage differentials between neurons, and then open paths for discharging some amount of electric charge. And why do these chemicals have different charges? That has to do with the fundamental properties of the physical particles of which the chemicals are composed: electrons, protons, etc. On the physical reductionist account, all that is "really" going on in what we might, out of convenience, call the "mind" is basic physics—the same physics that governs all matter anywhere: charges, spins, gravitation, etc.

This example, however, shows one of the crucial problems, for it seems that in following a strict reductionist logic, we have arrived at eliminative materialism, or, "the thesis that our common-sense conception of psychological phenomena constitutes a radically false theory, a theory so fundamentally defective that both the principles and the ontology of that theory will eventually be displaced, rather than smoothly reduced, by completed neuroscience."[27] This view, which takes its cues from Hume's concept of "useful fictions," entails epiphenomenalism, the "belief" that mental properties are without causal power.[28] While there are those who have supported this position, by and large it seems that eliminativism forbids any sort of realistic engagement with humans—perhaps even the end of any attempt to construe ourselves as "knowers" in any real sense.[29] Against eliminativism, it seems to most that mental causation must be preserved; even many physical reductionists acknowledge this and argue for species of physical reduction that preserve mental causation.[30] As neuroscientist and philosopher Terrence Deacon puts it: "Arguing that the causal efficacy of mental content is illusory is . . . pointless, given the fact that we are surrounded by the physical consequences of people's ideas and purposes."[31] Indeed, it is impossible to imagine a study of religion—to say nothing of biblical studies—constructed entirely without reference to any human intentions or beliefs. The eliminativism of strict reduction is a dead end.

Emergentism as a Trans-Ordinal Theory

As a trans-ordinal theory of scientific knowledge (that is, in its more ambitious sense, in contrast to the more modest account of "emergent properties" described above), emergentism is an attempt to navigate the Scylla and Charybdis of strict reductionism and dualism.[32] Historically, this has meant that emergentist thinkers have attempted to avoid the pitfalls of these two outlooks (both the "spookiness" of dualism, and the eliminitavist epiphenominalism of reductionism), while retaining the strengths of both. With dualism, emergentism shares a "realist" approach to phenomena like mental causation and biological life, but nevertheless holds to ontological monism. That is, the world, for emergentists, consists of just one kind of stuff, but any viable description of that world nonetheless has to give a more robust account of phenomena like thought, intention, and life than is possible when starting from reductionist principles.

With reductionism, emergentism shares the same stratified understanding of scientific knowledge, but suggests a different kind of relationship between these "levels" of knowledge—and, in some cases, between the corresponding "levels" of being in the world. As a result, the ground that contemporary emergence theory has laid out is fairly expansive, with plenty of room for competing theories. Indeed, just within philosophy of mind, in surveying the contemporary landscape, Robert Van Gulick discerns no fewer than ten versions of emergence.[33] However, while many, therefore, begin their work on emergence with a complaint about how no one really agrees on what the concept is supposed to mean, I am inclined to find this internal diversity advantageous in providing the Pauline scholar with a broad array of ways to construe and make sense of our complex world.[34] While I have preferences among the competing accounts of emergence, my strategy will be to build an argument as hospitable to as many different accounts as possible. Nevertheless, there is, among the diversity, a strong and meaningful set of intuitions. We will find that this extensive set of options shapes how certain important questions about complex systems are asked and answered—and how we may approach the trans-ordinal questions that have presented themselves in the scholarship on s/Sin in Romans. To get a sense of the scale and scope of various theories of emergence, I begin with a review of the history of such theories, and then consider the driving dialectic in the emergentist framework: supervenience and downward causation.

A Brief History of Emergence Theory

Emergentism as a trans-ordinal theory of scientific knowledge has had two seasons of ascendancy, the first being in the mid-nineteenth into the early twentieth century, largely in the work of John Stuart Mill and the so-called "British emergentists": George Henry Lewes, Samuel Alexander, and C. D. Broad. These men provided many of the basic building blocks of emergence which we've already discussed: Lewes coined the term "emergentism" and proposed the famous example of the chemical composition of water;[35] Alexander's Gifford Lectures represent an early and ambitious attempt at deploying emergence as a unifying trans-ordinal theory of everything;[36] and Broad first proposed the distinction between intra-ordinal and trans-ordinal laws.[37]

After a hiatus in the middle of the twentieth century, the current resurgence of emergentist ideas more or less began with the work of polymath Michael Polanyi and neurobiologist R. W. Sperry.[38] In his 1969 article, "A Modified Concept of Consciousness," Sperry bemoans the situation in neuroscience: "Most investigators of cerebral function will violently resist any suggestion that the causal sequence of electro-physico-chemical events in the brain, that they work with and are trying to analyze, could in any way be influenced by conscious or mental forces." This resistance leads to a common assumption: "Whatever the stuff of consciousness, it is generally agreed in neuroscience that it does not interact back causally on the brain's electrophysiology or its biochemistry." This amounts to eliminativist materialism, and requires one to hold that the human experience of consciousness is a mere epiphenomenon of cerebral biochemistry. Unwilling to accept this, Sperry proposes instead to "make consciousness an integral part of the brain process itself and an essential constituent of the action." He proposes that:

> First, conscious awareness . . . be a dynamic emergent property of cerebral excitation. As such, conscious experience becomes inseparably tied to the material brain process with all its structural and physiological constraints. At the same time the conscious properties of brain excitation are conceived to be something distinct and special in their own right. They are "different from and more than" the collected sum of the neuro-physico-chemical events out of which they are built.[39]

The license for claiming such a causal relationship from the higher level onto the lower is found on an analogy with chemistry. This passage is worth quoting at length:

> Although the mental properties in brain activity, as here conceived, do not directly intervene in neuronal physiology, they do *super*vene.[40] This comes about as a result of higher level cerebral interaction that involves integration between large processes and whole patterns of activity. In the dynamics of these higher level interactions, the more molar conscious properties are seen to supersede the more elemental physio-chemical forces, just as the properties of the molecule supersede nuclear forces in chemical interactions . . . The subjective mental phenomena are conceived to influence and to govern the flow of nerve impulse traffic by virtue of their encompassing emergent properties. Individual nerve impulses and other excitatory components of a cerebral activity pattern are simply carried along or shunted this way and that by the prevailing overall dynamics of the whole active process (in principle—just as drops of water are carried along by a local eddy in a stream or the way the molecules and atoms of a wheel are carried along when it rolls down hill, regardless of whether the individual molecules and atoms happen to like it or not). Obviously, it also works the other way around, that is, the conscious properties of cerebral patterns are

directly dependent on the action of the component neural elements. Thus, a mutual interdependence is recognized between the sustaining physico-chemical processes and the enveloping conscious qualities. The neuro-physiology, in other words, controls the mental effects, and the mental properties in turn control the neurophysiology.[41]

In this mutual interaction between the part and the whole, Sperry finds a third way, a middle path

> between older extremes of mentalism on the one hand and materialism on the other. The present [proposal] is mentalistic in accepting the existence of potent mental forces that transcend the material elements in cerebral function. It is materialistic in denying that these mental forces can exist apart from the brain process of which they are a direct property. This "emergent interactionism," or "idealistic materialism" as some would label the present compromise, permits proponents of both extremes to retain some of their more important concepts.[42]

Indeed, as we saw above, this is much the way emergentists continue to under-stand themselves, forging a middle way for those who want to hold both to an ontological monism and a robust sense of consciousness and personal agency.[43] This dialectic is established by the two basic principles in emergentism: *superve-nience* and *downward causation*.

The Generative Dialectic: Supervenience and Downward Causation

"Supervenience," writes emergentist sociologist R. Keith Sawyer, "refers to a relation between two levels of analysis and states that if two events are identical with respect to their descriptions at the lower level, then they cannot differ at the higher level."[44] Changes on the higher level correspond to changes on the lower level (but not necessarily vice versa—that is, two different states at the lower level may produce the same state at the higher level—this is known as the prin-ciple of multiple realizability). But, two identical states at the lower level (e.g., the same state at two different times) cannot produce two different states at the higher level.

An example might help here. Take the two different "levels" of analysis of a baseball game: the score and the outcome (win or lose). The outcome (win or lose) supervenes on the score. It is possible (in fact, quite common) that two different scores yield the same outcome. That is, the home team could outscore the visiting team 4–3 or 7–0, but either way, the outcome is the same: the home team wins. The outcome, "home team wins" is multiply realizable in terms of the score of the game. What is not possible is for the same score (e.g., Home Team 4, Visiting Team 3) to result in two different outcomes on two different days. In all cases, if the home team scores four runs and the visiting team scores three, the outcome will be that the home team (having scored more runs) wins. For this reason, we can say that the outcome supervenes on the score. This is the case for runs, but not for other metrics. The outcome does not supervene, for example, on the total number hits. By the rules of baseball, it is quite possible for a team that outhits the opposing team to win the game one day and, outhitting the opposing team by the same margin the next day, to lose.

The principle of supervenience means that higher-level entities are onto-logically dependent on their "supervenience bases." In the cases of the emergent properties we described at the beginning of this chapter, the fragility of the vase would be said to supervene on the micro-physical structure of its materials, the wetness of the water to supervene on the chemical characteristics of H_2O as well as the ambient temperature and pressure, and the blue color of the bird feathers to supervene on the nanostructures of the feathers. In the case of the mind-body relationship, "supervenience" describes the connection between mental proper-ties and entities, and their neurological bases; mental properties are said to super-vene on the physical structures and processes in the brain. Supervenience allows emergence to hold to ontological monism.

At the same time, while emergentists maintain that emergent properties, enti-ties, and processes (or simply "emergents") have a relationship of supervenience to the properties and entities at adjacent, "lower" (that is, more fundamental) lev-els, unlike their reductionist counterparts, they insist that these novel emergents are irreducible to their supervenience bases. So, true emergents are supervenient on structures at the lower level, but irreducible to those structures.

The character of this irreducibility is a matter of some disagreement. Some argue that this irreducibility has an epistemological character. That is, what is meant by "irreducible" here is that emergents at a higher level are not explain-able (at least not exhaustively) in terms of dynamics at the lower, more funda-mental level.[45] This view emphasizes emergentism's commitment to ontological monism, and shows the compatibility of a certain kind of emergence with modest reductionism. Others argue that this irreducibility is best thought of as onto-logical. That is, an emergent is "irreducible" to its supervenience base because it really exists, as a new thing in the world. Those who advocate so-called "strong emergence" tend to add this ontological understanding of irreducibility to the epistemological, and argue for ontological emergence based on epistemological irreducibility.[46]

However, there are those who argue for ontological irreducibility and also deny epistemological irreducibility, thereby arguing that this ontological emergence is, in fact, a more modest form of emergence even than epistemological emergence, inasmuch as it is compatible with reductionism at the epistemological level. Philosopher Mario Bunge writes:

"Contrary to a widespread opinion, [emergence] has nothing to do with the possibility or impossibility of explaining qualitative novelty. Hence, it is mistaken to define an emergent property as a feature of a whole that cannot be explained in terms of the properties of its parts. Emergence is often intriguing but not mysterious: explained emergence is still emergence."[47]

Social theorist Dave Elder-Vass argues in a similar direction for a "relational emergentism" which

allows higher level properties to be explained scientifically, but ... does not allow them to be replaced with properties of the parts in causal explanations because it is only when the parts are organized into this particular type of higher level system that the causal power exists.[48]

As a result, Elder-Vass, like Bunge, defines irreducibility in ontological, rather than epistemological, terms.[49] This argument for ontological irreducibility without epistemological irreducibility—counter-intuitive though it might seem at first—has substantial merits. Certainly, the fragility of the vase is no less the property of the vase as a structured whole—and not of its component parts at the smallest scale—just because a material scientist can explain how it is that the micro-structures of the porcelain give rise to these macro properties. Similarly, the pigment-less blue bird feathers are certainly blue, but only at the level of the structured whole; the materials that compose the feather are not blue, except in relation to their being structured as a part of a larger whole.[50] The blue color of the feathers supervenes on these materials—no materials, no blue color—but is not reducible to them in the ontological sense. Given that Prum has explained the mechanism by which the nano-structure of the component materials gives rise to a blue color at the macro level, the irreducibility of this blue color could not be said to be epistemologically emergent.

This seems rather straightforward for these cases of property emergence. The classic "strong emergence" case might have more to recommend it when we consider the more thorny examples that will preoccupy us in the next chapter: namely, in the cases of the mental and the social. The mind may be said to supervene on the brain (or some larger supervenience base; see discussion of "extended mind" theories below)—that is, no brain, no mind—but it is not *reducible* to it. Mind is, in some sense, "more" than just brain. However, this irreducibility may be thought of in several different ways. By some, it will be taken as epistemological; they would predict that psychological behavior will never be fully explainable through neuroscience, from the bottom up, as it were. Strong emergentists would argue that, because of this, we ought to understand the mind as really existing. Emergentists of Bunge and Elder-Vass's brand would wager that, over time, more and more of the mechanisms of relation between the neurological and the psychological will be understood by science, but that this gives no reason for us to be skeptical about the existence of the mind or of the mental.[51] Emergentists argue similarly that the social supervenes on the individual—that is, no individuals, no society—but that the social is *irreducible* to the individual. And, again, here we have the same set of options: either that means that the social is not explainable in terms of the interactions of individuals alone (with the option of concluding—or not—that we therefore ought to understand the social as real), or that means that the social is itself real and distinct from (though retaining the relationship of supervenience to) the actions of individual agents.

Relational emergentists who follow Bunge and Elder-Vass expose the immodesty of epistemological emergence—which we might have originally taken to have been the more modest form—inasmuch as epistemological emergence makes certain pessimistic predictions regarding the reach of scientific explanation in perpetuity. Furthermore, relational emergence—even while holding to ontological irreducibility—shows itself to be functionally compatible with epistemological reductionism; to that extent, I take it to be *functionally* compatible with so-called "weak emergence," that is, the view that emergents are useful simply as heuristic categories. So, for a weak emergentist, psychological entities will always remain useful units of analysis, but they do not exist in the same way that physical substances exist. I take it that, to the extent to which there is no essential difference between a heuristic and a "powerful fiction," there is little that would distinguish a weak emergentist of this type from a Humean reductionist.[52]

However they are conceived, the combination of supervenience and irreducibility means that emergents appear quite apart from any sort of intention, design, or externally imposed teleology.[53] That is, the paradigm cases of emergence are understood to describe instances of self-organization, so-called cases of "spontaneous emergence." Under the right conditions, complex systems at lower levels naturally give rise to irreducible emergents at a higher level of abstraction. Dissipative, or "nonequilibrium" systems—that is, physical systems that exchange energy with their surroundings as a necessity of their persistence, as all living systems do—especially seem to exhibit this sort of behavior, in exhibiting self-regulation at higher levels of structure.[54] Thus, in evolutionary theory, emergence theory offers some description of the *mechanism* of the appearance of order—and of humanly significant entities at higher levels of order, like organisms, life, and mind—which otherwise can seem to arise out of nowhere. This makes emergence theory quite compatible with evolutionary biology, as we will see below.[55]

The Problem of Downward Causation

Having arisen irreducibly from their supervenience bases, emergents then exert *downward causation* on their supervenience bases.[56] Social groups exercise constraint on the individuals of which they are composed. The needs of a hive organize the behavior of the individual bees in ways that serve the hive's needs. Downward causation is at once perhaps the most important feature of emergence theory, and at the same time its most controversial claim. The difficulty is that it seems to stand in considerable tension with the relationship of supervenience. The challenge of emergence is to describe the mechanisms through which causation at lower levels can give rise to higher- level causation, which then exercise constraint back on the components of those same systems. As central an issue—and a problem—as downward causation has been for emergence, it is no less central for my purposes. Inasmuch as the problems in the first chapter centered around issues of culpability, this study has very much to do with questions of causation—and particularly, to what extent causation can move downward, that is, from a higher level to a lower level (e.g., the social to the individual). Given the controversial role downward causation has played in certain classic discussions (philosophy of mind, social theory)—for example, this is where some philosophers of mind will complain that emergence starts to sound a bit "spooky"—perhaps it will be helpful to start with a more modest example of simple *property* emergence: the case of London's Millennium Bridge.[57]

When the Millennium Bridge opened on June 10, 2000, the crowds who walked across it were in for quite a surprise. The steel suspension bridge over the River Thames began to sway side to side with an ever-increasing magnitude, to the extent that pedestrian access was first limited and then eventually closed entirely for more than a year while the bridge was repaired.[58] The first question that had to be answered was, what was causing the motion of the bridge? Video footage of the opening day showed the crowd of pedestrians walking in step; this synchrony seemed to be driving the swaying motion of the bridge. But how did a disorganized crowd get in step? Eventually, it was discovered that the pedestrians on the bridge, in order to keep themselves from falling over due to the swaying motion of the bridge, had to alter their gait in a way that further drove the swaying of the bridge.[59] The crowd needed no "conductor," no external, centralized system of coordination in order to get in step. Once the crowd reached a critical size, random statistical variation would provide the initiating force and the feedback loop of causation would begin: the lateral force of the natural human gait on the bridge, the wobble of the bridge back on the human agents forcing them to alter their gait and get in step, the increasingly synchronized lateral force of the crowd back on the bridge, etc. Adapting models that describe the synchronization of biological systems like neurons, a collaborative team of engineers from Cornell University, the University of Cambridge, and the University of Maryland was able to predict precisely the rate at which the feedback system would cause an increase in the amplitude of the lateral swaying of the bridge.[60]

In the terms of emergentism, the swaying motion of the bridge is an emergent property of the system that includes the pedestrians and the bridge itself. This motion supervenes on both the bridge and the pedestrians: a crowd of pedestrians walking on a different surface causes no such motion and, without the perturbation of the crowd of pedestrians, the bridge similarly does not show such motion. However, while the pedestrians are part of the supervenience base of the lateral swaying, that swaying also exercises downward causation back on the individual pedestrians, forcing them to alter their gait, get in step, and further drive the motion of the bridge (as they are, after all, still part of the supervenience base of the bridge's swaying motion). The principles of supervenience and downward causation, then, form two sides of a feedback loop—a feature of systems that exhibit emergent behavior familiar to systems biologists and sociologists alike.[61]

Moving on to the more difficult case of philosophy of mind, the formal tools remain the same. In Sperry's proposal discussed above, the emergent mental properties are said to have causal effects at their own level that, in turn, because they are supervenient on the neurobiological level, bring about changes on the lower-level supervenience base. Ultimately, then, on this sort of account, supervenience and downward causation describe two sides of a relationship of mutual causation and determination between the emergent properties and their supervenience bases. Nevertheless, as Sperry states, "One should remember in this connection . . . that the conscious phenomena are in a position of higher command, as it were, located at the top of the organizational hierarchy." The causal ascendancy of the emergent properties is presumably related to Sperry's language which depicts an ontological emergence, describing various qualia as "real properties."[62] Nevertheless, the dialectic of supervenience and downward causation, which we saw in the case of the bridge, also holds for Sperry: the mind and mental qualia supervene on a neurological substrate on which they also exercise downward causation. Thoughts are understood to emerge from neurological processes, but also exercise constraint on those same processes: supervenience and downward causation form a feedback loop.

This particular case of downward causation has been met with substantial resistance from some philosophers of mind—and has driven many to question the coherence of the concept itself. The question of the reality of downward causation is in many respects the dividing line between philosophers who find in emergence grounds to talk about the mind as "an emergent property of the brain," and those who instead find in emergence reason to talk about the mind as "*only* an emergent property of the brain." This latter view is sometimes called "weak emergence."

The most vocal champion of "weak emergence" is Jaegwon Kim. Kim has written—against his earlier position—that emergent properties as described by emergentists are epiphenomenal, or, mere "symptoms" of the real, physical properties on which they supervene.[63] He rightly argues that, ever since Alexander's work, emergentism has staked its importance on its ability to ascribe causal powers to emergent properties.[64] Kim's attack on downward causation, therefore, strikes at the heart of the emergentist project. His critique is twofold. First, Kim argues that because of the principle of supervenience, emergent properties cannot be said to exert any causal power—even among themselves—unless downward causation is indeed possible. This is generally agreed upon, even by proponents of strong emergence. Second, Kim argues that, again, because of the principle of supervenience, every alleged higher-level cause would have a corresponding lower-level cause, with the result that "every case of downward causation involves causal overdetermination."[65]

Kim's flagship case is that of mental causation. Suppose that we want to say both that one mental state, M, causes another, M*, and that M and M* supervene on physical states, P and P*, respectively. We might diagram the situation as shown in Figure 2.1:

FIGURE 2.1. Supervenience, downward causation, and causal overdetermination.

If M* arises from P* and P* is caused by P (through the regular workings of the laws of physics), why not say that M* is caused by P, through its causing P*? Otherwise, P* seems to be caused by both M and P. Such overdetermination is highly implausible; and, if one were to decide that this is precisely what we mean by "downward causation,"

> this goes against the spirit of emergentism in any case: emergents are supposed to make distinctive and novel causal contributions. However, if there is systematic causal overdetermination in all cases of downward causation, emergents cannot fulfill their causal promise; anything they causally contribute can be, and is, contributed by a physical cause. This result, unless it is successfully rebutted, threatens to bankrupt one of the central claims of emergentism. If downward causation goes, so goes emergentism.[66]

On the basis of this argument (and other similar arguments), Kim has challenged emergentists to prove downward causation, or scrap the theory entirely.

Defense of downward causation comes from emergentists working in a variety of fields, from philosophy to chemistry to evolutionary biology to sociology. Philosophically, I take it that the question comes down to how we understand the diagonal arrow in the diagram from M to P*. I propose that we understand the first mental state as providing *necessary but not sufficient* conditions to bring about the physical state on which the second mental state supervenes. Michael Polanyi has described this "downward," inter-level causation as the principle of "marginal control": "the control exercised by the organizational principle of a higher level on the particulars forming its lower level." The key is *structure*. The mechanism of the control that higher-level emergents exercise is the *structural constraint* within which they restrict lower level mechanisms to operate. They provide the *context* within which lower-level entities indeed follow the laws relevant to their level of scale and complexity.

A *machine* is a simple case.[67] The parts of a machine, while they work together to function in ways that the constituent parts do not individually, nevertheless each behave according to the laws that govern their behavior when they are not a part of the machine. The functioning of a car's combustion engine does not require the fuel or the steel to break the laws of physics that govern their physical behavior—quite the opposite, the functioning of the engine depends on these materials and parts functioning according to the laws of chemistry and physics: the gasoline must combust at the appropriate temperature and pressure in the presence of enough oxygen; the piston must respond to the pressure differentials created by the combustion. But the functioning of the engine *as* an engine has everything to do with the structure of the parts that place gasoline and oxygen and the piston in a particular sort of arrangement such that when they do what they would always do, something novel happens: the engine produces power that drives the car forward (when subject to input decided by the driver, at yet a higher level of control).

In the case of biological systems, the biological structures shape "the boundaries of the lower level which is relied on to obey the laws of inanimate nature, i.e., physics and chemistry."[68] So, at the lower level, the laws of physics and chemistry are obeyed, but within the constraints provided by the *structure* regulated by the higher-level entity. Standard efficient causation holds at the lower level, but this leaves open certain "boundary conditions" that are only fixed by the structure provided by the higher level.[69] This allows Polanyi to speak quite straightforwardly of "dual control" without concern for causal overdetermination.[70] What is different in the case of biological systems—as opposed to machines—is that the higher-level constraints have not been imposed "from above," but rather have emerged "from below." This spontaneous appearance of an intrinsic teleology is one of the fundamental—and most remarkable—features of life in its various forms.[71]

So, within a given level, we can speak quite freely about one state "causing" another in efficient terms. But, across levels, we need to be more careful to nuance our language of causation such that it is sufficient to a mereology of complex systems (that is, our theory about how parts relate to composite wholes). What is sometimes called "upward causation" of emergents is not the same sort of causation.[72] "Downward causation" is a matter of "marginal control" or the establishing of "boundary conditions"—something like a *formal* cause, in Aristotelian terms.[73] Kim's challenge helps us nuance this language and refine what we mean when we talk about downward causation. Structure is the key.

Downward Causation in Chemistry

Recognizing the significance of this structural context allows us to recognize, against Kim, that, with regard to the sorts of regularities that are significant at the emergent level, physical causes are also themselves *necessary but not sufficient.* This is a point argued by the chemists and philosophers of chemistry.[74] It is a sort of return home for emergence. As we saw above, the original paradigm cases for emergence were drawn from chemistry in the nineteenth century. Joseph Earley, a philosopher of chemistry, criticizes Kim (and indeed most philosophers of mind) for having a view of material causation drawn exclusively from the field of (now-superseded Newtonian) physics. "It seems that Kim's physicalism could be paraphrased as: 'if an event of any sort has a cause at t, then it has only an elementary-particle-level cause at t.'" Yet, despite the claims of philosophers that total reduction of chemistry into physics (via quantum mechanics) has taken place—indeed, this is for some a paradigm case of reduction—Earley is not convinced.

First, Earley argues, Kim, like other philosophers, makes erroneous assumptions about the nature of physics itself. Kim assumes that the objects of physics on the smallest levels are undifferentiated wholes—this is the philosophical force of "elementary particle" for him. Earley points out, however, that physics continues to find that at smaller and smaller levels, each "elementary" particle turns out to be itself a composite. If even physics is constantly dealing with composite wholes (rather than atomistic simples), then Earley suggests we ought to interrogate the operating mereology in Kim's work. Kim's mereology, which Earley takes as more or less standard among reductionists, is deficient because "even though all sciences are greatly concerned with 'structure,' standard mereology cannot deal with 'structured' wholes. *Structured* wholes, such as chemical molecules, generally have causal efficacy in virtue of their 'connectivity'—*in addition to* the causal powers of their constituent atoms." Hydrogen molecules composed of the same sub-atomic particles exhibit different behavior—even "alone"—depending on their participation in different bonds. Crystal structures, networks, superconductivity, superfluidity, and the Hall Effect are all listed as phenomena that are "substantially *independent* of lower-level properties."[75]

Ultimately, the prevalence of downward causation at the frontiers of basic science research leads Earley to question the fundamental starting point of the reductionist project—that is, the reduction of chemistry into physics in quantum mechanical explanation. As Earley points out, philosopher of chemistry Robin Hendry has argued that in the case of quantum-level accounts of chemical molecular structure, "the gross molecular structure (atomic connectivity) is generally not a result of quantum-chemical calculations but is put in as an initial assumption based on chemical experience—and that no evidence or argument shows how to avoid invalidating the reductionist project by making such assumptions."[76] As downward causation is the principle on which emergence lives or dies, the reduction of chemistry into physics is no less central for the program of physical reduction. If even chemistry cannot be reduced to physics, much less so can biology, neurobiology, or the "special sciences." If downward causation is required in order to give an adequate account even of physical chemistry, the implication is that a mereology adequate to the world we live in will have to render an account of downward causation. In other words, it is philosophical accounts that *exclude* downward causation that are insufficiently "physical." The testimony of the chemists turns Kim's argument on its head.

Downward Causation in Biology

If chemists pose fundamental philosophical challenges to claims against downward causation, the testimony of biologists has a much more pragmatic flavor. In the practice of systems biology, the kinds of "feedback loops" that the dialectic between supervenience and downward causation describes are standard explanatory fare. For example, British biologist Denis Noble has noted that the processes that regulate cardiac rhythm cannot be described adequately without recourse to downward causation as an explanatory framework. Noble describes multiple layers of inter-level causation in biological systems between genes, proteins and RNAs, protein and RNA networks, sub-cellular machinery, cells, tissues, organs, and organisms, as Figure 2.2 shows:

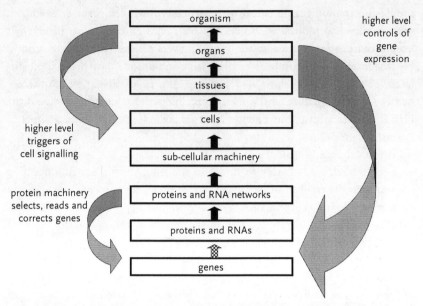

FIGURE 2.2. "The bidirectional causal structure of systems biology." Denis Noble, "A Theory of Biological Relativity: No Privileged Level of Causation," *Interface Focus* 2, no. 1 (2012), 59, by permission of the Royal Society (caption Noble's).

As a result, in biological systems, "Causation is, therefore, two-way, although this is not best represented by making each arrow two-way. A downward form of causation is not a simple reverse form of upward causation. It is better seen as completing a feedback circuit."[77] Noble even goes so far as to describe the mathematics of the interaction of these two directions of causation in terms of the differential equations that describe complex biological systems:

> One might think that, provided all the relevant protein mechanisms have been included in the model and if the experimental data are reliable, and the equations fit the data well, cardiac rhythm would automatically "emerge" from those characteristics. It does not. The reason is very simple and fundamental to any differential equation model. In addition to the differential equations you need the initial and boundary conditions. Those values are just as much a "cause" of the solution (cardiac rhythm) as are the differential equations.[78]

This prevalence of downward causation in systems biological explanation leads Noble to posit what he calls a biological theory of relativity, that is, that "there is, *a priori*, no privileged level of causality in biological systems."[79]

This means that even the *genetic* level—so often touted as the firm foundation of biological explanation—has no valid claim to causal hegemony. Rather,

Noble and others insist, contemporary research shows us again and again that genetic, upward causation is conditioned by downward, "epigenetic" factors that control gene expression. Despite the tremendous importance of the sequencing of the human genome, "the results have turned out to be somewhat underwhelming. One of the surprises was the relatively small number of genes that humans possess—perhaps as few as 22 000," biologist P. C. W. Davies explains. He goes on to explain, however, that

> It was already evident at the start of the project . . . that cataloguing genes *per se* was of limited value in explaining life's processes, because there is no way that even a billion bits of information can, on their own, specify the entire structure and organization of an organism . . . which contains exponentially more information than does the genome that is supposedly coding for it.[80]

Craig Venter, a key player in the sequencing of the human genome, reflects, "One of the most profound discoveries I have made in all my research is that you cannot define a human life or any life based on DNA alone . . . an organism's environment is ultimately as unique as its genetic code."[81] Thinking "emergently" means thinking "environmentally" and gives us good reason to question firm boundaries between the organism and the environment, the self and the world.

Ultimately, it is the *epigenome*—the set of environmental constraints that surround the genome at the molecular, cellular, organismic, and global levels—that supplies this extra information. As Davies explains, "In a nutshell, genetics deals with what genomes are and epigenetics deals with what they do."[82] Crucially, Noble insists, the epigenome includes the cellular machinery that makes use of DNA. Viewed in terms of information content, the structure of cells themselves contains more information than the DNA they contain. This is the site, then, of much of the data "missing" at the end of the human genome project—it is analog, rather than digital. Indeed, it is not a representation at all. "The rest of the cellular machinery does not need a code, or to be reduced to digital information, precisely because it represents itself."[83] But, of course, the epigenome is much more than this cellular machinery; it also includes the environment of the cell itself, or of the organism as a whole. As such, though rooted in the physical structures of the world, the epigenome is a virtual, rather than a physical, object. Davies writes:

> We will look in vain for any particular physical object within the cell that we can identify as "the epigenome." In the case of epigenetics, there is no physical headquarters, no localized commanding officers issuing orders, no geographical nerve centre where the epigenomic "programme" is stored and from where epigenomic instructions emanate to help run the cell . . . The epigenome is everywhere and nowhere; it is a global, systemic

entity. Expressed more starkly, *the epigenome is a virtual object.* Given that it calls many, if not most, of the biological shots, its non-existence as a specific physical entity is deeply significant.[84]

In other words, the epigenome is an *emergent* entity, and the causal powers it exerts over its supervenience base is a classic case of downward causation. Crucially, this "non-existence as a physical entity" in no way tempers the epigenome's causal powers. The epigenome, though a virtual object, regulates cellular biology through physical (or, better, chemical) processes that are better understood by molecular biologists every day. Davies points especially to research on the function of chromatin, which forms the structures of chromosomes. Existing in the "mesoscopic" realm (that is, larger than DNA, but smaller than whole chromosomes), "chromatin marks the intersection of upward and downward causation, because its structure and behaviour are influenced both by the genes it contains and by the macroscopic forces acting on it from the rest of the cell and the cell's environment."[85] Davies's description of biological causation, therefore, has much in common with Noble's:

> There is thus a web of causation, both upward and downward in length scale, with complex feedback loops leading to many possible stable and unstable states. Generally, an explanation for a biological process will entail both upward causation—such as when a gene is switched on and makes a protein that affects cell and organismal behaviour—and downward causation—when a change in the environment triggers a response all the way down to the gene level . . . The necessity to consider organisms as systems subject to both upward and downward causation complicates causal reasoning and presents a challenge to physical scientists used to thinking of step-by-step cause and effect. The subject of systems biology attempts to get to grips with this fundamental and unavoidable characteristic of life.[86]

If we are to take biological explanation seriously, we will have to adopt a trans-ordinal theory that allows for bi-directional causation, as emergence does. Indeed, the new hearing that emergence is receiving in contemporary culture as a whole may in part be attributable to the recent ascendancy of biomedicine (after a twentieth century largely dominated, in the realm of science, by physics—especially nuclear and particle physics). Reductionism, after all, is a common symptom of "physics envy." Learning to think in the terms of emergence may be necessary in order to make sense of the world in our biomedical age.[87]

Downward Causation in Sociology

As hinted above, many social theorists also find it necessary to talk about upward and downward causation. Social actors construct social systems that, in turn, constrain or even, on some accounts, construct those same social actors. James S. Coleman describes this as the central theoretical problem of sociology: "how the purposive actions of the actors combine to bring about system-level behavior, and how those purposive actions are in turn shaped by constraints that result from the behavior of the system."[88] Even Peter Berger, who insists that "despite the objectivity that marks the social world in human experience, it does not thereby acquire an ontological status apart from the human activity that produced it," nevertheless also argues that

> the relationship between man, the producer, and the social world, his product, is and remains a dialectical one. That is, man . . . and his social world interact with each other. The product acts back upon the producer . . . *Society is a human product. Society is an objective reality. Man is a social product.*[89]

This dialectical relationship is easily recognized as a causal feedback loop typical of complex systems, though Berger gives it an ontological flavor: "Social structure is produced by man and in turn produces him."[90] As nearly universal as the recognition of this dialectic is, predictably, social theorists of different stripes will emphasize one or the other of these poles of causation in social systems. Methodological individualists are inclined to reduce all causation at the social level to "real" individual causes, while methodological collectivists are inclined to ascribe causal ascendancy to the social level.[91] This division, of course, follows a familiar paradigm, falling more or less along the lines of the reductionist-dualist divide. Emergentist social theorists, then, work to explore a third way that recognizes the reality of both levels of analysis and also explores the mechanisms of their interrelation.

Margaret Archer has been carrying the emergentist banner in social theory for several decades. For Archer, emergence functions precisely to make sense of the causal feedback loops that arise in social systems:

> Emergent properties are relational, arising out of combination (e.g., the division of labour from which high productivity emerges), where the latter is capable of reacting back on the former (e.g., producing monotonous work), has its own causal powers (e.g., the differential wealth of nations), which are causally irreducible to the powers of its components (individual workers). This signals the stratified nature of social reality where different strata possess different emergent properties and powers.[92]

It is the particular *structure* of the relationships between individual social agents that give rise to the particular social systems that then act back down on these individual agents. This is what Archer calls the morphogenetic cycle. R. Keith Sawyer summarizes the distinct contribution emergence offers as a framework within which to theorize this generative dialectic of the social sciences:

> The Emergence Paradigm is a positivist, objectivist, scientific approach, and consequently it rejects subjectivism and interpretivism. It argues that the causal power of emergents cannot be explained solely in terms of individuals' representations of them, their demonstrated orientations to them, or their subjective interpretations of them. Properties at higher levels have autonomous causal force. They are unintended emergent effects, and they are causal even when individuals have no knowledge of them. Of course, in many cases individuals do have some knowledge of these emergents, and individuals' perceptions can have socially relevant effects. But in the Emergence Paradigm, most of the explanatory power comes from emergent properties and their processes of emergence, and individuals' subjective interpretations of emergents are generally not necessary in social explanation. The Emergence Paradigm attempts to explain the causal forces that originate in an emergent that was created by the participants. Emergence Paradigm research focuses on the micro-interactional mechanisms by which shared social phenomena emerge and on how those emergents constrain those mechanisms.[93]

Despite Sawyer's insistence on distancing the "Emergence Paradigm" from the interpretivist method, it is not difficult to rephrase Berger in emergent terms: the social world—"society"—supervenes on individuals without whose activity the social world does not exist, but, through downward causation, that same social world acts back upon those same individuals, so constructing their own subjective senses of themselves as to say that they are "created" by the social system of their own creation.[94] This cannot be far from how Sin is operating in Romans 5–8.[95]

This is not to minimize the substantive differences between different social theories, but simply to emphasize the dialectic that describes the lay of the land in which each theory is aiming to stake a claim. Emergentism is well-suited as a meta-theory in social theory, because it contains within it this dialectic between "bottom-up" and "top-down" causation. And emergentist accounts of social theory make room for both, and leverage the language of emergence to theorize the mechanisms that make such a both-and solution coherent—and, to my mind, more palatable. In an emergentist framework, we can affirm that the social does not exist without the participation of individuals who constructed society, but we can also insist that our sense—pervasive, on Berger's account—that society then acts down upon us is not illusory. "The product acts back upon the producer," indeed.

In sum, in considering the fate of downward causation and of emergentism in the face of Kim's challenge, it seems that there do exist satisfactory answers to the philosophical challenge laid down by Kim and, moreover, the discoveries of contemporary science—especially in biology—quite clearly require some idea of downward causation. In the introduction to a 2012 issue of the Royal Society's interdisciplinary journal, *Interface Focus*, dedicated to downward causation in the sciences, issue editors Denis Noble, Timothy O'Connor, and G. F. R. Ellis conclude that "there is solid evidence that top-down causation does indeed occur in the domains of all the sciences, ranging from physics to microbiology to physiology to sociology, in each of which the concept is deployed with considerable explanatory power."[96] In other words, even if the philosophical arguments of Earley and others do not satisfy us, we are still left with this simple response: downward causation is *possible* because it is *actual*. In the workings of complex systems—from the opening day of the Millennium Bridge, to the inner workings of cells, or the large-scale balancing acts of ecosystems—we see it happen. The more we understand the world as full of complex, self-organizing systems (as evolutionary theory encourages us to do), the more generative the dialectic of supervenience and downward causation becomes. And the explanatory power of emergence becomes that much more plain.

Case Study: Racism

To this point, while the discussion has certainly ranged across multiple disciplines, our comments have been limited to a single discipline at a time. However, emergence invites us to think in more integrative terms. In some sense, this is the intellectual inheritance of Samuel Alexander, seen in the ambitious "theory-of-everything" work of contemporary emergentists such as Philip Clayton, Stuart Kauffman, and Terrence Deacon. Indeed, to engage emergentism as a transordinal theory of knowledge is precisely to suggest not only that emergence explains the relationship between two adjacent levels of scale or abstraction or complexity, but that we can "link up" multiple of these levels and observe nesting dolls of supervenience and grand cascades of downward causation.[97] As a means of integrating much of the conversation from this chapter and leading us toward this kind of more integrative and ambitious emergentist analysis, let us attempt a multilevel analysis of a complex social system: racism in the United States. This analysis is intended to be suggestive—and certainly not exhaustive—in indicating the sorts of integrative analyses that are possible when the world is viewed through the lens of emergence. The fact that the example is one that certainly has some relation to the topic of this book—namely, sin—will of course be advantageous, because this case study will give us a taste of the complex, multi-level issues entailed in any realistic assessment of systemic sin and injustice.

It is common, of course, to conceive of racism as an ideological problem, as is plain from one of the first scholarly descriptions of racism, Ruth Benedict's in 1945: "the *dogma* that one ethnic group is condemned by nature to congenital inferiority and another group is destined to congenital superiority."[98] Indeed, to this day, in his standard textbook on race and ethnicity, Richard Schaefer defines racism as a "doctrine."[99] And certainly this ideological description of racism has substantial merit. Belief regarding the innate superiority of one group over another is evident in racist cultures. Racism has *at least* this individual, ideological character. From a certain viewpoint, what else could racism possibly be?

Of course, there are a number of problems with this analysis. First and foremost, stated in the simplest terms, this explication of racism as an ideology regarding "race" gives us the impression that the fundamental category of race somehow pre-exists racist ideology, and is simply available as "raw material" about which the racist can opine. Racism and race have a much more complicated relationship than this, as the history of the construction of race as a category tells us.[100] Race has a classic Foucauldian structure, "both an instrument and an effect of power," and racism is a classic Foucauldian discourse, which conspires to create the very concept it purports to describe.[101] Foucault would, of course, insist that this is the case of all objects of knowledge, all would-be "objects prior to discourse." Foucault's description of how such objects are in fact constructed has a necessarily *social* dimension, "on the basis of a complex field of discourse," which ultimately "allows the sovereignty of collective consciousness to emerge as the principle of unity and explanation."[102] Foucault's theory of knowledge, then, has something of an emergent structure. Objects of discourse supervene on complex social networks that give rise to a "collective consciousness," which accords these objects' status as autochthonous. These objects exercise downward causation on the participants in these discourses precisely through their (only-) apparent givenness. Foucault would urge us to resist this process, to look to the history of these processes for the fissures that allow us to resist the process by which power produces "knowledge" that further entrenches the powerful, but this is at the prescriptive level, not the descriptive—a strategy of resistance, set in sharp relief against the backdrop of a regularly (if certainly not "naturally") occurring process of social emergence of objects of discourse. Race lends itself well to this sort of description, indicating that racism has causes, not merely effects, at the social level.

While there is very little disagreement among sociologists about the truth of this constructivist account of racism, as Eduardo Bonilla-Silva points out, there are at least three different ways this perspective on race plays out in the social sciences. On the one hand, there are those who take it that because race is socially constructed, it is not "real," and therefore is not a valid category of analysis and must instead be reduced to the "real" social factors that adhere at the individual level: for example, socioeconomic status or education background. This position is readily recognized as an instance of reductive eliminativism: race supervenes on factors at the individual and social levels; therefore it is not "real." Second, there are those who, while dutifully reciting one or another constructionist formula, essentially reject the growing consensus regarding the constructionist approach to race. For this group, race is an essential feature of humanity. As Bonilla-Silva argues, their work, by failing to pay attention to the social structures that give rise to racial differences themselves, largely functions to reinforce the racial order. In treating race as an essential category, these scholars appear as sort of racial "dualists," writing as though race had some independent existence of its own outside or beyond the psychological or social. Finally, Bonilla-Silva advocates a third approach "which acknowledges that race, as other social categories such as class and gender, is constructed but insists that it has a *social* reality. This means that after race—or class or gender—is created, it produces real effects on the actors racialized as 'black' or 'white.'" Bonilla-Silva's argument is recognizably emergent. He argues *both* that race is socially constructed—that is, it *supervenes* on the actions of social agents—but *also* that race acts back upon those individual agents. In a classic emergentist move, Bonilla-Silva then argues—in part, on the basis of the reality of this downward causation—for the "reality" of the emergent entity: race.[103]

Sociologists like Bonilla-Silva, working with an understanding of the category of "race" as a constructed object of discourse, insist that racism requires a *structural*, rather than a merely *ideological,* account. Rather than holding, as others do, that "racism is ultimately . . . a psychological phenomenon to be examined at the individual level," Bonilla-Silva's account of racism begins not with racists but with "*racialized social systems*" (emphasis original).[104] It is these systems that lay the foundation for ideological racism as they "allocate differential economic, political, social, and even psychological rewards to groups along racial lines; lines that are socially constructed. After a society becomes racialized, a set of social relations and practices based on racial distinctions develops at all societal levels." It is only after this process of racialization that "races historically are constituted according to the process of racialization; they become the effect of relations of opposition between racialized groups at all levels of a social formation." This accords with what we would expect from a constructivist understanding of race.

With the category of race now constituted within the racialized structures, "there develops a racial ideology (what analysts have coded as racism)." This is not to minimize the importance of racism. Rather, Bonilla-Silva insists, "It becomes as real as the racial relations it organizes."This ontological aspect of the analysis is evident elsewhere: for example, when Bonilla-Silva insists that "after a society becomes racialized, racialization develops a life of its own." We see this ontological ambition also in Bonilla-Silva's ascription of a long line of active verbs to racism: "Racism crystallizes the changing 'dogma' on which actors in the social system operate, and becomes 'common sense'; it provides the rules for perceiving and dealing with the 'other' in a racialized society."[105] Of course, in the case of a well-respected, Western, modern sociologist like Bonilla-Silva, we are unlikely even to entertain the possibility that this language is intended as anything more than personification, but Bonilla-Silva's willingness to talk about racism's "relative autonomy" and reality ("as real as the racial relations it organizes") makes one wonder.[106]

Ultimately, this account permits Bonilla-Silva to conceive of "racism without racists," perpetuated through a new, "color-blind racism."[107] Nevertheless, for all that Bonilla-Silva asserts about the autonomy of racism and the perdurance over time of more or less stable racialized systems, "this does not mean," he insists, "that the racial structure is immutable and completely independent of the action of racialized actors. It means only that the social relations between the races become institutionalized (forming a structure as well as a culture) and affect their social life whether individual members of the races want it or not."[108] In other words, this is not a dualist description, no matter how "real" we understand racism to be. There remains a relationship of supervenience between the racialized structures that give rise to racialized ideology, and the racialized actors who participate in such systems. The autonomy of racialized systems emphasizes that these systems can exercise downward causation in acting back down on their supervenience base: namely, racialized actors.[109] Indeed, Bonilla-Silva sees this downward causation at work in all aspects of society—not just those most readily recognized as specifically "racial." All actors have been racialized. All actions take place within racialized structures. These structures put the interests of racial groups at odds with one another. Racial conflict is inevitable. "The process of racial contestation reveals the different objective interests of the races in a racialized system."[110]

This is a description of emergence. There is a bi-directional, causal relationship between racialized actors (racist or otherwise) and racialized social systems. The systems supervene on the individuals, and at the same time, the individuals are constrained by the systems, so much so that they are said to be constituted *as* racialized actors precisely *because* of the constraint exerted by these same racialized structures. This is the emergence relationship that is thought to exist between the psychological and sociological levels. We are quite familiar with the half of this relationship that reductionism would have us imagine: that is, the psychological explaining the social. This is the baseline explanation of racism against which Bonilla-Silva is arguing: racists give rise to racism. Rather, he would have us see the other side of the feedback loop: racialized systems give rise to racialized actors with racialized ideology (racism). Most strikingly, Bonilla-Silva argues, racialized structures can bring about negative outcomes for minority racial groups quite apart from any explicit, racialized ideology (racism without ideological racists).

But emergentism would not have us stop there. If racism is "real"—not just an epiphenomenon of a few irrational Archie Bunker-types—and it exercises causal effects back *down* on racialized actors embedded in racialized systems, does the cascade of effects continue on down the chain? Having seen downward causation cross the boundary between the social and the psychological, can we also see that cascade also cross the boundary between the psychological and the neurological? Recent research suggests that the answer is yes.

Two studies published in 2000 (Hart et al., and Phelps et al.) used functional MRI (fMRI) to study amygdala response in the brains of subjects who identified as white (and, in one study, black) when presented with white and black faces previously unknown to the subjects.[111] The amygdala, a part of the (evolutionarily) "reptilian" brain, is a brain structure known to be related to social and facial recognition, and is particularly related to fear conditioning—even if such fear is conditioned without direct negative experience, or, indeed, even if stimuli are presented subliminally.[112] In short, the amygdala is the part of the brain that quickly identifies reasons to be afraid, as the brain's "early warning mechanism"; its work seems to be entirely automatic.[113] Both studies showed increased amygdala activation when subjects were exposed to "out-group" faces (whites confronted with black faces, blacks confronted with white faces). In support of Bonilla-Silva's decreased emphasis on ideological racism, the study by Phelps et al. showed correspondence with two unconscious measures of race evaluation, but not with conscious expression of race attitudes. That is, it did not matter if subjects consciously adhered to racist ideology; all subjects exhibited elevated amygdala activation when confronted with unfamiliar faces of the opposite race.

These findings would, of course, be consistent with a reductionist account of race and racism: racial bias exists at the neurological level, and the consequences propagate upwards to the psychological level, in the form of racist ideology, and eventually to the social level, in the form of racist systems and structures. Ideological racism and racist social structures would, on this account, be an unfortunate but natural consequence of automatic neurological response to unfamiliar stimuli. However, two later studies suggest this is not what is happening. Lieberman et al., in 2005, showed that blacks exhibited the same heightened amygdala response to black faces as did whites. The authors concluded that "the amygdala activity typically associated with race-related processing may be a reflection of culturally learned negative associations regarding African-American individuals."[114] While universal fearful response to out-group faces could be explained without reference to learned social bias, a unilateral association of fearful responses to black faces would require an explanation that involved causation from the social level. Further strengthening this explanation, in 2008, Chiao et al. found that white Americans and Japanese study participants did not show any elevated responses to neutral out-group faces, concluding that "previous findings of greater amygdala activity for outgroup neutral faces may reflect cultural knowledge of negative stereotypes specifically about African–Americans, rather than general negative stereotypes about other outgroup members." They noted that "this finding provides novel and surprising evidence of cultural tuning in an automatic neural response"—surprising because the causal arrow is pointing the "wrong" way: *down* from the social level to the neurological, perhaps skipping the (conscious) psychological level entirely.[115] These kinds of results are surprising enough to have launched an entirely new field: social neuroscience.

This multilevel description demonstrates that any adequate analysis of racism in the United States will have to account both for "upward" and "downward" causation—that is, it will be best described in the language of emergence. Race as a category seems to be constituted and maintained through multiple feedback loops of supervenience and downward causation. The consequences of racism, in turn, propagate in all directions: "upward" from racist individuals to social institutions; "downward" from those institutions to racialized actors; and even to the unconscious neurological activity within their brains, whence come psychological impulses not unrelated to racialized ideology (racism). Accounts of culpability, simple within a reductionist framework, are complicated—and *expanded*.[116] Constraint "from above" is an irreducible part of any reasonable explanation, even if we concede that all such higher-level entities (societies, races, minds, brains) themselves supervene—indeed, depend for their being—on lower-level entities (individuals, raced persons, brains, brain structures, or neurons). This should be familiar by now: this is the both-and of emergence: downward causation *and* supervenience, irreducible emergence *and* ontological monism.

Conclusions

Our review of the literature on emergentism in the fields of philosophy of mind, and philosophy of science more generally, yields a few important impressions. First, and most significantly, we have in emergentism an account of structured complex systems that suggests that the apparent dilemma of metaphysical dualism, on the one hand, or physical reductionism (and attendant eliminativism), on the other, is illusory. I have not proven either option false, though I have briefly considered the substantial disadvantages to both approaches. Metaphysical dualism would run counter to the otherwise materialist assumptions about reality that scientific inquiry requires at least methodologically. And reductionist eliminativism would push our account of higher-order entities like the mind so far from our apparent experience that we might have to say that it ultimately doesn't really explain the "data" of experience itself. Emergence provides a framework within which to take seriously the unity of the world, and yet also adopt a realist stance toward our subjective experience of it, so much of which consists of interactions with higher-level abstractions like life and mind.

Second, we are amassing a certain vocabulary for discussing the interactions of complex structures. We have explored the relationship of supervenience that describes the emergence of higher-level properties from their lower-level bases. We have also explored the phenomenon of downward causation that these emergent properties exert back onto their lower-level bases. In this dialectical tension between supervenience and downward causation, we have seen a new picture of structure come into view. We have structure that isn't imposed "from above," but rather emerges "from below," yet nevertheless exerts causal power both on its own level and (as is logically required because of the relationship of supervenience) on its supervenience base.

Third, we have found a natural affinity between certain trans-ordinal theories and coordinating epistemologies. In the tripartite system we have proposed, essentialism is the epistemological counterpart of dualism, objectivism is the epistemological counterpart of reductionism, and a sort of Foucauldian constructivism is the counterpart of emergentism. This is an important set of correspondences for the scholar of religion, for whom both essentialism and objectivism are epistemologies in decline. For the intellectual already inclined toward at least modest flavors of constructivism, emergentism offers a certain elegance: it suggests that the world as it actually *is* corresponds—at the formal level—to the world as we have come to *know* it. It suggests that the world as it is materially constituted—in the mechanisms that describe the various joints and connecting tissue of the world from the level of particle physics, to chemistry, to biology, to psychology, sociology, and beyond—exhibits the same *formal* relationships that we find in our epistemology of the various concepts we must employ at each of these levels of description. There is a correspondence between ontology and epistemology. Race, the entity, is constituted formally in an analogous way to how "race," the concept, is constituted. Both are constituted through a dialectical process of "upward" and "downward" causation, both from the individual level and from the social level. Both exist "only" to the extent that they supervene on entities at the lower level, and yet one may assure oneself of the reality of this existence through appeal to the downward causation that they exercise on entities at lower, more fundamental levels (that is, lower-level concepts in the case of epistemology, lower-level entities in the case of ontology). Of course, elegance alone does not prove a case, but the connection here for the constructivist is more intrinsic than mere aesthetics. After all, the constructivist's instinct is precisely that ontology and epistemology have this sort of correspondence. Usually, this is expressed in something like Foucault's skepticism regarding ontology, regarding the "givenness" of objects prior to discourse, but of course it could just as easily be turned around: the fact that objects are constructed by discourse tells us precisely that epistemology *should* correspond to ontology. Any other ontology would be susceptible to a sort of essentialist or objectivist naïveté.

Finally, this discussion of the general philosophical problems posed by trans-ordinal theory—and the traditional solutions that present themselves—allows us to see the history of scholarship from the first chapter in a new light. For example, it is now clear, ironically enough, that the Vatican position, shared by Bultmann and Nelson, is a *reductionist* position. This position argues that all agency, no matter how much it *apparently* emanates from social systems, is always *reducible* to the agency of individuals. In fact, to the extent to which these positions amount to an outright denial of the existence of social agency, a claim that all apparent social agency is ultimately illusory, this view adheres to a particularly hard-line reductionist view: eliminativism. We see this even in the work of Derek Nelson who, in summarizing the debate between Liberationist and the Vatican, argues "If social sin is to be properly conceived and theologically explicated, it is nonetheless the social sin of *social individual sinners*."[117]

By contrast, in the terms of philosophy of science, the position of Käsemann and his contemporary advocates reveals itself as a *dualist* position (indeed, this is in part what made this position so distasteful to the modern-minded Bultmann). There are human sins, yes—but even more important is the reign of the cosmic power, Sin, which exists with so substantial a freedom from individual sins as to have an existence alongside the individual, as if the two were composed of two different substances. At any rate, inasmuch as this line of thinking is not overly concerned with the relationship between Sin and sins—and even less with the *mechanisms* of such a relationship—the dualist paradigm clearly holds sway: there are, on the one hand, terrestrial sins and, on the other, there is cosmic Sin. For the Käsemann school, this is construed much the same way the relationship between body and mind is construed on the dualist view: there exists the physical body on the one hand and the mental mind (with some relationship to soul) on the other—and there is a relative independence of these two entities.

The more radical liberationist positions, such as those espoused by Juan Luis Segundo, seem to advance a distinct dualism of the social and the personal, as opposed to Käsemann's dualism of the cosmic and the personal. By and large, however, the liberationists, for their part, seem to be advocating a third way, which, on the terms of contemporary philosophy of science, seems to be some form of emergentism. This is especially evident when liberationists like José Ignacio González-Faus describe causal feedback loops: "When human beings sin, they create structures of sin, which, in their turn, *make human beings sin*."[118] This emergentist account is able to describe social causation as quite "real," that is, able to exercise constraint on the human individuals, while also maintaining that these social structures are themselves constituted by the participation of individual human agents.

Mapping out these various positions from the first chapter in this way has several important consequences. First of all, as the preceding brief analysis demonstrates, we are now better able to relate the various proposals in the field and understand the various conflicts found therein. In this light, the conflict between Käsemann and more radical liberationists, on the one hand, and Bultmann and the Vatican, on the other, is entirely predictable: it is the conflict between dualists and reductionists.[119] Those more committed to modernist frameworks (Bultmann and the Vatican in this case) adopt the reductionist view.[120] Those more committed, largely for theological reasons, to the recovery or preservation of premodern frameworks (Käsemann, Gaventa, etc.) adopt a dualist view. Those less committed to modern or premodern Western frameworks (non-Western liberationists and postmodern Westerners) are inclined toward something that looks more emergent.

We can also now theorize this conflict in a far more sophisticated way than has been done heretofore. Armed with the various theoretical tools that come to us from the emergence debate, we can identify the dynamics of supervenience and downward causation that create the causal feedback loops that González-Faus describes and that, as Davies warned us, drive much of the confusion and conflict in the debate. The sins of social institutions do, indeed, supervene on the actions of individual agents. However, these sinful social structures also then exercise downward causation back on these agents, causing these same agents to sin. On the terms of emergentism, we can affirm *both* that "social sin is . . . the social sin of social individual sinners," as Derek Nelson insists, and also that sinful social structures *cause* individuals to sin, as Segundo insists. Nelson is describing the relationship of supervenience. Segundo is emphasizing downward causation. We can similarly describe the instincts of Bultmann and Käsemann. Bultmann, in insisting that "Sin came into the world by sinning,"[121] is rightly affirming that, however we ought to understand s/Sin for Paul, its supervenience base is the result of individual human agency. When Käsemann insists that the human agent embedded in sinful social systems "cannot choose freely," he is rightly describing the constraining power of downward causation back on that supervenience base.[122] An emergent account of sin can synthesize these views, finding in them a productive tension rather than an intractable paradox.

Finally, we can now also imagine extending González-Faus's proposal to include not only the individual and the social levels, but also the mythological as well. This extension would mean understanding the world to admit a "mythological" level of emergence. This level would emerge from the social, much like the psychological emerges from the biological. That is, "mythology" in this sense would describe the "psychologies" of social "bodies" (this will be defined in greater detail in the next chapter). As we saw in our case study (and as suggested by Noble's theory of "biological relativity"), as a trans-ordinal theory, emergentism does not merely give us tools to relate two adjacent levels of analysis; rather, it suggests that complex systems may be analyzed at any number of levels. So we might think of the cosmic power, Sin, itself supervening on a complex network of sinful social systems, which themselves supervene on the sinful exercise of individual human agency. This relationship of supervenience would describe the way that, as Bultmann says, "sin came into the world by sinning." The cosmic power, Sin, would not, then, have an existence separate from the sinful social structures built by sinful individual agents, any more than organisms exist apart from the organs, cells, and molecular machinery that compose a living body. Nevertheless, we would be free to take quite seriously the idea of causal constraint imposed by the emergent, higher-level entities, both at the social and cosmic level, as the liberationists and Käsemann school suggest. In both cases, we would simply be dealing with instances of downward causation.

On one point I have heretofore been intentionally evasive. And it is no small issue—indeed, it was one of the central concerns of the first chapter. That is, it is not yet clear whether an emergent account of the cosmic power, Sin, would give us license to describe such a power *as a person*. After all, Murphy-O'Connor described Sin precisely in terms of what I described as a classic case of emergence—"The sensation is that of being caught in a tightly packed crowd swept by a motion of panic"—but used this analogy precisely as a reason *not* to describe Sin in personal terms, that is, as "a supernatural evil power."[123] In the next chapter, we will consider what emergence and contemporary science have to say about *personhood,* and whether an emergent account of Sin would render Paul's language a case of personification or person-identification.

3   THE EMERGENCE OF PERSONS GREAT AND SMALL

Müsset im Naturbetrachten immer eins wie alles achten.

[When looking at nature, you must always consider the detail and the whole.]

—GOETHE

The driving question in the first chapter was: how can we tell personification from person-identification? I argued that answering this question inevitably involves importing some pre-existing framework for separating persons from non-persons: an ontology of persons. We have to know from the outset what does or does not qualify as a person, in order to know then whether a description of an entity as a person is metaphorical or not. Indeed, in the case of ἁμαρτία in Romans 5–8, interpreters have repeatedly shown themselves unable to refrain from importing their own (modern) frameworks for making this determination. Bultmann, Murphy-O'Connor, Nelson, and the Vatican—reductionists with an individualist ontology of persons—begin with the assumption that all "real" persons exist at the level of the individual human person, and therefore relegate all discussion of Sin's agency or personhood at the cosmic, or even social, level to the realm of metaphor. Lost on these readings are the levels of causation privileged by the liberationists, who privilege the social, and by the Käsemann school, who privilege the cosmic or mythological. Each of these two schools have an ontology of the human person that is largely determined "from above," as it were, imposed by the overriding constraints of social institutions, in the case of the liberationists, or cosmic powers, in the case of the Käsemann school. The Käsemann school, inasmuch as they hold a dualist ontology of persons, has no difficulty identifying real persons at the mythological level. The exegetical problem is that each school does justice to at least some aspect of Romans 5–8 which the others miss. What is needed is an ontology of persons, acceptable within our readerly horizon (to borrow from Gadamer), that can hold together these various readings of Romans 5–8. That is, we need a trans-ordinal ontology that facilitates a multilevel account of ἁμαρτία.

Therefore, the questions that need to be asked at this point are of two sorts—and in the first chapter we saw someone like Murphy-O'Connor beginning to ask questions of both kinds. First, there are questions such as: What does it mean for an entity to be a person, a self, an individual, or an agent—or to possess a mind?[1] How do human beings fit these criteria? What allows us to count human beings as "real" persons, potentially distinguishable from other only "fictitious" persons? These questions inevitably lead us into one of the oldest and most vexing questions of philosophy: what is the self? And in our contemporary context, in which the ever-expanding reach of neuroscience takes questions about consciousness, agency, and selfhood as proper to its domain, we will necessarily have to ask the fundamental question of contemporary philosophy of mind: how does the mind relate to the body? Indeed, even the givenness of the body—that is, the body's status as a simple whole—is brought into question by contemporary biology. Biologists are asking: At what level of scale is it proper to describe a biological system as an organism? What defines an organismic "whole"? How does one determine its boundaries? So, we will need to ask on what grounds we take the paradigmatic person's *body* to be a "real" thing. All these questions are oriented around the individual person or agent.

The second set of questions, prompted by the social readings of ἁμαρτία by both Murphy-O'Connor and the liberationists, goes further, asking questions about structured collections of individual persons and agents. We need to ask: Is the social real? Is social agency real? If so, how might complex social systems qualify as agents, or even as persons? These questions, of course, are some of the most fundamental in the history of social theory (we began to consider how emergentism might help us answer these questions in the last chapter), and our discussion will engage several social theorists, from Durkheim up to the present, who address such questions. But useful analogies will be found also in the study of other social species. Again, we will find that stimulating questions about the boundaries of the organism—that is, the boundaries of the body—are presented by contemporary biologists. Can collections of organisms be described as a single organism—a *unit* in some meaningful sense?

These two sets of questions—about the individual and about the social—have very much to do with each other. And when we pursue them along emergentist lines, we find that certain social systems ought to be considered just as "real" persons as individual human persons—and for precisely the same reasons. The argument here is that the eliminative individualism of Bultmann, Murphy O'Connor, Nelson, and the Vatican depends on an atomistic conception of the human person that, though it models itself after the great modernist scientific dogma of physical reductionism, is actually quite out of step with contemporary scientific descriptions of the human person—at both the biological and the psychological levels. If the human person, body and mind, were an atom—a simple unity easily distinguished from its environment—then individualists would be quite right to reduce all accounts of social sin to the "sin of social individual sinners," and any treatment of ἁμαρτία as a personal, cosmic power would indeed be the sole provenance of the "mind of simple people."[2] In that case, we could only refer to human social realities as "analogous" to persons—or, "real," human individuals having some much more stringent identity as atomistic persons. However, the human person—whether we think primarily in terms of the body or in terms of the mind—is not as atomistic as this reductive individualism would have us believe. Both body and mind are *internally composite* and *integrated externally* with their environments, to the extent that the very use of the categories "internal" and "external," and "individual" and "environment," become problematic. If the key to identifying literary personification is "a separation between the literary pretense of a personality, and the actual state of affairs," then we will have to admit that contemporary scientific reflection serves not to confirm, but rather to deny, this separation in the case of certain "personified" social realities.[3]

Ultimately, we will find that social realities *can* be described as personal on precisely the same grounds that individual human persons are. Indeed, my contention is that Sin, as described by Paul in Romans 5–8, is precisely one of these social realities. The distinction between "personification" and "person-identification" is demonstrated here to have no basis. We do not need any additional "figurative" language, or any extra layer of abstraction, to ascribe personhood to certain social realities. All of the abstractions and metaphors required to describe a social reality as a person are required to ascribe personhood to a human individual—whether conceived of biologically as an "individual" organism (that is, as a *body*) or neuropsychologically as an "individual" mind. Formally, the argument advanced here may be seen as an expansion of Durkheim's founding analogy of sociology, when he argued that "the relationship which unites the social substratum and the social life is at every point analogous to that which undeniably exists between the physiological substratum and the psychic life of individuals."[4] Or, to illustrate this in another way:

Physiological : Mental :: Individual : Social

Such an analogy serves as the basis for an emergentist account of social entities, and unites the discussion of emergence at the individual level with emergence at the social level. Durkheim employs familiar emergentist language:

> There is nothing more in animate nature than inorganic matter, since the cell is made exclusively of inanimate atoms. To be sure, it is likewise true that society has no other active forces than individuals. . . . Of course the elementary qualities of which the social fact consists are present in germ in

individual minds. But the social fact emerges from them only when they have been transformed by association since it is only then that it appears. Association itself is also an active factor productive of special effects. In itself it is therefore something new.[5]

In a letter to the editor of the *American Journal of Sociology* (1898), Durkheim further explained that:

> it is very true that society comprises no active forces other than those of individuals; but individuals, as they join together, form a psychological entity of a new species . . . Thus I do not deny in any way that individual natures are the components of the social fact. What must be ascertained is whether as they combine together to produce the social fact, they are not transformed by the very fact of their combination. Is the synthesis purely mechanical, or chemical? This is the heart of the question.[6]

The answer for Durkheim is clear: the synthesis is *chemical* (in J. S. Mill's sense). The social fact is real; this is ontological emergence. The entity that emerges is not simply epistemic—that is, the social *fact*. Rather, what emerges is "a psychological entity of a new species." Of course, this is the sort of ambitious language that has plagued Durkheimian scholarship for over a century now, but I will show that there are reasons to take the language quite seriously. Indeed, it is a natural consequence of Durkheim's analogy, which suggests we ought first give careful attention to the question of the emergence of individual human persons and the relationship between physiology and the psychological self.

An Emergent Ontology of Human Persons

We have conceived of emergentism as an alternative to two dualisms (and their modern reductionist counterparts): vital and mental. In turning to an emergent account of the human person, it can be tempting to think that a description of the human person has only to do with this second dualism. Inasmuch as an emergent account of human personhood entails the same ontological monism as the larger emergence paradigm, however, this cannot be the case. An emergent account of personhood must engage both the emergence of mind from body, and also the emergence of that same living body from biochemistry. The emergence of the living body is, in space and time, synchronous with the emergence of the mind from body. In short, both dualisms—mental and vital—will have to be addressed and both reductionisms—the eliminative reduction of biology to chemistry (in which living bodies—be they single cells or "whole organisms"—are only useful fictions) and the eliminative reduction of psychology to neurobiology (in which the mind is only a useful fiction)—must be avoided.[7] What we will find is that the same formal arguments required to make sense of the mind as emergent from the body are required to make sense of the body as emergent from its biochemistry. The body is no less an emergent entity than the mind. Whatever metaphysical misgivings we have about an emergent description of the mind, it is not possible for us to resolve our concerns by retreating to the "firm" ground of a material body. Upon closer examination, in the light of contemporary philosophy and physiology, the body reveals itself to be just as mysterious as the mind, presenting the same sorts of questions and requiring—formally, at least—the same sort of description. This formal symmetry exists in the objects themselves (that is, body and mind). The strongest argument in favor of the emergent account of human personhood lies in its attention to and description of this symmetry.

On the basis of this symmetry, philosopher James Haag, neuroscientist Terrence Deacon, and philosopher Jay Ogilvy (hereafter, Haag et al.) have tackled the difficult philosophical problem of identifying the human, subjective self by first addressing the (perhaps) simpler but analogous case of the organismic self.[8] That is, they argue that "the self experienced by creatures with complex brains is in many ways derivative (or rather emergent) from the self of organism existence." So, as a foundation for discussing the selfhood of the human person, they assert that "even organisms as simple as bacteria have properties that qualify them as selves, in at least a minimal sense," which "suggests that self is not just a subjective issue."[9] The question of selfhood leads Haag et al. to begin with more basic questions about the ontology of an organism, which turn out to be more complex than one might first suppose.

As Haag et al. observe, "the organism is in a constant state of renewal in which new organization is produced (formed and reformed) that allows it to maintain itself. At every moment an organism's material constitution is different."[10] To paraphrase Heraclitus's old maxim: "you never wake up in the same body twice."[11] So, the first difficulty we must address in locating a minimal organismic self is defining a site of continuity in a dynamic complex system. As it turns out, it is nontrivial to describe the continuity of identity of even some apparently simple entities—for example, a flame, a wave, or a river.[12] To take Heraclitus's classic example: what grants continuity of identity to a river? There is no sustained identity of its constituent components; water is constantly flowing in and out of the system. But a wave is perhaps yet more perplexing. A wave is precisely distinguished from the medium through which it propagates; a wave travels through the ocean but is in no sense constituted by the ocean or even by the water that swells as the wave passes through. Nevertheless, without a medium, there is no wave (with, of course, the notable exception of light waves and other quantum phenomena conceived of as waves).[13]

Of particular import are examples of the type of the flame—that is, non-equilibrium or dissipative systems. Other examples include vortices (think of tornadoes or water draining in a bathtub) and, crucially, living organisms. Most of the spontaneous appearances of order in the natural world are dissipative systems; they are called "dissipative" because they naturally dissipate energy and therefore depend on a constant supply of energy in order for the structure to persist.[14] These structures are significant to any discussion of minimal selfhood because their energy structures exhibit a certain reflexivity. As philosophical cognitive scientist Mark Bickhard explains, "a candle flame maintains above combustion threshold temperature; it melts wax so that it percolates up the wick; it vaporizes wax in the wick into fuel; in standard atmospheric and gravitational conditions, it induces convection, which brings in fresh oxygen and gets rid of waste."[15]

Bickhard characterizes this reflexive behavior as minimal "self-maintenance."[16] The flame is an emergent entity; its self-maintenance is a result of its exercising downward causation upon its constituent parts. This reflexive behavior qualifies the flame, for Haag et al., as a sort of proto-self, but not yet even a minimal self.

Compared to the flame, a minimally complex organism like a bacterium exhibits not just self-maintenance, but recursive self-maintenance. An organism "is not merely a self-organizing process, but a reflexively organized constellation of self-organizing processes, each of which contributes in some way to the conditions that make the others possible."[17] This has an impact on how one thinks about the ontology of the organism and its parts. The parts of the organism "are in a continuous state of turnover . . . The molecular 'parts' of this organism do not even enjoy any kind of existence as parts independent of this organization, since each is dependent on the interactions among others. So although the parts constitute the whole, the whole also generates each part."[18] Haag et al. (like Bickhard), then, understand the part-whole relationship in emergence in *process* terms: the "wholes" that emerge are processes composed of component processes. The "self" of the organism—and, indeed, the "self" of the human person—then is revealed to be a set of *constraints* on those component processes. Haag et al. identify the self with "*the intrinsic constraints that organize the physical work (e.g., of the brain or body of an organism) with respect to functional ends and the requirements of a system that confer this capacity.*"[19] This identity of the emergent self makes good sense within the frame of emergentism. After all, on emergent terms, the "self" is that higher-level entity that exercises downward causation on its supervenience base. As we saw in the last chapter in cases as diverse as molecular structure, the Millennium Bridge, and cardiac rhythm, downward causation appeared in the form of *constraint* on lower-level systems and entities—*boundary conditions* for the differential equations that described these systems in mathematical terms.

Indeed, as far back as 1968, Michael Polanyi suggested that the boundary conditions of differential equations were the places to go looking for downward causation in action.[20]

If the organismic self—the body—is a set of constraints, then it is the case that this self is, in fact, an abstraction.[21] But Haag et al. insist that this is not a Humean abstraction, incapable of being a source of causal power. Rather, they argue, if we conceive of the "self as the source of constraint on the physical processes generated by an organism," then "it can introduce asymmetric causal properties such as are a necessary defining attribute of end-directedness."[22] It is this end-directedness that allows the organism to be "recursively self-maintenant" in the sense that Bickhard distinguishes the selfhood of organisms from that of simpler dissipative systems. This introduction of teleological language into their description of biological systems might set off alarms for anyone well-schooled in evolutionary theory, but it is important to distinguish the *agential* teleology they are describing from the *design* teleology that evolutionary theory explicitly denies. That is, the organism's teleology does not come extrinsically from its form in a Platonic sense. Rather, the structure of the organism as a self-organizing process gives rise to its own spontaneous, intrinsic teleology.

How this intrinsic teleology spontaneously emerges from the non-teleological is a central problem in evolutionary cognitive science, and is the central concern of Deacon's own work; it is also addressed by emergentist evolutionary biologist Stuart Kauffman.[23] Both point to Kant's concept of "natural ends" as a starting place for answering this question. Describing the appearance of "natural ends"— life—from non-teleological material reality, Kant writes that "a thing exists as a natural end if it is both cause and effect of itself."[24] Kauffman argues that Kant's description of organisms as "autopoetic wholes in which each part existed both for and by means of the whole," now appears especially prescient in light of contemporary research that suggests that life first appeared in autocatalytic chemical "soup."[25] Indeed, Kauffman argues, this sort of autocatalysis may prove to be the origin of organismic agency in contrast to the "central directing agency" suggested by certain DNA-centric ways of thinking about the organism:

> A collectively autocatalytic set of molecules—at least in silica, as we have seen—is capable of reproducing itself, dividing into two "blobs" capable of heritable variation, and hence, following Darwin's argument, capable of evolution. But in a collectively autocatalytic set, there is no central directing agency. There is no separate genome, no DNA. There is a collective molecular autopoetic system that Kant might have been heartened to behold. The parts exist for and by means of the whole; the whole exists for and by means of the parts. Although not yet achieved in a laboratory beaker, an autocatalytic set is not mysterious. It is not yet a true organism. But if we stumbled on

some evolving or even coevolving autocatalytic sets in a test tube or hydro-thermal vent, we'd tend to feel we were looking at living systems. Whether or not I am right that life started with collective autocatalysis, the mere fact that such systems are possible should make us question the dogma of a central directing agency. The central directing agency is not necessary to life. Life has, I think, an inalienable wholeness. And always has.[26]

Organismic agency—that reflexive self-maintenance that gives even the simplest organism a minimal self—need not come from DNA, as though it were the smuggler of all the teleological information lost when we surrendered the idea of teleological design. Rather, this agency emerges from the reflexivity of autopoesis itself. This reflexivity—understood as constraint—is at once deeply material in the sense that it does not come from the "outside," but rather emerges spontaneously from the system itself and yet is ultimately immaterial, an abstraction of the type Haag et al. describe. Kauffman summarizes:

> I believe that life itself is an emergent phenomenon, but I mean nothing mystical by this . . . No vital force or extra substance is present in the emergent, self-reproducing whole. But the collective system does possess a stunning property not possessed by any of its parts. It is able to reproduce itself and to evolve. The collective system is alive. Its parts are just chemicals.[27]

If life itself is an emergent entity, Haag et al. argue the same for the organismic self:

> If the organism is continually reproduced via synergistically interacting self-organizing processes, then defining self in substantive terms is problematic. Many self-organizing processes in living organisms are multiply realizable, that is, not limited to a single type of molecule or even any specific chemical reaction. So any search for the essential "stuff" of the organism will inevitably fail. Morever, the organism is not even any single type of organized process, since these too can change over the course of a lifetime. Instead, the unit of continuity that is the self of an organism is the synergistic relationship between numerous self-organizing processes that constitutes this tendency to preserve the synergy. It is then this special reflexive organization of form—(constraint-)generating processes that determine the closure to formal influences—that we recognize as a kind of autonomy. Precisely because organized systems spontaneously tend to degrade, a system that actively regenerates and replaces its components and maintains their interrelationships intrinsically has itself as an end. As Kant suggested, when the end is the means and the means is the end a kind of intrinsic teleology comes into being.[28]

What defines the organismic self—what persists over time, even as the material that composes the organism changes—is a form, not in the Platonic sense, but rather in the sense of a spontaneously appearing *structure*. This structure is abstract, best understood as a system of constraints, or, better yet, a multilayered network of self-reinforcing constraints. The result is that the organism, the body, cannot be defined in substantive terms. The body is not the refuge from metaphysics one might have imagined.

With this conception of the organismic self in place, Haag et al. then move to offering an analogous description of the subjective self. They posit that the physiological difference between organisms with only a rudimentary organismic self (bacteria, plants, etc.) and those with subjective selves (humans, primates, and other animals) lies with the latter group having complex brains. The operations of complex brains entail yet higher-order reflexive dynamics, and therefore higher-order properties emerge, including a higher-order teleology: *intention*. So, while simple organisms in fact *do* take actions (in the simplest sense of doing work) to counter the entropic forces that would destroy the persistent order that is the organismic self, the subjective selves of organisms with complex brains not only do these actions, but the higher-order reflexivity of their complex brains means they can from time to time be said to *intend* to do them. The capacity for symbolic description emergent from human brains then adds a final level of reflexivity: the self-conscious self, which allows for higher-level forms of work, "e.g., the construction of narratives, the creation of obligations, obedience to principles, and so forth—not available to simpler forms of life."[29]

At every point, this subjective self is understood to be constructed in precisely the same way as is the organismic self. Both are complex systems of reflexive constraints on constituent processes. They are the boundary conditions that maintain order within these dissipative structures. This means that they are both physical and nonmaterial. Therefore, Haag et al. argue that "we abandon our search for a substantial self in favor of a self that is constituted by constraints, and constraints are not something present, but the boundary conditions determining what is likely."[30] No more substantial self—but rather, a self that is emergent from the complex dynamics that it constrains. This is a thick description of what emergentists from Broad to Sperry to Clayton are suggesting when they imagine that mind emerged from the body.[31] This description bears all the hallmarks of those earlier emergentist accounts, not least of which is a strong commitment to the physicalism of ontological monism, but also to the reality of nonmaterial emergents. Haag et al. conclude:

> The complex and convoluted dynamical processes we believe to be the defining features of self at any given level are reciprocal limitations on dynamics, not the processes themselves nor the materials and energy that

are their instantiation. So, ultimately, this view of self shows it to be as nonmaterial as Descartes might have imagined and yet as physical and extended as the hole in the hub of a wheel, without which it would just be a useless disk.[32]

"Nonmaterial" and yet "physical": this description of the self explodes these categories. Where we might describe the body as physical and the mind as nonmaterial, the organismic self (i.e., the body-as-unity) is revealed to be just as nonmaterial as the subjective self (i.e., the mind). Indeed, inasmuch as these two categories obtain in single entities, Haag et al. invite us into a world in which "nonmaterial" and "physical" can no longer serve as antinomies for us in the ways they typically do.

The Self Out of Bounds

To an extent, Haag et al.'s proposal serves as a meditation on the fact that the self is not simple—that is, it is internally divisible. Both the human mind and the human body are *internally composite*. They are structured wholes—whether we conceive of them as structured systems of parts, as do conventional emergentists, or as structured systems of processes, as do Haag et al. The perhaps surprising conclusion that the self—both as body and as mind—is both nonmaterial and physical is a result of the fact that neither is simple: both are *emergents*. They are physical inasmuch as they have a relationship of supervenience on the component systems from which they emerge, and they are nonmaterial inasmuch as they nevertheless are ontologically irreducible to those same systems, shown by their exercising downward causation on their supervenience bases in the form of constraint, providing boundary conditions for these lower-level systems. Counter to the atomism of eliminative reductionists, human persons—both as bodies and as subjects—are *internally composite*. So the atomistic description fails internally. It also fails externally. "No man is an island" is no mere slogan. Contemporary scientific description shows human persons to be integrated externally (that is, indivisible from their environments) as well—at both the biological and psychological levels. This integration further problematizes an atomistic conception of the human person, and shows that treating social realties as persons requires no new metaphysical or literary innovation that is not already required for a basic ontology of the individual human person.

The body—the organismic self—as we saw above, is indubitably composite. But whereas a systems approach to the human body might, at first glance, suggest to us a simple mereology of nested parts and wholes, the reality is not so simple.

A 2012 *Scientific American* cover story summarizes the contemporary picture of the human body as a complex system quite well:

> The human body is not such a neatly self-sufficient island after all. It is more like a complex ecosystem—a social network—containing trillions of bacteria and other microorganisms that inhabit our skin, genital areas, mouth, and especially intestines. In fact, most of the cells in the human body are not human at all. Bacterial cells in the human body outnumber human cells 10 to one . . . This mixed community of microbial cells and the genes they contain . . . offers vital help with basic physiological processes—from digestion to growth to self-defense. So much for human autonomy.[33]

As a result, full biological description of these basic, "internal" human physiological processes necessarily requires an account of these "external" (in the sense of being genetically non-human) organisms. Restricting oneself to only the human tissue would make a description of functions as basic as digestion and immune defense impossible. As a result, an evolutionary account of the development of human physiology requires a parallel account of the evolution of these microbial symbiotes. Human DNA is not the only DNA necessary for a full account of human evolution.

Even the attempt to demarcate the boundaries of the human body at the cellular level breaks down. The contemporary theory of the origin of mitochondria—one of the basic structures of all eukaryotic cells—contends that mitochondria once existed outside their eukaryotic hosts as independent prokaryotic bacteria.[34] In short, mitochondria have revealed themselves to be aliens within: "endosymbionts." They are the "outside" inside our insides, problematizing the very notion of "inside" and "outside" when it comes to the body.

On analogy to this theory of the origin of mitochondria, Richard Dawkins suggests that we think of our very genes (which, on some accounts, would describe the biological essence of the atomistic, individual person) as interlopers that use our bodies to reproduce.[35] This is "the selfish gene" for which Dawkins is famous. On this account, the goings on of the human body as a biological individual organism are themselves epiphenomenal to what is "really" going on: the persistence or death of individual genes. The account of human personhood that results is another brand of eliminative materialism; if our bodies themselves are epiphenomenal, our subjective experiences are only more so. But the fact that even our genes can be thought of as somehow "external" to us drives the point home: the fact that our bodies are irreducibly internally composite means that, at the microbiological level, it becomes difficult to distinguish the boundaries of the body.

If the account of endosymbiosis in the body confounds the identity of the self from what we might reasonably take to be the "inside," recent accounts of human cognition stemming from the work of cognitive scientist Andy Clark raise similar difficulties in excluding what we might otherwise consider "outside" the human mind.[36] Clark's thesis has come to be known as the "extended mind" hypothesis, the theory that human cognition is neither limited to the brain, nor to the nervous system (which also participates in cognition).[37] Rather, Clark argues, human cognition naturally extends out into the mind's environment. In their seminal article, "The Extended Mind," Clark and David Chalmers analyze a number of mental processes that lead them to suggest that some physical objects function as extensions of the mind itself, inasmuch as they function as an integral part of "a process which, were it done in the head, we would have no hesitation in recognizing as part of the cognitive process."[38] Their flagship case is a thought experiment involving an Alzheimer's patient who uses a notebook to supplement his memory. Other examples include

> the use of pen and paper to perform long multiplication (McClelland et al. 1986, Clark 1989), the use of physical re-arrangements of letter tiles to prompt word recall in Scrabble (Kirsh 1995), the use of instruments such as the nautical slide rule (Hutchins 1995), and the general paraphernalia of language, books, diagrams, and culture.[39]

Clark and Chalmers argue that, in certain cases, these external resources do epistemic work for the mind that engages them to the extent that distinguishing these resources from the mind proper becomes difficult to justify.[40]

Consider David Kirsh and Paul Maglio's research on human subjects playing Tetris.[41] Subjects found it 70 percent faster to rotate a piece through the game (two-tenths of a second to select the button, one-tenth for the shape to change on the screen), than to rotate the piece "in their heads" (which took them on average a full second). As a result, in playing the game, subjects regularly used the rotation function of the game not just when they needed to do so in order to correctly place a piece, but also in order to help determine which orientation of the piece yielded the best fit. Kirsh and Maglio call this kind of action "epistemic action." Which of these actions are undertaken "internally"—that is "within" the mind (conceived as brain-bound)—and which are undertaken via certain "external" epistemic actions is a pragmatic choice for the individual. There is no essential difference. Clark and Chalmers conclude:

> In these cases, the human organism is linked with an external entity in a two-way interaction, creating a *coupled system* that can be seen as a cognitive system in its own right. All the components in the system play an active

causal role, and they jointly govern behaviour in the same sort of way that cognition usually does. If we remove the external component the system's behavioural competence will drop, just as it would if we removed part of its brain. Our thesis is that this sort of coupled process counts equally well as a cognitive process, whether or not it is wholly in the head.[42]

Clark and Chalmers are right to insist that examples of these sorts of coupled systems need not be especially high-tech, but the steady march of technology's advancement yields ever-increasingly vivid examples of these sorts of coupled systems.[43] Chalmers gives an especially relatable high-tech example in his foreword to Clark's 2008 book:

> A month ago, I bought an iPhone. The iPhone has already taken over some of the central functions of my brain. It has replaced part of my memory, storing phone numbers and addresses that I once would have taxed my brain with. . . . Friends joke that I should get the iPhone implanted into my brain. But if Andy Clark is right, all this would do is speed up the processing and free up my hands. The iPhone is part of my mind already.[44]

The iPhone is, of course, not a part of the physical brain—but it *is* a part of the mind, serving, as it does, as a functional component of the user's cognition.[45] This is the mind beyond the bounds of skull and skin, a mind both physical and nonmaterial.

Clark's work has found a number of supporters, including Mark Rowlands, who argues, on the basis of Clark's work, for seeing consciousness itself as extending beyond the individual human body and including these "external" extensions of the mind.[46] Given that defining consciousness itself remains a "hard problem" of philosophy, Rowlands's work can only be speculative, but it is nevertheless evocative. Moving in a similar direction—and owing a debt to the emergentist tradition—Deborah Perron Tollefsen has suggested that if physical objects can be understood as extensions of mind, so, too, could other people (and thus, other minds).[47] As a trivial extension of the extended mind thesis, Tollefsen suggests that we might imagine a dependable spouse swapped in for the notebook in the case of Clark and Chalmers's Alzheimer's patient. Tollefsen calls the resultant mind "collective," rather than merely extended, including, as it does, more than one human mind. "When minds extend to encompass other minds, there is a collective system formed," a system which may qualify, Tollefsen argues, as a collective mind. Her work bridges the Extended Mind and Group Mind theses, demonstrating how the tendency of the "personal" mind to break boundaries of skull and skin opens us to taking quite seriously the possibility of emergent minds at the social level. Tollefsen is not alone in speculating regarding group minds, as we will see below; indeed, she engages much of the contemporary debate regarding group mind in her article on extended mind.[48] But to make the jump too quickly to the group or collective mind thesis would be to miss the most profound feature of Tollefsen's suggestion. Tollefsen has not merely suggested that groups of individual minds can form integrated, complex systems from which group minds might emerge (this is more or less the group mind hypothesis that I will consider at length below). Rather, Tollefsen has suggested that, in giving an adequate account of the individual mind, extended as it is into the mind's natural environment, we are always already describing "a mind" that is integrated into larger systems. Just as the boundaries of the body—that is, the organismic self—irreducibly entails that which is genetically "other" than the organism itself, the mind, too, necessarily engages that which lies beyond the boundaries of the body, including technology such as pen, paper, and language, but also "other" minds. The minds of human persons always already "extend to encompass other minds."[49]

Roger Sperry himself—the grandfather of the modern rebirth of emergence in philosophy of mind—described a mind fundamentally in community. While we have heretofore focused on his emergent theory of consciousness, Sperry is most noted for his work on the differentiation of the two hemispheres in the brain, or so-called split brain research (work for which he was awarded a Nobel Prize in 1981). Working with patients who, in order to relieve persistent, debilitating seizures, had the two hemispheres of their brains surgically disconnected, Sperry and his colleagues noted striking behavioral results:

> Instead of the normally unified single stream of consciousness, these patients behave in many ways as if they have two independent streams of conscious awareness, one in each hemisphere, each of which is cut off from and out of contact with the mental experiences of the other. In other words, each hemisphere seems to have its own separate and private sensations; its own perceptions; its own concepts; and its own impulses to act, with related volitional, cognitive, and learning experiences. Following the surgery, each hemisphere also has thereafter its own separate chain of memories that are rendered inaccessible to the recall processes of the other.[50]

While the experimental results obviously give us unique insight into the functioning of the divided brain, what is most significant is what they suggest regarding the "normal," connected brain. With the two hemispheres disconnected, Sperry observed for the first time that, in fact, the "individual" human brain is itself far from unitary. Rather, it appears that at least two "streams of conscious awareness" are constantly functioning within themselves and in dialog with one another. In his patients, Sperry saw a duplication of all major mental functions: sensation, perception, concepts, impulses, volitional, cognitive, and learning experiences. In addition to the duplication of other mental functions, Sperry observed a duplication of the memory; each hemisphere had "its own separate chain of memories." In the case of the disconnected brain, these were "inaccessible to the recall process of the other," but in the connected brain, these two memories function as one.

Sperry's observations amounted to the "the presence of two minds in one body"—what neuroanatomist Jill Taylor, reflecting on her own personal experience of a stroke that temporarily divided the two hemispheres of her brain and alternatively isolated "her" in one hemisphere and then the other, describes as "the 'we' inside of me."[51] And while the surgical intervention in the cases Sperry observed allowed for his observation of the separate functioning of these two minds, the typical case, of course, involves the mutual interaction of these two minds, and their participation in what we typically understand to be a single mind. Sperry's research provides what is tantalizingly close to objective evidence of the emergence of a group mind, albeit counterfactually in the case of his subjects. In normal cases, Sperry's research suggests that all human persons regularly provide evidence for emergent group minds—at the very least, communities of two minds that have already extended to encompass other minds, ready to extend further to encompass even more minds as well. In this sense, the observation of the two hemispheres of the typical human brain offers us a simple test case— indeed, the simplest possible test case—of what emerges from more than one mind in intricate interaction: that is, you get a mind—even though the component minds continue to experience a conscious awareness completely isolated from one another, as Sperry's research shows.

The isolation that Sperry's research suggests is quite important for distinguishing what sorts of minds groups may exhibit from the likes of science fiction (or, as we will see, the likes of social theory at the turn of the twentieth century). There is no sense of a "higher consciousness" into which all member minds are taken up. Rather, these component consciousnesses continue unabated, and a new consciousness emerges. This consciousness impacts component consciousnesses, but it does so through downward causation, rather than through some sort of Borg-like imposition of uniform consciousness.[52]

Ultimately, the extended mind thesis fundamentally challenges our conception of "mind" in the first place. Tollefsen writes:

> "Mind" is not a name for a substance; rather it names a whole host of cognitive processes, dispositional states, connotative and agential behavioral dispositions. The picture of mind that comes out of [Clark and Chalmer's] work is that some of these states and processes supervene on features outside of the body.[53]

Escaping from the grips of substantialism in the case of our concept of mind means that there are several levels of analysis at which we might find minds. Sperry's work suggests that there exists "mind" at least at the hemispherical level. Then, of course, there is the "individual" mind we often unthinkingly take as bounded by "skull and skin." But, Clark and Chalmers insist, even an "individual" mind has a supervenience base that pushes beyond these borders. Then, finally, we may have collective or group minds. So, there are at least four possible levels of analysis, and correspondingly, four different boundaries of "mind." There is no essential bounding of mind that can tell us which level demands our attention; rather, the recognition of "mind" at one or more level is a matter of analytical convenience, and is determined by the questions we are asking. Let this serve as prolegomena for the moment. I return in earnest to contemporary theories of group minds below. First, however, let us consider again the organismic self: that is, the body.

The Social Self: Superorganisms and Group Minds

Up to this point, we have seen remarkable symmetry between the non-atomistic features of the organismic self (the body) and the subjective self (the mind). Each is best described as physical and yet nonmaterial: a nonmaterial set of constraints on the physical. These systems of constraints persist while the materials that compose the tissues on which both body and mind supervene turn over. This is just as true of the body as it is of the mind. Both body and mind reveal themselves to be internally composite, the body being emergent from a complex structure-of-structures-of-structures of cells, tissues, organs, and systems, the mind emerging from a similar multilevel structure of neurons, brain structures and hemispheres. Both spill "out of bounds," the body incorporating (pun intended) multiple "foreign" bodies as "internally" as one could imagine, the mind "encompassing" (to use Tollefsen's problematic term just once more) technologies, abstractions, and other minds into its machinery of cognition. If the eliminative individualism of Bultmann, Murphy-O'Connor, Nelson, and the Vatican depends on an atomistic human person, we should have to suggest that this sense of personhood is itself quite out of step with "the actual state of affairs" as described by much contemporary science. This latter description leaves us with a sense of the essentially combinatorial, social nature of body and mind, of the human person—internally composite and always already poised for further combination.

Organisms, Superorganisms, and Biological Relativity of Scale

If my reading of Tollefsen and Sperry is correct in suggesting that the idea of a group mind is difficult to exclude, on the grounds that the would-be atomistic individual mind one would otherwise champion is itself irreducibly composite, even minimally "social"—leading one to leave the basic unit of analysis, "mind," as something best determined pragmatically as each case requires—then we would do well to note that a parallel argument is made in biology regarding the basic unit of biological analysis, the *organism.* Given that the organism is internally composite in the manner I have described—nested and overlapping sub-units of organization—what justification do we have for describing a single level of analysis as the "whole" "organism"? What makes the biological whole the whole and what makes the parts parts? While this argument has spilled over into broader debates in philosophy of biology, the impetus for this discussion comes from entomology.

The "eusocial" insects have long served as objects of fascination for those who studied the natural world because of their social form of life.[54] Indeed, Aristotle described insects like bees and ants as "social" or "political."[55] As we will see below, Aristotle was by no means the last to interpret these insects in terms of human social systems (and vice versa). Bees, he took it, were led by a "leader," the "king of the bees"; ants were among the "anarchic" insects.[56] The proper number of "king" bees (which Aristotle mistakenly thought was typically more than one per hive) was important to maintain, lest the hive become factious (in the case of too many), or unable to reproduce (in the case of too few).[57] Only in the seventeenth century would the sex of the "king bee" be discovered by Jan Swammerdam, and the correct feminine language of "queen bee," adopted. Swammerdam, too, avails himself of political language in describing the life of the hive, calling it the "wonderful republic of Bees, which is founded upon affection only, and excludes all kind of superiority."[58] This "republic" is such an irreducible feature of the life of bees and ants that one begins to wonder at which level one is encountering the organismic "whole": at the level of the "individual" insect; or at the level of the hive or nest?

In a seminal 1912 article, the father of modern entomology, William Morton Wheeler, suggested that the ant colony was itself best understood as an organism.[59] In prescient language quite similar to that of Haag et al., Wheeler laments that an adequate definition of "organism" is difficult to determine, since "the organism is neither a thing nor a concept, but a continual flux or process." The best Wheeler can give is a functional definition:

> An organism is a complex, definitely coordinated and therefore individualized system of activities, which are primarily directed to obtaining and assimilating substances from an environment, to producing other similar systems, known as offspring, and to protecting the system itself and usually also its offspring from disturbances emanating from the environment.[60]

These functions are most clearly present in the bee hive or ant colony at the level of the collective. This is particularly clear when it comes to reproduction, in which most individual bees and ants never participate, but every healthy hive and colony do. As a result, Wheeler insists, the "colony is a true organism and not merely the analogue of the person."[61]

Given this functional definition, any number of biological systems at any number of levels might be considered organisms. Entities both smaller and larger than the "person"—the paradigmatic case of the organism—qualify as organisms. From sub-cellular systems, to cells, to "persons," to various kinds of social systems (insect, human, or otherwise), to the earth, or even the universe as a whole, each level can be understood in organismic terms: "all of them are real organisms and not merely conceptual constructions or analogies."[62] The fact that the living world is composed of these nested structures is revelatory of a fundamental aspect of life itself:

> If the cell is a colony of lower physiological units, or biophores, as some cytologists believe, we must face the fact that all organisms are colonical or social and that one of the fundamental tendencies of life is sociogenic. Every organism manifests a strong predelection for seeking out other organisms and either assimilating them or coöperating with them to form a more comprehensive and efficient individual.[63]

As a result of this predilection, Wheeler maintains that "our biological theories must remain inadequate so long as we confine ourselves to the study of the cells and persons and leave the psychologists, sociologists and metaphysicians to deal with more complex organisms."[64]

The most recent inheritor of Wheeler's Harvard chair and legacy, E. O. Wilson, affirms Wheeler's instinct that such larger structures properly lie within the purview of biology. In his 2012 tour de force, *The Social Conquest of Earth*, Wilson aims to explain not just the evolution of eusocial insect colonies, but also the origins of human sociality, the story of the coevolution of the human genome and human culture. Wilson argues that "eusociality, the condition of multiple generations organized into groups by means of an altruistic division of labor," is nothing less than "one of the major innovations in the history of life." This organization "created *superorganisms*, the next level of biological complexity above that of organisms."[65] However, just as Wheeler before him, Wilson finds reason to resist any facile distinction between "individual" organisms and "collective" superorganisms. The givenness of the "organism" as that central level of biological analysis is undercut by the composite nature of our paradigm cases of "individual" organisms. Wilson describes the superorganism as an organism on analogy to the human body itself as a complex biological community:

> The queen and her offspring are often called superorganisms, but they may equally be called organisms. The worker of a wasp colony or ant colony that attacks you when you disturb its nest is a product of the mother queen's genome. The defending worker is part of the queen's phenotype, as teeth and fingers are part of your own phenotype . . . Each of us is an organism made up of well-integrated diploid cells. So is a eusocial colony. As your tissues proliferated, the molecular machinery of each cell was either turned on or silenced to create, say, a finger or a tooth. In the same way, the eusocial workers, developing into adults under the influence of pheromones from fellow colony members and other environmental cues, are directed to become one particular caste.[66]

The genetic revolution that has taken place since Wheeler's work gives Wilson new, yet more precise, ways of describing this analogy between the superorganismic body of the colony and the individual human body. The workers in the colony are genetically identical; their differentiation into different castes is simply a matter of *epigenetic* variation—certain genes are "turned on" or "turned off" via exposure in the nest environment to certain pheromones.[67] This differentiation is impossible to distinguish formally from the differentiation of tissues within the human body, which proceed according to similar epigenetic forces (recall Denis Noble's research from the previous chapter). As a result, "the origin and evolution of eusocial insects can be viewed as processes driven by individual-level natural selection. It is best tracked from queen to queen from one generation to the next, with the workers of each colony produced as phenotypic extensions of the mother queen."[68] The colony is itself "an organism in which the working parts are not the usual cells but pre-subordinated organisms," an *individual*, if you like, the "extrasomatic projection" of the queen's genome.[69] On this analysis, disruptions of the social system of the hive are understood as being something like the case of cancer in the human body, in which defense mechanisms exist for the eradication of runaway cells, but if they are not contained, the "whole" organism sickens and dies.[70]

In describing the origins of superorganisms, however, we are faced with a problem: How does a collective of "individual" organisms evolve to operate in this way? What is the evolutionary advantage to the worker never to participate in reproduction? Fortunately, the insect world gives us examples of various degrees of eusociality that help us imagine how the maximally integrated eusociality of the colonies Wilson described above came to be. Crucially,

Wilson argues, the evolution of these colonies can only be described by appeal to *multilevel selection*—that is, natural selection at (at least) the "individual" and "group" levels. (Indeed, a fully integrated multilevel theory of natural selection will problematize the givenness of these levels as either "individual" or "group.") That is, natural-selection pressures will both select in favor of the fittest individuals (among different individuals), but also in favor of the fittest groups (among different groups). This simple idea goes back at least to Darwin and, while it fell out of favor in the middle of the twentieth century, during the heyday of reductionism, it is currently experiencing a resurgence of interest.[71]

Darwin's interest in group selection arose from a riddle posed to him many times in response to the inherent "selfishness" seemingly implied by the evolutionary rule "survival of the fittest" and language of evolutionary "competition": Wherefore cooperation? What is the evolutionary benefit of altruism?[72] The answer: individuals cooperate for the good of the group—that is, for the evolutionary advantage of the group. "There can be no doubt that a tribe including many members who ... were always ready to give aid to each other and to sacrifice themselves for the common good, would be victorious over most other tribes; and this would be natural selection."[73] While Darwin was thinking specifically of altruism in human society, the impact of group-level selection goes much further back. Martin Nowak describes the advent of multicellular life some 3.5 billion years ago as an early result of group selective forces. Nowak cites chains of filamentous bacteria that survive because "every tenth or so cell commits suicide for the benefit of this communal thread of bacterial life."[74] This behavior is disastrous, of course, for the individual bacterium, but highly advantageous for the group. Ultimately, Nowak argues, "group"-level selective forces became so strong, and the advantages of cooperation so decisive, that these bacterial communities became the first multicellular life. The advent of the endosymbiosis of mitochondria in eukaryotic cells and the endosymbiosis of photosynthesizing plastids fit quite neatly as examples of this process of (in this case, inter-species) "group-level" fitness being so successful that what we now consider new organisms and new cell-types emerge. The result is that all life follows "the Russian doll logic of groups within groups within groups within groups."[75]

In the case of primitive insect colonies, the story Wilson tells is very similar. Individual wasps, bees, ants, or termites begin nesting together, and the result is increased survival for the individuals who nest, as opposed to those which do not. Evolutionary individualists would argue, of course, that this is explainable in terms of selection at the individual level, and Wilson would agree. Wilson's argument isn't, properly, in favor of group selection (only), but rather in favor of multilevel selection, or, the interplay between individual- and group-level selection.[76]

The key to this both/and, of course, is emergence. On Wilson's account, group-level selection acts on

> the emergent traits due to the interaction of [a group's] members. These traits include cooperation in expanding, defending and enlarging the nest, obtaining food, and rearing the immature young—in other words, all the actions a solitary, reproducing insect would normally perform on her own.[77]

When groups perform all the functions that an individual insect would normally perform, it becomes difficult, from a functionalist point of view, to distinguish the "individual" and the "group," and the "organism" and the "superorganism." Both are subject to this tension between individual- and group-level selection. Wilson concludes, "Natural selection is usually *multilevel*: it acts on genes that prescribe targets at more than one level of biological organization, such as cell and organism, or organism and colony."[78]

In the group setting, individual selection promotes "selfish" behavior, whereas group selection promotes "altruistic" behavior. "Cheaters may win within the colony, variously acquiring a larger share of resources, avoiding dangerous tasks, or breaking rules; but colonies of cheaters lose to colonies of cooperators . . . Individual-versus-group selection results in a mix of altruism and selfishness, of virtue and sin, among the members of a society."[79] The tension between these two forces is the productive tension of multilevel selection. Again, Wilson turns to cancer as an instance of this same dynamic on the cellular level:

> An extreme example of multilevel selection exists in cancer. The cancerous cell is a mutant able to grow and multiply out of control at the expense of the organism, which is the community of cells forming the next higher level of biological organization. Selection occurring at one level, the cell, can work in the opposite direction from that of the adjacent level, the organism. The runaway cancer cells cause the larger community of cells (the organism) of which it is a member, to sicken and die. Conversely, the community stays healthy when the growth of the cancer cells is controlled.[80]

The result, as in Wheeler's work (and Haag et al.), is that, in terms of evolutionary theory, the "organismic" level is more or less arbitrary, a matter of analytical convenience. At times, as in the example of cancer above, it will be most advantageous to describe the human body as a group and the cells within the body as the "individuals," with group selection operating on the body as a whole and individual selection operating on the cells. At other times, it will be better to describe individual selection operating on the human body and group selection operating on a familial or societal level. This outcome is reminiscent of physiologist Denis Noble's theory of biological relativity of scale, that "in multilevel systems, there is no privileged level of causation."[81] Indeed, Wilson's principle would seem to be a straightforward application of Noble's general theory; in multilevel systems, there is no privileged level of selection.

Such is the case for Wilson, especially for human evolution. If, in the case of the most highly evolved eusocial insects, group selection wins out so completely that the colony becomes the "extrasomatic projection" of the queen's genome, then in human evolution, Wilson sees a more delicately balanced state of affairs.[82] Of course, the genome of the individual remains the unit affected by both selection forces. The targets of the selection, however, are different. In individual selection, the targets are the traits that emerge from the genome and epigenetic environment of the individual, whereas in group selection, the targets are the traits that emerge from the genomes and epigenetic environment of the group. In this latter context, Wilson understands culture to be an epigenetic force on human evolution.[83] His story of human evolution is one of "gene-culture coevolution," in which the human cultural group functions as an adaptive unit.[84]

A simple example of gene-culture coevolution at the individual level is the appearance of lactose tolerance in the relatively recent evolutionary past (three- to nine-thousand years ago), in response to the innovation of cattle-herding among some human cultures in Europe and East Africa.[85] Previous to this time, all humans had stopped producing the enzyme necessary to digest milk after they were weaned, but the cultural innovation of herding cattle made it advantageous to be able to metabolize milk later in life. Dairy farming—a cultural revolution—changed our genes. Wilson argues that this simple example is multiplied many times over when we look for gene-culture coevolution at the group level. For example, Wilson examines the case of incest avoidance, known as the Westermarck effect. As it turns out, there is a universal rule to avoid sexual contact with anyone with whom you were well-acquainted by two-and-a-half years old. This rule is innate and appears even in cultures without a conscious belief about negative consequences of inbreeding.[86] Color vocabularies are similarly "hardwired," and fMRI studies have shown top-down control of the language center (in which these vocabularies reside) over the visual cortex.[87] Even such fundamental aspects of human nature as the ability to read intentions are provided for genetically, with the brain having structures specifically given over to these tasks. What drove the development of these structures?

It appears to have been group selection. A group with members who could read intentions and cooperate among themselves while predicting the actions of competing groups, would have an enormous advantage over others less gifted. . . . Morality, conformity, religious fervor, and fighting ability combined with imagination and memory to produce the winner.[88]

Citing the work of Michael Tomasello (with whom Wilson has collaborated), Wilson argues that the innate human language capacity evolved under similar pressure at the level of group selection, language itself being a "set of coordination devices" that "derives from the uniquely human abilities to read and share intentions with other people."[89] In short, group-level selection is an irreducible aspect of human evolutionary history. When group-level selection takes the primary place, human groups function as adaptive units from an evolutionary perspective.[90]

What we have, then, is this: life is fundamentally combinatorial.[91] Organisms are systems all the way down. The level of the organismic "individual" is not easily determined. Indeed, through evolutionary history, what we have is a history of "individuals" becoming parts of groups, on which, in some cases, group-level selection exerts ever-increasing force until the "individuals" have become "parts"—organelles, cells, tissues, organs—and the group, Nowak's "society of cells," appears to be the "whole," or the "individual"—in Ernst Haeckel's language, the "person." Each of these moments marks what John Maynard Smith and Eörs Szathmáry famously called a "major transition" in evolution.[92] David Sloan Wilson describes these major transitions:

> When between-group selection dominates within-group selection, a major evolutionary transition occurs. The social group becomes a higher-level organism and the members of the group acquire an organ-like status. This idea was first proposed to explain the evolution of eukaryotic (nucleated) cells, not by small mutational steps from prokaryotic (bacterial) cells but as highly integrated symbiotic associations of bacteria. The idea was then generalized to include other major transitions, including the first cells, multicellular organisms, social insect colonies, and even the origin of life as groups of cooperating molecular interactions.[93]

All eukaryotic cellular life is the result of one of these major transitions; and all eukaryotic multicellular life is a result of these transitions at least twice over. Multicellular life of the likes of a human "person" is, diachronically, a result of these transitions recursively through evolutionary history and, synchronically, as Nowak suggests, a "Russian doll" of groups within groups.[94]

When we look at a beehive, we see a snapshot of evolutionary development teetering on the brink of another nested whole—as multiple "individuals" become simply specialized tissues for the group, diverse phenotypic expressions of the queen's genotype, the "extrasomatic extension of the queen's genome." No doubt, sociality among humans operates in different ways evolutionarily, but the effect of group-level selection is nonetheless discernible—indeed, much of what makes us who we are: language, culture, our very nature, is a result, in part, of evolutionary pressures not just on individuals, but on groups. As D. S. Wilson insists, each of these major transitions causes

> the higher-level unit to become an organism in every sense of the word. Ironically, given group selection's previous pariah status, it is now the concept of groups as organisms that stands on a firm scientific foundation. Moreover, it is likely that human evolution represents such an evolutionary transition, and this has profound implications for psychology and all other human-related subjects.[95]

In short, the more we understand organisms as groups, the more reason we have to understand groups as organisms.[96] This is particularly true of human social groups:

> It is likely that early human evolution represented a major transition, turning our ancestral groups into the primate equivalent of bodies or beehives. . . . The consequences were momentous; mere individuals and less coordinated groups were no match for the new superorganisms, which spread over the globe, eliminating other hominid species and thousands of other species along the way.[97]

The evolutionary advantages of social life were so great that these new social bodies swiftly attained the supremacy on the planet that, for better and for worse, is a major feature of the world as we know it. The social conquest of the earth is now well under way.

Group Minds

If these human social groups qualify as organisms "in every sense of the word"—that is, as organismic selves—what ought we say about the mental lives of these organisms? Are there corresponding mental selves for these superorganisms? D. S. Wilson suggests so:

> If the individual is no longer a privileged unit of selection, it is no longer a privileged unit of cognition. We are free to imagine individuals in a social group connected in a circuitry that gives the group the status of the brain and the individual the status of the neuron.[98]

Indeed, Wilson argues, not only are we free to imagine groups this way, this analogy describes precisely how cognition works at the group level.

> Just as individual cognition is based on interactions between neurons, with any particular neuron playing a limited role, group cognition is based on social interactions, with any particular individual playing a limited role.[99]

The logic is familiar from the discussion of groups as organisms. Once we have a composite picture of "individual" cognition, imagining group cognition is only so difficult. This is the basic fundamental insight of Durkheim's analogy.[100]

Once again, the flagship cases come from the social insects. D. S. Wilson points to T. D. Seeley's work on group-level cognitive adaptations in bee hives.[101] For example, Seeley and his colleagues demonstrated that bee colonies can quickly adapt to changing qualities of food sources, opting for richer sources even when no individual bee has visited all of the relevant sources. The comparison was done at the group level. A group mind emerges that has cognitive capabilities that far outstrip the component parts:

> Many aspects of the group mind are remarkable for their lack of sophistication as far as individual behavior is concerned. The individuals respond to environmental cues and each other in a simple fashion, but the interactions have emergent properties that result in complex and adaptive behaviors at the colony level. For example, the colony acts as if it is hungry when its honey supplies are low, sending more workers to collect nectar, yet no individual bee is physically hungry.[102]

Seeley and Buhrman have described a similar process in a colony identifying a new site in the case of colony multiplication (or split). Again, each worker visits only one site and the decision is made through precise interactions within the swarm. Intriguingly, the algorithm employed in this interaction is equivalent to the decision-making algorithm employed by individual humans in making a "best-of-n" decision. "The algorithm is the same, regardless of whether it involves a group of neurons or a group of bees."[103] The "hive mind" is much more than mere metaphor. The neural network that gives rise to the mind of a human individual is formally indistinguishable from the network of bees in the hive, just as the bees' epigenetically determined phenotypic variation is formally indistinguishable from the epigenetically determined differentiation of various tissues within an individual human body.

Other species also exhibit group-level cognitive adaptations. As Wilson describes, H. H. T. Prins's research on the behavior of African buffalo reveals similar group-level decision- making processes.[104] Prins observed a distinct voting behavior among female members of the herd simply by directing their gaze in a particular direction that determines where the herd is to move next. When the average direction of the gaze of the female members of the herd is compared with the subsequent movement of the herd, the average deviation is only three degrees. When the voting is complete, the entire herd moves in unison, though without an individual leader. Wilson notes that similar voting behavior has been observed among baboons and schools of fish.[105] He concludes: "It is an important scientific achievement to show that group minds actually exist and are not just fanciful metaphors."[106] A full account of evolutionary history requires giving a full account of the minds of groups conceived as adaptive units.

Indeed, this scientific achievement extends to cognition performed by human groups.[107] Edwin Hutchins's classic example is of the traditional navigation practices of a U. S. Navy ship as it comes into port.[108] The crew of the ship functions together as a single cognitive whole. Some crew members are responsible for taking precise sighting measurements from various locations on the ship, others for communicating these measurements back to the navigator. Others are responsible for communicating the navigator's subsequent orders to various crew members who change the orientation of the ship's rudders and the thrust of the engines. In addition to the various crew members, this elaborate cognitive process depends equally on the alidades used by those sighting the shore, the ship's gyrocompass, the navigator's chart, and the specialized tool the navigator uses to place the ship on the chart by means of the sightings communicated via the ship's telephone. This is precisely the heterogenous cognitive system Tollefsen describes. This is a mind both *extended* in Clark's classic sense—by the incorporation of various material artifacts—and *collective* in the way Wilson describes: the individual has begun to function like a neuron in a group mind.

Hutchins's research has become canonical for a large number of researchers working on group cognition in human social institutions, among them philosophical political theorist Philip Pettit.[109] While denying "that our minds are subsumed in a higher form of Geist or in any variety of collective consciousness," Pettit nevertheless argues that

> There is a type of organization found in certain collectivities that makes them into subjects in their own right, giving them a way of being minded that is starkly discontinuous with the mentality of their members. This claim in social ontology is strong enough to ground talk of such collectivities as entities that are psychologically autonomous and that constitute institutional persons.[110]

Pettit begins by describing the famous doctrinal paradox in jurisprudence.[111] The paradox arises because of the multiple ways a court can synthesize the opinions of multiple contributing judges.

Suppose there are multiple disputed premises on which the judges have to rule before reaching any conclusion. If the judges' rulings disagree on these premises (and on the conclusion), how are their rulings to be synthesized? Do the judges vote on each premise and then compute the conclusion, or should they vote on the conclusion itself? In the case of a simple two-premise ruling, these two different procedures can render different rulings. Pettit gives the example of a case in which a conclusion of liability depends on two premises, whether the defendant was the cause of harm and whether the defendant had duty of care to begin with. If a three-judge court (judges A, B, and C) rule as follows, the paradox shown in Table 3.1 appears:

Table 3.1. Paradox of judgment-centered versus premise-centered voting in a two-premise case

	Cause of harm?	Duty of care?	Liable?
Judge A	Yes	No	No
Judge B	No	Yes	No
Judge C	Yes	Yes	Yes

If the judges vote on each premise, the court will rule that the defendant was the cause of harm and had the duty of care and was therefore liable, even though only one judge (C) had individually concluded that the defendant was liable.[112] In the case of a three-premise ruling on a court with three judges, it is possible for a court that resolves each premise individually to issue a ruling that *none* of the judges advocated individually. This is possible if all three premises have to hold in order to lead to a particular conclusion, as illustrated in Table 3.2:

Table 3.2. Paradox of judgment-centered versus premise-centered voting in a two-premise case

	Premise 1	Premise 2	Premise 3	Conclusion
Judge A	Yes	Yes	No	No
Judge B	Yes	No	Yes	No
Judge C	No	Yes	Yes	No
Premised-Centered Result	Yes	Yes	Yes	Yes

In such a case, it is clear that the (minimally complex) structure of the collectivity of the court is not only doing cognitive work but that the results of that cognition are impossible to ascribe to any individual judge on the court—despite the court consisting only of these judges and the rules that govern their interactions. Pettit goes on to argue that these sorts of processes of collective decision-making are not unique to courts and in fact arise in any sufficiently organized group, which Pettit calls a "social integrate."[113] As demonstrated by the doctrinal paradox, the positions adopted by the social integrate are demonstrably the positions of the integrate itself and *not* necessarily those of the members of the group. What's more, because the institution exists through time, the decision-making processes that the group adopts must allow for the emergent institutional subject to appear as a rational agent in its own right. Because social integrates are accountable diachronically as rational subjects, Pettit insists that they constitute real institutional persons.

> I have no hesitation in arguing that this means that they are institutional persons, not just institutional subjects or agents. Integrated collectivities bind themselves to the discipline of reason at the collective level, and that means that they are open to criticism in the event of not achieving rational unity in relevant regards. They avow judgments, intentions, and actions and prove able to be held responsible for failures to achieve consistency and other such ideals in their associated performance. They are subjects that can be treated as properly conversable interlocutors.[114]

Pettit argues that this position is not inconsistent with a certain sort of individualism, such that consistent "with being individualistic we may also oppose the singularism that insists on the primacy of the isolated agent and claims that we can describe collectivities as persons only in a secondary sense."[115] Ultimately, the individualism Pettit affirms is the sociological equivalent of an emergentist's ontological monism. That is, we can hold both that groups are composed of individuals and their interactions, and also that these groups are nonetheless real and, furthermore, that individuals do not have a privileged claim to personhood.

Perhaps the most striking instance of group cognition in the modern world is the practice of science itself.[116] Like Hutchins's ship, modern scientific research projects entail the development and deployment of large, distributed, and (sometimes surprisingly minimally) coordinated collections of individual human subjects and their specialized tools. Karin Knorr Cetina points to modern experiments in high-energy physics (HEP), like those conducted at the European Organization for Nuclear Research (known as CERN), as examples of especially large, distributed group-level cognitive processes. In her ethnography of HEP experiments, Knorr Cetina argues that "besides building up an understanding of the deepest components of the universe, high energy physics also builds 'superorganisms': collectives of physicists, matched with collectives of instruments, that come as near as one can get to a—post-romantic—communitarian regime."[117]

Knorr Cetina points to the shifting authorship conventions observed in papers resulting from these massive collaborations involving thousands of scientists. Rather than citing a lead researcher or in any way highlighting an individual's role, papers are published with every project member's name listed in alphabetical order. (Knorr Cetina notes that for some projects at CERN, this means that the listing of authors amounts to three printed pages listing hundreds of co-authors.) This reveals far more than a mere shift in academic practice:

> Naming, then, has shifted to the experiment, and so has epistemic agency—the capacity to produce knowledge. The point is that no single individual or small group of individuals can, by themselves, produce the kind of results these experiments are after—for example, vector bosons or the long "elusive" top quark or the Higgs mechanism. It is this impossibility which the authorship conventions of experimental HEP exhibit. They signify that the individual has been turned into an element of a much larger unit that functions as a collective epistemic subject.[118]

The experiment—conceived of as a social and mechanical whole—is a collective epistemic subject that exhibits self-knowledge and self-care (i.e. self-maintenance) of the type that Haag et al. would readily recognize. This largely comes in the form of reports given by team members to one another and to the scientific community at large. It is "within the experiment's conversation with itself," understood in terms of these reports, Knorr Cetina argues, that "knowledge is produced."

> The stories articulated in formal and informal reports provide the experiments with a sort of consciousness: an uninterrupted hum of self-knowledge in which all efforts are anchored and from which new lines of work follow. The communitarian structure of experiments may rule out the individual epistemic subject as a procurer of knowledge. But it does not rule out all traits of subjectivity; in particular, it does not rule out self-knowledge as a form of (partly material) cognition distributed among participants about the states of experimental components.[119]

Knorr Cetina goes on to invoke Durkheim's "conscience collective," which she says emerges in HEP experiments not, as Durkheim suggested, "from social likeness or common sentiment, but from the reflexive integration of objects."[120] This allows for a substantially heterogeneous collective that nevertheless functions as a superorganismic whole.

This reflexively organized system—a self of the type Haag et al. describe—then also gains what Pettit insists is the sine qua non of a person: the necessity to defend one's rational unity and significance over time.[121] The start of a new HEP research project, then, is literally the birth of the personal, superorganismic experiment:

> During the birth of an experiment this work of separation, through which the experiment becomes constituted as a distinctive and powerful struc-
> ture in its own right, is carried out. It is not just the work of rearranging groups and technologies and resources, or of reshuffling networks. It is the work of rearranging the social order, of breaking components out of other ontologies and of configuring, with them, a new structural form. The repackaging of efforts accomplished during the birth of a new experi-
> ment is also the repackaging of social composition and the creation of a new form of life.[122]

In the birth process as well as in the processes that begin new sub-projects, new tissues for the superorganism (physicists) are selected based on their ability to be trusted to work for the good of the whole. In this sense trust functions as a "selection mechanism" for the superorganism in precisely the way multilevel selection theory predicts, selecting individuals who cooperate and connecting them in "confidence pathways."[123] The language of "pathways," of course, evokes the neurological concept of neural pathways and, indeed, these confidence pathways function for the experiment in the same way pathways between neurons function in the brain. They connect various substructures within the system, crossing between groups that otherwise function as more or less separate cognitive subsystems: in the case of HEP, across technology groups, institutes, even across experiments themselves.

This is one important place in which Knorr Cetina's description varies from Pettit's. Pettit's account of institutional persons depends heavily on the institu-
tional structure, on its rules that impose "discipline of reason at the collective level." This is why, for Pettit, a political party counts as an institutional person, but a populace does not. The populace does not have structures by which to police its own rational unity, and therefore cannot be accountable as a rational interlocutor in the same way as the party.[124] In other words, for Pettit, institutional personhood is legislated "from above," as it were; it is a matter of design. Knorr Cetina, on the other hand, describes HEP experiments as emerging "from below" and existing without the sorts of legal structures Pettit's institutional persons depend upon: "In my view, the hallmark of the HEP experiments I saw is not

that they organize a work force of employees in industry-like ways but that they bring about truly collective forms of working: they entice participants into some form of successful cooperation."[125] These participants are, in fact, involved in legal structures, but these are independent physics "institutes": university departments, government-finances research facilities, and the like. The experiment as a collective entity sits "on top" of these structures and functions as a post-traditional communitarian structure. The experiments exist legally only through non-binding memoranda of understanding and in order to function depend on continued trust among individual collaborators who together constitute confidence pathways *across* institutional lines. Ultimately, these individual relationships and patterns of collaboration and mutual trust—*not* the independent institutes—are the base on which the collective epistemic subject supervenes. This is why the birth of the experiment is such a rupture for the existing social ontologies. Of course, divided allegiances still exist. Just as an individual scientist can (in part) alternate between operating as a part of the collective epistemic subject and his or her status as an individual human epistemic subject, so, too, participating institutes can sometimes reassert their own social ontologies on their members from time to time. Nevertheless, Knorr Cetina argues, for the lifetime of the experiment, these ontologies have been subjugated to the emergent ontology of the experiment itself, built through confidence pathways forged among individual collaborators.

I take it that this "bottom-up" account is to be preferred inasmuch as it better conforms to our expectations of how mental entities come to be. Rather than being designed, as in Pettit's description, Knorr Cetina's experiments emerge spontaneously and do not depend on a lawgiver for their self-sustaining logic. Instead, as Haag et al. would suggest, HEP experiments generate their *teloi* through their own internally recursive self-maintaining activities.

Knorr Cetina's description is vivid and ambitious, and makes the most of the superorganism and Durkheimian traditions. She has been criticized on the grounds that one need not make an epistemic subject out of the experiment itself. Rather, one could simply ascribe any true knowledge produced by the experiment to team members or, frankly, to anyone with training to read the reports and reason to trust their reliability.[126] I take it, however, that this individual epistemic agency is secondary (diachronically and logically) to the collective epistemic agency exercised by the experiment (conceived of as a social-and-mechanical whole). The superorganism analogy (if, indeed, it is an analogy) is particularly helpful on this point, for the individual knowing in this case would be analogous (or even formally identical) to the knowledge that an entomologist might have regarding the outcomes of the collective cognition of an ant colony.[127] Presumably, this is clear enough in the case of the peer scientist who reads the results of an HEP experiment in a journal. But I would insist that the knowledge gained by the team members of the experiment itself is of the same type—the only difference being that, in the case of CERN, the individual members of the superorganism possess cognitive capacities and symbolic faculties to appropriate the knowledge produced by the system in which they participate, while the individual ants are not individually able to appropriate the knowledge produced by the colony.

This disanalogy is at the crux of perhaps the greatest difficulty in the superorganism tradition in group mind theory and is evident all the way back to the tradition's beginnings: how does the group mind interact with the individuals who comprise the group?[128] Philosopher Robert Wilson traces the history of the group mind thesis back to the late nineteenth-century reflection on the French Revolution and the Paris Commune. These works focused on the psychology of mobs or crowds. Wilson highlights particularly Gustave Le Bon's *La Psychologie des Foules* (in English, *The Crowd*). Le Bon describes a certain kind of emergent psychology—"new psychological characteristics" that appear spontaneously "from the mere fact of their [the members of the crowd] being assembled."[129] These new psychological characteristics fundamentally alter the psychologies of the individuals.

> The sentiments and ideas of all the persons in the gathering take one and the same direction, and their conscious personality vanishes. A collective mind is formed, doubtless transitory, but presenting very clearly defined characteristics ... It [the organized crowd] forms a single being, and is subjected to the law of the mental unity of crowds.[130]

This is typical of turn-of-the-century thinking about crowds: "This putative law [the law of the mental unity of crowds] claims that crowds destroy the individuality of those that belong to them, psychologically unifying and homogenizing them so that they act as one." It is, Le Bon argues, as if the individual members of the crowd have been hypnotized.[131] This, of course, has much more to do with the dim view European elites took of crowds of non-elites than with the "data" themselves. But Le Bon's work nevertheless provides something of a baseline against which later authors refine what is and, more importantly, what is not meant in the superorganism tradition by a "group mind."

In the superorganism tradition, there is a sharp distinction drawn between cognition at the group level and cognition at the level of the individual.[132] This is necessary in the superorganism tradition because, in many cases, one is dealing with a group of organisms (e.g., social insects) that, individually, are not understood to possess minds. Because the group mind is emergent from the interactions of the individual members of the group, the group mind is conceived of operating at a higher level of abstraction in relative independence from the minds of the individuals. As D. S. Wilson argues:

> Group-level adaptations are usually studied in the context of physical activities such as resource utilization, predator defense, and so on. However, groups can also evolve into adaptive units with respect to cognitive activities such as decision making, memory, and learning . . . At the extreme, groups might become so integrated and the contribution of any single member might become so partial that the group could literally be said to have a mind in a way that individuals do not, just as brains have a mind in a way that neurons do not.[133]

This is especially clear in the case of insect colony cognition, though it becomes more complicated in the case of human group cognition. After all, human individuals *do* have minds in ways neurons do not. So, giving an account of cognition of human groups necessarily involves giving a multilevel account of cognition that makes sense of both the cognitive activity happening at the group level, and the cognition of the human individuals that compose the group.

Robert Wilson separates these two levels of analysis. First, Wilson argues, there is the true "group mind hypothesis" which holds "that groups have properties, including mental properties, which their individual members do not have, and which are not reducible to the properties of those members." So far so good. However, Wilson goes on to argue that this "emergentist view of group properties" also entails the manifestation of these same properties at the individual level, which is what later causes him problems, as we will see. Logically independent from this first hypothesis is what Wilson calls the "social manifestation thesis," which is simply "the idea that individuals have properties, including psychological properties, that are manifest only when those individuals form part of a group of a certain type."[134] Framing the analysis this way leads Wilson to conclude:

> Clearly, the social manifestation thesis could be true without entailing the group mind hypothesis if group minds did not exist. Conversely, the group mind hypothesis could be true without entailing the social manifestation thesis if the relevant groups were comprised of individuals that did not have minds at all.[135]

In the second case, Wilson is presumably thinking of cases like colonies of social insects. In the case of human groups, he concludes that contemporary advocates of the group mind thesis like D. S. Wilson and Mary Douglas (see below) are "better understood as somewhat confusing attempts to state a version of the social manifestation thesis."[136] Le Bon's excesses have made Robert Wilson overly cautious. His concern is to protect recent group mind advocates from having to conclude that group members in cognitive groups have their minds taken over by the group mind in the style of science fiction.[137] However, it seems quite possible to render a truly multilevel account of cognition in human groups that affirms the insights of D. S. Wilson, Hutchins, and Knorr Cetina about the cognitive properties of groups while also affirming the relative local sovereignty of individual minds within groups.[138]

Of course, multilevel descriptions of complex systems are the strong suit of emergentism and, within the emergence paradigm, it is not hard to imagine a formal solution: human group cognition emerges from and supervenes on the cognition of contributing members (no members, no group mind) and exercises downward causation back upon the cognition of these same members through placing "boundary conditions" on the cognitive activities of group members— *not* by collapsing group members' mind into an undifferentiated whole at the individual level. I take it that this is what D. S. Wilson has in mind in the case of human group cognition when he suggests that "the group could literally be said to have a mind in a way that individuals do not, just as brains have a mind in a way that neurons do not."[139] That is, though human individuals have minds, their minds, their cognitive activities, are distinct from the cognitive activities of the group. They are shaped, rather, through downward causation, which yields the phenomena Robert Wilson describes in terms of his "social manifestation thesis." This downward causation, this placing of boundary conditions on the cognition of individual group members, becomes especially clear when we consider the impact of the social context on individual cognition.[140]

In *How Institutions Think*, Mary Douglas argues for the "social basis of cognition" along the lines of what one finds in the work of Emile Durkheim and Ludwik Fleck. Like Robert Wilson, Douglas takes her role to be that of defending Durkheim and Fleck from having their positions on group minds misconstrued. She writes, "There is a tendency to dismiss Durkheim and Fleck because they seem to be saying that institutions have minds of their own. Of course institutions cannot have minds. It is worth spending time understanding what these thinkers really said."[141] Of course, we have seen that there is ample reason to take human groups—if Pettit is right, *especially* institutions—to have minds of their own. Nonetheless, Douglas, writing in 1986, has reason to need to rehabilitate these social theorists:

> The very idea of a suprapersonal cognitive system stirs a deep sense of outrage. The offense taken in itself is evidence that above the level of the individual human another hierarchy of "individuals" is influencing lower level members to react violently against this idea or that. An individual

that encompasses thinking humans is assumed to be of a nasty totalitarian sort, a highly centralized and effective dictatorship ... Many subtle and able thinkers are made so nervous by the crude political analogy between individual mind and social influences on cognition that they prefer to dismiss the whole problem. Anthropologists cannot dismiss it.[142]

For Douglas, the fact that institutions cannot think is not a reason to discard all Durkheimian thought, but rather a reason to fear all the more the institution's power. Given institutions' regulatory power, it is "no wonder" that

> they easily recruit us into joining their narcissistic self-contemplation. Any problems we try to think about are automatically transformed into their own organizational problems... For us, the hope of intellectual independence is to resist, and the necessary first step in resistance is to discover how the institutional grip is laid upon our mind.[143]

For Douglas, the process of unveiling the institutional grip was the center of Durkheim's and Fleck's work. So, in describing how institutions think, Douglas turns her attention to how institutions influence the thought lives of individuals.

Douglas notes that Durkheim's goal in arguing for collective representations was precisely to describe the ways in which the collective enables, and at the same time constrains, cognition at the individual level, supplying the basic categories of time, space, and causality that make human cognition possible.

> They represent the most general relations which exist between things; surpassing all our other ideas in extension, they dominate all the details of our intellectual life. If men do not agree upon these essential ideas at any moment, if they did not have the same conceptions of time, space, cause, number, etc., all contact between their minds would be impossible, and with that, all life together. Thus, society could not abandon the categories to the free choice of the individual without abandoning itself. . ... There is a minimum of logical conformity beyond which it cannot go. For this reason, it uses all its authority upon its members to forestall such dissidences. . . . The necessity with which the categories are imposed upon us is not the effect of simple habits whose yoke we can easily throw off with a little effort; nor is it a physical or metaphysical necessity, since the categories change in different places and times; it is a special sort of moral necessity which is to the intellectual life what moral obligation is to the will.[144]

In the language of emergence, this is downward causation, the placing of boundary conditions on the mental lives of individuals.

Fleck, Douglas argues, pursues this Durkheimian intuition in his account of cognition in modern science. In his 1935 work on the scientific identification of syphilis, *The Genesis and Development of a Scientific Fact*, Fleck, himself a medical doctor and bacteriologist who worked on the identification of syphilis, argues that scientific facts have social histories. More than sixty years before Knorr Cetina's work on HEP experiments, Fleck highlighted the generative role of laboratory culture itself in generating scientific research: "Many workers carried out these experiments almost simultaneously, but the actual authorship is due to the collective, the practice of cooperation and teamwork."[145] Fleck described this thought collective, or *Denkkollektiv*, in emergent terms: "Although the thought collective consists of individuals, it is not simply the aggregate sum of them."[146] The thought collective produces and reinforces a "thought style" that, as Douglas describes, "sets the preconditions of any cognition, and . . . determines what can be counted as a reasonable question and a true or false answer. It provides the context and sets the limits for any judgment about objective reality."[147] This is the process through which the emergent social whole is constituted as a self: through the application of boundary constraints that constitute the self as a self-maintaining entity by "determining what is likely."[148] As a result of the universal presence of these constraints, Fleck argues, "the individual within the collective is never, or hardly ever, conscious of the prevailing thought style, which almost always exerts an absolutely compulsive force upon his thinking and with which it is not possible to be at variance."[149] Thus, the "downward" pressure exerted by the group mind on its constituents is at once both imperceptible and coercive—indeed, it is coercive precisely because it is imperceptible, hence Douglas's admonition. Recalling Durkheim's description of the collective representations, we see that this downward pressure is both enabling *and* destructive, both establishing the grounds of the possibility of cognition and coercively regulating its enactment. This is a far cry from the "hive mind" of Le Bon, but not nearly so rosy as the superorganism tradition's language of foundational "altruism."

Taking Fleck's and Knorr Cetina's work together, we see that science itself places constraints on social agents that both enable cognition and coercively reinforce social categories. In other words, it is the emergent social superorganismic body and group mind (in the most vivid, Durkheimian sense) that exercises constraint on individual social actors. This constraint is *not* in terms of the science-fiction mind-meld imagined by Le Bon, but rather through the standard mechanisms of downward causation we have come to expect from emergence in general. Douglas argues that this is not just true of modern scientific practices, but in fact true of all human interactions. The social cognitive machine is constituted by "founding analogies," lists of opposites that provide a framework for the foundational concepts of distinction and sameness.[150] In considering the origins of these founding analogies, we find the familiar feedback loop of emergence: individuals, "as they pick and choose among the analogies from nature those they will give credence to, are also picking and choosing at the same time their allies and opponents and the pattern of their future relations ... In short, they are constructing a machine for thinking and decision-making on their own behalf."[151] Individuals construct the social machine which then thinks and makes decisions on their behalf through the downward causation it exercises through the maintenance of founding analogies.

To return one last time to D. S. Wilson's suggestion that a "group could literally be said to have a mind in a way that individuals do not, just as brains have a mind in a way that neurons do not," we might perform a thought experiment: if a neuron *did* have a mind, how aware would it be of its participation in a brain and of that brain having a mind? My suspicion is, very little. As one of tens of billions of neurons connected to at most merely thousands of other neurons, an individual neuron would have very little sense of the scale of the structure to which it belonged.[152] Of course, from our point of view, this structure explains almost all of what is going on in an individual neuron—providing "inputs" and receiving "outputs" from the neuron, and, at a higher level of abstraction, "using" the neuron (and its 86 billion neighbors) to "think" with. The individual neuron—even endowed with a mind in our thought experiment—presumably would have no sense of this. Its only sense of belonging to a superstructure at all would come through its communications with that smaller community of neurons with which it was connected. Surmising that the structure had some impact on its own "thought process" would require attention to patterns of its own interaction with its environment and the constraints that environment placed on its thinking—an environment that was always already its context. Such an insight would require stepping outside the neuron's own sense of what was "given" or "natural." In short, it seems to me that Douglas's description of the covert grip institutions have on our minds is more or less the experience an intelligent individual neuron would have—the experience we would expect to have were D. S. Wilson's hypothesis correct.

In sum, we have very good reasons to take seriously the existence of personal collective entities emergent from large networks of human individuals. Bodily—even biologically—these groups constitute superorganisms that differ only by degree from those observed among the eusocial insects. Like any organism, these superorganisms' bodies supervene on structures at lower levels of biological organization. Selection pressures at the "group" or "superorganismic" level counteract selective pressures at lower levels, selecting for cooperation in the superorganism's emergent, adaptive behaviors. These adaptive behaviors include cognition, which is evident at the level of the group/superorganism. These cognitive behaviors demonstrate that these superorganisms have minds of their own and are epistemic subjects in their own right. The result is that the mental life of human individual persons is as inseparable from the mental life of the groups to which the person belongs as the biological life of any biological unit is from the workings of the larger biological structures to which it belongs. In each case, the influence "from above," as it were, comes through downward causation, through the placing of boundary conditions on individual-level behavior.

Conclusions

What extended mind and group mind do at the level of the mind (and here mind is important primarily as a seat of "real" personal agency) biological theory about the communal nature of the individual organism, on the one hand, and about superorganisms, on the other, does at the level of the body. Even what we instinctively call "individual organisms" turn out to be internally and externally social, to the extent that even the definitional boundaries of the body seem less clear than we often imagine. Every simple organism is a superorganism when viewed at a lower level, and will appear as an organ or a component of a larger organism at a higher level of abstraction. In other words, both personal agency and the personal body—crucially, the two most salient aspects of personhood that Paul ascribes to ἁμαρτία—have what we might call a fractal geometry.[153] That is, they are self-similar at different levels of scale. (Recall Nowak's Russian nesting dolls.) This is the geometry of complexity and the shape emergentism predicts, and is reflected in Durkheim's definitional analogy of sociology. In a world that exhibits emergence at every level of scale, there is a recurrence of the formal relationships at different boundary markers of scale, abstraction, and scientific discipline.

What emergentism gives us is an anthropology that describes the human person as a node in a network of multiple scales. On the "bottom-up" view, the human person is describable as the whole that is more than the sum of its parts, the entity emergent from the complex biological systems of which it is composed. At this level of description, the human person is the top of the pyramid, the singular "whole" that is constituted by its component parts. However, as we have seen, this view is only a rough approximation. The boundaries of this "whole" are difficult to draw and the human person "leaks" beyond its presumed borders. The biological systems that compose the individual person's body are made up of non-human cells. The individual mind extends beyond the head and beyond the "individual body" itself. We must ultimately come to the conclusion that the self-contained human individual person—even as a biological entity—is a fiction. Simply at the level of a material description, the human individual is not an island. Therefore, to say that the human individual is constituted "from without" or "from above" as well as "from below" is not a matter of socio-anthropological dogma; it is a requirement of a complete material explanation of the human individual. "From above," the human individual person, then, is describable as a node in a network of which it is just one component part and is constituted as a node of that network.[154]

The power of Durkheim's analogy is thus apparent. The social emerges from the individual in the same way the mind emerges from the body, with the result that the social collectivity reveals itself to be a complex system with a body and a mind, a "psychological entity of a new species."[155] This is where the real strength of the emergentist model appears. As critical as what emergentism has to say about collectives (within social theory) is what it has to say about individuals (in philosophy of mind). Individuals, according to emergentist accounts, are slippery, supervenient on physical reality. This is where we get the intricate connection between what we can say about individuals and what we can say about collectives. Emergentism "works both sides," undercutting the atomistic understanding of the self even as it promotes a more robust, agential sense of the collective. Emergentism assigns causation and agency to individuals and to collectives by precisely the same arguments. However one works out the details, the discourse of emergentism suggests that analogies drawn between the mental and the social are far from being "mere metaphors." Instead, Durkheim's strongest language—that of the social as a "psychological entity of a new species"—seems most adequate to the task.

Of course, as always, Humean skepticism is still possible. It could be that all emergents are illusory, second-class citizens ontologically. But, if Durkheim's analogy holds, note what is *not* possible: it is *not* possible that individuals are real but the social is not. This is because of the intrinsic relationship between the two middle terms of Durkheim's analogy:

Physiological : **Mental :: Individual** : Social

It is hard to imagine how, if the mental is illusory, the "individual," in the sense described by methodological individualists in the social sciences (that is, as a conscious, subjective, decision-making center), could be real.[156] Indeed, as we have seen, even if we wanted to take "individual" in a bodily sense, we would run into this same problem. Rather, if we are to follow the Humean critique, the individual would also be a useful fiction. The force of this argument only increases if we recall that reductionism—given that it operates with the same hierarchy of "levels" as does emergentism—also predicts that something very much like Durkheim's analogy should hold, namely:

Biological : Psychological :: Psychological : Sociological

In this case, the identity of the two middle terms is obvious, and the strictness of physical reductionism's eliminativism becomes apparent: for both the analogy and reductionism to hold, all four terms must be Humean fictions. Emergentist sociologist Dave Elder-Vass makes much this same argument. His reasoning is worth quoting at length:

> individualists often deny causal power to social structure on the basis of the reductionist argument that we can always explain the effects of the structure in terms of causal contributions of the individuals concerned and the relations between them, but they consistently fail to apply this argument recursively to human individuals. If they were to do so, they would have to argue that we can always explain the effects of an individual in terms of the causal contributions of their cells and the relations between them, the effects of cells in terms of the causal contributions of the molecules that are their parts and the relations between them, and so on. They could not be individualists but would have to successively become cell-ists (!), molecule-ists, atom-ists, and so on. Causality, on this account, would seem to drain away—either to the lowest physical level, if there is such a level, or entirely, if there is not. In neither case are humans causally effective, hence we can assert that the emergentist argument advanced here is more coherent than the individualist one.[157]

If causality and being are to be denied to social structure on the basis of reductionist argument, then they must be denied to the human individual—and for the same reasons. Either the social is real or the individual is not. Ontological individualism is incoherent. If persons are always and everywhere Humean fictions, then the distinction between personification and person-identification disappears. Descriptions of *anything* in personal terms is a fiction.[158]

In the final analysis, if we like, we can adopt a charitable agnosticism regarding the Humean analysis of the person (the subjective self) as a useful fiction. As Daniel Dennett explains:

> Since the dawn of modern science in the seventeenth century, there has been nearly unanimous agreement that the self, whatever it is, would be invisible under a microscope, and invisible to introspection, too. For some, this has suggested that the self was a nonphysical soul, a ghost in the machine. For others, it has suggested that the self was nothing at all, a figment of metaphysically fevered imaginations. And for still others, it has suggested only that a self was in one way or another a sort of abstraction, something whose existence was not in the slightest impugned by its invisibility. After all, one might say, a center of gravity is just as invisible—and just as real. Is that real enough?[159]

Dennett later reprises this final refrain with more flair: "Are pains real? They are as real as haircuts and dollars and opportunities and persons, and centers of gravity, but how real is that?"[160] Fortunately for us, the question of personification does not require an absolute answer about the reality of persons generally.[161] Rather, we just need to do away with our suspicion that Sin has less claim to the category of "real" than do you or I. The contention of this chapter is that Sin—if it is a person emergent from complex networks of human social interaction—is as real as haircuts, dollars, opportunities, persons, and centers of gravity. So long as I am correct to include persons on that list, we can join Dennett in asking "how real is that?" with the fundamental question already solved. Ultimately, we don't have to know how real that is. Money, human persons, Sin-as-cosmic-tyrant—it can all be baloney. The point is simply that it's the same *kind* of baloney.

Of course, I *don't* think it's all baloney. I take it that persons, minds, and bodies are real.[162] And emergentism gives us an ontology that describes the reality of these entities. Given that we can render the same account of the reality of persons, minds, and bodies at the social level (if we accept the former cases as cases of ontological emergence), we have to take seriously the reality of these social entities as well. Pettit wonders,

> Why might someone deny that an entity that displays the functional marks of an intentional subject, as the integrated collectivity does, is not really an intentional subject? One ground might be that intentionality requires not just a certain form of organization, but also the realization of that form in inherently mental material, whatever that is thought to be. Few would endorse this consideration among contemporary thinkers, however, because there appears to be nothing inherently mental about the biological material out of which our individual minds are fashioned.[163]

In other words, rejecting mental dualism—the existence of an "inherently mental material"—necessarily opens one up to taking other functionally equivalent cognitive systems seriously as intentional, epistemic subjects—that is, as *persons*. To privilege the "individual" human cognitive system over a composite system is to fall into the same sort of crypto-dualism as the person who believes that a nutritional supplement from a natural source is inherently superior to a chemically identical supplement sourced artificially. The end of vitalism meant the end of privileging organic materials. The end of mentalism means the end of privileging psychological individuals with brains as though they possess some special "mental material."

As it turns out, mind, like the self-organizing processes that Haag et al. identify as the supervenience base from which both the organismic and subjective self emerge, is multiply realizable. That is, it can supervene on various different lower-level processes and entities. There is no "essential mental stuff." Rather mind,

which, as Tollefsen suggests, is shorthand for "a whole host of cognitive processes, dispositional states, connotative and agential behavioral dispositions," can
emerge from various different supervenience bases.[164] In the paradigm case, mind
emerges from a complex neurological system in contact with various objects in
its environment (including other minds). In the case of group-level minds, mind
emerges from a complex, overlapping network of these systems. And where there
is body and mind, I am inclined to say there is a person.

In other words, what we have found is that the social is both a biological
and a psychological entity of a new species. That is, these social "psychological" entities—corporate persons or collective epistemic subjects—supervene on
social "biological" entities—superorganisms. In this sense, we find that this use
of the term "social" is more than a bit imprecise. We might use it to describe the
organismic self emergent at the social level, but, in Durkheim's terms, we would
also use the same word to describe the subjective self emergent at this same level.
Both sorts of "social selves" seem to emerge. That is, Durkheim's "social" contains
within it what might more naturally be described in emergentist terms as two levels. Therefore, we would perhaps be better served by introducing some nomencla-
ture to distinguish the two. I propose that we retain the use of the word "social" to
describe these superorganismic selves—social *bodies*—but that we use the word
"mythological" to describe subjective selves—social *minds*—that emerge from
these bodies. This suggestion, of course, has everything to do with my anticipat-
ing that this new emergent level, the "mythological," is precisely the category that
will help us theorize some entities like Sin that the Bultmann school dismisses as
"*merely* mythological." Adopting this usage, we would say that the mythological
is to the social precisely as the psychological is to the biological. Mythological
entities are (at least minimally) subjective selves. They perform cognitive functions. They are intentional subjects. Indeed, their cognition exercises downward
causation upon the superorganisms from which they emerge, and, further, upon
the individual psychologies of the members of these superorganisms (and upon
their biology, and so on).

Now, because we know that mind and body are a "psychosomatic unity" (that
is, we hold to ontological monism for such entities), just as we refer to the unity
of the mind and body as the individual "person," so also we may think of the unity
of the mythological psychology and the superorganismic body as a "mythological
person." Discussion of personhood on an emergentist account will always be multilevel, because the human person exists as a nexus of both "upward" and "downward" causes at various levels.[165] That is, just as it would be folly to distinguish the
individual human body too precisely from the individual human mind—rather
than talk simply about unified persons—so, too, we may find it appropriate to
talk about unified persons emergent at the social-and-mythological levels. We
will find it useful to talk about such persons as "mythological" given the way we

common-sensibly prioritize psychology in conceptualizing the person.[166] In this sense, we might say that a "mythological person" has a "social body." We now have technical language to describe mythological persons.

Sin as a Mythological Person: A Superorganism with a Group Mind

At long last we may return directly to the topic at hand: s/Sin in Paul's letter to the Romans. My hypothesis is that the multilevel account of human persons and social groups presented in this chapter is conducive to holding together at once the description of s/Sin at the personal, social, and mythological levels.[167] In short, I take it that all three can be held together through an understanding of ἁμαρτία in Romans 5–8 as a mythological person: that is, a superorganism with a group mind emergent from a complex network of individual human persons. On this account, individuals participate in the life of the superorganism through sinning—thus vindicating Bultmann's slogan, "Sin came into the world by sinning."[168] Sinful behavior—"sins" in the plural—happen in the context of social institutions which take on, to one or another degree, this sinful character. This vindicates the liberationist instinct that it is appropriate—indeed, necessary—to talk about sinful social structures. The superorganism, Sin, emerges from the resultant complex interaction of sinning individuals and sinning institutions and exercises downward causation back upon institutions and individuals. This vindicates the Käsemann school's instinct that Sin constrains the freedom of the human subject. Inasmuch as this downward causation "trickles down" to the individual level via the social, it also vindicates the liberationist instinct that the freedom of the human subject is largely constrained by the power of sinful social structures. At this point, we may imagine that this downward causation takes the form of the various species of social constraint described by Durkheim, Fleck, and Douglas—that is, as the coercive influence of *collective representations, thought collectives*, or *founding analogies*, respectively. The case study of racism in the United States from the second chapter would serve as an example of this sort of downward causation, and will be taken up again in the next chapter.

There is much more to say about both the emergence of and downward pressure exerted by this mythological person and we will come to it in due course. But there are at least two problems with the hypothesis presented by this chapter that deserve attention at this point. The first problem regards the *moral* character of emergent social collectivities. At various points in this chapter, we have seen scholars argue that there is an inherent moral value in these sprawling social systems. For Le Bon and his compatriots, the answer was obvious: the crowd is an enemy, robbing the human person of individuality and rationality. Collectives are inherently morally suspect. On the other extreme, Knorr Cetina regularly praises the selflessness of HEP scientists and this aligns well with the recent revival of the superorganism tradition. For many of the evolutionary biologists (e.g., Nowak, E. O. Wilson, D. S. Wilson), the tendency is to contrast the inherent "selfishness" of individual-level selective pressures to the "altruism" of group-level selection (owing, no doubt, in part to the force of the language "*eu*social insects"). Indeed, we saw above, E. O. Wilson suggests that the fact that the human person sits at the nexus of these two sorts of selective pressures explains the origins of human nature, concluding that "individual selection is responsible for much of what we call sin, while group selection is responsible for the greater part of virtue. Together they have created the conflict between the poorer and the better angels of our nature."[169] Certainly the majority of current opinion would suggest that the emergence of group-level attributes is the triumph of altruism and cooperation.[170] Perhaps I am fundamentally mistaken in identifying Sin itself as one of these emergent entities.

Even E. O. Wilson himself, however, recognizes a dark side to group selection and its products. After all, for Wilson, the essence of the human is rooted in the tension between the will and intentions of the individual, and the will and good of the group. Therefore, any sort of "hive mind" that might emerge from a true human superorganism would require component members to be less-than-human, as the individuality of the group members would have to be entirely suppressed. Ironically for our purposes, Wilson claims that this is precisely what happens in the case of religion, which he takes to be the pinnacle of human tribalism and ethnocentrism. Rather than promoting a healthy balance of self-interest and the good of the group, "the goal of religions," he says "is submission to the will and common good of the tribe."[171]

Of course, this sort of ethnocentric tribalism was well-known to Paul. But Paul would describe this kind of social arrangement as Sin, especially in Romans, where tribalism and ethnocentricity are on trial.[172] All to say, despite the overwhelmingly optimistic language of "altruism" and "cooperation" among advocates of group selection, the fact is that human cooperation is morally ambivalent, depending on the ends of the cooperation. Indeed, I will argue in the next chapter that Paul has in mind not one, but two emergent social entities of roughly the type described in this chapter—the Body of Sin and the Body of Christ. Certainly these two bodies are of substantially different moral value for Paul.

Finally, I want to offer some initial remarks regarding the relationship of Sin to identifiable social institutions. Ought we imagine Sin itself as an identifiable social system? Are there particular social institutions that together constitute Sin in its social manifestation? Could we make a list of such institutions? This is a topic that will reappear later, but there are some insights—particularly those from Knorr Cetina—that are worth noting before moving on. First of all, I take it that while Sin has certainly been (and will continue to be) identified with specific institutions from time to time, doubtlessly Sin-with-a-capital-S has a greater scope. If the liberationists are to be believed, Sin certainly employs structures, even takes them up into itself from time to time, but we would be inclined to think that Sin is not identical to any single institutional structure, but rather supervenes on a number of social structures. This is where Knorr Cetina's account of overlapping social ontologies is potentially quite helpful. A CERN physicist is a member of a home institute, but also a member of a CERN experiment. Both identities are social. Each social entity could rightly be considered a collective subject of some sort.[173] The individual subject is sometimes caught in conflicts with one or both supervening collective subjects.

I take it that Sin is a collective subject of the species of the experiment, rather than the institute—more like what Knorr Cetina describes than what Pettit describes. Like an HEP experiment, Sin supervenes on multiple institutions that participate more or less exclusively in its cognition and agency. Presumably the same is true at the individual level as well. Just as HEP scientists have multiple affiliations with their home institute, perhaps even with multiple experiments, we can imagine human agents with divided allegiances to multiple social institutions, to Sin, or to other larger, emergent entities. It is likely that any honest assessment of the human individual on the moral landscape described in Romans will have to account for hybrid identities and conflicting commitments. Indeed, Paul's ardent rhetoric regarding the impossibility of hybrid allegiance to Sin and to Christ is proof positive of the practical reality of such hybrid allegiances.

Let all these concluding comments serve, at this point, as parts of a hypothesis regarding a synthetic, multilevel account of ἁμαρτία in Romans 5-8—a hypothesis that must now be tested exegetically.

4 AN EMERGENT ACCOUNT OF SIN IN ROMANS

Power is tolerable only on condition that it mask a substantial part of itself. Its success is proportional to its ability to hide its own mechanisms.

—MICHEL FOUCAULT, *History of Sexuality I*

From the beginning, what we have wanted to know is this: when Paul speaks of ἁμαρτία in personal terms in Romans, is he speaking literally or figuratively? The difficulty is due to the fact that we lack criteria for making this distinction.[1] In the first chapter, we concluded that this question could not be solved exegetically—that is, historically or philologically. The process of discerning unmarked metaphors necessarily engages the horizon of the reader, to use Gadamer's term. We inevitably rely on our "understanding of the subject matter" as a key to decode when an author is writing literally or figuratively.[2] When the author clearly speaks in contradiction to our understanding of the subject matter, giving the benefit of the doubt to the author, we take the speech to be figurative. So, in order to answer the question about Paul's language, we have to examine the subject matter itself: what it is to be a person—and whether ἁμαρτία, as an entity with causal powers at the psychological, sociological, and mythological levels, is the kind of entity that could be a person.

The turn to emergent accounts of scientific and philosophical research on what it means to be a person—to be a self—at the biological, psychological, and sociological levels, is an attempt to address these issues. Through this lens, modern scientific research yields a perhaps surprising view of the self which is entirely incompatible with the atomistic individualism of modernity.[3] Rather, on this account, the self is internally composite. The boundary between the self and the other is difficult to draw and, depending on the criteria for drawing that line, often runs right through the heart of what we would common-sensibly take to be the "interior" of the self. Selves are fundamentally combinatory and open externally to integration into larger wholes. The selves, the persons, we know best—human individuals—turn out to be "selves made of selves." And, given that these selves are "defined by constraints, not by particular material or energetic constituents," nor "the generation of an exterior skin," selves may—and in fact do—emerge at ever higher levels of scale and abstraction "with more variable degrees of individuation and correlation with physical boundedness."[4] These higher-order selves—be they the group minds of David Sloan Wilson, the institutional persons of Philip Pettit, or the collective epistemic subjects of Karin Knorr Cetina—are all around us, providing the basis of our cognition, and constraining our thought patterns.

With this emergent "understanding of the subject matter"—that is, with an emergent understanding of personhood and the self as a framework—we now return to the text of Romans itself. How does this understanding of the self reframe not only our questions about the personal language Paul employs with regard to ἁμαρτία, but also our questions about the overlapping agencies at the individual, social, and mythological levels?[5] How do these discourses overlap? The hope was that careful consideration of the trans-ordinal theory that we bring to the text would provide a better framework within which to make sense of these convoluted agencies operating within and across various boundaries of scale, abstraction, and academic discipline. This chapter provides the opportunity to return to these agencies as they appear in the text of Romans, and to employ the tools of emergentism to see if we can tame the beast, as it were.

A return to the Romans text also necessarily involves an engagement with history—not because there is any hope of getting inside Paul's head by blind application of historical method, but because we, the readers, are people with modern historical consciousness. For us, part of "the actual state of affairs" is that this text was composed almost two thousand years ago. Even if we recognize that we can understand this text only on our own terms, we still have to admit that our own terms include some sense that this text once had a home in a place and time quite different from ours. We want to know what this text might have meant in that place and at that time—even if all we can do is construct an approximation of that time and place in our own time and place in order to test the fit. Furthermore, I share with Troels Engberg-Pedersen the hunch that at least one way our time and place differs from that ancient time and place is that we are far quicker to resort to metaphor—that is, to the extent that we retain physical reductionist instincts, we have a rather narrow sense of what can count as being literally the "actual state of affairs."[6] So, in some sense, this desire to hold the whole text together, to find a way to hold Paul's personal discourse together with his moral or social ideas, is ultimately an historically driven desire: the desire to resist our modern (reductionist) drive to resort to metaphorical interpretation.

These historical contexts (for there will be more than one construction we will encounter), of course, are not truly ancient. The past is gone.[7] All we have at our disposal are modern constructions of the past; therefore, the "ancient" contexts which will serve as at least one pole of my interpretation of Romans are—undoubtedly—contexts of my own construction (and the constructions of other modern historians). In that sense, they are decidedly modern—constructed in the twenty-first century according to (at least some of) the practices of twenty-first century historiography, for the needs of twenty-first century readers, whose own readerly horizon involves this basic historical consciousness.[8] In this way, I take it that we can imagine that these "historical" contexts are much more certainly part of our own readerly horizon than they are representations of the horizon of Paul's text in itself. That is, these ancient contexts in no way give us "shortcuts" to the text of Romans. It is not as though we have finally arrived at the "secret key" that will unlock the meaning of Romans. These ancient contexts are not to be privileged over the other resources brought to bear in this reading. The instinct remains, rather, that the only means for sorting out Paul's text is to pay close attention to our own sense of the "actual state of affairs." It is for this reason that we will engage the liberationist tradition at some length. Liberationist readers like Elsa Tamez and Franz Hinkelammert quite self-consciously engage with the "actual state of affairs"—that is, the first-hand experience of Sin in its political and psychological manifestations—as a crucial context for biblical interpretation. The fact that their insights are particularly helpful at this point should not at all be surprising, given the trajectory of the study so far.

The downward spiral of Romans 1-7 is a story of enslavement to s/Sin through law that results in death. The task at hand is to render a multilevel account of this story that makes sense of it at the individual, social, and mythological levels. Crucial to this account is a description of the overlapping agencies which are at play at multiple levels. First, I will narrate the origin of s/Sin in Romans, paying close attention to the story of decline that Paul tells, and to the transition from an emphasis on ἁμαρτάνω (sinning) and similar actions on the one hand, to ἁμαρτία (s/Sin) on the other. This will be an account of the emergence of the personal and cosmic power, Sin, from a supervenience base of human sinners and sinful social structures. Then I will give an account of the superorganismic Body of Sin as described in Romans 6:6. There, we will pay close attention to the ways Paul's addressees constitute a social body *before* they become the Body of Christ in baptism, and consider the antinomy between the Body of Sin and the Body of Christ in terms of their constituting two competing cosmic bodies (in roughly Stoic terms).

Finally, with these preliminary matters in place, I will turn to the heart of the matter: the dominion of Sin through the law that brings about death and the convoluted, overlapping sets of agencies involved. This is where the language of emergence will serve us particularly well, supplying terminology to describe the feedback loops caused by the intersections of individual, social, and mythological agencies. The dominion of Sin will be presented as an instance of downward causation (Polanyi's marginal control) and its effects traced through the social level (through Douglas's "founding analogies") to the level of individual moral psychology. Elsa Tamez and Frank Hinkelammert will provide insight into the social dynamics of this dominion, and the role of the law in bringing about death. Throughout, the fundamental proposal is that we understand Sin as a super-organism with a group mind, emergent from a complex network of individual human persons and social institutions.

The Emergence of the Cosmic Power, Sin

By Rom 5:21, the personhood and agency of ἁμαρτία—whether we understand that literally or figuratively—is quite plain. In 5:21, Sin has achieved the position it will hold for most of the next two chapters: Sin is a slave master, exercising dominion over those under its power. The main task of this chapter is to describe this dominion, for Sin as a cosmic power is most clearly seen in its exercise of agency in the world. But so far as it is possible, I begin by making a couple of simple observations about the origin of this power. It seems to burst onto the scene, but if we dig a bit, we find that we actually have two stories of the origins of Sin: 1:18–32, and the classic pericope, 5:12–17. In both cases, we see that the origin of Sin is coincident with the sinful activity of human beings. On these grounds, I suggest that the cosmic power, Sin, emerges from a supervenience base of human sins.

Romans's story regarding s/Sin begins in Paul's description of the decline of the Gentiles in Romans 1, beginning with the invention of idolatry. As Stanley Stowers has demonstrated, such a decline narrative (including the invention of iconic worship)—while certainly found in Jewish literature such as Wis 12–15 and *Sib. Or.* 3.8–45—is a broad Greco-Roman commonplace.[9] Stowers cites multiple ancient philosophers to support this claim, but Seneca's *Ep.* 90 is his most important source. In it, Seneca praises the original, bucolic human condition and recounts the onset of moral decline. In the beginning, true knowledge of the gods flows naturally from wisdom. It is wisdom who "discloses to us what the gods are and of what sort they are." Such worship needs no icon and, indeed, no temple. Regarding this natural revelation of the gods and their worship, Seneca writes, "Such are wisdom's rites of initiation, by means of which is unlocked, not a village shrine, but the vast temple of all the gods—the universe itself, whose true apparitions and true aspects she offers to the gaze of our minds."[10] For Seneca, as for Paul, the cosmos declares the true nature of divinity; worship of images is a step away from this original ideal.

Seneca is not alone. The Cynic author Pseudo-Heraclitus writes what sounds like typical Jewish invective (so much so that he has occasionally been misidenti-fied as a Jewish author), but he is clearly expressing a Greco-Roman philosophical commonplace: "You stupid men, teach us first what god is, so that you may be trusted when you speak of committing impiety. Also, where is god? Is he shut up in temples? ... You ignorant men, don't you know that god is not wrought by hands, and has not from the beginning had a pedestal, and does not have a single enclosure? Rather, the whole world is his temple."[11] The argument is, of course, quite close to Paul's:

> Ever since the creation of the world his eternal power and divine nature, invisible though they are, have been understood and seen through the things he has made. So they are without excuse; for though they knew God, they did not honor him as God or give thanks to him, but they became futile in their thinking, and their senseless minds were darkened. Claiming to be wise, they became fools; and they exchanged the glory of the immortal God for images resembling a mortal human being or birds or four-footed animals or reptiles. (Rom 1:20–23)

Whether an author is a Jew like Paul, a Stoic like Seneca, or a Cynic like Pseudo-Heraclitus, the decline of humanity involves the invention of idol worship.

For Paul, however, the onset of idolatry was not merely one step in a long chain of moral decline; it was *the* sin of the Gentiles, the fountainhead of their decline into all manner of debauchery, which climaxes in 1:29–32. While the appearance of iconic worship does appear in Seneca's account of the decline of human beings, and we can cite other ancient Greco-Roman philosophical invective against idolatry, the onset of idolatry does not seem to have had the same weight for these philosophers. Rather, if there is an "original sin" for the philosophers, it is desire and its cognates. As Seneca describes in *Ep.* 90, the original fellowship between humans and divinity, mediated by wisdom, "remained unspoiled for a long time, until desire [*avaritia*] tore the community asunder and became the cause of poverty, even in the case of those whom she herself had most enriched."[12]

This onset of avaricious vice first brought about the need for law. Originally, wisdom had governed through benevolent dictatorship, "but when once vice stole in and kingdoms were transformed into tyrannies, a need arose for laws and these very laws were in turn framed by the wise."[13] Despite the framing work of the wise, according to Seneca, the laws "could not stem the general development of wickedness."[14] Instead, Seneca, like Paul (in Rom 3:20), describes law as functioning merely to deepen human culpability. Of the original humans, Seneca writes, "It was by reason of their ignorance of things that the men of those days were innocent; and it makes a great deal of difference whether one wills not to sin [*peccare*] or has not the knowledge to sin."[15] Stowers concludes:

> In spite of the massive amounts of ink that have been spilled on asking how in Romans 5 Adam's sin was causative of human sinfulness, Paul follows extant Jewish sources in showing no interest in that question. Rather,

his interest is in epochs in the history of sin and salvation. Paul's mention of sin and death—beginning with Adam, and then sin being in the world before the law, the period from Adam to Moses (5:12–14), and then on to his big point about the universality of Adam and Christ—clearly envisages sin as having the kind of history seen in Jewish and other forms of primitivism. Sin began, it "spread," it was not reckoned in the period before the law, Adam sinned in one way, later people in another, and law came in to make the trespass greater. This is not a view of sin from the perspective of a moment in the pre-mundane heavenly realm or in the Garden that changed human nature.[16]

Indeed, Stowers does well in describing the history of s/Sin in Romans and provides ample evidence to suggest that this story was intelligible to Paul's Gentile addressees.[17] The story Paul is telling is a story of moral decline. Sinning—idolatry and all the wickedness that flows from it—comes first and, as we will see, throughout Romans there is never a sense that ἁμαρτία, even understood in personal terms, is ever fully separated from this basic sense of individual misdeed.

Yet there is a dynamic of this early decline narrative that shows the integration of this narrative with Paul's later, vivid, mythological language regarding Sin. Following the Gentiles' initial sin of idolatry, Paul says that God "hands them over" to the desires of their hearts (1:24), to dishonorable passions (v. 26), and to a debased mind (v. 28). Παραδίδωμι here retains the technical sense of handing one over to a jailer. The Gentiles find themselves "imprisoned" to a deformed moral psychology. These sequential imprisonments anticipate the language of enslavement (6:6, 16-20, 22; 7:6, 25; 8:15, 21) and domination (5:14, 17, 21; 6:9, 12, 14) at the hands of Sin, which comes to the fore later in the letter. This deformed moral psychology is a mechanism of Sin's dominion. This account of a chain of psychological imprisonments, then, is the story of the emergence of the dominion of Sin experienced at the psychological level.

From an emergent point of view, however, the emergence of this agency is coincident with the emergence of an entity. In the convoluted collective moral psychology of those who function as the supervenience base for the emergent cosmic tyrant, Sin, we have the establishment of the sorts of processes of recursive self-maintenance that ground Sin's being as a self. Given human cognition's social basis, one person's desires (1:24) and passions (1:26) set the boundary conditions for the desires and passions of another. The residue of past transgressions become the built environment in which future transgressions flourish as natural. There is no "architect"; the buildings build themselves. (Of course, Paul is quite aware that intentional, "top-down" social artifice—in this case, law—can be imposed, but his contention is that this imposition is not so external as to be able to avoid serving to solidify and embolden s/Sin.) The natural social-cognitive processes that facilitate the spread of desire and degrading passions themselves become the constitutive processes that give rise to the single, "debased mind"—the collective epistemic subject—that has emerged (1:28). Those who participate in this subject's constituent thought styles—the *Denkkollektiv* of Sin—are "given over" (παρέδωκεν) to thinking within the boundary conditions established by its cognition. In such a calamitous psychological state, doing "that which ought not be done" (τὰ μὴ καθήκοντα) is part and parcel of the sentence.

At the mythological level, we would describe it this way: the dominion of Sin is established through the rebellion of human beings, the natural consequences of which are permitted by God.[18] This is a picture of the power, Sin, emerging from the sinful rebellion of human beings.[19] This rebellion provides the base on which the cosmic power, Sin, supervenes. Human beings then ironically experience the real dominion of this creation of their own hands. There is no conflict between Paul's story of decline and his later mythological language. We are the authors of our own tragedy, demiurges of a slave master that holds us in bondage. The turn to idolatry is, in a certain sense, ironically successful. The story of the advent of idolatry is the story of the creation of a real, superhuman power that truly does exercise dominion over its human subjects. As Beverly Gaventa describes it:

> Some scholars posit a tension between what Paul affirms in this passage about human refusal to acknowledge God and later sections of the letter that speak of Sin as a power. The beginning point of this grand depiction of Sin is certainly humanity's willful choice to deny God, even to create its own gods. Paul's depiction of humankind opens with an action taken by humanity itself rather than by another power. With the claim that God delivered up humanity to impurity, passion, and debased mind, however, there may be at least a hint of some larger conflict. An as-yet-unnamed someone or something challenges God for humanity. That is not to overlook the initial action: humanity's refusal of God's lordship meant that God conceded humanity for a time to the lordship of another.[20]

Already in Romans 3:9, long before the Adam story is introduced, "all, both Jews and Greeks," are described as being ὑφ᾽ ἁμαρτίαν, "under Sin." Paul previously used this phrase in Gal 3:22, and uses it again in Rom 7:14. This is language of dominion. Whatever advantage Jews have over Gentiles in having the "oracles of God" (Rom 3:2), there is universal equality in this fact: all humanity lives under the dominion of Sin.[21] The scriptural catena in 3:10–18 describes the universality of this reign and its consequences. While it would be hard to build a Pauline conception of the dominion of Sin on the strength of this phrase alone, it is worth noting that from early on, in the midst of the extended decline narrative, Paul is already quite happy to use language that describes Sin as a dominator, a slave master to whom human beings are subject. Paul is able to do this without in any sense detracting from the story of moral decline. The onset of Sin's dominion and the increase of sin, of transgression, and of moral decay are one and the same thing, and Paul can adopt at least these two different discourses—moral decline or personal, enslaving power—as they suit his rhetorical needs.

We now turn to the classic pericope, Romans 5:12–21. To a large extent, the puzzle about the origins of ἁμαρτία lies in 5:12: "Therefore, just as through one man Sin came into the world and through Sin came death, and so death spread to all people, because all sinned." Sin entering [εἰσῆλθεν] is just the first of a long string of actions that Sin performs. From here, Sin increases (5:20), exercises dominion (5:21, 6:12, 14), produces desire (7:8), revives (7:9), and dwells in the bodies of sinners (7:17, 20).[22] In other words, Rom 5:12 constitutes the second creation account of Sin in Romans: the creation of the cosmic tyrant, Sin. If the early account of the origins of s/Sin focus largely on the level of moral psychology, here the focus is on the mythological level—the development of Sin as a mythological power that exercises dominion over the creation.

For many Christian interpreters since Augustine, this passage serves as the textual "hook" for an expansive doctrine of original sin, beginning with the sin of the first man, Adam, and constituting a fundamental change in anthropology. More recently, scholars have argued that 5:12 simply indicates a spread of sin—that is, of sinful behavior—of the type that we saw in the moral decline narrative in chapter 1.[23] Käsemann points to 2 Bar. 54.15, 19 as indicating that this tension could be tolerated within ancient Judaism: "For although Adam sinned first and has brought death upon all who were not in his own time, yet each of them who descended from him has prepared for himself the coming torment . . . Adam is, therefore, not the cause, except for himself, but each of us has become our own Adam."[24] Adam brought death upon all—and yet, each of us becomes our own Adam.

All this is made clear in Rom 6. As plain as Paul's language is about Sin's dominion, he is equally clear about human cooperation. Sin's dominion involves our participation. So, in v. 12, Paul can command the addressees: "Do not let sin reign (Μὴ . . . βασιλευέτω)." Despite Sin's reign, there is an exercise of agency involved. In v. 16 we have: "Do you not know that to whomever you yield yourselves [παριστάνετε ἑαυτοὺς] in obedience as slaves, you are slave of the one whom you obey, either of Sin resulting in death, or of obedience resulting in righteousness?" Enslavement to Sin is a result of an act of presenting oneself as a slave—"yielding," as Jewett suggests.[25] One lives under a master of one's own selection—or, to take the emergentist language one step further, of one's own creation.[26] Paul's plea to the addressees is: yield your members to righteousness and become a slave of obedience.[27]

In summary, the decline of human beings into sin—in archetypical Adam (5:12–21), in each person's imitation of that archetypical sin (as in *2 Bar*), and in the history of the nations in Romans 1:18-32—is coincidental with their being handed over to Sin and then living under its dominion. On an emergent reading, this is precisely where the power, Sin, is coming to be, where the transition from sinning to Sin is happening. At the individual level, each is subjected to desires (1:24) and to dishonorable passions (v. 26); their very psychology is corrupt. At the social level, this leads to a subjection to a collective debased mind (v. 28). Sin supervenes on these properties and entities at the individual and social levels. Read in an emergent framework, Romans 1:18–32 appears as a rather straightforward account of Sin's *autopoiesis*. The account of moral decline is an account of the generation of ever more convoluted processes of self-maintenance and regulation of lower-level processes (in this case, psychological and social) that give rise to the emergence of a "self" at a higher level of organization (in this case, mythological). This is a "bottom-up" description of Sin. It is not evidence, as Stowers claims, that there is no understanding of Sin as a power in Romans.[28] Rather, it is evidence that the power, Sin, emerges from a complex system of human transgression, of human moral psychology run amok.

However much Sin might function as a cosmic tyrant in Romans, Sin's power develops with the cooperation of its subjects. Romans is everywhere insisting, as did Bultmann, "that sin came into the world by sinning."[29] In emergent terms, Sin arises from a supervenience base of human transgressions, of human sinning. Sin as a cosmic power emerges from the exercise of individual human agencies—paradigmatically Adam's, but subsequently the contingent, historical, and destructive behavior of people. Walter Wink's summary of the emergence of "powers" serves quite well as a summary of the emergence of Sin (which neither Wink nor I take to be a member of Paul's category, δυνάμεις or "powers"):

> It is far from the case, then, that human beings create their gods. The "spirits" of things emerge with the things themselves and are only subsequently divined as their inner essence. The gods, spirits, and demons are not mere personifications or hypostatizations. That is the language of reductionism; it means that these entities are not regarded as real, but only as poetic fictions or shorthand for speaking about realities the historian knows how to describe more precisely with his analytical tools. Personification means illusion. The Powers we are speaking about, on the contrary, are real . . . To be sure, we do establish new structures and modify old ones. Insofar as we share in the creative process and bring new consciousness to it, we help create the spirituality of things. There is a reciprocity, so we could argue that it is as true to say that the gods create us as to say that we create the gods.[30]

Wink's language vividly evokes the language of idolatry with which Paul begins his invective. The original instinct to create new gods in the images of human beings or animals is, as we have noted, ironically successful. A new "divinity" does come into being, and exercises a dominion that reflects the essential difference between it and the true God: it is *mortal,* as opposed to the immortality of God (1:23) and so it reigns in death, rather than in life (5:14). Jesus's obedience (5:19) reverses this dire situation (5:17).

This conception of Sin as a cosmic power answers one of the critiques of this view posed by Stanley Stowers when he argues that, "Paul thinks that the age is dominated by masses of people who have allowed themselves to serve evil beings. But such cooperation is not what scholars have in mind when they speak of sin as a power."[31] Whether or not Stowers is right in characterizing what advocates of Sin as a power have in mind, I cannot know—nor can he. But if Stowers's concern is that whatever we mean by "power," it ought to be compatible with individual freedom, or at least culpability, that concern is spot on. An emergence framework captures this dialectical relationship between human and suprahuman agency, and suggests that this convoluted mesh of processes is precisely what constitutes a new self at the higher level of scale, abstraction, and analysis. On this account, Sin not only gains power over people's lives through their cooperation, but also, Sin depends ontologically on this cooperation, as Sin's supervenience base consists precisely of this cooperation. This is the founding, ontological nature of the causal feedback loop which is examined in detail later in this chapter. This is as predicted within an emergence framework: namely, that in the case of the emergent self, the dynamics *are* the ontology. The self as a locus of "dynamical reciprocity" is a self in which ontology cannot be separated from dynamics, in which being cannot be separated from agency.[32]

The Body of Sin

In the previous chapter, I described these sorts of selves at both the organismic (bodily/biological) level and at the subjective (mental/psychological) level. At both levels, we found the same basic emergent logic at work; the emergence of organismic selves—living bodies—from non-life was a model for the emergence of subjective selves—minds—from organismic selves. At very large scales and high levels of abstraction, we found that organismic selves were best described as superorganisms: organisms composed of organisms, selves made of selves, communities within which group selective pressures are so strong that a new order of self begins to emerge. Is, then, Sin a superorganism, composed of human individuals and/or their sinful actions? This is not far from what

Anders Nygren understands Paul to be describing when he talks about the Body of Sin in Romans 6:6:

> "In Adam" we all belonged to the same *organism*. As human beings we are members of one body ... But now, through baptism, we have been incorporated into Christ. That means that we are henceforth not merely members in the great organism of humanity; we are members in "the body of Christ".[33]

In other words, Nygren describes the Body of Sin as a collective body—a superorganism—analogous to Paul's other collective body, the Body of Christ. While Nygren's suggestion is followed by Schmidt, by and large it has been otherwise dismissed.[34] I find good reasons, however, to take it up again—and the reasons have everything to do with the conception of selves and bodies—both singular and collective—in Romans and in the broader Greco-Roman context.

As Dale Martin and Michelle Lee have illustrated, Paul's use of the term σῶμα (roughly, "body") functions against an extensive background in the ancient philosophical world.[35] Particularly for the Stoics, who supplied many of the learned "common senses" of the first century, σῶμα was a central concept. The Stoics denied that anything could exist which is not a body or the state of a body; whatever was acting or being acted upon must be a body.[36] Diogenes Laertius attests that Archedemus, Diogenes, Antipater, and Chrysippus held that "everything that acts is a body [σῶμα]."[37] Paul's contemporary, Seneca, states the matter just as plainly: "that which acts is a body [*corpus*]."[38] Seneca's intuition is quite similar to that of a modern ontological monist: namely, that the causal world must consist only of things of one type. For modern ontological monists, this type is "physical," while for the Stoics, this type is "corporeal"—though, of course, we ought not take the fact that these categories function for these two groups in similar ways as an indication that they are the same; they are not. Seneca writes at length on the question "is the good corporeal?":

> Now the good is active: for it is beneficial; and what is active is corporeal. [*Bonum facit; prodest enim; quod facit corpus est.*] ... You will have no doubt, I am sure, that emotions are bodies [*corpora sint*] ... like wrath, love, sternness; unless you doubt whether they change our features, knot our foreheads, relax the countenance, spread blushes, or drive away the blood? What, then? Do you think that such evident marks of the body are stamped upon us by anything else than body? And if emotions are bodies [*corpora sunt*], so are the diseases of the spirit [*morbi animorum*]—such as greed, cruelty, and all the faults which harden in our souls, to such an extent that they get into an incurable state. Therefore evil is also, and all its branches—spite, hatred, pride.[39]

All these "abstractions" (from our point of view) are *bodies* for Seneca. Crucially for our purposes, vices of all kinds are bodies; they are diseases of the spirit. They are bodies because they have bodily effects. Given Paul's quasi-fatalistic language in Romans 7, Seneca's summary is worth quoting at length:

> Furthermore, any object that has power to move, force, restrain, or control, is a body [*corpus est*]. Come now! Does not fear hold us back? Does not boldness drive us ahead? Bravery spur us on, and give us momentum? Restraint rein us in and call us back? Joy raise our spirits? Sadness cast us down? In short, any act on our part is performed at the bidding of wickedness or virtue. Only a body can control or forcefully affect another body. [*quod imperat corpori corpus est, quod vim corpori adfert, corpus.*] The good of the body is corporeal; a man's good is related to his bodily good; therefore, it is bodily.[40]

The fact that Seneca is an ancient "materialist" does not prevent him from arguing that the human agent is subject to the rule (*imperium*) of outside moral forces.[41] Rather, precisely because of his commitment to Stoic materialism (or, perhaps better, "corporeality"), Seneca has to accept the bodily existence of these moral forces and their corporeal constraint of the agencies of human individuals. In other words, it is because of Seneca's commitment to bodily causal closure—not in spite of it—that Seneca concludes that "any act on our part is performed at the bidding of wickedness or virtue." Clearly, *body* is something very different for Seneca than it is for us. Paul's conception, we will see, shares more in common with Seneca.

Ancient materialism turns out to be just as surprising as modern non-reductive physicalism. But our questions about bodies, about organismic selves, have all focused on issues of mereology—that is, how bodies are constituted "internally." The Stoics had a tripartite mereology for bodies. First, there were bodies composed of separated (διεστώτων) parts, like a flock, army, or senate; second, bodies composed of contiguous parts (συναπτομένων) which form a single structure, like a house; and third, unified bodies (ἡνωμένα), like stone, wood, or people, unified by a spirit (πνεῦμα) or set of habitual practices (ἕξις).[42] This mereology makes it possible to have *social* bodies, bodies made of bodies—indeed, *all* bodies are such bodies; the only variation being the degree of the integration of the components. As I have suggested is the case on an emergent account, this set of nesting dolls goes all the way up. At the most grand level, the Stoics took the entire cosmos to be a living being. Lee cites Diogenes Laertius, *Vit. Phil.* 7:139, citing Antipater of Tyre's *On the Cosmos*: "The whole world [κόσμος] is a living being [ζῷον ὄντα] endowed with soul and reason [ἔμψυχον καὶ λογικόν], and having aether for its ruling principle [ἡγεμονικόν]."[43] The same work attests to Chrysippus assigning the role of ruling principle, ἡγεμονικόν, to heaven or—without contradicting himself—to the "purer part of the aether; the same which they declare to be preeminently God and always to have, as it were in sensible fashion, pervaded all that is in the air, all animals and plants, and also the earth itself, as a principle of cohesion."[44] This is typical of Stoic cosmology, freely switching back and forth between material (aether), cosmological (heaven), and mythological explanations (God).[45]

That the world itself constituted a living body was an idea inherited from Platonic tradition. For Plato, "The universe is a living creature, composed of a bodily and visible Heaven, through which is woven the invisible Soul; there is also a correspondence between the human body and the cosmos in the fact that both are composed of the same elements."[46] While this idea appears elsewhere, the most significant text was of course the *Timaeus*, in which it is reasoned that because God "wanted to produce a piece of work that would be as excellent and supreme as its nature would allow . . . divine providence brought our world into being as a truly living thing, endowed with soul and intelligence."[47] This cosmos is "a single living thing that contains within itself all living things, mortal or immortal."[48] As a result, the human body could be understood in terms of the cosmic body and vice versa. The significance of this conception of the universe as a body was such that, for the ancients "the human body was not *like* a microcosm; it *was* a microcosm—a small version of the universe at large."[49]

Social bodies came in smaller sizes as well. The next step down from the one, cosmic body, was the universal human body, which supplied the foundational principle for Stoic social ethics. Seneca writes, "I can lay down for mankind a rule [*formulam*], in short compass, for our duties in human relationships: all that you behold, that which comprises both god and man, is one [*unum*]—we are the parts [*membra*] of one great body [*corporis*] . . . Our relations with one another are like a stone arch, which would collapse if the stones did not mutually support each other, and which is upheld in this very way."[50] Note that Seneca states that all humanity *is* a body, but is only *like* an arch. The somatic language is not metaphor. There also existed yet smaller civic bodies—including the body politic. So, Seneca writes of "two commonwealths [*dues res publicas*]—the one, a vast and truly common state" (the single unified body of humanity) and "the other, the one to which we have been assigned by the accident of birth . . . the commonwealth of the Athenians or of the Carthiginians."[51] This social body, then, became a *topos* by which one could lobby for social unity within a particular political entity. These *homonoia* speeches were so common that they became a genre unto themselves.[52]

One particularly striking example of the appeal to corporeal unity in a *homonoia* speech is Seneca's description of the Roman Empire itself as a body with the emperor, Nero, as its ruling spirit. Seneca writes to Nero:

> The whole body is the servant of the mind [*animo*], and though the former is so much larger and so much more showy, while the unsubstantial soul remains invisible not knowing where its secret habitation lies, yet the

hands, the feet, and the eyes are in its employ; the outer skin is its defence; at its bidding we lie idle, or restlessly run to and fro; when it commands, if it is a grasping tyrant, we search the sea for gain; if covetous of fame, ere now we have thrust a right hand into the flame, or plunged willingly into a chasm. In the same way this vast throng, encircling the life of one man [*unius animae*], is ruled by his spirit [*spiritu*], guided by his reason [*ratione*], and would crush and cripple itself with its own power if it were not upheld by wisdom [*consilio*]. It is, therefore, their own safety that men love [*Suam itaque incolumitatem amant*], when for one man they lead ten legions at a time into battle when they rush to the forefront and expose their breasts to wounds that they may save the standards of their emperor from defeat. For he is the bond [*vinculum*] by which the commonwealth is united, the breath of life [*spiritus vitalis*] which these many thousands draw, who in their own strength would be only a burden to themselves and the prey of others if the great mind of the empire [*mens illa imperii*] should be withdrawn.

> If safe their king, one mind [*mens*] to all;
> Bereft of him, they troth recall.[53]

In this passage, Seneca evokes the ancient analogue of Durkheim's founding analogy of sociology, stated in its plainest form by Isocrates: "Every polity [πολιτεία] is the soul (ψυχή) of the state, having as much power over it as the mind (φρόνησις) over the body."[54] The emperor is the animating spirit of the empire, which is his (social) body. He endows this body with all it needs: reason, the breath of life, a unifying bond. What the emperor wills, the individual bodies in the empire will do, even to their bodily harm, whether thrusting hands into flames, diving into chasms, or exposing their breasts to wounds in battle. The language is precisely as we would expect in an emergent account; the complex system of the Roman state is constituted as a superorganism with a group mind—in this case, identified, "incarnated," if you will, in a single individual: Nero. Seneca even invokes the social insects as a comparison: the lines from Vergil (*Georgics* 4.212) describe a hive of bees' devotion to their "king." And, in fact, Seneca's description of Nero's relationship to the empire sounds very much E. O. Wilson's description of the insect colony as the "extrasomatic projection of [the queen's] personal genome."[55] This is group selection run amok, overpowering individual-level concerns.

The passage quoted emphasizes the dependence of the imperial body on Nero as its ruling principle. But the organic unity works both ways. The image quickly becomes the basis for Seneca's plea to Nero to exercise restraint in dealing with what is, in actuality, his very own body: "if—and this is what thus far [this discourse] is establishing—you are the soul of the state and the state your body (*corpus*), you see, I think, how requisite is mercy; for you are merciful to yourself when you are seemingly merciful to another."[56] Seneca's rhetoric makes it plain: this is no mere metaphor. What is merely *apparently* the case is the emperor and citizens' individual differentiation. This is an illusion that threatens to obscure their literal corporeal unity. Our modern instinct toward individualism in social analysis is completely inverted. As David E. Hahm notes:

> There seems to be nothing hypothetical about the Stoic use of the biological model. Nor did the Stoics ever suggest that the biological model is in any way analogical. For the Stoics the biological model possessed as much ontological reality as did the phenomena it explains. Thus it not only explains phenomena; it is itself a phenomenon. This makes the Stoic biologistic cosmology quite different from the "likely tale" of Plato's *Timaeus* or the countless analogies in Aristotle's scientific works.[57]

As a result, Michelle Lee argues, the social body was not something that needed to be argued for; rather, it was the ontological basis from which ethical arguments could be constructed. Describing Cicero's invocation of "body" language in his ethical works, she writes:

> Cicero is not saying what people should do, but rather describing what people naturally do and are. Thus he uses the body metaphor to stress an ontological point by describing the unity of humanity. The point he is illustrating is less a desired behavior or prescribed course of action than a description of who they are and what they are like . . . He does not tell the members to act like a body, but that they are like a body . . . It is not something that they can accomplish; but rather something they are.[58]

Lee slips into the language of metaphor and simile, but the evidence is quite clear: it is the fact that humanity as a whole and smaller communities *are* in fact real, material, unified bodies that supplies "the ontological principle for their ethical precepts . . . the already-existing bond among people prior to the formation of any concrete communities."[59]

The material unity of these real, social bodies was facilitated by the pervasiveness of πόροι ("pores")—"channels that enable external material to enter and pervade the body and constitute passageways within the body for psychic and nutritive (or destructive) matter"—which allowed the unifying πνεῦμα to pervade the bodies of members (μέλη). Πόροι were the basis of one ancient ideology of disease, which was understood in terms of invasion by external bodies. (Social "illness" or discord was conceived similarly.) The pervasiveness of πόροι meant that the boundary between an "individual" body and the cosmos was constantly being crossed.[60]

The result, according to Martin, is a concept of body that will sound at once counterintuitive and yet, at this point in the study, quite familiar: "the nonexistence of the 'individual,' the fluidity of the elements that make up the 'self,' and the essential continuity of the human body with its surroundings."[61] This statement is affirmed by the modern scientific reflection reviewed in the previous two chapters. What else are we to conclude once we have come to know our "own" bodies as more than 90 percent non-human at the cellular level, when we see that our minds extend beyond the boundaries of skin and skull, when cognition itself—the *cogito* core of Decartes's individualism—is revealed to have a social basis? The modern-scientific and the ancient come together to point the way in orienting ourselves to the strange sorts of bodies—the strange sorts of "selves"— we encounter in Romans.[62]

Of course, the flagship social body in the Pauline corpus is the Body of Christ, invoked in Romans in 12:4–5.[63] The explicit invocation of social-body discourse comes on the heels of a more subtle invocation in 12:1-2. The addressees are to present their *plural* bodies as a *single* living sacrifice (παραστῆσαι τὰ σώματα ὑμῶν θυσίαν ζῶσαν). They are to be transformed by the renewal of their single, collective mind (μεταμορφοῦσθε τῇ ἀνακαινώσει τοῦ νοὸς). With this collective language invoked, 12:4–5 makes explicit what is already implicit: "For as in one body we have many members, and not all the members have the same function, so we, who are many, are one body in Christ, and individually we are members one of another." As in the many *homonoia* speeches cited in Martin and Lee, the invocation of the social body provides an ontological foundation for the ethical argument advanced in the larger pericope. The existence of the social body is not argued for, but rather, argued *from*. The addressees already know themselves to be a body. Indeed, Paul has already invoked this collective identity that they share in bodily terms in Romans 8:23: "and not only the creation, but we ourselves, who have the first fruits of the Spirit, groan inwardly while we wait for adoption, the redemption of our [pl.] body [sg.] [τὴν ἀπολύτρωσιν τοῦ σώματος ἡμῶν]."[64] They were constituted as the Body of Christ in baptism (invoked explicitly in Rom 7:4), when they entered *into* Christ (6:3), such that they now live *in* Him (6:11, 8:1–2, 39, 12:5). Because of the social body that they are, they ought to behave in a particular way.

This is all straightforward enough, but given what Hahm, Lee, and Martin have demonstrated, we might ask: what of the social identity *before* baptism? While commentators have worked hard to imagine the depth of social identity constituted in the Body of Christ, they tend to imagine an original (modernist) individual who opts in to this odd (from a modern point of view), socially conditioned life in the Church.[65] Jewett describes the Body of Christ as the place where "the various congregations and individual members are to find their unity."[66] Dunn contrasts a possibly "individualistic concept of salvation" with "its communal character."[67] Käsemann (Käsemann!) holds that factions can dissolve the unity of the body and return its members to a(n original?) state as "religious individuals."[68]

Yet time and again in Romans we find language that describes even the pre- (or simply non-) baptismal state in collective terms. In 1:28, Paul writes of the gentiles that "God handed them [pl.] over to a [sg.] debased mind. (παρέδωκεν αὐτοὺς ὁ θεὸς εἰς ἀδόκιμον νοῦν)." The moral degradation of the gentiles results in a social body with a debased corporate mind. This is a social body, a *Denkkollektiv* in Fleck's terms, unified by a common habitual practice: sinful rebellion against God.[69] In Rom 6:6, as we have already seen, we get collective language used of the addressees' former state: "We know that our [pl.] old self [sg.] [ὁ παλαιὸς ἡμῶν ἄνθρωπος] was crucified with him so that the Body of Sin [τὸ σῶμα τῆς ἁμαρτίας] might come to nothing [καταργηθῇ], and we might no longer be enslaved to Sin." The phrase ὁ παλαιὸς ἡμῶν ἄνθρωπος (literally, "our old human") has long troubled interpreters, but it need not trouble us too much. This is the "self," the whole "person" that supervenes on the Body of Sin.[70] The characteristic genitive plural personal pronoun in possession of a singular noun (ὁ παλαιὸς ἡμῶν ἄνθρωπος) gives us the sense of Sin having a social body—the Body of Sin—united by a shared habitual practice: sinning.[71]

In Rom 6:12, we find similar language used of the addressees' former state. They are not to return to their former state: "do not let Sin reign in your [pl.] mortal body [sg.] [τῷ θνητῷ ὑμῶν σώματι], to make you [pl.] obey its [sg.] passions." This singular "mortal body" does not refer to each individual's body.[72] When Paul uses this phrase to refer to the constituent individual bodies, he is quite happy to use the plural for the exact same phrase in 8:11: "he who raised Christ from the dead will give life to your mortal bodies [τὰ θνητὰ σώματα ὑμῶν]." Rather, the body referred to in 6:12 is the collective, social body of Sin, of which they are members. It is "mortal" inasmuch as it is subject to Sin, and therefore subject, at the mythological level, to Death, the consort of Sin.[73] The collective nature of this Body is made explicit in 6:13, where Paul invokes language of *members* (μέλη), usually, in Paul, an image for the constituent bodies of a collective (save for in Rom 7:23–24, in which the macrocosm of the Body of Sin has become a microcosm within the constituent's individual body).[74] At any rate, μέλη ("members") is parallel to ἑαυτούς "yourselves," later in the same verse, further suggesting that the "members" in view are precisely the "individual" members of the corporate body of the Roman church. "No longer present your members [τὰ μέλη ὑμῶν] to Sin as weapons of wickedness, but present yourselves [ἑαυτοὺς] to God as those who have been brought from death to life—that is, present your members [τὰ μέλη ὑμῶν] to God as weapons of righteousness. For Sin will not rule over you, since you are not under law but under grace."[75] This is martial language reminiscent of Plutarch's description of Stoic bodies of separated parts (διεστώτων), in which he cites armies (στόλον καὶ στρατόπεδον) as chief examples. The recipients of Romans are being recruited into two armies, each of which constitutes a collective body. Their individual bodies are enlisted as members of these collective bodies and deployed as weapons to two very different ends: either wickedness or righteousness. These two armies constitute two different dominions. Here we see the structure of the dominion of Sin that I will discuss at length in the pages that follow: Sin rules over those members of its own social body through legally encoded social customs, the legal expressions of the regnant thought style that "sets the preconditions of any cognition, and . . . determines what can be counted as a reasonable question and a true or false answer."[76] That is, Sin's rule through law constitutes a socially-mediated marginal control of the moral psychology of its members.

Against the modernist instinct of an "original" individuality only later joined into a communal identity in Christ, one rather gets the sense, as Troels Engberg-Pedersen has noted, that "there is no self-conscious notion of 'the self' in Paul . . . he thinks in terms of membership of groups: Jews, Gentiles, Christ followers."[77] We may now add to this list "sinners": those who constitute the Body of Sin by their submission to Sin's rule through their cooperation in committing sins. The Body of Sin in this sense is a *cosmic* body, that is, it constitutes a *cosmos* within itself, a degraded version of the cosmos God established and through which God's true nature is revealed (Rom 1:20). The cosmic consequences of Sin are evident not just in human sinners but in the natural world around them:

> For the creation waits with eager longing for the revealing of the children of God; for the creation was subjected to futility, not of its own will but by the will of the one who subjected it, in hope that the creation itself will be set free from its bondage to decay and will obtain the freedom of the glory of the children of God. We know that the whole creation has been groaning in labor pains until now; and not only the creation, but we ourselves, who have the first fruits of the Spirit, groan inwardly while we wait for adoption, the redemption of our Body. (Rom 8:19–23)

The creation itself is in slavery (δουλείας), under the reign of Sin, to whom, like the Gentiles in Rom 1, God has subjected it, allowing the natural consequence of human sin: the emergence of the cosmic Body, the cosmic agent, Sin. Only through the redemption of the social Body will creation be set free.

Romans is not the only place where we find Paul talking about the cosmic scope of corruption. In Galatians, for example, Paul describes the very "elements of the cosmos [τὰ στοιχεῖα τοῦ κόσμου]" as enslaving powers themselves.[78] The rule of the elements is closely tied to the rule of Sin which, while certainly less pronounced in Galatians, is not absent entirely. As in Romans, the dominion of

Sin is established with divine permission (Gal 3:22). But the rule of Sin is largely exercised through the perversion of law (about which, in Romans, see below) and the cosmic elements. J. Louis Martyn has persuasively argued that these elements are to be understood as consisting of corresponding lists of opposites, which Pythagorean and Stoic philosophy understood to serve as the very foundations of the world. Read this way, these elements share much in common with Mary Douglas's founding analogies, which provide the basis for collective thinking and decision-making.[79] These antinomies, such as "Jew and Greek," "slave and free," or "male and female," provide not just the foundations of cognition, the horizon where it is possible to assign significance to objects of discourse; rather, they provide the foundations of the (corrupted) cosmos itself.

It is this cosmos that is brought to nothing through baptism into the death of Christ in which "there is no longer Jew or Greek . . . slave or free . . . male and female" (Gal 3:28). In Romans, Paul describes baptism bringing about the death of the Body of Sin (about which, see below). In Galatians, Paul describes baptism effecting the dissolution of the corrupt "present evil age" (Gal 1:4). Inasmuch as the Body of Sin—which emerges from and recursively reenforces the antinomies that ground corrupted collective cognition—constitutes a cosmos, these two expressions amount to more or less the same thing. Sin establishes its Body as a cosmos. The maintenance of the elements of that cosmos (the founding analogies of the social cognition regulated by Sin) is a constituent process of self-regulation through which Sin emerges.

Again, this cosmic story has precursors in Seneca's story of decline. The moral decline of human beings goes hand in hand with a decline in the condition of the world itself. Seneca writes, "the very soil was more productive when untilled, and yielded more than enough for peoples who refrained from despoiling one another."[80] If Paul ever heard a similar sentiment within his cultural milieu, the resonance with Genesis 3:17–19 would be hard to miss. There is a symbiosis to the relationship between humankind and cosmos. If human beings have altered the quality of the earth, the world in turn is now churning out worse humans: "there is no doubt that the world [*mundus*] produced a better progeny before it was yet worn out."[81] Thus, the cosmic drama that Pauline scholars routinely find in Romans is not at all at odds with the philosophical elements within Paul's intellectual environment. Rather, given the proper cosmological framework, the cosmic consequences of Sin are intelligible within the ancient environment.[82]

The dominion of Sin is so strong, its organic unity so universal—because all have sinned, all have participated in its unifying habitual practice (Rom 2:12, 3:9, 12, 23; 5:12)—that the only way out is death. This is precisely what Paul says happens in baptism. Those who have been baptized *into* Christ Jesus (that is, into the Body of Christ), have participated in his death (6:3–5). This was "so that the body of sin might be destroyed [καταργηθῇ]" (v. 6). Καταργέω here is a typical Pauline word for epoch-change. For example, in 1 Cor 2:6, Paul writes of the rulers of this age (τῶν ἀρχόντων τοῦ αἰῶνος τούτου), who are doomed to perish (καταργουμένων).[83] The language in Rom 6:6 is similarly in an apocalyptic key.[84] In the death of baptism, the cosmic Body of Sin is coming to nothing as its members fall off necrotic, having died with Christ in baptism and been raised to new life "in Christ," that is, in the Body of Christ. So the addressees must consider themselves dead to Sin and alive to God in Christ Jesus, that is, in the Body of Christ.

The Body of Christ, then, constitutes a rival cosmos, the new creation breaking in, bringing about the end of the old creation which, for the time being, is constituted by the Body of Sin. The rivalry between these two entities appears in regular contrasts and comparisons between the two, most notably in describing the dominion of each and their constellation of related concepts and ideas. Sin's consort, Death, exercises dominion in Rom 5:14 and 17—though v. 21 clarifies that this dominion is Sin's dominion in death. In parallel, grace exercises dominion in v. 21, and the promise is that those who receive the grace available in Jesus Christ will reign in life in v. 17. Similarly, 6:16-22 compares the slavery to Sin (vv. 16, 17, 20) and impurity and ever greater lawlessness (v. 19), to slavery to obedience (v. 16), to righteousness (vv. 18, 19), and to God (v. 22). The summary in 6:23 indicates that this second set of masters is a part of "life in Christ Jesus our Lord"—that is, in the Body of Christ. Each social body comes with its own *hegemon,* expressed in these various forms. As Käsemann explains:

> Because the world is not finally a neutral place but the field of contending powers, mankind both individually and socially becomes an object in the struggle and an exponent of the power that rules it. His basic definition derives from the category of belonging. He is no more neutral than the place where he stands. If creation has already set a lord over him, he is in no sense autonomous in the fall. Even though the Creator maintains his claim to him, he falls under another lordship. Concretely he falls under sin and death.[85]

Of course, Käsemann's language of "the fall" is anachronistic, but the general point stands: as Bob Dylan said, "you gotta serve *somebody.*" My contention is that "field of contending powers," this contested lordship, is expressed concretely, *corporeally* in the antithesis between these two cosmic bodies, the Body of Christ and the Body of Sin. The addressees find themselves, as Seneca says, citizens of at least two commonwealths (*dues res publicas*).[86] One is their local citizenship, their *ekklesia,* the other is a cosmic body—either the Body of Sin or the Body of Christ. Paul's concern is for the fate of this local, social body in its alignment with one or the other cosmic body. Again, Käsemann is helpful when writing about 6:12-14: "If in such a context Paul speaks of our members, or even our bodies themselves are called members, it is clear that we are never autonomous, but always participate in a definite world and stand under lordship."[87] What is true of each individual body is true also of the social, cosmic body. Even the Roman community itself is not autonomous. It, too, is subject to one or the other of these cosmic bodies.

We find further support for the idea of Sin and Christ constituting two dominions in 6:2. Here it is suggested that at some point "we" were living *in* Sin, which Robert C. Tannehill takes to be parallel to the ubiquitous Pauline, "in Christ [ἐν Χριστῷ]" (Rom 3:24; 6:11, 23; 8:1–2, 39–9:1; 12:5; 15:17; 16:3, 7, 9–10). He writes:

> The importance of this phrase becomes clear when we see that the idea of living "in" sin is part of a broader Pauline pattern of expression . . . The connection of this form of expression to Paul's idea of the two dominions is clear. The two dominions are different because they are ruled by different powers. It is the powers operative in the dominion which determine its nature, which mark it off from another dominion where other powers are operative. Such a dominion is a power field. It is the sphere in which a power is at work.[88]

Taking Tannehill's observation one step further, we could suggest that these two "power fields" are nothing other than two cosmic bodies. These two bodies provide two different sets of boundary conditions for those who exist within these bodies and, indeed, form their supervenience bases.

The Community Rule from Qumran (1QS 3.13–4.26) describes two competing spirits with two distinct dominions: the Prince of Light and the Angel of Darkness.

> The authority of the Prince of Light [שר אורים] extends to the dominion [ממשלת] over all righteous people [בני צדק]; therefore, they walk in the paths of light. Correspondingly, the authority of the Angel of Darkness [מלאך חושך] embraces the dominion [ממשלת] over all wicked people [בני עול], so they walk in the paths of darkness. The authority of the Angel of Darkness further extends to the corruption of all the righteous [בני צדק]. All their sins, iniquities, shameful and rebellious deeds are under his dominion [בממשלתו], a situation God in His mysteries allows to continue until His era [עד קצו] dawns.[89]

Rather than the body, the image here is of family. The domain of each power is a set of *siblings*, the "children of righteousness [בני צדק]" or the "children of wickedness [בני עול]." This is a discourse, of course, that Romans takes up in the case of the children of God (Rom 8:14, 16, 17, 19, 21), but not in the case of the Body of Sin.[90] Regardless, the dualism is typical of certain apocalyptic strands of Second Temple Judaism and certainly fits with the symmetries Paul highlights between the Body of Christ and the Body of Sin.[91] The claim that the dominion of the Angel of Darkness extends to include the "children of righteousness," accounting for *their* sins, however, is a claim Paul is unwilling to make. It should not be possible for one who has died to Sin (in baptism) to go on living in it (6:2). Implicitly, however, Paul concedes that Sin's dominion may indeed extend even to members of the Body of Christ, as he pleads with the (baptized) Romans no longer to allow Sin to exercise dominion in their midst (6:12).

For all the symmetries, Paul also insists on a fundamental asymmetry in these two master-slave relationships. Right in the middle of his series of comparisons of enslavement to Sin and enslavement to Christ, Paul apologizes for the imprecision of the comparison: "I am speaking in human terms [Ἀνθρώπινον λέγω] because of the weakness of your flesh [τὴν ἀσθένειαν τῆς σαρκὸς ὑμῶν]. For just as you once presented your members as slaves to impurity and to greater and greater iniquity, so now present your members as slaves to righteousness for sanctification" (6:19).[92] These two slaveries are quite distinct, though Paul speaks what they know, given the weakness of their collective flesh. Drawing out the contrast is the focus of vv. 21–23. In the case of enslavement in the Body of Sin, the outcome is shame, whereas in the case of "enslavement" in the Body of Christ, the outcome is sanctification. Ultimately, the "wages" of sin are death; but the "end" of enslavement to God is eternal life—offered as a gift.

We might theorize this difference in terms of the kind of social body, or the kind of superorganismic system, in which each Body is constituted. In the case of the Body of Sin, the outcome is precisely what E. O. Wilson predicts: the death of the individual for the sake of the larger body.[93] On the other hand, in the case of the Body of Christ, Elsa Tamez insists that Paul's language of slavery misses something: "To affirm that the God of life takes possession of the human being does not imply that the latter returns to being a slave—now a slave of God—with no space of one's own to be a subject. To say that God takes possession of the human being is probably a poor choice of words"—a choice for which, as we've seen, Paul apologizes.[94]

In summary, in the ancient philosophical context constructed by Hahm, Lee, and Martin, the Body of Sin appears as a marriage of two philosophical concepts: the idea that virtue and vice were themselves bodies; and the concept of the social body. The second concept is by far the more important, though the first gives us some sense that the Body of Sin is the body of this vice become a social reality. The point of connection is the hierarchical relationship that holds in both cases (the ruling principle of the corporate body and the vice over the weak moral agent), and the agency that it exercises. Of course, there is also an important contribution from Paul's apocalyptic antinomy between this age and the age to come, the old and new creations, this world and the world to come—an antinomy that shares affinities with 1QS and other Qumran texts.[95] What we have, then, in these two locutions—"Body of Sin" and "Body of Christ"—is a Pauline syncretism: Paul's apocalyptic dualism meets a popular philosophical doctrine of a world body, and we have two world bodies as a result.[96] In emergent terms, each of these bodies is superorganismic, constituted by the particular set of practices—disobedience in the case of the Body of Sin, obedience in the case of the Body of Christ. Each of these bodies involves a group mind—in the case of the Body of Sin, the debased mind of 1:28, in the case of the Body of Christ, the renewed mind of 12:2. Each of these minds emerges from and in turn coercively regulates through downward causation a particular *Denkkollektiv* among its members. We now finally have our basic materials for addressing the main difficulty: the dominion of Sin and the complex of agencies entailed.

The Dominion of Sin

The primary role Sin plays in the cosmic drama of Romans is that of exercising dominion over the members of its Body. Indeed, as we saw in the first chapter of this book, this dominion, this enslavement, this constraint of human agents is what drives interpreters from Bultmann to Ratzinger toward metaphor. If this difficulty has slipped our minds, we can allow Stowers to refresh our memory:

> The challenge comes from the incoherency of the idea of powers, including sin as a power, as it has been developed in this scholarship. It is extremely difficult to know what claims these interpretations are making. What is a power and how does it affect humans? . . . The claim seems to be that describing sin as a power means more than that all sin and that this error against God dominates human life. But what is that "more"? The problem comes not only from the vague idea that sin is some sort of cosmic being or force. This incoherency, I think, comes also from the fact that the writers in question have not supplied a coherent psychology from the letters to explain how these powers work on humans. Thus, the modern talk of powers in Paul's letters stands in sharp contrast to ancient and medieval doctrines of sin and original sin that had coherent moral psychologies, even if they featured humans struggling with the Devil and demons.[97]

We already have some answers as to what this power, Sin, is. Sin is a *self*, emergent from a complex system of human transgressions—the "all" who sin and live the dominated human life. Sin is a superorganism, a body made of bodies, a self composed of selves. I have begun to suggest that this body has a mind—also emergent from this supervenience base of human sin; I will have more to say on this topic later in this chapter. But Stowers puts his finger on the most difficult issue: how does this power affect humans? Stowers is right when he says that the hinge here is (moral) psychology. Our explorations in emergence, social cognition, ancient philosophy, and thus far in Romans have suggested a psychology that is constituted both "from below" (from within) and "from above" (from without). That is, the fact that cognition itself has a "social basis" means that the psychological "individual" exists at the nexus of what we common-sensibly call the "self" and the "other." The self is constituted precisely in this dialectic, and the interface to the social is cognitive or psychological, precisely because it is *bodily*. This embodied self is externally integrated in the social environment and, therefore, is incorporated into selves that emerge at higher levels of social organization—that is, the sort of selves of which I take Sin to be an instance. Ultimately, then, if we want to offer an account of how the cosmic power, Sin, affects humans, we will need to give a multilevel account: that is, an account of such an agency at the mythological, social, and psychological levels. This will involve a synthesis of all that has been said to this point.

The mythological account is more or less straightforward; this is what lies on the surface of the text of Romans. We have already recounted the domination language. Sin is said to have ruled (ἐβασίλευσεν) through death (Rom 5:21). Participation in the death of Christ in baptism is described as an end to this rule (Rom 6:6, 9, 12, 14). This rule is described in terms of a master-slave relationship (Rom 6:6, 16-20, 22; 7:25; 8:21). At the social level, we may understand this in terms of the fact that "each is sufficiently determined by the social poison of sin that choices of evil deeds remain inevitable."[98] The characteristic outcome of this master-slave relationship—its "wages" (6:23)—is death.[99] Death so characterizes Sin's dominion that Paul can talk instead about Sin's dominion as the dominion of death itself (Rom 5:14, 17). Indeed, liberationist Franz Hinkelammert concludes: "This is then the criterion for distinguishing what is sin, the only one Paul is aware of: causing death. Whatever causes death is sin; and sin lives by sucking the life out of those it kills."[100] Sin, understood in terms of its deadly agency, is easily identifiable at the social level. It is what Óscar Romero identifies as "structures of sin," which are identifiable as "sin because they produce the fruits of sin: the deaths of Salvadorans—the swift death brought by repression or the long, drawn out, but no less real, death from structural oppression."[101] This is the social Body of Sin. It exercises coercive control at the social level and it works death through the social system.

At the social level, Sin's structural oppression functions through its usurpation of law. Indeed, this is as Isocrates's dictum would predict: "Every polity [πολιτεία] is the soul [ψυχή] of the state, having as much power over it as the mind [φρόνησις] over the body."[102] The polity, the legal structure of the state, is its animating principle; a corrupted law brings about a corrupted social body. Now, early in Romans the law does not function as a tool of Sin; Paul's early interests in law in Romans are relatively tame. He invokes the law as a distinguishing feature between Jews and Gentiles, and therefore the cause of their "separate but equal" standing before God as sinners (Rom 2:12-27). As in Seneca's narrative of decline, the advent of law deepens culpability and initiates the reckoning of sin as transgression (4:15; 5:13). Beyond a mere reckoning, however, law is also that which produces *wrath* (4:15). For all this, law is ultimately ineffective in controlling sin (5:20). This latter discourse regarding the law (and, presumably, the reputation he's earned from letters like Galatians) require that Paul then defend himself against charges of antinomianism (6:1–4; 6:15–19).

The crucial turn comes in Rom 7, in which the law is taken over by Sin and begins to have directly adverse effects. Law works to arouse sinful passions within our members "to bear fruit for death" (7:5).[103] The law's effects are so extreme that Paul must ask in v. 7: "What then should we say? That the law is sin?" "Μὴ γένοιτο!" is Paul's adamant response, but nevertheless he concedes:

> Yet, if it had not been for the law, I would not have known s/Sin. I would not have known what it is to desire if the law had not said, 'You shall not desire.' But Sin, seizing an opportunity in the commandment, produced in me every desire. Apart from the law Sin lies dead. I was once alive apart from the law, but when the commandment came, Sin revived and I died, and the very commandment that promised life proved to be death to me. For Sin, seizing an opportunity in the commandment, deceived me and through it killed me. (Rom 7:7–12)

This is the first account of Sin's usurpation of law (a second follows soon after). To be sure, it is primarily mythological in register—that is, it is an account of the cosmic power, Sin. At this level of analysis, the story is more or less plain. The commandment (the individual instance of law) is intended to produce the eradication of desire. But Sin wields law as a weapon (as it wields its members in 6:13) and uses it contrary to its intended purpose. Sin here is a deceiver, not unlike the serpent in Gen 3.[104]

At the social level, law is the tool that Sin uses for its coercive control. Hinkelammert writes:

> The text speaks of sin, but it is not a question of the violation of any law. It is in the law, it acts through the law, it uses the law. In the fulfilled [or enforced] law, sin acts. Now, Saint Paul speaks of a law and of commandments institutionalized in structures. It is law that is in force, which is the

other face of a structure. Sin operates through the structure and its law that is in force, and not through the transgression of the law. This Sin is a substantive being [*un ser sustantivado*], from which the law derives its own existence and which is present in this law. It is a structural sin [*un pecado estructural*].[105]

Sin is a substantive being—that is, a mythological being—precisely as a social power embedded in institutional structures. Sin's usurpation of law, therefore, has real, material impact for how we think about life in institutions. Ethics are rendered suspect. Institutional norms cannot be taken for granted. Law enforcement cannot be trusted. "Therefore," Hinkelammert concludes, "Paul is faced with the fact that law enforcement [*el cumplimiento de la ley*] leads to death."[106] The flagship example of this general principle—that the enforcement of laws corrupted by Sin brings about death—is the crucifixion of Jesus at the hands of Roman law enforcement.

Race, the Law, and the Dominion of Sin

Indeed, (white) Americans have become increasingly aware in recent years of the ways that law enforcement, corrupted by Sin in the form of racialized structures, brings about death. (African Americans have been quite aware of this dynamic for some time.) The 2014 death of Michael Brown, an unarmed African American man, at the hands of a white police officer, Darren Wilson, was an especially striking case. It is not too hard to extend the arguments I have made here to see that this was a death brought about through the dominion of Sin exercised through the perversion of law. After all, what marked Michael Brown's death as distinct from, for example, the 2015 deaths of nine African American worshippers murdered in the basement of Emanuel AME Church in Charleston was that Brown's death was deemed *legal*. The fact that this legal determination was made by a grand jury and not through a criminal trial is, of course, significant, but it does not change the fact: the shooting of this black man was committed without consciousness—even after careful examination—of the violation of any law. Rather, Wilson argued successfully that he had acted in self-defense, motivated by *fear*.[107]

The fMRI studies examined in the racism case study in chapter 2 suggest that Wilson's experience of fear is entirely explainable on the basis of Brown's race alone.[108] However, since establishing self-defense has everything to do with the (jury's belief in the) defendant's reasonable belief in the need to exercise deadly force, Wilson's experience of fear (and the jury's willingness to treat this fear as reasonable)—a pre-cognitive response based on social conditioning in the context of a racialized society—becomes a legally acceptable defense. This is the operation of the corrupt collective moral psychology in action. Sin, operative in the racist systems that alter the psychology of individual members (who themselves participate in these systems and therefore underwrite these same systems' power), through the corruption of law that cannot recognize the racial character of the experience of fear, brings about death. The shooting of Michael Brown was deemed legal essentially because he was black. Sadly, Brown's death is hardly the only example.[109]

The effective "law" is that the killing of a black person is more likely to be self-defense than the killing of a white person, as the unequal application of Florida's "Stand Your Ground" law attests.[110] Aside from ideological racists, no one would support *this* idea in the abstract, but in practice, this is the "law that is in force [*vigente*]." The abstract legal principle is that one may use lethal force when one reasonably fears for one's life. This may be an ethical law. However, the mechanism that transmutes this ethical law into the corrupt law that is actually in force, is the *environment*. Sin establishes the boundary conditions, the environment, in which the law is put into practice. Among these conditions is the fact that unfamiliar black faces induce fear in subjects socialized in the racialized United States. In this environment, then, the explicit law—which may well be "holy and just and good" (Rom 7:12)—is corrupted. Sin, seizing an opportunity in the legal principle, deceives those of us who imagine law as impartial and through the legal principle—and our culpable credulity—Sin *kills* (7:11). The cognition that matters—the cognition that generates the general principle that the death of a black person is more likely to be excusable on the grounds of self-defense—cannot be located in any individual's mind. Indeed, the majority of minds would explicitly reject this principle. This cognition is performed *collectively*; it emerges from the interplay of individuals, legal principles, and the racialized environment that establishes the boundary conditions in the context of which individual and institutional cognition is performed. What then should we say about this cognition? It is Sin's cognition. This thought—that black lives matter less—is *Sin's* thought.[111] It is the product of Sin's mythological psychology, working death through the enforcement of law.

Law and the Dominion of Sin

For Paul, law is revealed as a *sine qua non* of the life of Sin: "apart from the law, sin lies dead" (7:8).[112] From an emergent perspective, this makes tremendous sense, because law is the medium through which the cosmic power, Sin, connects to its supervenience base. Law—in the sense of Douglas's "founding analogies," which regulate institutions and through which institutions regulate their constituents—is the social glue that regulates sinners' relationships to one another and to Sin. Tamez writes:

> In this situation the law is imposed as legitimator of the anti-life dimension that is called "sin." "Law" is used in the broad sense to refer to the logic of the entire socioeconomic and cultural system which includes the laws of the market, judicial law, and the implicit and explicit norms of a way of life. Similarly, sin is understood as a social and historical fact, including the absence of brotherhood and sisterhood and of love in relationships between people, the breaking of friendship with God and with other human beings, and, consequently, inner division within the human being as well. All who live within this logic turn into slaves. They do not have the ability to decide or to act on their decisions. The law has usurped its place because sin has taken command over the law, and consequently the law functions according to the standards of sin.[113]

On this account, law is the neck of the Body of Sin—that which connects the head to the body. To sever Sin from law would amount to decapitation. In terms of "upward causation," the causal structures that constitute Sin ontologically would be ruptured. In terms of "downward causation," the result would be the end of Sin's dominion (if there could be such a thing, Sin being cut off from its supervenience base). As it is, armed with law, Sin's victory yields its characteristic "fruit": death.

This inversion of the purpose of the law elicits another rhetorical question: "Did what is good, then, bring death to me?" Again, Paul answers "μὴ γένοιτο!" "Rather," Paul insists, "it was Sin, working death in me through what is good" (7:13).[114] The perversion of law is the work of Sin—not the work of the law itself. The result is that in our institutions, sin and "transgression" are no longer aligned. Tamez writes, "In this complete inversion of society, to fulfill the law is an act of sin, for sin is expressed in the law. Sin 'acts through the law and uses the law . . . Sin operates through the legal structure and its prevailing law, and not through the transgression of the law.'"[115] The one who sins within such a system does so "without any transgression of the law. He is a sinner when he identifies with the structural sin. Of course, it is he who is the sinner, not the structure. But he is [the sinner] when he submits to Sin, which acts through the structure. He makes himself a slave of Sin . . . That, at least, is the teaching of Saint Paul."[116]

What follows in Romans is an analysis of the psychology of s/Sin.[117] Through the law, Sin's dominion has reached its peak. The individual self is unable to carry out that which it wills (v. 15).[118] The conclusion is obvious—there is an enemy within: "Now if I do what I do not want, I agree that the law is good. But in fact it is no longer I that do it, but Sin who dwells within me" (vv. 17–18). The cosmic power, Sin, in exercising its downward causation through the social and down to the psychological levels, is a "foreign" presence embedded deep within the individual mind itself. Of course, the "foreignness" of this presence is not so straightforward, as it is the presence of a power that has emerged from the participation of the human self and is now deeply embedded within the socially conditioned cognition of the self. Its presence is a puzzle that must be reasoned out. The regular experience of the self embedded in the Body of Sin, suffering as a slave under its dominion, is precisely *not* to recognize this constraint.

We do well to recall that constraints placed by Sin on the freedom of the individual agent is not some science-fiction replacement of the individual's mind with the mind of the collective Body of Sin. (This was Le Bon's conception of crowd psychology, rejected in the previous chapter.) Rather, Sin's dominion operates through Polanyi's "marginal control," setting boundary conditions for cognition at the individual level—establishing what is likely. In its usurpation of law, Sin shapes the normative ethics of a society, which provide the basic categories for cognition for the individual, and therefore mask Sin's dominion. Distinguishing between "the Sin" as structural Sin which has a substantive being and individual "sins," Hinkelammert writes:

> there are sins in the sense of transgressions of some law, and there is Sin, a being who kills through the very fulfillment [or enforcement] of the law ... But there is a big difference between this Sin and the many sins. The many sins are transgressions, and whoever commits them is conscious of the fact that he is transgressing an ethical norm. Sin is distinct. Ethics confirm it, it demands that it be committed. It has to do so, because any ethics demands fulfillment [or enforcement] and orients the consciousness of sin around transgressions. For the normative ethic, only sins exist; Sin as structural sin does not exist. Since it is located within the ethic and its fulfillment, the ethic cannot denounce it. It can only denounce transgressions. For this reason, Sin consisting in the identification with structural sin is necessarily committed without consciousness of sin. Its own character brings about the elimination of the consciousness of Sin. This sin is committed with a clean conscience, which is to say, with consciousness of complying with ethical demands.[119]

Sin has so reframed the thought style that sin is hardly ever experienced as such. Fleck's prediction that "the individual within the collective is never, or hardly ever, conscious of the prevailing thought style, which almost always exerts an absolutely compulsive force upon his thinking and with which it is not possible to be at variance" is vindicated.[120] The law serves both as a tool and as a cover for Sin's dominion over its subjects—its material constituents.

Nevertheless, Paul insists that the enemy is *within*: "For I do not do the good I want, but the evil I do not want is what I do. Now if I do what I do not want, it is no longer I that do it, but Sin who dwells within me" (7:19-20). What are we to say about this insistence that Sin's dominion is experienced *internally*? Does this not contradict our working hypothesis that the dominion of Sin is socially mediated?[121] One possible answer would be to suggest that Rom 7:19–20 essentially concurs with the fMRI studies measuring amygdala response in the brains of racialized subjects reviewed in chapter 2 and referenced above.[122] In that case, we observed that what was constructed socially (racism) now acted back down upon the psychology of its constituents, even embedding itself in the flesh—that is, in the neurobiology—of its members. These studies provide "evidence of cultural tuning in an automatic neural response"—a cultural force has been inscribed materially in establishing the boundary conditions of a biological process. This is as we should expect given the account of the self that emerges from modern scientific reflection—and its analog in the ancient world. The self open to the world is subject to invasion from forces from the outside, because the "outside" is not fundamentally other than this self which constitutes its environment and is in turn constituted by it. Here the "individual" self, functioning as a member of the Body of Sin, is no more separable from Sin's agency—even at the biological level—than an organ is from the rest of the body. A struggle against Sin is a war within the self, even within the individual body.

Stowers has highlighted the extensive ancient background for this ideology of self-mastery (ἐγκράτεια) in Romans.[123] The ideology is found with slight variations in every major ancient philosophical school. The key to the moral life is the defeat of desire (ἐπιθυμία) and the passions (πάθη) by the mind (νοῦς). Aristotle discusses ἐγκράτεια at length, contrasting it with its opposites, which include concepts used in the Pauline corpus: unrestraint (ἀκρασία, 1 Cor 7:5), softness (μαλακία, 1 Cor 6:9) and weakness (ἀσθένεια, Rom 8:26, etc.). These are the conditions that allow one to fall prey to desire and the passions. Aristotle writes of the weak in particular: "The weak deliberate, but then fail to keep their resolution because of their passions."[124] Stowers points to Euripides's *Medea* as a cultural source for the popularization of this moral psychology: "I am being overcome by evils. I know that what I am about to do is evil but passion is stronger than my reasoned reflection and this is the cause of the worst evils for humans."[125] This agonistic struggle finds expression also in Epictetus: "For since he who does wrong [*hamartein*] does not want to, but to be right, it is clear that he is not doing what he wants to do [*ho men thelei ou poiei*]."[126] It is hard not to hear Paul's words in Rom 7 as an echo. This is the classic moral struggle of ancient moral psychology; the *ego*, the "I," is losing.

The result is the ironic law of Sin, namely "that when I want to do what is good, evil lies close at hand. For I delight in the law of God in my inmost self, but I see in my members another law at war with the law of my mind [νοός], making me captive to the law of Sin that dwells in my members" (vv. 21–23). As a result, there is an experience of conflict between the true self—the "innermost self"—and this foreign presence that invades through the members, through the flesh, the material interface with the larger Body of Sin.[127] The distinction between these two cognitive faculties is expressed in 8:7: There exists both a φρόνημα—a pattern of thought—of the flesh and a φρόνημα of the Spirit. The first yields death, the second brings life and peace. As the cognitive pattern of the self dominated by the foreign power (because it is the material interface with the social body that constitutes this foreign power), "the pattern of thought [φρόνημα] of the flesh is hostile to God; it does not submit to the law of God, for it cannot," with the result that "those who are in the flesh cannot please God" (8:7–8). Rescue comes in the form of the Spirit of God, available to those "in Christ" (8:1–2), which grants victory to the mind, which serves the law of God (v. 25), restoring its natural freedom and power.[128] This is nothing less than the transfer of the self from one cosmic body to another: from the Body of Sin to the Body of Christ, from enslavement to the law of Sin to enslavement to the law of God (7:25). Since Sin depends for its existence on the members that constitute its supervenience base, once these members of the Body of Sin are put to death with Christ in baptism, the Body of Sin comes to nothing (6:5–6). When this happens, "Sin can no longer keep itself alive by leading the body toward death, but rather the death of sin now enables the body to live in freedom."[129] Sin has been put to death. The elements of the corrupted cosmos have been toppled. The self is free to choose the good.

If Paul's, Tamez's, and Hinkelammert's critiques of law evoke defensiveness, Mary Douglas has a theory as to why. It has everything to do with our "sacred" commitment to our theories of justice:

> [Hume's] idea that justice is a necessary social construct is exactly parallel to Durkheim's idea of the sacred, but Hume clearly refers to us, ourselves. He brings our idea of the sacred under scrutiny. Our defensive reaction against Hume is exactly what Durkheim would predict. We cannot allow our precepts of justice to depend on artifice. Such teaching is immoral, a threat to our social system with all its values and classifications. Justice is the point that seals legitimacy. For this very reason, it is difficult to think about it impartially. In spite of a wide belief in the modern loss of mystery, the idea of justice still remains to this day obstinately mystified and recalcitrant to analysis. If we are ever to think against the pressure of our institutions, this is the hardest place to try, where the resistance is strongest.[130]

This is only more so the case when it comes to life and death decisions, says Douglas.[131] These, of course, are precisely the sorts of stakes Paul is talking about.

The Transmission of Sin

In Christian hamartiology, describing the origins of s/Sin means that one is likely to be understood as offering an account of "original sin." Of course, the standard line from Pauline scholars about "original sin" is to defend Paul from all claims that he taught any such idea. Augustine, it is said, invented this doctrine from a Latin mistranslation of Romans 5. And there is certainly some truth to that; doctrines seem disinclined to appear fully formed in biblical texts. Nevertheless, there are opportunities here to talk about at least one of the theological questions answered by doctrines of original sin, namely: how is sin *transmitted*? That is, what are the conditions that incline human agents toward sin, and how are those conditions transmitted? The emergent account of s/Sin that I have offered suggests new ways to navigate this very old question.[132]

Augustine located the transmission of original sin in the male seed, contributed by the father at conception. This was important for Augustine, in part because it explained our ontological solidarity with Adam. That is, Augustine makes an argument not unlike the author of Hebrews, who argues that Levi tithes to Melchizedek because he is "still in the loins of his ancestor" (Heb 7:9–10). All humanity is in this sense "in Adam" when he sins. Locating this propensity toward sin in this way makes procreation—and sexual desire—the locus of the transmission of sin.[133] This gives Augustine both a psychological and a biological way of talking about sin's transmission. This biological inheritance model has a strong reception history through Calvin, the Augsburg Confession, and beyond.

In modern times, as scientific models of biological inheritance have become more sophisticated, scholars have attempted to use these biological models to ground theories of the inheritance of original sin. David L. Smith, for example, suggests that the "tendency which leads to actual transgression" is transmitted *genetically*: "Each infant born into the world possesses that gene, as it were, that predisposes toward sin."[134] That is, original sin is refigured as a genetic disease. However, for many scholars, this "gene," and the nature of the disease itself, remains rather abstract. For some, however, the genetic model offers an opportunity to be quite specific about the character of our disposition toward sin. Biologist Daryl Domning, for example, argues that the " 'stain of original sin' " is "that innate tendency to act selfishly which drove our entire evolution right up to and beyond the moment we became human—evolutionary 'business as usual.' " The selfishness of our genes is mirrored in the selfishness of our hearts; rather than talk about "original sin" we ought rather, on this account, talk about "original selfishness."[135] This suggests that sin is inherited less through a "sinful gene" than through the fact of *having genes* in the first place. In this view, the process of evolution itself has made us selfish individuals; something else, then, must make us altruistic.[136]

In contrast to the biological account of the transmission of sin, on the whole, modern authors have exhibited a preference for accounts of *social* trans- mission. Augustine himself had already hinted at the possibility of something like a theory of the social transmission of sin.[137] But Friedrich Schleiermacher provided the seeds for the modern theory that has come to dominate Catholic and much Protestant hamartiology. While rooted in the individual conscience, Schleiermacher's understanding of sin has a much more potent *social* dimension than those that come before him. Sin is realized in concentric circles of social solidarity—"families, clans, tribes, peoples, and races; the form which sinfulness takes in any of these can be understood only in connection with the rest." This social concept of sin, then, provides grounds for a theory of social transmission of sin: "The like holds good also of time. What appears as the congenital sinful- ness of one generation is conditioned by the sinfulness of the previous one, and in turn conditions that of the later; and only in the whole series of forms thus assumed, as all connected with the progressive development of man, do we find the whole aspect of things denoted by the term, 'original sin.'"[138] Albrecht Ritschl seized upon this social account of sin and developed it more fully, invoking what he calls the "kingdom of sin." Ritschl's "kingdom of sin"—nearly synonymous (at the individual and social levels) with what I've called the "Dominion of Sin"— encompasses a wide scope of habitual sin that forms a "vast complexity of sinful action" and establishes a "power of common sin," most notably in the blunting of "our moral vigilance and our moral judgement."[139]

The social mechanisms of the kingdom of sin obviate, for Ritschl, any need to struggle with the traditional Augustinian doctrine of original sin and its account of the biological transmission of sin.[140] After all, Ritschl argues,

> Paul neither asserts nor suggests the transmission of sin by generation, he offers no other reason for the universality of sin or for the kingdom of sin than the sinning of all individual men. For the sinful bias, which he discovered as present in himself when the negative commandment drew him into his first conscious act of sin (Rom. vii. 7-11), is not described by him as inherited, and can with perfect reason be understood as something acquired.[141]

For Ritschl, abandoning the theory of biological transmission of sin is not just good theology; it is good exegesis. All that remained to consolidate in Ritschl's account of the social transmission of sin was to fully articulate the role of *struc- ture*, which, from the work of Walter Rauschenbusch through the work of the liberationist theologians, eventually established something like the contemporary consensus, expressed by Monika Hellwig in her introduction to Domning's *Original Selfishness*:

> The focus has been on the notions of "social sin" and "sinful structures" as the real issue of the traditional doctrine of original sin ... The complex structures of our societies set limits to what we can see, understand, and choose to do. We are caught in the web of relationships, expectations, economies, cultural activities, acculturation to particular contexts, political and administrative arrangements which seem to take on a life of their own, larger, more enduring, and more resistant than the efforts of any individual or group of individuals to change or act in opposition to such forces. Here, then, is the concrete presence of original sin or the sin of Adam, the force for evil that precedes the choices of those who appear to be choosing, preempts the actions of those who appear to be acting, and tends to crush out of existence any who persist in acting in critical opposition.[142]

The loss of freedom rightly invoked by the doctrine of "original sin" comes not from within—from a biological source—but from the social environment.

So, we have two theories: the biological transmission of sin; and the social transmission of sin. The biological model locates the transmission of sin at the individual level. In this account, sin is the selfish drive of the evolutionary "individual," which has to be modulated by the sociocultural advantages of altruism. The individual is the villain; the drive to sociality is the hero. But this cannot be the full account. As I argued in the previous chapter, not all social cooperation is moral. Complex human sociality can be—and often is—tuned to inculcate vice just as much as it promotes virtue. Nor is all evolutionary "altruism" morally altruistic; one can lay down one's life for the sake of an evil cause. These are the crucial insights of those who advocate the theory of social transmission. On this account, we have the argument that sin is transmitted through social structures, from which the individual must be rescued by higher consciousness. Here, society is the villain; the elevated individual consciousness is the hero.

It is possible, of course, to synthesize these two views. Recognizing that the story of humanity is one of gene-culture coevolution, E. O. Wilson, for example, argues that "Human nature is the inherited regularities of mental development common to our species. They are the 'epigenetic rules,' which evolved by the interaction of genetic and cultural evolution that occurred over a long period in deep prehistory."[143] A theory oriented around the *epigenetic* transmission of sin would emphasize the interplay of genetic and cultural mechanisms of transmission. The genetic predispositions of individuals within cultural systems will impact the shape that these cultural systems take. Likewise, the cultural systems themselves will shape the phenotypic expression of the genetic structure of individuals. In very large timescales, genetic evolution may take place that has real impact on the moral horizons of individuals. In shorter timescales, the impact of cultural evolution will be more pronounced.

What is missing in both theories—and the proposed epigenetic synthesis—is the mechanism of transmission that is most prevalent on the surface of Paul's text: the dominion of Sin. Ritschl's "kingdom of sin" comes close, but his is a kingdom without a king. The mythological level is missing; s/Sin is reduced to the social level alone. To the account of epigenetic transmission, we must add a theory of the mythological transmission of sin. Generation after generation is bound to sin because each generation is bound—that is, enslaved—to *Sin*. It is the dominion of this cosmic tyrant that accounts for the persistence of human sin. Of course, this mythological account of the transmission of sin is a multilevel account. That is, claiming that the transmission of sin is mythological does not make sin's transmission any less social or biological.

The tyrant, Sin, owes its longevity through the ages to the stability of its biological and social bases, which it recursively maintains. Social systems function as mechanisms for the regulation of the psychologies of Sin's individual members by, as Hellwig argues, setting limits—boundary conditions—on "what we can see, understand, and choose to do." Through this marginal control, Sin establishes the conditions of the possibility of its own cognition—the institutional thinking upon which its constituents depend to make life and death decisions. These social facts—including, crucially the "founding analogies," the basic antinomies (e.g., racial categories like "black" and "white" or gender categories like "masculine" and "feminine") that establish the world as we experience it as humanly significant—outlive any human individual. Though certainly these analogies shift over time, their relative constancy is what lends the tyrant Sin its apparent immortality.

As we have seen, these sociocultural facts do not simply sit on top of the biology of Sin's constituents; rather, because the environment is never cleanly separable from the organism or person, the sinful sociocultural environment shapes the bodies of individuals. Autonomic responses are socially conditioned. The founding analogy, "black/white," reconfigures the neurobiology of the racialized subject. The "immortality" of these analogies means that the individuals that make up the Body of Sin refresh one another as surely as new cells replace dead cells in the healthy human body. Each new "cell" is born ready to take on the epigenetically determined phenotypic variation as they are deployed as differentiated "tissue" within the Body of the superorganism. As a result, the Body of Sin is no less biological than an "individual" body. The transmission of sin is no less biological for being social. On the emergent, multilevel account, the transmission of sin is biological, social, *and* mythological. Each level of the complex structure recursively reenforces the function of the others as the mythological self engages in its processes of recursive self-maintenance, transmitting its epigenetic constraint across the generations.

Conclusions

Taking together the emergence of Sin from a supervenience base of human transgression and the dominion of Sin over that same base through downward causation, what we find is a causal feedback loop of the kind we saw in chapter 2 in the examples of crowd dynamics, cardiac rhythm, and social systems. As I argued in that chapter, causal feedback loops are not telltale signs of logical incoherence, but rather signs of complexity that reveal themselves when we try to synthesize our understanding of the world at multiple levels. Such is the case when it comes to Sin, a self emergent from a complex of human sinners and sinful social structures. At the mythological level, the ontological account of the cosmic person of Sin runs along the lines familiar from chapter 3. Sin is a superorganism—a self made of selves—with a group mind. Sin is an institutional person. Along the lines of Knorr Cetina's account of HEP experiments, Sin operates as a collective epistemic subject, depending ontologically on the participation of its constituents but nevertheless functioning as a distinct locus of epistemic activity. Like all selves, Sin is not bounded by the "generation of an exterior skin," but rather by the fuzzy boundaries of its own "dynamical reciprocity."[144] Because this reciprocity is ontologically constituent of Sin (as it is of all selves), as we saw time and again in this chapter, Sin's being depends on the participation of its members. This constitutes the "upward causation" side of the feedback loop. The "downward causation" side takes the form of the establishment of boundary conditions at the adjacent level of the structural hierarchy—namely, the social. At the mythological level, we can describe this as Sin's dominion over its own body. Sin's operation through law mediates the social manifestation of Sin's dominion. My sense is that this concept of social coercion is familiar to us from experience.

We ought to pay special attention to the propagation of the effects of the individual agent's sins through the system. These dynamics are key to trying to unravel the sticky question of culpability that haunts any reading of Romans that takes Sin's tyranny seriously—including my own. The agent's sins constitute the self as a constituent of the Body of Sin and, as such, contribute to the being and agency of the cosmic power, Sin. That cosmic power then exercises downward causation back on its constituents. This downward causation is socially mediated, establishing the boundary conditions for the constituent's moral reasoning. Indeed, this in turn contributes to future exercises of sinful agency on the part of the constituent— but this contribution could hardly be construed as entirely "external," resulting, as it did, in part from the agency of the constituent. On this account, culpability, if anything, is expanded, for now I know that my sin, inasmuch as it contributes to the being and agency of Sin, contributes to the likelihood—if not inevitability—of others' sins. Of course, these causal chains are impractical (impossible?) to trace in the vast, convoluted social systems in which we exist—hence, the advantage of adopting an emergent approach to theorizing these systems at the mythological level.[145] Nevertheless, I take it that concerns about culpability—which we saw time and again in the first chapter—are resolved by the emergent framework.

Finally, we should return to Stowers's concerns about the lack of a coherent moral psychology in the "powers" reading of s/Sin. The emergent framework provides this account of moral psychology by taking seriously the social basis of cognition, locating the power's agency in the establishment of boundary conditions of individual cognition. Stowers's hunch is that for the "cosmic power" reading of Sin to make sense, s/Sin must be demonstrated to be "an external power or inherited internal power that is something in addition to 'normal' human psychology."[146] But the emergence argument is that we can account for Sin precisely in terms of normal human psychology. Sin is the self that emerges from a vast network of such psychologies and, as such, exercises downward causation back on—that is, defines the boundary conditions that provide the condition of the possibility of—the cognition performed by such psychologies.

Mary Douglas's account of moral psychology demonstrates the point. When it comes to our most important moral reasoning, "no private ratiocination can find the answer. The most profound decisions about justice are not made by individuals as such, but by individuals thinking within and on behalf of institutions."[147] Indeed, on the emergent account, this is precisely how Paul describes the situation: moral cognition is conducted within the constraints of one or the other social body. If moral reasoning takes place "in Christ" and with the aid of the Spirit (8:1–2), conclusions will be sound. If moral reasoning takes place in the Body of Sin—that is, with Sin ruling within—it turns into tortured convolutions (7:20, 23) as the collective cognition performed by the unified depraved mind of 1:28 exercises marginal control over the cognition performed at the individual level.

The major question then becomes: to which Body should we submit ourselves—our members (6:13)? Properly engaging the νοῦς (7:23, 25), or "choosing rationally, on this argument, is not choosing intermittently among crises or private preferences, but choosing continuously among social institutions. It follows that moral philosophy is an impossible enterprise if it does not start with the constraints on institutional thinking."[148] Taken together with what we gleaned in the previous chapter from David Sloan Wilson, Philip Pettit, and Karin Knorr

Cetina regarding group minds, institutional persons, and collective epistemic subjects, respectively—all of which give us every reason to take these institutions seriously as *persons*—Douglas summarizes the dynamics of the constraint of Sin quite elegantly.

In the final analysis, I take it that Stowers has done well to capture some of the ancient moral psychology—especially with his identification of the centrality of the discourse of self-mastery. However, the "moral psychology" that Stowers "recovers" (or rather constructs) is exclusively the moral psychology of moral *individuals*—making it an ironically modern(ist) psychology. Granted, Stowers has a "thin" social moral psychology in that he describes how social norms provided the basic frameworks within which ancient individuals strove for moral improvement. But his moral psychology does not consider how society itself—as a material body—actually makes many of these moral decisions for the individual, how the social body itself becomes a moral actor. In practice, Stowers treats the social as an aggregate of individuals rather than an organic unity—a shocking anachronism, given the ancient evidence regarding social bodies. Stowers describes, of course, how these social groups were imagined to have the same agonistic struggles with one another and how the same logic of self-mastery rules the fate of these social entities. But Stowers nowhere in his consideration of Paul's discourse of self-mastery considers the letter's addressees' collective Body's own struggle for self-mastery. The next chapter provides precisely such an account.

5 SIN, GENDER, AND EMPIRE

Tissue *is not* text, but there is tissue only because there *is* text.

—GRAHAM WARD, *Cities of God*

We now turn to the ideological representation of the cosmic tyrant, Sin. In pursuing this ideological analysis, this chapter pulls together two important threads from the previous chapter. First, there is the rhetorical function of the ideology of self-mastery, which Stowers has described.[1] This chapter expands upon what was said in the previous chapter about this ancient ideology and its relevance for understanding the dominion of Sin. Second, there is the instinct (drawn from Hinkelammert and Tamez) that the operation of Sin has everything to do with the coercive constraint exercised on moral psychology by the power of the dominant sociopolitical system. So, this chapter explores the ways in which Paul's discourse about Sin as a person is situated within the dominant sociopolitical system of his day—that is, the Roman Empire. We will find that the ideology of self-mastery and the ideology of empire are, in fact, one and the same. Their shared foundation, in many respects, is ancient gender ideology. And so in this chapter, for the first time, we will consider the fact that Sin—Ἁμαρτία—has not only a body, but, per Paul's account, a gendered body—specifically, a female body, enslaved as it is to appetites, passions, and desires. (It is at this point that Sin will take on a personal name: Hamartia.) The chapter explores the ways Paul's rhetoric exploits this gendered body in describing Hamartia's dominion and, in the process, both employs the categories of Roman imperial ideology, and thereby comments on that ideology.

In placing the Body of Hamartia within the context of Roman imperial ideology, I compare Hamartia to two colonial representations of Roman political power: the goddess Roma, and Mark's Legion (Mark 5:1–20). These entities, I argue, exhibit similar ontologies as entities emergent from complex social systems. But Roma in particular provides an important *comparandum* for Hamartia, given their shared status as socially emergent women exercising political dominion—a problematic identity indeed, given that the dominant ideology gendered *imperium* (dominion) as masculine.[2] This problematic then frames the rest of the chapter, in which I describe the dominion of Hamartia in the context of ancient ideologies of sex, gender, and empire. Finally, I consider Paul's second world body, the Body of Christ, and the ways this body both fulfills and subverts the expectations of dominant ideology. I conclude the chapter by exploring this rhetorical ambivalence and its significance for Christian hamartiology.

Up to this point, we have worked hard to take Paul's mythological language seriously—in both his context and our own. And nothing I say now should be taken to suggest that this seriousness is about to wane. But saying that Paul takes the emergence of the cosmic tyrant, Sin, seriously—and that perhaps we ought to do the same—is not to suggest that such a tyrant is immune to historically contingent ideological description. In fact, all "real" persons are subject to such treatment—such explanation and elaboration—by other persons. If Paul, indeed, describes Sin as a person—if Sin *is* a person—then that description must itself take place within a "thought style," that is, an ideological framework in which the significance of selves as persons is made clear. This chapter examines Paul's description of Sin as a person embedded within ancient discourses of gender, empire, and self-mastery. As we will see, all persons in the ancient world were describable in these terms; if Sin is, indeed, a person, we should expect to find such description embedded in these discourses. So, we now ask: how does Paul describe Hamartia as a gendered *person* struggling for self-mastery and dominion as defined by Roman imperial ideology? Let us pick up again where we left off at the end of the last chapter, with the ancient ideology of self-mastery.

Ancient Ideology of Self-Mastery

Foucault frames self-mastery as a particular species of a broader agonism that dominated the ancient Greco-Roman environment. He cites the beginning of Plato's *Laws*, where we see this struggle against the self framed precisely in terms of struggles in the social sphere.[3] I quote at length:

> *Clinias*: The legislator's position would be that what most men call "peace" is really only a fiction, and that in cold fact all states are by nature fighting an undeclared war against every other state . . .
>
> *Athenian*: But if this is the right criterion as between states, what about as between villages? Is the criterion different?
>
> *Clinias*: Certainly not.
>
> *Athenian*: It is the same, then?

Clinias: Yes.

Athenian: Well now, what about relations between the village's separate households? And between individual and individual? Is the same true?

Clinias: The same is true.

Athenian: What of a man's relations with himself—should he think of himself as his own enemy?

Clianias: Well done, my Athenian friend! ... not only is everyone an enemy of everyone else in the public sphere, but each man fights a private war against himself [καὶ ἰδίᾳ ἑκάστους αὐτοὺς σφίσιν αὐτοῖς] ... This, sir, is where a man wins the first and best of victories—over himself [Κἀνταῦθα, ὦ ξένε, τὸ νικᾶν αὐτὸν αὑτὸν πασῶν νικῶν πρώτη τε καὶ ἀρίστη]. Conversely, to fall a victim to oneself is the worst and most shocking thing that can be imagined. This way of speaking points to a war against ourselves within each one of us. [ταῦτα γὰρ ὡς πολέμου ἐν ἑκάστοις ἡμῶν ὄντος πρὸς ἡμᾶς αὐτοὺς σημαίνει].[4]

Self-mastery is a "private war" each man fights against himself. John J. Winkler argues that this is

> not a Platonic peculiarity but a faithful reflection of the common moral language which praised a good man as "stronger than himself," (*kreittôn heautou*) that is able to manage and control his various appetites, and a bad man as "weaker than himself." (*hêttôn heautou*, Foucault 1985:63–77) The temptations in question are food, drink, sex, and sleep. At all levels of practical morality and advice-giving we find the undisciplined person described as someone mastered or conquered by something over which he should exert control, usually conceived as part of himself.[5]

This transition from conqueror to conquered can happen in an instant. Winkler cites Xenophon's apology of Socrates, the *Memorabilia*, in which he recounts Socrates warning of the catastrophic effects of giving in to lust in the form of kissing Alcibiades's son: "What do you think will happen to you through kissing a pretty face? Won't you lose your liberty in a trice [αὐτίκα μάλα] and become a slave [δοῦλος μὲν εἶναι ἀντ᾽ ἐλευθέρου], begin spending large sums on harmful pleasures [βλαβερὰς ἡδονάς], have no time to give to anything fit for a gentleman, be forced to concern yourself with things that no madman even would care about?"[6] Xenophon moralizes after recounting Socrates's sage advice:

> Thus in the matter of carnal appetite [ἀφροδισιάζειν], he held that those whose passions [ἀφροδίσια] were not under complete control should limit

themselves to such indulgence as the soul would reject unless the need of the body [δεομένου τοῦ σώματος] were pressing, and such as would do no harm when the need was there. As for his own conduct in this matter, it was evident that he had trained himself to avoid the fairest and most attractive more easily than others avoid the ugliest and most repulsive.[7]

Socrates couldn't possibly be guilty of the charges leveled against him at Athens; he was a sage of self-mastery—which meant he was a practitioner of self-mastery as well.

Xenophon's example of sexual appetite is, of course, by no means arbitrary. As Stowers notes, "gender hierarchy lies close to the heart of the discourse of self-mastery." According to the discourse, women innately lack ἐγκράτεια and live dominated by the passions and desires. In contrast, the masculine life

is war, and masculinity has to be achieved and constantly fought for. Men are always in danger of succumbing to softness, described as forms of femaleness or servility. In the ancient Mediterranean construction of gender, the sexes are "poles on a continuum which can be traversed." To achieve self-mastery means to win the war; to let the passions and desires go unsubdued means defeat, a destruction of hard-won manliness.[8]

As a result, *femaleness* was not simply an innate quality of women. On account of the "odd belief in the reversibility of the male person, always in peril of slipping into the servile or the feminine," femaleness was a threat to men, as "the cultural polarity between the genders is made internal to one gender, creating a set of infra-masculine polarities."[9]

Indeed, ancient gender ideology assigned gendered meanings to—and read gendered physiological implications onto—what Thomas Laqueur famously described as "a one-sex body."[10] Femininity was not one of a pair (or more) of stable gender identities, as has generally been posited in modern times. Rather, "In the hegemonic Roman gender script, femininity is the given, the a priori, the default state, while masculinity is what must be achieved and maintained. It is the hard-won product of (self-)conquest."[11] Gender (undifferentiated from "sex" in ancient ideology) was simply a descriptive category indicating sufficient or insufficient attainment to a masculine ideal. As Laqueur argued, "In a public world that was overwhelmingly male, the one-sex model displayed what was already massively evident in culture more generally: man is the measure of all things, and woman does not exist as an ontologically distinct category."[12] Losing the battle of self-mastery meant losing the battle for manhood—a loss which could have physiological consequences.[13] The quest for virtue (as the etymology of the term would suggest) is a fundamentally gendered quest—the process by which the "vir" (simply, "man," but also the one who exhibits "*vir*tue") proves himself through winning the battle against the lower, feminine urges: appetites, passions, and desire.

The broader, agonistic justification meant that this battle of self-mastery corresponded (in both directions) with contests in the social sphere; only those who achieved self-mastery were to be trusted with political or household leadership. As Stowers has argued, the very founding of the Roman Empire, in Octavian's victory over Antony, was framed by imperial propagandists

> not as a civil war between Roman factions but as an epic conflict between ancient Roman values and the moral degeneracy of the East, where women and castrated men ruled. Octavian's propaganda made Antony into a lesson of what would happen to Romans who succumbed to the decadence of the East. Above all, Antony had lost his self-mastery, allowing himself to take the subordinate position to a woman. According to Dio (50.28.3), Octavian expressed his goal as "to conquer and rule all humankind, and to allow no woman to make herself equal to a man." The charges manufactured against Antony included drunkenness, sexual indulgence, a life of luxury, and abandonment of the ancestral traditions of Rome. Antony's relation with Cleopatra allowed Octavian to associate femaleness with foreignness, lack of self-mastery, and failure to master inferiors.[14]

In short, Stowers argues, in the hands of Octavian's propagandists, the dawn of the empire was the dawn of "an ethic and an ideology of imperialism rooted in the ancient ethic of self-mastery."[15] This set the terms for both centuries of political ideology, and an ethical standard for what sufficiently masculine *imperium* looked like at the individual level.[16] That is, there was, as in many ancient ideologies, an assumption of a microcosm-macrocosm correspondence. If the ruler (the microcosm) was master of himself—if he embodied a hard, Roman masculinity—then the state (the macrocosm) would be strong. The reverse was true as well. Those who lacked self-mastery were ideologically "servile"—a microcosmic projection of the macrocosmic understanding of conquered people as typically lacking in self-mastery. As Craig Williams has demonstrated, the central issue was *control*: "Masculinity meant being in control, both of oneself and of others, and femininity meant ceding control."[17]

Of course, if Octavian's triumph marks an important moment in the history of the development of the ideology of self-mastery, his propagandists nevertheless owed their success to the ancient prejudices and anxieties they tapped into. For example, Aristotle could casually mention "the hereditary effeminacy [μαλακία διὰ τὸ γένος] of the royal family of Scythia, and the inferior endurance of the female sex as compared with the male" as examples of innate tendencies against self-mastery (ἐγκράτειαν).[18] There was a longstanding tradition of stereotyping women and the political other as lacking in self-mastery. The propaganda machine of the early empire, however, enshrined this tradition as *the* justifying ideology of the empire.[19] The "servile" and the "feminine" were synonyms that described the polar opposite of the ideal of self-mastery: the conquering male. To succumb to desire and the passions (ἐπιθυμία and πάθη), and thus lose the war against oneself, was to become at once servile *and* effeminate. This was because the war against oneself could be theorized as a war between the feminine and masculine natures that resided within the individual. As Cicero describes in *Tusculan Disputations*:

> Now, the soul is divided into two parts, of which one partakes of reason [*rationis*] and the other does not. Thus, when we are told to control ourselves [*imperemus*], we are really being told to see to it that reason restrains impetuousness [*ratio coerceat temeritatem*]. In nearly every soul there is something naturally soft [*molle*], abject, abased, in some way or other spineless [*enervatum*] and listless. If that is all there were, nothing would be more repugnant than humanity; but reason stands ready as sovereign of all [*domina omnium et regina*]—reason, which, striving on its own and advancing far, finally becomes perfect virtue [*virtus*]. That reason should give orders to [*imperet*] the other part of the soul, the part that ought to be obedient [*quae oboedire debet*]—that is what a man [*viro*] must take care to do. "But how?" you will ask. The way a master gives orders to his slave, or a commander to his soldier, or a father to his son. If that part of the soul which I previously called soft [*mollem*] behaves disgracefully, if it gives itself over in womanish fashion [*muliebriter*] to tears and lamentation, let it be bound and constrained by friends and relatives. For we often see broken by shame those who would not be won over by any reasoning.[20]

Cicero concludes: "Thus everything comes down to this: that you rule yourself. [*Totum igitur in eo est, ut tibi imperes.*]" This is the crucial task. Cicero is describing the ideal orientation of the masculine subject. This struggle is deeply embedded in ancient ideology of gender and *imperium*: "Do nothing in a base, timid, ignoble, slavelike, or womanish way."[21] As we saw in the previous chapter, this ideal was paired with a decline narrative that described the habitual failure of subjects to achieve this mastery. It is this story of failure that Paul tells in Romans 1–2.[22]

Paul was not the first Jewish writer to seize upon the opportunity latent in the rhetoric of self-mastery for articulating classical Jewish moral philosophy. Philo of Alexandria, in recounting Genesis 3, uses this constellation of coordinated stakes to interpret the mythological account allegorically. Philo casts Eve as the senses, Adam as mind, and the Serpent as pleasure:

> And pleasure [ἡδονὴ] encounters and holds parley with the senses first, and through them cheats with her quackeries the sovereign mind [ἡγεμόνα νοῦν] itself ... Reason [λογισμός] is forthwith ensnared and becomes a subject instead of a ruler [ὑπήκοος ἀνθ’ ἡγεμόνος], a slave instead of a master [δοῦλος ἀντὶ δεσπότου], an alien instead of a citizen [ἀντὶ πολίτου φυγὰς], and a mortal instead of an immortal [θνητὸς ἀντ’ ἀθανάτου].[23]

In Philo's hands, Adam and Eve function as two halves of a single subject at war with him(her)self. Of course, the idea that Adam and Eve are two halves of an original androgyne was a given in ancient thought.[24] Against this background, Philo's interpretation of Genesis is hardly "allegorical" at all. This is a quite literal reading of the text; Adam and Eve *are* the two halves of this subject at war. Their interaction in the decline narrative of Gen 3, then, is a window into the physiology of the ideology of self-mastery, the mechanism by which the feminine enticement—pleasure—through the use of the feminine parody of the reasoning faculty—the senses—unseats the masculine, rational, ruling principle: the mind (ἡγεμόνα νοῦν).

It is here that Philo's account bears striking resemblance to the passage cited above from Xenophon. While Philo gives a more detailed philosophical description of what happens, in both cases, the decline is more or less instantaneous, the defeat absolute: once the feminine takes the upper hand, the entire physiology of the ideal, masculine subject is thrown out of order. In short, this is the process by which men become women—a very real, very literal possibility in the ancient imagination.

Because the ancient world was a "world where at least two genders correspond to but one sex, where the boundaries between male and female are of degree and not of kind," where women "are inverted, and hence less perfect, men," where biology does not determine gender, but rather, "only records a higher truth," gender transgression carried with it the very real possibility of physical transformation.[25] As Laqueur argues, in the ancient Mediterranean, "anatomy in the context of sexual difference was a representational strategy that illuminated a more stable extracorporeal reality. There existed many genders, but only one adaptable sex."[26] And, that more "stable extracorporeal reality" had everything to do with the ideology of *imperium* described above. A man was one who could master himself and therefore function as master of his social domain; a woman was all that fell short of this ideal. As Williams notes, "in the inexorably oppositional logic of Roman masculinity, if one is not manly one is womanly."[27]

Sexual intercourse, in which the masculine is the penetrating dominator and the feminine is the penetrated passive, enacted this "natural" hierarchy (as we saw in Aristotle).[28] This meant that for the ancients, sex—not just gender—was performed. On the dominant ancient account, a "man" who was a sexual passive was a man no longer, but had rather succumbed to what Philo called the "disease of effemination."[29] If one's sex/gender (the two were coextensive in ancient ideology) wasn't properly performed, if one were happy "to lose the (internal) battle of the sexes," the consequences were, as Paul suggests in Rom 1:27, experienced in one's own body.[30] Diana Swancutt has demonstrated that this was the plain sense of Paul's text to ancient readers: that effeminating sex had changed the biology of the participants. As Clement of Alexandria asserts in interpreting the passage, "desire can alter the character of somebody already formed."[31] It was not only masculine "gender" that was at stake in the war with oneself; it was the physiology of the hard, penetrating-but-never-penetrated masculine body as well. To succumb to desire was to fall into femininity, the consequences of which were experienced physiologically. It is this physiological transformation that Philo describes in his retelling of Gen 3, as the νοῦς is dethroned and subjected to the senses. (For the philosophically educated Philo, the νοῦς was, of course, a body, a material thing, composed of material πνεῦμα.)[32] This is the transformation of the body from an appropriately hierarchical masculine form to a disordered feminine form, no longer subjected to the rule of νοῦς, but rather at the mercy of desire (ἐπιθυμία) and the passions (πάθη). It is precisely this transformation that Paul describes in his decline narrative—at both the personal and the mythological levels. That is, Paul describes both the bodies of individual sinners and the social Body of Sin as disordered, effeminate/feminine bodies.

Desire and the Passions vs. the Mind in Romans

As we saw in the previous chapter, enslavement to desire and to the passions characterizes Paul's narrative of decline of the Gentiles. It is to the "desires [ἐπιθυμίαις] of their hearts" that the Gentiles are handed over in Rom 1:24. Enslaved to these effeminating desires, the consequence is a degrading of their "individual" bodies among one another. The same handing over is resumed in v. 26, this time invoking the language of "degrading passions [πάθη ἀτιμίας]"; the exercise of these passions again entails consequences that accrue "in their own persons." This enslavement to the desires and the passions results in a corruption of the masculine ruling principle, the mind (νοῦς). Gentile men—Roman *viri*—are thereby exposed as less-than-men who have lost the battle against the self, enslaved to their lower nature in the form of the desires and passions. Their bodies are re-/dis-ordered; they take on a different physiology and function in a fundamentally different way.

But this does not merely describe the dynamics of the individual in the decline narrative described by Stowers (the physiological consequences of which Swancutt makes clear). This same enslavement to desire typifies the physiology of the (social) Body of Sin, for, as we should expect, in the case of s/Sin, what is true of the individual (the microcosm), is true of the social (macrocosm) as well.[33] In Rom 6:12, Paul says that at one time, Sin exercised dominion in the collective Body (τῷ θνητῷ ὑμῶν σώματι) through demanding obedience to its desires (τὸ ὑπακούειν ταῖς ἐπιθυμίαις αὐτοῦ). Obedience to desire is precisely what constitutes this social Body as the Body of Sin.

Once we see clearly the central importance of the reign of desire within the Body of Sin, it becomes plain that the appearance of Ex 20:17 in Rom 7:7–8 is by no means an arbitrary selection from the Decalogue. The commandment would be quite plain to Gentiles in Paul's audience and would garner approval: "You shall not desire [οὐκ ἐπιθυμήσεις]." English translations that render this command in its more familiar form from Exodus, "You shall not covet," obscure entirely the force of this example within the flow of Paul's argument.[34] Paul's point here, in Chapter 7, is to describe how Sin uses the law to enforce the reign of desire throughout its Body, including within the bodies of its members, and then in the members of their bodies as well (Rom 7:23, 25). In this reign, the (masculine) mind is usurped by Sin, through its law, which enforces obedience to desire.

The social Body of Sin, then, is a body in which desire runs rampant; Sin's dominion is the ascendancy of (naturally subject) desires over the (naturally hegemonic) mind.[35] This is why Paul can contrast the law of Sin with the law of "my mind" in 7:23. In 7:25, "in the mind" the ἐγώ is enslaved to the law of God; it is only "in the flesh" that the self (ἐγώ) is enslaved to the law of Sin. The deposed mind (νοῦς) leaves the "mindset" (φρόνημα) vulnerable. In Rom 8:6–7, Paul summarizes the predicament of the self: the "mindset" can be set either on the flesh (and its desires) or on the πνεῦμα, the Spirit, the higher-order principle. In other words, the body can be ruled (rightly) by the Spirit and pneumatic things like the mind or (wrongly) by the flesh and fleshly things like desire (Rom 13:14). As we saw in Douglas's observations at the end of the previous chapter, the law to which the self is subject corresponds to the body of which it is a member. One who is subject to the law of fleshly desire is part of the disordered, feminine (those two are more or less synonymous ideologically) Body of Sin.[36] One subject to the law of the Spirit is part of the properly ordered, masculine (again, these are ideological synonyms) Body of Christ. This is why Paul's ultimate solution to the Romans' enslavement to Hamartia is a renewal of the corporate mind—"be transformed by the renewing of your mind"—that rehabilitates their functioning as a collective epistemic subject—"that you [pl.] may discern what the will of God is" (Rom 12:2). So, at the mythological level, the narrative arc runs from the enslavement of the corporate Body, to desire (in 6:12), to the renewal of the corporate Mind, resulting in a renewed collective cognitive faculty.

In other words, in Romans, the Body of Sin is precisely a female Body.[37] Hamartia is a woman, enslaved by her desires, enslaving others by means of those same desires. This is the usurpation Philo described, the trans-gendering decline into femininity writ large and small all at once in the multilevel dominion of Hamartia through enslavement to desire. In living subjected to the desires of their corrupted social Body, Paul's Roman audience constitutes a radically disordered, feminine social body. They are not just losing the battle of self-mastery, but also suffering the (naturally unnatural) social consequences of that defeat: they are subject to a woman's rule. This is the dominion/domination of Hamartia.

The irony—terrifying for Paul's first readers—is that this female corporate person is described so vividly and so often as exercising dominion (most vividly in 5:21, 6:12). Her exercise of dominion is her defining characteristic—indeed, this is presumably what has driven many modern scholars since Dibelius to adopt that enigmatic term "power" to describe her. Hamartia dominates. She enslaves. She subdues even the law and the mind under her power. The subjugation of these essences of masculine *imperium* would have formed the core of the distaste that Paul's audience would have felt in his description of the emergence of Hamartia. She fulfills every hypermasculine ideal externally while being totally out of order, totally "feminine" internally. Her masculine rule and reign come precisely through her enticement to feminine desire and passions. She makes others servile (and thus "feminine")—that is, she becomes "masculine"—but she does so as a body totally out of order. Ideologically, she is an impossibility.[38] Historically, she is the goddess Roma.

The Emergence of the Goddess Roma

The worship of the goddess Roma (Θεὰ Ῥώμη) in the Greek East provides an important analog to Paul's Hamartia, both in terms of her ontology with respect to her social body, and in terms of the gender trouble latent in her exercise of ideologically masculine *imperium*. Invented by those on the colonial margins of Roman political influence as the personification of a complex social system, Roma bears a striking resemblance to Hamartia at a formal level. Perhaps unsurprisingly then, modern scholarship on Roma exhibits some of the philosophical difficulties with which we are by now quite familiar. Before returning to Roma's problematic gender identity, I suggest that we understand Roma as a real person emergent from a complex social system—namely, the Roman state—not entirely unlike Seneca's depiction of the genius of the emperor discussed in the previous chapter, nor dissimilar to Mark's Legion (Mark 5). A conception of Roma as an emergent person solves many of the problems that have plagued scholarship on the deity, and provides a rich ancient parallel to Paul's Hamartia—another suprahuman woman who exercises *imperium* over her social body. Furthermore, inasmuch as the gendered Roman ideology of self-mastery is the justifying ideology of Roman *imperium*, situating Hamartia in the context of Roman imperial ideology—especially as represented at the colonial margins—will be quite helpful to our discussion of Hamartia's location within that field of signification.

Much the way twentieth-century scholarship on s/Sin in Romans was obsessed with the question of whether to understand the personification of s/Sin literally or figuratively, Roma scholarship for much of the twentieth century struggled with questions about the sincerity of belief in the goddess. In his classic monograph on Roma, Ronald Mellor argues that the goddess functioned for the Greeks who invented her as a useful fiction. Establishing a temple to Roma (as was done for the first time in Smyrna in 195 BCE), was a savvy diplomatic and political move.[39] For Mellor, therefore, the question of sincerity has everything and only to do with the sincerity (or lack thereof) of the diplomatic sentiments communicated. And, certainly, Greek sentiment vis-a-vis Roman expansion was mixed:

> [The Greek cities] were enthusiastic at Rome's first appearance, and some Greek cities continued to be genuinely grateful for Roman favors. But many found the *amicitia* proffered by Rome something much less than true friendship. So the cult of Roma covered the entire range of political emotion: enthusiastic affection, servile flattery, gratitude, suspicion, naked fear. It was a cult based on political, rather than religious, experience.[40]

In other words, for Mellor, Roma is reducible to the social level. The Roma cult is a matter of politics, not of religion.[41]

And yet, the Roma cult took an undeniably religious form. So Mellor himself insists also that "Roma was not merely a personification; she was a goddess with the trappings of divinity: cults, priests, temples, epithets."[42] S. R. F. Price, in his landmark work on the imperial cult, offers to save Mellor from himself by means of exploding his facile distinction between religion and politics:

> A Christianizing theory of religion which assumes that religion is essentially designed to provide guidance through the personal crises of life and to grant salvation into life everlasting imposes on the imperial cult a distinction between religion and politics. But a broader perspective suggests that religions need not provide answers to these particular questions, and the imposition of the conventional distinction between religion and politics obscures the basic similarity between politics and religion: both are ways of systematically constructing power.[43]

For Price, questions about the sincerity of belief are quite beside the point, and certainly don't help us isolate Roma devotion (or the later imperial cult) as either completely religious or completely political. James Knight summarizes Price's argument as follows: "The religiosity of the cult of Roma, then, should not be defined in terms of individuals and 'their interior mental states' but as a 'public cognitive system' that was manifested in the public sphere."[44] Roma was a feature of the *Denkkollektiv*—or, even more, a person emergent from that system, the mythological manifestation of the system that reinforced this thought world.

But Price's answer to Mellor's question only drives us further into a yet more familiar problem: namely, how we are to identify Roma's relationship to the political institutions which grant her power and whose power she represents. The problem here is precisely one of "personification." And, while in the case of Roma, both Mellor and Price are inclined to say that we have personification in the earlier, more credulously mythological sense, this agreement still leaves the relationship between Roma and the various eponymous political entities undertheorized.[45] The appearance of Roma devotion is roughly contemporary with the appearance of a variety of cults to the Roman people themselves, the Roman Senate, or even certain Roman prefects.[46] Should we take this as evidence that Roma is distinct from these entities—even within the discourse of "religion"—or rather as evidence that Greek religion is proposing various answers to one and the same question: namely, how ought Greek cities represent Roman power to themselves?

Mellor argues persuasively for the latter. In Ephesus, we find two related inscriptions which refer to the same statuette variously as *urbs Romana* (The Roman City), ὁ δῆμος ὁ Ῥωμαίων (The Roman People), and Ῥώμη ("Roma" or "Rome").[47] Combined with several other cases where Greek sources refer to what must be statues of Roma as statues of the Roman people (δῆμος), it seems fairly clear that Roma ought to be identified precisely with this collective social entity.[48] Mellor concludes:

> Roma was not a living man, a king honored as a god; she was the personification and deification of the Roman state, the *res publica Romana* (Livy 7, 6, 3). Personification had long been used as one of the principal Greek modes of apprehension. It was a direct, graphic presentation of forces, phenomena, or concepts and was therefore not amenable to explanation by systematic analysis. Though places, cities or even countries, were often personified, Roma was not the city personified. She was the personification (and deification) of a collective, the Roman state.[49]

Roma, despite the fact that her cult partook of the forms of the personifications of Greek cities, was not of the same species as these deities. Roma embodies something more visceral—the experience of an irresistible power emergent from the vast machinery of a burgeoning empire. Nor, of course, was the Roma cult a ruler cult, though there was obviously some borrowing that took place between the Roma cult and imperial cult. For Mellor, while Roma was not a human king, her cult adopted the forms of the Seleucid ruler cults and preserved them for the Roman imperial cult that followed:

> Roma was the transmitter; through her the forms of the ruler cult were kept alive between the fall of the Hellenistic dynasties and the deifica-tion first of Roman proconsuls and later of Roman emperors. Epithets like ἐπιφανής passed from the kings to Roma and thence to Julius Caesar and his successors.[50]

On this account, the Roma cult was merely a stopgap measure, a bridge between the Seleucid and Roman ruler cults. This leaves Mellor, however, with a nagging question he cannot answer: why did the Roma cult persist alongside the Roman imperial cult?[51] In the end, Roma—as "Roma Aeterna"—outlived the Roman imperial cult by more than a millennium.[52] Why? Mellor's "bridge theory" of the function of the Roma cult cannot provide an answer. Roma ought to have disap-peared once a ruler cult (re)appeared.

However, Mellor's own theory of the function of Roma suggests an answer; we simply need to grant his language of personification a bit more ontological weight. Mellor more or less suggests that personification, as we have seen, can function as an effective cognitive strategy for recognizing and describing real per-sons at higher levels of emergence. And that is precisely what is happening in the case of the Roma cult: a Roman social body whose mereology is sufficiently con-voluted to subvert any attempt to analyze it systematically is rationally cognized instead at the mythological level as a goddess, Roma. The goddess herself—the collective person, Roma—emerged from the increasingly convoluted structures that supported the burgeoning Roman state. That state constituted a very real social body—and, as we saw in the previous chapter, was recognized by ancient philosophers as such. As Mellor himself insists, "through the goddess the Greeks honored that rather inaccessible body—the Roman people."[53] This is the super-organismic body of Roma.

In other words, in Roma, we have the peripheral colonial depiction of what we saw Seneca describing from the imperial center.[54] Both are descriptions of an imperial social body. Seneca needs to find a place and role for the emperor, and imperial ideology supplies the answer: Nero is the hegemonic mind, the masculine ruler of his own body, which is the Roman state. But this account makes plain the primacy of the ideology of the social body—rather than of the ruler cult—in the complex of ideas. This is why Roma persists alongside the ruler cult, and in fact outlives it: she represents most transparently the heart of the intuition—grasped both in the imperial center and from the periphery—of the existence of a suprahuman personal entity emergent from the social body of the Roman state. It is the Roma cult that more transparently captures this reality emergent from the convoluted complex systems of colonialism. True, the advent of Roman emperors demanded that this emergent person be identified with a single figurehead, and the imperial cult was (re)born. But for a two-hundred-year period during the Roman Republic, the Roma cult expressed this insight quite transparently. And the persistence of the Roma cult—often literally alongside the imperial cult, as the two statues would be paired together in temples—suggests that Roma devotion retained its utility as a description of the "actual state of affairs."[55] Mellor's "bridge theory" ought therefore be inverted: the imperial cult was an adaptation of the Roma cult's more fundamental religiopolitical expression. So Stephen Moore can rightly describe the emergence of Roma without recourse to analogy to the imperial cult:

> In essence, the cult of Roma represented a solution to a problem. The problem for the Hellenistic cities in which the cult originated was that of coming to terms with a power that was at once irresistible and external to the city, emanating from a place far distant from it, yet extending deep within it, and a permanent source both of potential devastation and essential benefaction. In all of this, that power was structurally similar to that of the traditional gods, and the cults of the gods thus became the logical model for the inhabitants of the cities for managing and placating that power, but also for representing it to themselves, in terms that were not imposed from without but adapted from their own traditions.[56]

Moore invokes the language of "models," but of course there is no need for this recourse to metaphor. Within an emergentist framework, the ontological significance of this metaphor is apparent: the effectiveness of this cognitive strategy suggests that we ought to take seriously the being of the person emergent from this complex social system. Roma was not so much invented, as recognized. "Deification"—that is, the founding of a cult—was a strategy to represent this real person and engage with her.

If Roma was the dominant Greek strategy for representing this emergent person, Mark's "Legion" was a Palestinian analog (Mark 5:1–20). The political imagery in the passage is hard to miss. The demon, asked by Jesus to reveal his name, uses military language: "My name is Legion; for we are many" (Mark 5:9b). The awkward shift from the singular pronoun "my" to the plural subject "we" is a telltale marker of the presence of a collective mythological emergent.[57] The demon(s) in some sense represent(s) the integrated social body of the Roman army. (An army, as we noted in the previous chapter, was one of the Stoics' prime examples of an integrated body.) The casting of this/these demon(s) into swine in verse 13 also has important political resonances. The banner used by Caesar's tenth legion (Legio X *Fretensis*)—stationed in northwestern Syria from 17–66 CE and later involved in the Jewish war—used a boar on its seals.[58] Jesus's casting of this (Roman) Legion (back) into the sea is, therefore, both political theater *and* literal spiritual-political warfare.

John Dominic Crossan has described this exorcism as "a brief performancial summary . . . of every Jewish revolutionary's dream." Crossan argues that for many in first century Jewish circles, "Roman imperialism meant that God's people were possessed by demons on the social level." This results in what Crossan describes as a sort of social schizophrenia, for social possession "indicates a power admittedly greater than oneself, admittedly 'inside' oneself, but that one declares to be evil and therefore beyond any collusion or cooperation." This is the social crisis prompted by the imposition of imperial power (and, for what it's worth, sounds strikingly similar to the way Paul describes the dominion of Hamartia). Invoking the ideological macrocosm-microcosm correspondence, Crossan suggests that this possession on the social level was also experienced by individuals— hence the possession of the Markan demoniac.[59]

Crossan explains this possession by way of a comparison to mid-twentieth-century Rhodesian practices of deliverance prayer against possession by colonial spirits.[60] According to anthropologist Barrie Reynolds, in the colonial context, the traditional concept of possession by ancestral spirits (*mahamba*) was extended to include the possibility of possession by the spirits of a European (*bindele*).[61] Exorcising the *bindele* was a means of freeing an individual from spiritual possession, but also a means of resisting colonial oppression. Crossan concludes: "Legion, I think, is to colonial Roman Palestine, as *bindele* was to colonial European Rhodesia."[62] Crossan rationalizes this phenomenon via the modern (Western) discourse of mental illness. In this description, mental illness, statistically more prevalent in colonial contexts, appears both as a microcosmic projection of the macrocosmic disorder, but also, as Paul Hollenbach argues, as "a socially acceptable form of oblique protest against, or escape from, oppressions."[63]

Of course, one no more need choose between Rhodesian mythological and Western psychological explanations than one must choose between political and religious explanations of the function of Roma. Rather, we can see both Legion and the *bindele* as entities emergent from the complex sociopolitical systems on which they supervene, exercising downward causation back on their constituents' psychologies.[64] Understanding the interface of imperialism and demonization in this way allows us not to have to choose between seeing the Markan episode as either figurative or literal. Instead, like the Rhodesians, Jesus and his followers are representing the foreign Roman power to themselves "in terms . . . adapted from their own traditions."[65] The irresistible Roman force is therefore cognized mythologically—demonologically—as a supra-individual, superorganismic *person*, an "I" whose name reveals itself to be a "we." Exorcising this demon is therefore an intervention at the mythological level hoped to have consequences that "trickle down" to the sociopolitical level.

Seneca's ideology of the imperial body, Greek devotion to the goddess Roma, and the Markan exorcism of the Palestinian Legion all constitute various strategies for cognizing the very real person emergent from the Roman state. Each draws on the various philosophical, theological, and demonological resources available in different cultural locations, both at the imperial center and at its periphery. But Roma deserves special attention, not only because she emerges in the Greek East in which Paul did his work, but also because, unlike Seneca's imperial body and Mark's Legion, Roma exhibits the sort of gender trouble we see in the case of Hamartia.[66]

Roma's Gender Trouble

Roma's gender trouble begins with the folk etymology of her name—that is, the name of the city—which, transliterated in Greek (Ῥώμη), was identical to the word for "strength" (ῥώμη). And, indeed, the identification of this new unstoppable military force with the word for its basic attribute—strength—made good sense. It proved impossible for Greek authors to resist punning on this etymological accident.[67] However, the noun ῥώμη contained within it a gender problem. While undoubtedly ideologically masculine, it was grammatically feminine. Grammar won out in assigning Roma a visible gender (what we might call "female sex"): Roma was a woman. But what kind of woman was this? Stephen Moore describes the source of the problem: "the deity created to symbolize the irresistible [masculine] strength of Rome was not a god but a goddess, one whose very name was 'Strength.'"[68]

The collision of masculine identity and female form is highlighted by John Stobaeus's inclusion of Melinnos of Lesbos's hymn to Roma in his fifth-century anthology in the section entitled "On Courage [περὶ ἀνδρείας]." With some overemphasis on etymology, we could translate this title as "On Manliness."[69] The hymn is full of the language of ideologically masculine *imperium*. Roma is praised with ideologically paradoxical language as a "warlike mistress [δαΐφρων ἄνασσα]." She possesses "the royal glory of everlasting rule [κῦδος ἀρρήκτω βασιλῆον ἀρχᾶς]" that she "may govern with lordly might [κοιρανῆον ἔχοισα κάρτος ἀγεμονεύης]." The poet declares: "with a sure hand you steer the cities of peoples [κυβερνᾷς ἄστεα λαῶν]."[70] Not only does she exercise political *imperium*, she brings forth "the strongest men [κρατίστους ἄνδρας]" and "great warriors [αἰχματὰς μεγάλους]." This goddess, in other words, epitomizes Roman man-liness (as Stobaeus's editorial decision confirms), defined as it was by the all-encompassing logic of *imperium*.[71]

This tension in Roma's gender identity plays out vividly in her iconography. Her depiction draws from that of Athena, the Greek goddess of war, and also that of the Amazons. Indeed, the "girdle of gold" which Melinno describes Roma wearing is a feature she shares with Amazon dress. She is the paradigmati-cally paradigm-breaking warrior woman: "Roma typically appears in military dress (sometimes with bared breast, Amazon-style) . . . wearing a crested Roman helmet, and occasionally holding a spear but more often clutching a parazo-nium, the ceremonial short sword or outsized dagger that was symbolic of mili-tary rank." The possession of the parazonium connects Roma's iconographic representation to that of the Roman Emperors, Mars, and Virtus—"the divine personification of military valor and manly virtue, and a figure who fuses with Roma: they are frequently all but indistinguishable in their representations."[72] Indeed, Cornelius Vermeuele, in the standard work on Roma iconography, defines a single "Roma-Virtus type."[73] Virtus—grammatically feminine while ideologically masculine—exhibits the same sort of grammatical-ideological con-fusion that we have in the case of Roma. "Grammatical gender yields, of course, to the overarching imperative of masculine ideology," as Williams observes, but we are nevertheless left with a complicated emblem of Rome and its militant, hypermasculine power.[74]

As a complex artifact of ancient gender ideology, Roma's significance is mul-tivalent, and pregnant with all sorts of possibilities. Roma's multivalence is all that much more significant given her origins at the imperial margins. We must ask, "What does it mean that *this* is the image of imperial Rome that the prov-inces choose to reflect back to the metropolis? What is actually being said?"[75] Given that, as we saw above, "Roman masculinity is always tenuous, fragile, fluid always threatened, always incompletely achieved, ever under siege, ever liable to lose its footing on the greased gender gradient sloping down to femi-ninity and hence irrevocable shame, irredeemable disgrace," Moore describes Roma as

a figure in perpetual deconstruction. She holds the terms "femininity" and "masculinity" in constant, warring tension (no wonder she is so heav-ily armed), without ever reconciling them, without ever merging them into a harmonious synthesis. Each term perpetually threatens the other; each is the always unrealized negation of the other.[76]

Read in this way, Roma may be seen as a figure who represents the ultimate vic-tory of the subject's "war with him/herself," or "the most fully realized example of that relatively rare but highly symptomatic Roman gender type, the woman who 'overcomes' her femininity to act as befits a man."[77] Moore summarizes:

> A female body overlaid with the trappings of Roman military discipline, Roma may be read as the uncritical celebration of a masculinity that constructs itself through the unceasing suppression of femininity. As such, Roma may be read as a visual allegory of hegemonic Roman gender ideology. Roma's iconography may be interpreted to say—indeed, to repeat incessantly—that masculinity is the defeat of femininity.[78]

In this reading, the colonial construction of Roma represents an insightful echoing back, to the imperial center, the basic contours of its own ideology.

But Roma may also be read quite differently, as a sort of colonial protest of imperial domination that takes the form of what Moore calls "gender masquerade":

> Roma—female but not feminine, masculine but female—might be read as saying that the Roman ideology of masculinity is a self-contradictory and self-subverting impossibility. Or it might even be read as a satiric assertion that Roman masculinity is always threatening to shrivel back into the femininity on which it is erected, and which is always showing through its armor, Roma thus dismantling the hard/soft, Roman/Asian dichotomy on which the denigrating stereotype depends.[79]

These various lines of critique all seize upon the possibilities latent in Roma's queer gender identity. "Roma is Rome in double drag: phallic masculinity masquerading as female flesh masquerading as hegemonic masculinity." It is this function of Roma as a possible site of critique of Roman hegemony that Moore argues the author of Revelation exploits with his character, the Whore of Babylon, whom Moore takes to be none other than Roma herself, thinly veiled. In this appearance, then, "Babylon is Rome in triple drag: phallic masculinity figured as female and clothed as virtuous and victorious warrior, then reclothed as depraved and defeated prostitute."[80] Moore's reading of the function of Roma ideology in Revelation is vivid and compelling. We will see that Paul may be doing something similar with Hamartia. But before we turn back to Romans, there is one more ancient gender category I propose we consider to make sense of Roma—and that may well have helped to shape the Seer's depiction of the Whore of Babylon (and thus have contributed to his critique of Roma): that of the *tribas*.

In Soranus's *On Chronic Diseases*, the *tribades* are those who practice both kinds of love, rush to have sex with women more than with men and pursue women with an almost masculine jealousy [*et easdem invidentia paene virili sectantur*], and, when they are freed from the disease or temporarily relieved, they seek to accuse others of that from which they are known to suffer, then, in their baseness of spirit, worn out by their twofold sexuality [*tum in animi humilitate duplici sexu confectae*], as though often ravished by drunkenness, they, bursting forth into new forms of lust that have been nourished by shameful custom, rejoice in the outrage to their own sex [*sui sexus iniuriis gaudent*].[81]

The problem with the *tribas* was not that she desired to have sexual relations with women per se, but that she desired to play the active, penetrative—that is, masculine—role.[82] She pursues her sexual object with an "almost masculine jealousy [*invidentia paene virili*]." It is this out-of-place masculinity that causes injury to her own sex (*sui iniuriis*)—an injury in which the *tribas* ironically finds joy. The *tribas* was a "gender-monster" because she was seen as a usurper of phallic privilege.[83] This meant that her transgression was as much sociopolitical as it was sexual.

Indeed, as noted above, in ancient Roman sexual ideology, intercourse was treated "as a sociopolitical act of penetration (masculine) or submission (feminine) that helped to define a subject's gender."[84] Sex was by no means a private affair. It (re-)inscribed social difference and social hierarchy—the dominance of the penetrator over the penetrated. The primary offense of the *tribas* was in inverting this hierarchy. This meant that the sexual activity of a *tribas* with a man's wife (as described in the elder Seneca's *Controversies*) brought (sexual) shame upon the husband, emasculating him.[85] In this agonistic sexual ideology, the *tribas* struck at the core of Roman (gendered) political ideology and (masculine) imperial anxiety.[86] And Roman men had reason to be anxious, given that legal reforms instituted by Julius and Claudius were giving women increased autonomy.[87] For elite Roman men, these social reforms suggested that, in fact, Roman matrons were on the move along the ancient gender spectrum. Seneca the Younger laments that many women of his day are taking on masculinity, evident in their appetites for food, drink, and sex. More worrisome than the drinking and carousing, of course, was their penchant for playing the active role in sexual encounters. "Although they were born passives [*pati natae*] . . . they devise the most impossible varieties of unchastity [*adeo perversum commentae genus inpudicitiae*] and penetrate men [*viros ineunt*]." As a result, their "feminine nature has been conquered . . . they have put off their womanly nature."[88] These sorts of women exemplify only masculine disease and weakness—not masculine strength. After all, these are the only "feminine" aspects of masculinity—the aspects a true man must conquer. A woman pretending to masculine status can only partake in these lesser (ideologically feminine) attributes. Such a woman is the very nadir of the decline of the women of Seneca's day; she is the *tribas* who manages to penetrate not only women, but also men.[89]

The danger of such women was, at least in part, that they might somehow achieve (unnatural, monstrous) masculine *imperium*, and in so doing acquire the physiology to match.[90] The concern throughout—in ancient literature written for and by elite Roman males—is that such masculine pretenders, wielders of ideologically impossible feminine *imperium,* would ultimately threaten the natural (though hard-won) *imperium* achieved by Roman *viri*.[91] Watching their proximate others—elite Roman women—achieve increased degrees of influence and *imperium*, elite Roman males deployed the charge that these women were assuming the form of the literally phallus-usurping *tribas*, "an imperial stereotype of androgynous Greek gender-monsters enervating the empire."[92]

According to Valerius Maximus, the effeminating consequences of such an impossible *imperium* were routinely experienced in the effeminate Greek East. The supreme example of such Eastern effeminacy was to be found in Cyprus:

> But even more effeminate [*sed tamen effeminatior*] was the male population of Cyprus [*multitudo Cypriorum*], who patiently allowed their queens to climb into their chariots on top of their women's bodies [*mulierum corporibus*], which were arranged as steps so that they might tread more softly [*quo mollius vestigia pedum ponerent*]. It would have been better for those men—if they were in fact men [*viris enim, si modo viri erant*]—to die than to submit to such a delicate dominion [*tam delicato imperio optemperare*].[93]

As Craig Williams notes, the entire passage turns on the impossible possibility of the "delicate dominion," wielded by the Cyprian queens over their male subjects.[94] This dominion has disastrous, effeminating consequences for the Cyprian men. Valerius isn't even sure what to call them; when he calls them men, he has to qualify this with "if they were in fact men."

But such Eastern, feminine (and effeminating) dominion was coming home. Marc Antony's infamous seduction by Cleopatra, and his subsequent descent into Eastern luxury and softness (as his opponents described it), retained within it an important political lesson, but the vociferousness with which it was still condemned indicated that this sort of Eastern, feminine, and effeminating *imperium* was considered a very real and present danger.[95] And, as we saw Stowers note earlier, the rhetorical strategy of painting one's political foe as an "Antony" was quite effective.[96] The rising tide was undeniable: Roman matrons were amassing influence that posed a threat to Roman *viri* right at the center of Roman *imperium*. Cato the Elder pointed out the irony, complaining that "all men rule over their women, and we rule over all men, but our women rule over us."[97] In this context, Swancutt concludes:

> the term *tribas* referred not to a person with a particular sexual or gendered identity. It was rather a Roman imperial gender-stereotype, a propaganda tool that deployed a variety of images: unnatural androgyny, portentious eastern lust, sexual dominion, illicit masculinity, adultery and husbandly humiliation to enable imperial Roman men to communicate with each other about the potential loss of their virile hegemony and to encourage the control of Roman matrons and Greeks as groups.[98]

Roma, a representation of the nature of Roman *imperium* constructed on the margins of the empire and reflected back to the center, would look suspiciously like the *tribas*. One need only consider the reliefs at Aphrodisias to see the problem. These reliefs present two very different femininities. First, throughout the ethnic reliefs, there are the figures of subjugated nations—including Judea—represented by women, as they ought to be ideologically.[99] These reliefs declare that, in being penetrated by Rome's masculine *imperium*, these ἔθνη have revealed their collective social identities—their social bodies—to be passive, feminine bodies. Collectively, they are women. As we may have come to expect by now, a recent handbook identifies these figures as "personifications of conquered nations."[100] But we now know to ask the question: "personification" in what sense? Given the ancient ideology of the (very real) social body, we have no reason to suggest that these figures represent anything other than the very real social bodies of conquered peoples.[101] And, as very real living bodies, they were assigned genders according to the dominant gender ideology. In being conquered, being penetrated, these bodies have become female. By playing the passive role in the sociopolitical-sexual encounter with hyper-masculine Roman *imperium*, these nations' social bodies—perhaps at one time penetrating and virile—have become passive and feminine. This is the inevitable consequence of political intercourse with the impenetrable penetrator that was the Roman *vir*, writ large on the masculine, Roman imperial body, represented in various ways in the imperial reliefs on the second story of the structure, above the ethnic reliefs.

These imperial reliefs also exhibit a second "femininity" and disclose the ideological problem posed by Roma. For, on the one hand, these reliefs follow the Roman gender script in depicting Augustus as the one wielding masculine Roman *imperium*, conquering even time and space itself.[102] But the second story also contained a relief of Roma standing in triumph over the Earth.[103] This in no way mitigates the emasculation of the nations paraded below; rather, as we noted in the discussion of the *tribas*, the active, penetrative action of the *tribas* results in a yet more complete emasculation of the would-be man in question. Read from the imperial center, this depiction of Roma is "femininity conquered" (precisely as one who conquers)—Moore's proposed "uncritical" reading of Roma. But, from the periphery, this depiction of a feminine-but-conquering Roma poses dangerous questions. What are we to make of Roma standing in victory over the earth? Is this proper femininity? Or is this "femininity conquered" in the sense Seneca means the phrase in describing the tribadic women of his day—that is, femininity run amok and transgressing into monstrous, hyper-feminine androgyny?[104] This gets to the heart of the gender problematic that Moore describes. The fact that Roma was to represent the very essence of masculine *imperium* could make her problematic gender identity that much more dangerous. To represent Roman *imperium* with the goddess Roma directed a rather pointed question at the very heart of Roman imperial ideology: is Rome's *imperium*, despite all the hyper-masculine rhetoric, a feminine and effeminating "*imperium delicatum*"? The Seer's depiction of the Whore of Babylon answers with a hearty "yes." The one who "has dominion over all the kings of the earth [ἡ ἔχουσα βασιλείαν ἐπὶ τῶν βασιλέων τῆς γῆς]" (Rev 17:18) is none other than a woman in abject service of her own desires (17:1–6), who enslaves her subjects by making them obedient to those same desires (17:2).

Hamartia as Tribadic Roma

Is Rome's *imperium*, despite all the hyper-masculine rhetoric, a feminine and effeminating "*imperium delicatum*"? We may never know Paul's answer about Roma.[105] But it is clear that he has presented Hamartia as exercising precisely this sort of *imperium*, as I will now demonstrate. Having invoked gender-transgressive, stereotypically Gentile, sex in Romans 1 (especially vv. 26–27), in Romans 5–8, Paul presents a collective entity, a mythological character, Hamartia, who embodies the sociopolitical significance of this transgression. Hamartia, as we have seen, is described by Paul precisely in terms of her feminine alliance with desire, and also in terms of her paradoxical exercise of masculine *imperium*. In exercising *imperium* over her subjects, she, like the tribadic queen of Cyprus, effeminates the men under her dominion—the evidence of which is their enslavement to her desires (Rom 6:12). Thus, for Paul's audience, part of the rhetorical effectiveness of Paul's description of Hamartia in personal terms lies in the horror they experience in being told repeatedly that Hamartia—a woman—exercises dominion over them—and additionally, as I have argued, Paul contends that, apart from Christ, they constitute the feminine social body of their tribadic mistress. Only death to this Body, through baptism, makes possible their submission to the natural hegemony of masculine mind as the Body of Christ.

Ironically, this masculine Body of Christ is organized precisely around ideologically feminine obedience of the sort Paul boldly proclaims that he is seeking to bring about among the Gentiles in Rom 1:5. So, at the individual level, much of what Paul must do in chapters 5–8 is demonstrate that the apparent masculine hegemony—when it results in transgression—is, in fact, effeminate (and effeminating) slavery. At the same time, at the mythological level, he must expose the apparently masculine *imperium* of Hamartia as a monstrous fraud: the tribadic authority of a woman. Thus, for Paul, Hamartia's *imperium delicatum* reinforces Greco-Roman ideology of sex and gender, thereby undermining that same ideology's alignment with the ideology of empire. The careful (modern) reader can easily find therein a critique of the whole ideological complex: gendered, sexual, social, and political. Whether Paul himself grasps these implications is unclear. The triumphant exclamation in Rom 8:37 that "we hyper-conquer [ὑπερνικῶμεν]" may be read as a declaration that true masculine *imperium* is found in Christ-like obedience, or it may be a declaration that, through Christ, the hearers have conquered conquering itself—that is, they have transcended *imperium* entirely.

The specter of gender-transgression, as I have noted, is initially raised in 1:26–27: "For this reason God gave them up to degrading passions. Their women exchanged natural intercourse for that which was beyond nature, and in the same way also the men, giving up natural intercourse with women, were consumed with passion for one another. Men committed shameless acts with men and received in their own persons the due penalty for their error." As Swancutt has ably demonstrated, it is clear from patristic interpretation that what is at stake in these verses has little to do with "homosexual orientation" (as such a concept was not known to ancient readers, nor to Paul), but rather gender-deviance with (individual) somatic and social (also somatic?) consequences.[106] Swancutt cites many examples, but for our purposes two will suffice. The first is Clement of Alexandria, who, in *Paed*. 2.10, finds in these verses a warning against "excessive desire, mutual intercourse [ἐπαλλήλων συνουσιῶν], relations with pregnant women, reversal of roles in intercourse [ἀλληλοβασίας], corruption of boys, adultery, and lewdness."[107] Clement's concerns about mutual intercourse and reversal of roles in intercourse align with the ancient anxiety with tribadic sex that we examined previously. The danger here is women assuming the active role in intercourse. Chrysostom balances the picture, focusing on the threat posed by men assuming the passive role:

This [1:27a] is clear proof of the ultimate degree of corruption, when the genders are abandoned. Both he who was called to be a leader of the woman and she who was called to become a helpmate to the man now behave as enemies to one another.... what shall we say of this insanity [1:27], which is inexpressibly worse than fornication? ... Not only are you made [by it] into a woman, but you also cease to be a man. Yet neither are you changed [fully] into that nature nor do you retain the one you had. You become a betrayer of both . . . for it is not the same thing to be changed into the nature of a woman as it is to become a woman while yet remaining a man or, rather, to be neither one nor the other.[108]

This sort of gender-deviance can land one physiologically in "no man's (or woman's) land," as an androgynous gender monster, an example of which we saw above: namely, the *tribas*. Sexually aggressive women challenge the sociopolitical *imperium* of men, which these same men voluntarily abdicate in playing the passive sexual role. Given the irreducible role of *imperium* for masculine identity, such men can no longer be called "men." They are less-than-men.[109] The common thread throughout this decline narrative, as noted above, is the enflaming role of desire: "the desires of their hearts [ταῖς ἐπιθυμίαις τῶν καρδιῶν αὐτῶν]" (v. 24) and the "degrading passions [πάθη ἀτιμίας]," (v. 26) to which God gave them over, reach their climax in "their passion [τῇ ὀρέξει αὐτῶν]" for one another with which men were consumed. This obsession with feminine desire means that the "debased mind [ἀδόκιμον νοῦν]" of v. 28 is nothing other than an effeminate mind, of the sort Philo said resulted from the unseating of the masculine ruling principle.[110] As I argued in the previous chapter, this mind is the foil for the collective mind of Rom 12:2—the corporate mind of the Body of Christ. The corporate nature of this debased mind pervades Paul's text, through his transition from the plurals of v. 24 and v. 26—"ἐπιθυμίαις" and "πάθη"—to the singular in v. 28: "God gave them [pl.] to a debased mind [sg.]." "Their [shared] appetite [τῇ ὀρέξει αὐτῶν]" in which they burned, in v. 27, anticipates this transition to a more integrated corporate structure of effeminate overindulgence.

This collective effeminate-and-effeminating, debased mind is none other than the mind of Hamartia. Given that "ancients treated the mind as the highest aspect of the physical body, not as an element or entity distinct from the physical body," we ought not be surprised that this mind fundamentally alters the physiology of Hamartia's Body, which Paul describes as "the Body of Sin" (6:6) and "your [pl.] mortal body [sg.]" (6:12).[111] The effeminate mind of Hamartia exercises its ironic tribadic dominion through the reinforcement of its own enslavement to desire. Hamartia exercises *imperium* (βασιλευέτω) in the collective Body precisely through forcing obedience to the collective Body's passions (6:12). She is a woman whose passions have run amok, and have driven her to exercise *imperium* over her now-emasculated subjects. This is the ultimate consequence of the decline narrated in Rom 1, the microcosmic effemination of 1:27–28 writ large on the macrocosmic Body.

As noted in the previous chapter, Paul goes on to describe the *imperium* of Hamartia not simply in terms of political rule, but in terms of enslavement.

The combination of these two images—politics and slavery—yields something very much like the triumph procession discussed above. We can picture Hamartia standing, as Roma at Aphrodisias, in triumph over her vanquished, emasculated foes, both as individuals and conquered social bodies. Paul's hearers, before baptism, were obedient slaves [δούλους εἰς ὑπακοήν] of Hamartia (6:16). The phrase "slaves of Sin [δοῦλοι τῆς ἁμαρτίας]" is repeated twice more in just a few sentences (6:17, 20). This language had gendered implications. As Jonathan Walters has shown, the slave was explicitly excluded from the category *vir* (man):

> What characterized the status of slaves was that they were not autonomous: they were under the control of their owner, to do with as he or she wished. Slaves could be beaten, tortured, killed, and the fact that a slave, male or female, was at the disposal of his or her master for sexual use was so commonplace as to be scarcely noted in Roman sources. It was this lack of autonomy on the corporeal level, this availability of the body for invasive assaults, which characterized the status of slavery. Conversely, this equation of slavery with having, or being, a body at the disposal of another for penetration meant that having one's body penetrated was seen as slavelike. To allow oneself to be beaten, or sexually penetrated, was to put oneself in the position of the slave, that archetypal passive body.[112]

To be a slave was to lose one's status as a man.[113] Hamartia, in making slaves of her subjects, effeminates them, makes them less than men; she makes them into passives. This is the height of Hamartia's offense. It is also precisely what drove first-century paranoia about *tribades*. In making slaves of her subjects, Hamartia enacts the role of the *tribas*, emasculating her male subjects through her expression of phallic *imperium*. Hamartia, like the queens of Cyprus, has made her subjects less than men.

But Paul's image is yet more complex. The power that Hamartia exercises over her slaves is nothing other than the *imperium* one exercises over the members of one's body. Hamartia "rules [κυριεύσει]" over the "members [μέλη]" of her Body (6:13–14). And yet this social Body is explicitly depicted in militaristic terms; these members are deployed as "weapons [ὅπλα]" (6:13). In terms of the reliefs at Aphrodisias, Hamartia is both Roma above, ruling her army, and, in some sense, the conquered women below—composed of the subjected "members" of her body. That is, the *imperium delicatum* wielded by Hamartia is both external and internal to her subjects.[114] Parasitic as she is on those who participate in the complex systems of transgression from which she emerges, Hamartia's effeminating *imperium* is nothing other than the natural consequence of—or, "the due penalty for [τὴν ἀντιμισθίαν ἣν ἔδει]" (1:27)—her subjects' own individual submission to the enchantments of (ideologically feminine) desire. In short, in his depiction of Hamartia, Paul exploits the identification of effeminating conqueror and effeminate conquered in Roman imperial ideology manifest in tribadic Roma (that is, in Roma-read-as-*tribas*). The implication is this: perhaps the *imperium* of Roman ideology is not the paradigm of an impenetrable masculinity, but rather the natural consequence of greater and greater degrees of enslavement to feminine desire.

And, indeed, the pairing of Roman "masculine" *imperium* with the sort of dissolute life enslaved to desire would not be unique to Paul. Neil Elliott has traced the recurring charge of effeminating incontinence leveled by historians against the emperors of Paul's time: Gaius Calilgula, Claudius, and Nero.[115] This critique came from the imperial center—a policing of the unending quest to secure Roman masculinity. Suetonius complains that "it was seldom that Claudius left a dining-hall except gorged and sodden [*distentus ac madens*]; he would then go to bed and sleep supine with his mouth wide open—thus allowing a feather to be put down his throat, which would bring up the superfluous food and drink as vomit."[116] The language is familiar from Seneca's rant regarding the masculine excesses experienced by *tribades* in *Ep.* 95. Suetonius describes Gaius Caligula's sexual appetites not dissimilarly:

> He had regard neither for his own chastity nor for that of others. He is said to have had sexual relations with Marcus Lepidus, the actor Mnester, and a number of hostages—giving and receiving pleasure in turn [*mutui stupri*]. Valerius Catullus, a man of consular family, proclaimed publicly that he had buggered [*stupratum*] the emperor and was quite exhausted by his sexual demands.[117]

The accusation that the emperor—ideologically, the one who was to be the most impenetrable penetrator—assumed the passive role in intercourse strikes at the core of the Roman gendered ideology of *imperium*. Philo, in attacking Gaius's pretense to divinity, attacks the emperor precisely in gendered terms:

> A man, indeed, may expect anything rather than that a man endowed with such a body and such a soul, when both of them are effeminate [μαλακὰ] and broken down, could ever possibly be made like to the vigour of Mars in either particular; but this man, like a mummer transforming himself on the stage, putting on all sorts of masks one after another, sought to deceive the spectators by a series of fictitious appearances.[118]

The effemination of Gaius's body goes hand in hand with that of his soul. Both are caused by an overindulgence of desire. Philo's litany, describing the causes of Gaius's eventual death, should sound familiar:

> But in the eighth month a severe disease attacked Gaius who had changed the manner of his living which was a little while before, while Tiberius was alive, very simple and on that account more wholesome than one of great sumptuousness and luxury [πολυτέλειαν]; for he began to indulge in abundance of strong wine and eating of rich dishes, and in the abundant license of insatiable desires [ἀπλήρωτοι ἐπιθυμίαι] and great insolence, and in the unseasonable use of hot baths, and emetics, and then again in winebibbing and drunkenness, and returning gluttony, and in lust [λαγνεῖαι] after boys and women, and in everything else which tends to destroy both soul and body, and all the bonds which unite and strengthen the two; for the rewards [ἐπίχειρα] of temperance [ἐγκρατείας] are health and strength, and the wages [ἐπίχειρα] of intemperance [ἀκρασίας] are weakness [ἀσθένεια] and disease [νόσος] which bring a man near to death [γειτνιῶσα θανάτῳ].[119]

Philo's language is startlingly close to some of Paul's own. For Paul, the enslavement to Hamartia—chiefly to her desires—results in weakness, such that he can summarize the state before Christ's intervention simply as "weakness" (5:6)—which Philo names as the natural consequence of intemperance. Philo's description of the rewards (ἐπίχειρα) of temperance and intemperance sound a fair bit like Paul's declaration in 6:23 regarding the wages (ὀψώνια) of Hamartia and the free gift (χάρισμα) of God. For both Paul and Philo, the result of effeminating indulgence of desire is death (6:23).

In short, the tribadic dominion of Hamartia sounds not unlike the effeminate dominion of the Caesars—Gaius Caligula, in particular—as described by Suetonius and Philo.[120] The effect for Paul's rhetoric is twofold—and the position of Roma as the middle term is meaningful in both aspects. On the one hand, Paul's depiction of Hamartia as a phallic-privilege-usurping gender monster gives substantial rhetorical force to his repeated pleas for his audience to be set free from their tribadic mistress (Rom 6:11–13, 19). The resonances with Roma would further strengthen the rhetorical force of Paul's description of Hamartia's overwhelming power; his audience had experience with this sort of insatiable dominating power. On the other hand, the resonance could turn the rhetoric in the other direction, and raise questions about how best to understand Roma's dominion in terms of regnant gender ideology. Paul's description of the consequences of Hamartia's reign in terms that would resonant so deeply with contemporary critiques of the Caesars would suggest that the dominion of the Caesars is nothing other than the dominion of Hamartia—that is, the dominion of Sin. If one begins to collapse the Roma-Hamartia identification, then perhaps Caesar is not the animating soul of the empire; perhaps Roma-Hamartia plays that role (as I argued Roma did originally and most straightforwardly for those who invented her cult). Caesar—any Caesar—is merely an Antony, seduced by Roma-Hamartia, a tribadic woman. This is the true nature of the Roman social body. This is "the complete inversion of society" that Tamez and Hinkelammert describe: the sociopolitical Body of Sin.[121]

The Body of Christ and the Obedience of Faith

As I have indicated already, this disordered, feminine Body of Hamartia is implicitly and explicitly contrasted with the well-ordered Body of Christ. In a certain sense, this contrast functions according to the expectations of the dominant ideology. The Body of Christ is ruled by a renewed collective mind (Rom 12:2). Participation in this masculine social body facilitates the attainment of masculine physiology at the individual level. Members of Christ's Body partake in a unifying Spirit which allows them to access a higher (pneumatic) mindset (φρόνημα) (8:1-8). This Spirit solves the effeminating usurpation of masculine mind (7:23, 25) by feminine desire (7:5, 7–8). This is done through inclusion "in Christ Jesus" (8:1, 2)—that is, in the Body of Christ—which is unified by a common habitual practice, the "law of the Spirit of life" (8:2). The result is that feminine desire no longer holds sway, because the believer is "clothed" in the (masculine) "Lord Jesus Christ" (13:14).[122] With Hamartia thus deposed, those who participate in the masculine Body of Christ "exercise dominion in life" (5:17). Masculine *imperium* is restored to those who had previously been the subjects of tribadic Hamartia.

In short, the fundamental role of gender ideology in Roman moral philosophy means that what Mary Douglas describes as the most important decision to make in moral philosophy—"choosing . . . among social institutions"—is, for the ancients, a decision about which social body has most achieved masculine self-mastery.[123] That is, it is a decision about the gendered physiology of the social body. For a man, the solution to realizing that he is living within a disordered, feminine social body is to join a masculine, well-ordered social body. Paul suggests that the Body of Christ is precisely this sort of alternative to the tribadic Body of Hamartia.

However, the Body of Christ, as Paul describes it, is not so straightforwardly masculine. While the Body of Christ makes good on the promises of life in a sufficiently well-ordered, masculine body—at the very least, the possibility of moral virtue and *imperium* "in life" (5:17)—Christ (and his followers) are hardly presented, in Romans, as paragons of Roman masculinity. This has everything to do with the way Paul deploys the category of obedience. In dominant Roman ideology, obedience was gendered as feminine because it was a marker of (ideologically feminine) servility. Cicero, in describing the ideology of self-mastery called the soft [*molle*], feminine part of the soul "the part that ought to be obedient [*quae oboedire debet*]."[124] In aligning the feminine with the obedient, Cicero trades on the ideological alignment of the feminine with the slavish. Language of "obedience" was so strictly tied to slavery in the Roman world that higher-status Romans created elaborate ways to avoid talking about the concept amongst higher-status individuals.[125] So significant was "the stigma which slavery cast on such relations," that J. E. Lendon identifies an "audible quiet of the ancient sources on the subject of aristocrats' obedience."[126] Lendon writes:

> Although it was understood that a gentleman official had to obey his chief's orders, he might be insulted if another gentleman official presumed actually to give him an order. Thus even the emperor was extremely tactful, phrasing his directives to his grand officials as suggestions and advice. Letters of appointment for his equestrian officials, where, of all places, a modern reader expects some reference to obedience, avoided all mention of it.[127]

In sum, Lendon finds an "antipathy to seeming to obey" encoded in elite Roman ideology.[128] Indeed, Paul's phrase in Rom 6:16, "δούλους εἰς ὑπακοήν [slaves unto obedience]," casually presumes upon this common-sense association of slavery and obedience.

This does not mean, however, that advocacy of obedience is absent from ancient literature. Rather, as an expression of social inferiority within a hierarchical society, elite writers were well aware that obedience (precisely *as* slavish and feminine) was a necessity for the proper functioning of the body politic. Without obedience rendered by the lower classes, Dio Cassius writes, the social fabric breaks down, citing ancient Roman experience as evidence:

> Those whose money gave them influence desired to surpass their inferiors in all respects as though they were their sovereigns [βασιλεύοντές], and the weaker citizens, sure of their own equal rights, were unwilling to obey them even in the smallest particular [οὐδὲν αὐτοῖς οὐδὲ σμικρὸν ... πειθαρχεῖν ἤθελον] ... So it was that they sundered their former relations, wherein they had been wont harmoniously to assist each other with material profit, and no longer made distinctions between the citizen and the foreigner. Indeed, both classes disdained moderation, the one setting its heart upon an extreme of authority, the other upon an extreme of resistance to servitude.[129]

This, to the elite Roman mind, is the problem with populism: in erasing class distinctions, it does away with the basic foundations of social order.[130] Without social inferiors obeying their social superiors, the social body would be in disarray. After all, in the social body, such people were that "something naturally soft [*molle*], abject [*demissum*], abased [*humile*]"—that is, "the part that ought to be obedient [*quae oboedire debet*]." If it weren't for the obedience of this lower, feminine aspect of the social body, the higher, masculine, rational part— the part that "stands ready as sovereign of all [*domina omnium et regina*]"— would not be able to effect, through its exercise of *imperium*, the perfection of virtue—"manliness."[131]

Given the social markers, it is then especially shocking that, for Paul, obedience is the distinguishing mark of Christ and his Body—this despite Paul's introduction of "Jesus Christ our Lord [κυρίου]" as a Davidic king (1:3) given posthumous divine honors (1:4). In the Body of Christ, both sovereign *and* subjects are marked by obedience. Indeed, in 5:19, it is Jesus's (effeminate) obedience that is the linchpin of the Pauline story of liberation from the tyranny of tribadic Hamartia: "just as by the one man's disobedience [παρακοῆς] the many were made sinners [ἁμαρτωλοὶ], so by the one man's obedience [ὑπακοῆς] the many will be made righteous [δίκαιοι]."[132] For Paul, the paradigmatic moment of this obedience is at the cross, when Jesus "became obedient [ὑπήκοος] to the point of death—even death on a cross" (Phil 2:8). It is easy for modern readers to miss the gendered significance of this declaration. Yet, as Jonathan Walters has shown, "sexual penetration and beating . . . are in Roman terms structurally equivalent."[133] On the cross, Jesus was exposed as less-than-*vir*—as effeminate. Swancutt's language is especially vivid: "As a Galilean Jew the Romans crucified as a royal pretender, Jesus embodied everything the Roman man was not—dominated, penetrated, scourged, and humiliated. To Roman eyes, therefore, the crucified Jesus was not king of the Jews, but a barely-man whom Rome nailed as a queen."[134] Indeed, the centrality of the slavish, effeminating crucifixion of Jesus in Paul's gospel means that Paul has to declare from the very beginning of Romans that he is "not ashamed of the gospel," and that despite all appearances to the contrary, the gospel is the "power of God for the one who believes [τῷ πιστεύοντι]" (1:16)—that is, for the one who exercises mimetic obedience: the obedience of faith (ὑπακοὴν πίστεως) (1:5, cf. 15:18, 16:19, 26). This ideologically effeminating mimetic obedience is linked back to Jesus's emasculating crucifixion, through co-crucifixion with Christ in 6:6.[135] As it was for Jesus, emasculating obedience to crucifixion is the turning point for the believers, the result of which is an end to their slavery to Hamartia, her disordered feminine social body coming to nothing as the members of the Body of Hamartia fall off, necrotic, and are raised to new life in the Body of Christ.

Ironically, it is within this effeminate Body of Christ that true masculine self-mastery is possible (as described earlier). The effeminate Body of Christ delivers what the tribadic Body of Hamartia could not: mastery of the passions (6:12, 13:14), the renewal of mind (12:2), and the establishment of *imperium* (5:17). Obedience in imitation of the "dominated," "effeminate" Christ yields everything that the masculine Roman ideology was supposed to deliver. And the *imperium* it makes possible includes liberation from enslavement to Hamartia. It is being "in Christ Jesus" that means that the hearers ought no longer let Hamartia exercise dominion (βασιλευέτω) in their mortal body (6:11–12). Rather than presenting their members as weapons in the unjust army of Hamartia, they become weapons in the just army of God (6:13).[136] If and when they make the move to the Body of Christ, Hamartia will no longer exercise dominion (κυριεύσει) (6:14).

It is at this point that Paul gets to the heart of the issue regarding obedience, for life in the Body of Hamartia seemed to promise high-status, masculine "freedom"—the opposite of slavery, the opposite of low-status, feminine obedience: "When you were slaves of sin, you were free in regard to righteousness." (Rom 6:20) But, Paul argues, this was not freedom, but rather a form of slavery. Disobedience—"freedom" from obedience—is itself the most slavish form of obedience. It is an obedience to the passions, to appetites, and, ultimately and most fundamentally, to Hamartia, the entity emergent from the cascade of disobedience begun with Adam. It is a matter of enslavement to the base passions, the consequence and evidence of a catastrophic defeat in the war that every man wages against himself. This enslavement, Paul argues, is perhaps even more easily identifiable as "feminine" on the terms of the dominant discourse: an enslavement to ἐπιθυμία. The more desirable obedience is the form of obedience that leads to δικαιοσύνη: the tautological obedience to obedience (6:16), which leads to freedom from Hamartia and her enslavement to desire through what Paul insists can only in the loosest sense be called "slavery" to δικαιοσύνη (6:19). This "slavery" yields eternal life (6:22–23), in which they will exercise true *imperium* (5:17). Thus, in the Body of Christ, paradigmatically *feminine* "obedience" is revealed as masculine. In the Body of Hamartia, paradigmatically masculine "freedom" is revealed as feminine. The so-called "masculine" has a feminine core; the so-called "feminine" has a masculine core.

Conclusions

Paul's rhetoric exhibits a complex relationship to the Roman gendered ideology of empire. On the one hand, Paul certainly trades on the gender stereotypes supplied by this ideology and deploys them for his purposes. Paul paints Douglas's choice among institutions—the choice between Social Bodies—as a choice between the disordered, irrational, unjust, feminine Body of Hamartia and the ordered, rational, just, masculine Body of Christ. His portrayal of Hamartia as a *tribas* trades on a particular stereotype of femininity attempting to reach above its "natural" place—a stereotype assembled from the same imperial masculine insecurity that formed the core of Roman imperial ideology of masculinity.

On the other hand, his deployment of the *tribas* type for Hamartia—modeled as it may well have been on a particular reading of Roma as *tribas*, and so resonant with Suetonius's and Philo's critique of Gaius—seems to offer an opportunity for critique of the dominant ideology. By showing Hamartia as so clearly exercising a thoroughly masculine *imperium* precisely through her feminine enslavement to desire, Paul's use of Hamartia, while leveraging certain aspects of dominant Roman gender ideology, also ends up critiquing that same ideology's assumed correlation between self-mastery and sociopolitical *imperium*—domination. In other words, in terms of Stowers's two-stage schema for the development of the ideology of self-mastery, Paul more or less ascribes to the ancient Greek notion, but he is dubious of the Octavian deployment of this ideology as the founding analogy of empire. Of course, the fact is that even the earlier, "Greek" ideology was agonistic—militaristic, even (recall Plato's *Laws*)—and contained within it the core intuitions that Octavian's propagandists exploited. Therefore, a critique of the ideology's ability to deliver lasting *imperium* strikes at the heart of even that ideology's Greek core. For the one with ears to hear, Paul's rhetoric reveals that there was something fundamentally intemperate about temperance conceived of agonistically—militaristically.[137]

Then again, the goods that even the "effeminate" Christ delivers are, decidedly, the goods of the dominant ideology of masculine self-mastery. And the core of the critique of tribadic Hamartia—even if it amounts to a critique of Roma, the emperors, and therefore the ideological complex as a whole—never culminates in a systematic critique of the whole. Indeed, it depends on many of the categories it would have to deconstruct if it were to render such a thoroughgoing critique. That is, Paul would seem to have fallen into the same trap that the Seer does in Moore's reading of Revelation: "While overtly resisting the Roman Empire, John covertly replicates it, constructing an Empire of God on its model."[138] Whatever Paul says in the field of ancient gender signification, he seems mostly to repeat the hegemonic themes. Perhaps Price would suggest that Paul simply demonstrates, once again, the fundamental inseparability of religion and politics as "ways of systematically constructing power."[139]

According to Judith Butler, this sort of repetition is unavoidable: "All signification takes place within the orbit of the compulsion to repeat."[140] Even attempts to critique take place in this orbit and participate in repetition. The crucial ethical question, then, is: what sort of repetition is this? I take it that Paul's rhetoric can be read at least two very different ways. Each reading offers valuable insight into the character of the dominion of Sin that he describes.

In one mode, we might begin with the observation, made by many deconstructionists, that interpretation inevitably involves a performance—a repetition—of what it seeks to describe.[141] This would seem to hold true for an account of the dominion of Sin.[142] That is, in the description of the coercion of Sin, we might expect to find the coercive constraint of Sin on full display. Mary Douglas suggests that it is precisely when we try to understand the cognitive constraint placed upon us by systems that these same systems, within which we operate, most forcefully exert their constraint upon us, preventing us from describing their coercive power.[143] Since Paul is precisely describing the coercive constraint of Sin upon the moral psychology of its members, we ought to expect Paul's account to reflect this coercive constraint. And the repetition that Butler predicts—and that we've already noted—is quite evident in Paul's interpretation of Sin as tribadic Hamartia. Paul's language in describing Sin's coercive constraint on the moral psychology of its members inevitably betrays Paul's own subscription to many of Sin's cognitive structures.

On Hinkelammert's account, this is the sin that reveals itself to be "the Sin" because it precisely is *not* transgression of social norm. Rather, "the ethic confirms it, demands that it be committed."[144] In rendering his account of Sin in terms of essentially feminine enslavement to desire, Paul re-inscribes the norms of what can only be one of the coercive structures through which Sin operates in his culture. In so doing, Paul ironically validates—by enacting—what he describes in Rom 7:18: "I can will what is right, but I cannot do it." This ironic performance confirms what a careful reader suspects throughout Romans 5–8: namely, that it is quite possible to live (as Karin Knorr Cetina describes and ancient ideology of the social body presumed) as a member of more than one social body. Paul insists throughout Romans that this is not the case when it comes to the Body of Sin and the Body of Christ (e.g., Rom 6:2). The straightforward Pauline narrative is: you have died to Sin and risen to new life in Christ. The transfer from one social body to the other is instantaneous and complete. You cannot belong to both bodies; it is impossible. But Paul regularly asserts this impossibility precisely in issuing moral imperatives to the Roman churches to live, paradoxically, in the only way that, the narrative says, is possible for them (6:11–13, 19). Paul's felt need to repeat these imperatives, of course, makes clear that what is impossible within the compact narrative from which Paul argues, is in fact precisely the lived experience of many in the church in Rome: life in the "now-and-not-yet" of this transfer from one social Body to the other. Thus, even if Rom 7 is not intended by Paul to provide an account of the struggle of the believer caught between social bodies—something like Luther's *simul justus et peccator*—Paul's performance in these chapters of an explication of the social coercion of Sin, that itself shows evidence of that coercion, illustrates Luther's point brilliantly. Here is Paul, *simul justus et peccator*, nevertheless daring to name what Douglas warns may be unnameable.[145]

On the other hand, returning to Butler, we might read Paul's repetition of the dominant ideology as parodic. Given the inevitability of repetition, Butler argues, "agency is to be located within the possibility of a variation on that repetition"—that is, through subversive parody, specifically, parody that "reveals that the original identity after which gender fashions itself is an imitation without an origin."[146] It is certainly possible to see Paul's repetition of Roman gender categories in tribadic Roma and effeminate Christ as this sort of parody, so convoluted do the categories become in the process of his repetition. In championing an effeminate, obedient Christ—and inviting members to engage in emasculating, mimetic, obedient, co-crucifixion—Paul's Body of Christ performs a subversive parody of Roman (hyper-) masculinity. Ironically, only *this* effeminate body can deliver the "goods" of Roman masculinity. Therefore, on this reading, the lordship of the Davidic messiah, Jesus—declared son of God (1:4)—does not just question the lordship of Caesar; rather, it calls into question the entire ideological machinery that justifies Caesar's *imperium*. That ideology, as we have seen, was expansive, incorporating ideologies of gender, sex, ethnicity, class, and, of course, politics into a single ideology capable of justifying such massive imperial machinery. The coming reign of the crucified Jesus—and the reign of those crucified with him and with whom he shares his imperial benefactions (5:17)—calls each of these ideologies into question, and exposes them as structures through which Sin exercises its coercive dominion. As the instruments of Sin, Roman masculinity and empire are each exposed as an "imitation without an origin." Butler's words provide a near perfect statement of the ontology of s/Sin. The effeminate Body of Christ's parodic performance of masculine *imperium* exposes the slipperiness of these categories—even more, exposes that each participates in the slippery ontology of Sin.[147]

The ambivalence of the rhetoric of Romans is likely to remain resistant to simple resolution—even or especially by appeal to questions of Paul's intentions. One need only consider the inability of scholars to come to consensus on the significance of Rom 13:1–10 in resolving the question of Paul's political intentions in Romans—a passage which one might naively assume would rather straightforwardly solve the question in favor of an empire-friendly Paul.[148] Rather, the crucial questions are returned to the readers: how are we to name Sin and expose its dominion? If Butler and Douglas are to be believed, naming Sin will necessarily involve "repetition" of various sorts. Inevitably, perhaps, subject as we are to Sin's dominion, it will involve repetition of the "reinscription" type. This is the result of the coercive constraint of the dominion of Sin in which we still participate. Sin has framed the terms of the debate. We can use no other language than Sin's language. This is "prejudice" in Gadamer's sense. Using this language will always have the character of repetition. But we may also hope that our repetition may have a parodic, subversive, liberating—redeeming—character. Within Christian theology, this will have to do with the way the crucifixion functions as a moment of rupture, a moment in which we are "pulled up short," to use Gadamer's language once more.[149] Indeed, Moore's critique of the Seer's would-be parody of the imperial cult in Revelation is most damning if and only if the crucifixion is entirely comprehended without remainder within Moore's reading—if there is no parodic power left in the image of the "lamb who was slain."[150] If and when there is no parodic leverage left in the cross, Christian theology is impotent, unable to exercise "agency" in Butler's sense.[151] About this, Paul is, no doubt, correct: co-crucifixion is the linchpin of Sin's undoing (Rom 6:6). But if the cross retains its parodic power, it is the power of God for salvation (Rom 1:16).

CONCLUSIONS

A man was taken to the Zoo and shown the giraffe.
After gazing at it a little in silence: "I don't believe it," he said.

—DOROTHY L. SAYERS, *Clouds of Witness*

A friend once described this project as an exploration of what happens when exegesis reaches its limit. At the end of the day, that may be as good a description as any. Certainly, the methods employed here have hardly been restricted to those of a typical, modern exegete. While Paul's text was our starting point, the questions it raised about what counted as a "person" led us to visit the disciplines of evolutionary biology, philosophy of mind, entomology, cognitive science, and more. In Chapter 1, I proposed the justification for this trajectory: the interpretive decision about whether the personal language Paul uses to describe s/Sin is metaphorical or not has inevitably to do with our sense of the "actual state of affairs."[1] Our sense of what counts as a person necessarily informs our decision of how to interpret Paul's description of s/Sin as a person. Bultmann's demythologization allowed him to present a Paul consonant with a modernist, atomistic, individualist self, and Käsemann exposed this decades ago.[2] But while Käsemann's description of man under the authority of cosmic powers captures more of Paul's language, it seems to render that language irrelevant to the experience of modern Westerners, just as Bultmann predicted. What is this coercion under which Käsemann insists we live? Where in modern life should we look to see this coercion in operation? The phenomenology is missing.

Liberationists offer the missing phenomenology. The liberationist transposition of Pauline language of the coercion of s/Sin to a social register delivers an excellent phenomenology of the injustice and human brokenness that we experience everyday. Furthermore, if paired with a sophisticated ontology of both individuals and social structures, the liberationist account makes space for Bultmann's account of individual responsibility. But, there is a substantial potential cost. The liberationist account might simply amount to a new demythologization of Paul's concept of s/Sin—a socialist, structuralist repetition of Bultmann's individualist, existentialist demythologization. At stake is Paul's vividly mythological language, which Käsemann recaptured so well. Jerome Murphy-O'Connor's description of s/Sin's tyranny exemplifies the essence of this danger.[3] For Murphy-O'Connor, if s/Sin's tyranny is experienced in terms of the social constraint on individual freedom, then it is not a person—not an agent at all. This raises another question, to put alongside the more general question about personhood: what is the relationship of personhood to systems?

These, then, were the two questions that needed answering within our readerly context: what is personhood, and what is its relationship to systems? The hope from the outset was to find answers that would yield opportunities for synthesizing Bultmann's account of individual responsibility for sin, Käsemann's account of Sin's tyranny, and the liberationist phenomenology of unjust structural coercion. Emergentism provides precisely such answers, by supplying an account of personhood emergent from complex systems. That is, if Murphy-O'Connor suggests that systems cannot appropriately be described as exhibiting "intelligence" or personhood, emergentism suggests precisely the opposite: namely, that *every* intelligent, personal agent we know emerges from complex systems. This is true of the paradigm case of personhood, the individual human person, whose organismic self (body) and subjective self (mind) both emerge from complex biological systems.[4] These are "selves made up of selves," which are open to further combination into yet more complex wholes—more complex selves. This account of the human person—internally composite, and externally integrated into the environment—provides the necessary critique to Bultmann's atomistic individual. This same account yields a description of Käsemann's self—always under the rule of outside forces—that is nonetheless integrated with biological and psychological accounts of the self.

This is possible because this emergent ontology suggests the existence of a "mythological" level of reality that supervenes on the social. Here we may have nothing less than the solution to Käsemann and Bultmann's decades-long argument over mythology. In the account I have offered, mythology is to sociology as psychology is to biology. That is, "mythology," in the way I have used the word, describes the psychology emergent from social bodies. Mythological entities are subjective selves that emerge from social organismic selves. Various accounts of social cognition and corporate personhood—from Philip Pettit to Karin Knorr Cetina—offer what we might call "mythologies": that is, accounts of the cognition performed by social bodies.[5] As we would expect on an emergent account, these mythological "psychologies" exhibit characteristic downward causation on the cognition of the individual members of their social bodies, as described by Durkheim, Fleck, and Mary Douglas. As we observed in the racism case study in Chapter 2, such downward causation can trickle down even further, to the neurobiological level and beyond.

The central interpretive proposal for Romans, then, is this: we can make sense of Paul's language about Sin as a cosmic power by understanding Sin as a mythological person emergent from a complex system of human transgressions. In this sense, Sin would have a body—a (super)organismic self. It is this Body which Paul describes in Rom 6:6. This Body is ruled by the collective depraved mind of Rom 1:28, dominated, as it is, by passions and appetites (1:24, 26; 6:12). With a collective psychology emergent from a social body, Sin qualifies as precisely the sort of mythological person I described. Paul's description of this sort of social body fits within an ancient, quasi-Stoic, philosophical, common sense that social bodies, especially when united by shared habitual practices, were very real bodies, with collective minds and spirits. Paul's language in Romans shows that he considered the Romans to constitute a local social body, both before and after baptism (6:12). But, the fate of this local social body lies in its incorporation into one of two global bodies: either the Body of Sin or the Body of Christ. The existence of these two world bodies is the material manifestation of the overlap of the ages in which Paul understands himself and his churches to be living (1 Cor 10:11). Sin exercises its dominion through the control of the moral reasoning of members of its body—a process recognizable as downward causation, in the terms of emergence. Liberationist phenomenological accounts of this dominion describe it as socially mediated precisely through Sin's usurpation of law (Rom 7:8–9, 23). It is Sin's perversion of the law which reduces the moral psychology of the members of Sin's social body to futility (Rom 7:21–23). And, it is precisely the legalization of sin—or, even more, the outlawing of righteousness—that liberationists describe as the apex of the dominion of Sin. Sin's dominion is exercised—as predicted by Douglas—through the "founding analogies" that provide the social basis for individual cognition.[6]

Paul's account of Sin, of course, is itself subject to precisely this social coercion. His depiction of Sin as the insatiable woman, Hamartia, trades on stereotypes drawn from the dominant ideology of the Roman Empire. Paul describes her physiology precisely in terms of her enslavement to feminine desire. Her dominion is described in terms that would threaten Roman men who would submit to her rule with especially scandalous emasculation. But Paul's preaching of the obedient, crucified—that is, effeminate—Son of God, Jesus, embodies a parodic repetition of the dominant ideology's penetrating-and-impenetrable masculinity. The cross, exercising parodic agency against the founding analogies established by Sin, makes Paul's gospel both potentially shameful and yet also powerful (Rom 1:16). Mimetic obedience of this parodically masculine Christ in baptismal co-crucifixion marks the dissolution of the Body of Sin, and the possibility of new life in the Body of Christ (6:6).

Modern-Day Mythological Persons?

This account of Sin, in finding space for emergent mythological persons within a modern scientific worldview, raises important questions not just for Paul's context, but for the modern reader's context as well. Having made room for Paul's language within our sense of the "actual state of affairs," we have come to perhaps surprising conclusions about the world in which we live. The dominions of various emergent mythological persons, mediated through the social constraint on individual cognition, now seem like a very real possibility. The phenomenology provided by the liberationists, to the extent to which it resonates with our experience of the world's systems, perhaps seals the deal; this may well be the world we live in. But there is something in the modern Western mind that instinctively pushes back against such a conclusion. I have intentionally poked at these instincts by using the word "mythological" to refer to the level at which these persons emerge. In part, I do so precisely because the sorts of entities which, I have argued, emerge at this level—Sin, Roma, Mark's "Legion"—are entities that have been dismissed by modern Westerners as "merely mythological." If such entities have been demythologized through reduction, I would seek to re-mythologize them, through providing an emergent ontology to describe their existence.

To this point, the examples—liberationist phenomenology and the racism case study notwithstanding—have stayed safely in the ancient past. But if the "actual state of affairs" is as I have described it, we may have to ask: who or what are the persons emergent at the mythological level in *our* world? What social structures are sufficiently complex to give rise to emergent psychologies that exhibit cognition at the mythological level? In the case of *Roma*, I argued that we have not a "top-down" instrument of imperial control, but rather a "bottom-up" strategy for meaningful intercourse. For us, as modern people, we are immersed in a world of similarly complex—if anything, more complex—sprawling and convoluted systems of overlapping and reinforcing agencies that exhibit these same emergent, novel behaviors. As a result (as in the case of the citizens of the Greek East in the days of the Roman Senate), we find ourselves under the influence—indeed, under the tyranny—of agencies that overflow the bounds of individual human agents, even individual human institutions.

Ultimately, my instinct is that the mythological discourses we engage in are just as useful for us as they were for the ancients. Indeed, as I have argued throughout, this approach is probably more than a mere strategy. At the very least, it is a very familiar strategy, a foundational strategy—a strategy that we employ when we engage with one another, when we put to one side for a moment all of the biochemical goings-on of the human bodies around us and engage one another as higher-order emergent entities: that is, as human persons. We can see in various modern discourses that, regardless of how metaphorically we take ourselves to be speaking, we have found it useful, necessary even, to engage in personal discourse about entities emergent from very complex social, economic, and technical systems. Is it possible that in reading our world—as in reading Romans—we have mistaken "person-identification" for personification? I think so. When it comes to mythological persons, we modern Westerners are very much like Sayers's man at the zoo in the epigraph to this chapter. We regularly gaze at these sorts of persons—we even give them names, discuss their dispositions and plans—and then simply state, "We don't believe it." I would like to present just three cases—two quite briefly, the other in a bit more extended form: The Network, "The Man," and The Market.

I began this book with a quote from an AT&T marketing campaign that invokes mythological language in describing "The Network."[7] Is this mere literary personification, or is there some more immediate connection between this language and the "actual state of affairs"? Marketing is not the only discourse in which we find this sort of language applied to the vast Network that now connects everything from computers, to cellphones, to gym shoes, to coffee makers, and beyond. As individual "users" of this Network, we increasingly treat it as an entity with knowledge. This knowledge is gathered from other human users, but, at sufficiently large orders of complexity, it is simpler to conceive of the Network, or parts of the Network, as subjects in themselves. In this sense, the Network is at once "external" and yet "internal" to us—precisely because we are "internal" to it; we are members of its body, on which it exercises downward causation.[8] From the Network have emerged what Knorr Cetina certainly would call "epistemic subjects": communities that "know" before—and differently than—any individual does.[9] With the increased prominence of automated trading on the stock market, such epistemic subjects play an increasingly important role in whatever we might want to say about "The Market." Such features of the Network have driven some to write about the awakening of a "global brain."[10] It seems to me that the sort of emergent ontology of "mythological persons" that I have laid out in this project could be quite useful in theorizing these features of "The Network" in its sprawling, convoluted complexity.

Of course, mythological entities that emerge from entities at the social level also exert downward causation back on these structures and, through them, on the individuals within those structures, as well as their psychologies, and even their physiologies. Recall the example of the downward causation exercised by systemic racism on the neurobiology of American subjects.[11] While that example traced such causation beginning from the social level, we might observe that we often resort to mythological language in describing the collective agency exercised by various racist social systems as the agency of "The Man." A thorough account of racism, then—in its variegated incarnations in economic, educational, political, formal, informal, local, and national systems—might quite appropriately render an account of the emergent agency of these various systems in personal, mythological terms. "The Man" may be no matter of mere metaphor. We can see this, in part, in how useful this phrase has been to many different constituencies expressing various constructions of power. Hippies in the 1960s used the term to describe the federal government specifically, but also the various power systems that perpetuated the Vietnam War and racial discrimination. These were social facts that, in light of widespread culture opposition, appeared to enact Rom 7:15–20 at the social level. Racial discourse adopted the phrase specifically in order to describe the faceless power that keeps blacks in the United States from achieving socioeconomic parity. In feminist hands, the appellation also contains within it the power to name patriarchy as the "founding analogy" that lies behind any number of constructions of power, including racial, political, and gendered. These discourses of power take over our language and our cognition, and therefore conform to the description of institutional coercion offered by Douglas, Fleck, and Durkheim.

The startling disbelief in the face of first-hand evidence to the contrary is perhaps nowhere more evident than in modern Westerners' treatment of "The Market."[12] Modern popular economic discourse exhibits the same dynamic that initially caught our eye in Romans when it regularly positions "The Market" as the subject of active verbs. "The market corrected itself," we say, or, "The market reacted positively to today's news from the Fed," among many possible examples. Even subjective states are attributed to the Market: "the market showed a modest upside bias over the short-term."[13] Personification of this one entity quickly spills over into a profusion of vivid, mythological language: "There is a massive amount of liquidity on the sidelines but it's sitting behind a dam of fear," Stephen Leeb, president of Leeb Capital Management, reported during the 2008 financial crisis, personifying the "sidelined" liquidity and depicting it as lying behind what one can only describe as a mythological "Dam of Fear."[14]

Yet more intriguing, we use mythological language regardless of how we characterize the market, or what sort of economic theory we subscribe to. As we saw in the case of the various depictions of the mythological person emergent from the Roman state—depictions that varied depending on one's political location at either the center (Cicero's depiction of Nero as the empire's ruling spirit) or the imperial margins (the Greek East's Roma or Mark's "Legion")—the mythological depictions of the Market are certainly shaped by the location of commentators within the modern economic landscape. The most familiar discourse, perhaps, is that which claims Adam Smith as its spiritual father. This discourse holds that the Market is fundamentally rational, and therefore fundamentally trustworthy. This Market is guided by an invisible hand; it demands adherence to this orthodoxy. As Harvey Cox notes, the mythology of this Market is complete enough to ground a functional religion. Writing in 1999, not long after the "Asian Flu" financial scare, Cox describes the discourse surrounding this Market, which demands nothing less than religious faith:

> The East Asian financial panics, the Russian debt repudiations, the Brazilian economic turmoil, and the U.S. stock market's $1.5 trillion "correction" momentarily shook belief in the new dispensation. But faith is strengthened by adversity, and the Market God is emerging renewed from its trial by financial "contagion." Since the argument from design no longer proves its existence, it is fast becoming a postmodern deity—believed in despite the evidence. Alan Greenspan vindicated this tempered faith in testimony before Congress last October. A leading hedge fund had just lost billions of dollars, shaking market confidence and precipitating calls for new federal regulation. Greenspan, usually Delphic in his comments, was decisive. He believed that regulation would only impede these markets, and that they should continue to be self-regulated. True faith, Saint Paul tells us, is the evidence of things unseen.[15]

Cox goes on to describe capitalist orthodoxy's dominant doctrine of the Market God in terms of process theology. On this account, the Market does not possess the classical attributes of God—omnipotence, omniscience, and omnipresence—but rather wills to have them. Cox's discussion of the Market's will to omniscience is especially insightful, and resonates deeply with what I have already said about the social cognition of mythological persons: "The Market, we are taught, is able to determine what human needs are, what copper and capital should cost, how much barbers and CEOs should be paid, and how much jet planes, running shoes, and hysterectomies should sell for."[16] In the classical model, the Market performs this cognition through the aggregation of the choices of individual rational market participants—not unlike H. H. T. Prin's buffalo herd, voting on where the herd ought to go next through the individual gazes of the female members.[17] These are but the lower-level behaviors from which the Market's mythological cognition emerges. Individual rational actors are the neurons from whose interaction the classical Market's divine wisdom naturally emerges.

As we saw in the case of Bultmann and Käsemann's dispute, differing opinions on the nature of the mythological entity emergent from economic systems—the Market—are profoundly shaped by the model of the self which they work. And the (neo-)classical account of the individual rational human subject is being questioned by economists. John Coates cites economic orthodoxy's Cartesian account of the self as one reason to suspect deeply the classical account of the Market's fundamental rationality: "Today Platonic dualism . . . is widely disputed within philosophy and mostly ignored in neuroscience. But there is one unlikely place where a vision of the rational mind as pure as anything contemplated by Plato or

Descartes still lingers—and that is in economics."[18] In place of the classical rational agent, Coates argues instead for a model of the individual economic agent driven as often as not by what John Maynard Keynes called "animal spirits."[19] George Akerlof and Robert Shiller describe these animal spirits as "a restless and inconsistent element in the economy," one which sometimes paralyzes, and at other times energizes, market players and observers.[20]

In a certain sense, by "animal spirits" Akerlof and Shiller simply mean "emotions," or other such non-rational psychological states.[21] And in this sense, their use of "animal spirits" to explain large-scale economic phenomena is simply an attempt to include a richer account of the individual agent in a nevertheless reductionist macroeconomics. But when they talk about animal spirits at the group level, they can't keep from talking about group psychological states—for example, in describing the collective memory that allows various groups to form the stories that they say are irreducible to explaining macroeconomics.[22] These spirits contribute to the cycles of euphoria and pessimism that manifest in bull and bear cycles. Crucial to these cycles are feedback loops in which, for example, high prices and the confidence they inspire in traders become runaway trains, so-called "bubbles." These feedback loops mean that classical economic theory fails to explain the real activity of the market. Akerlof and Shiller conclude: "If then we are living with a system of feedback from price to animal spirits to price, we are in a world that is very difficult to predict."[23] Cycles of boom and bust are emergent properties of a sufficiently complex system—one that exhibits psychological states not simply at the individual level, but at the collective level as well.

These social-psychological states—what I have defined as properties of mythological entities, in this case, the Market—emerge from the convoluted interaction of individual manifestations of these animal spirits and the machinery of the market (the price-to-animal-spirit-to-price feedback). Coates describes this dynamic vividly when he insists that "a trading floor acts as a large parabolic reflector, and through the bodies of its thousand-odd traders and salespeople it gathers information from faraway places and registers early signals from events that have yet to happen."[24] For Coates, it is precisely the bodies of the trading floor personnel that collectively function to know something that the individual traders realize consciously only later. This is what Coates describes as the "biology of the market," or, the collective superorganismic body of the Market. This body can develop pathologies at the group level, becoming, for example "price and interest-rate insensitive" in the way that an individual body might become insensitive to a drug therapy.[25] This superorganism, of course, exercises downward causation on the bodies of the individuals who compose the superorganism. Coates has demonstrated this downward constraint all the way down to the hormone levels in traders' bodies. "Financial risk-taking is as much a biological activity, with as many medical consequences, as facing down a grizzly bear," he argues.[26]

Similarly, Coates extends the feedback loops that Akerlof and Shiller describe to include the feedback loops that exist between the psychological states and hormone levels of individual traders.[27] The result is that "during bubbles and crashes the financial community, suffering from chronically elevated steroid levels, may develop into a clinical population."[28] In the case of a runaway bull market, Coates describes cycles of pathological confidence inspired by testosterone. The sense of invincibility these cycles generate in the trader inspires Coates to offer a mythological (dis-)analogy:

> The ancient Greeks believed that at archetypal moments in our lives we are visited by the gods, that we can feel their presence because these moments—of battle, of love, of childbearing—are especially vivid, are remembered as defining moments in our lives, and during them we seem to enjoy special powers. But alas, it is not one of the Olympian gods, poor creatures of abandoned belief that they are, who touches us at these moments: it is one of our hormones.[29]

Of course, given that these hormones are both causes *and* results of the group-level cognition and agency exhibited by the Market, we might suggest that elevated hormone levels are themselves evidence precisely of (pseudo-)divine visitation, the downward causation exercised by the Market's social body on its constituents.

The Market's premonitions, realized on the bodies of the traders—computed through the precognitive secretions of various hormones—are only later realized at the individual, conscious level, as Coates's description of the floor manager at the moment the trading floor performs its collective prognostication demonstrates: "The head of the trading floor looks up from his papers and steps out of his office, surveying the floor like a hunting dog sniffing the air. An experienced manager can sense a change in the market, tell how the floor is doing, just from the sight and sound of it."[30] This is precisely how I suggested we might understand the ways in which individual scientists come to appropriate the knowledge first produced by the collective epistemic subjects emergent from high-energy physics experiments described by Knorr Cetina.[31] The system produces knowledge that the individual participants only later come to understand, "second-hand," as it were. The Market—through its quite material superorganismic body, composed as it is of biological organisms—performs the primary act of cognition at the mythological level.

As it turns out, just like Roma and Hamartia, the Market's superorganismic body has a gender problem.[32] But unlike Roma and Hamartia, the problem is excess masculinity, rather than femininity. Given the prominent role of testosterone in the feedback loops that generate the destructive boom and bust cycles that have defined our age, as well as Keynes's Depression era, Coates suggests that the clinical pathologies from which the Market suffers are directly correlated to the preponderance of young male bodies that constitute the trading floor superorganism. The result is that, in order to defuse "the explosive mix of hormones and risk-taking in the market," one must find a way of "changing its biology."[33] Coates's primary suggestion is that more women—who make up just 5 percent of the average trading floor—be introduced to the trading floor superorganism.[34] With testosterone levels of only 10 to 20 percent of those of men, women (as well as older men, whose testosterone levels naturally decline after age fifty) might possess the very real biological antidote to the Market's collective fever in bullish seasons, when irrational levels of risk-taking consume the hyper-masculine trading floor.

In sum, the neo-Keynesian reformation of classical economic ideology led by Shiller may provide yet more reason to view the Market as a mythological person, emergent from the convoluted machinery of global economic systems. So, when Akerlof and Shiller suggest that the only way forward is to "pay due respect in our thinking and in our policies to the animal spirits," one is left with a sense that the task is mythological.[35] And, indeed, as we saw in the case of Legion in Mark, and its echoes in the modern sub-Saharan colonial context, adopting mythological language to describe a complex system can be the foundation of a strategy of resistance to the deleterious coercion of mythological entities. Indeed, Walter Wink and Mary Douglas both argue precisely this case. Wink writes:

> By virtue of their greater duration in time and their immense magnitude of power, institutions take on a momentum of their own. They are suprahuman, and some of their characteristics are a heritage from the animal kingdom, as I have already remarked. They have their own spirits and tend to preserve themselves through all the shifts of personnel. They can be changed, but genuine change is a function of the change of both structure and spirit. It is not pious talk to say that to affect an institution you must touch its soul; it is shrewd advice. Otherwise, the more things change the more they stay the same. There must be a "conversion" of the spirit to the vision of its place in the larger Whole.[36]

Mythological language is no matter of "pious talk"; rather, it speaks to the "actual state of affairs," and is therefore essential to any viable strategy of social resistance. Mary Douglas concurs: "Only changing institutions can help. We should address them, not individuals, and address them continuously, not only in crises."[37]

Douglas would have us take this yet one step further. For it is not simply that we shoot ourselves in the foot, as it were, if we fail to recognize the loci of agency, the persons, that emerge from these complex systems—no, much more than that,

Douglas argues that it is the strategy of institutions to prevent us from identifying their agency. Douglas describes the persistent failure of scholarly projects that seem to want to target the institutional constraints on human cognition, and concludes that these failures are no coincidence.[38] Rather, they are the evidence of a persistent agency of our institutions themselves, seeking always and everywhere to keep their agency hidden. Douglas concludes: "So let no one take comfort in the thought that primitives think through their institutions while moderns take the big decisions individually. That very thought is an example of letting institutions do the thinking."[39] The institution's best defense is its invisibility. As we saw in chapter 4, this is how Sin operates, working through institutions and institutional norms ("law") such that we sin without consciousness of having sinned.[40] Naming the group-level minds, the institutional persons, the collective epistemic subjects that emerge from the machinery of globalization is the first step in any strategy of resistance against their (often ill) effects.

Toward an Emergent Hamartiology

I take it that there is a substantial constructive, Christian hamartiological program suggested by this emergent account of Pauline sin. While this program lies outside the scope of the present project, I would like to sketch out the general shape of that program, and suggest some avenues worth exploring. Perhaps most importantly, there is the contemporary Christian call to look with fresh eyes at the complex social structures of the contemporary world, and consider where and whether we are interacting with emergent mythological persons—or, indeed, where we are interacting with Sin. In some respects, I take it, this would be an update of the prophetic, social-theological aspect of Walter Wink's work, begun, in part, earlier, in my discussion of the Network, "the Man," and, especially, the Market. There is certainly much that remains to be said.

Similarly, while I concluded chapter 4 with a brief discussion of the implications of my emergentist account of the tyranny of Sin for individual culpability, a fuller systematic discussion yet remains. I suggested that an emergent account of Sin, for example, expands culpability. If this is true, how might this shape practices of confession and repentance? What would it mean to repent for contributing to the being and tyranny of Sin, under which all human beings are held hostage? Presumably, this universal culpability could be localized in terms of repentance for participation in sinful systems—but this may be selling Sin's dominion short. I have suggested that Douglas's "founding analogies" are a helpful picture of one of the mechanisms of Sin's dominion.[41] What would it mean to recognize that cognition, meaning-making, itself involves participation in Sin's dominion? In many respects, this would require wrestling with Paul's instinct that the Body of Sin is, in fact, a *world* body—that the creation itself has been subjected under

Sin's dominion (Rom 8:20). The world—especially when understood as "the world of signification"—in its entirety is subject to Sin.[42]

Such a truly cosmic scale of Sin's dominion makes Douglas's choice between institutions seem like an impossible choice. What sort of phenomenology of justification might we offer that would comport with the emergentist account of Sin's dominion which I have offered? The severity of the problem requires Paul to suggest a drastic solution: death through baptismal co-crucifixion with Christ (6:6). Sin's tyranny is, in a certain sense, inescapable. The only feasible option, therefore is to die to that world and be raised to new life in a new world-body, the Body of Christ. At the end of the last chapter, I began to explore how the concept of co-crucifixion contains within it the seeds of parodic "agency" of the sort that Judith Butler describes precisely in the context of prevailing "founding analogies" that make repetition of established norms inevitable. This is presumably a first step toward describing the social "trickle-down" of the mythological account of justification Paul offers in Rom 6. I have already suggested, however, that Paul's own language betrays the fact that a phenomenology of justification would not be quite so neat and clean as this death-and-resurrection narrative would suggest. "Dual membership" in these two world bodies seems to be possible. How is this to be understood? If the unifying habitual practice of the Body of Christ is cruciform parodic repetition of the prevailing thought patterns coercively maintained by the Body of Sin, then the slippery line between parody and naïve repetition would be the line that defines membership in one cosmic body or the other. While oppressive gender norms would presumably number among the thought patterns that ought be a target of cruciform parodic repetition, they would certainly not be the only one. The "Kingdom of God," while not particularly central to Paul's letters, is important enough in the gospels that dominant constructions of power and politics would presumably be targets of such cruciform parodic repetition. Market ascriptions of value, similarly, would require such treatment.

Any sustained reflection on an emergent account of justification would immediately run into questions about the fundamental analogy that, I have suggested, Paul makes between the Body of Christ and the Body of Sin. I suggested in Chapter 4 that while there are analogies to be drawn between the Body of Christ and the Body of Sin as cosmic, collective, social bodies, Paul also hesitates and insists that there are, of course, important disanalogies (Rom 6:19). Paul's apocalyptic dualism does not imagine a perfect balance of good and evil, of dark and light. These two bodies are opposite but not equal. No matter the symmetries, the Body of Christ and the Body of Sin are disanalogous, unsurprisingly, on the basis of the disanologies that exist between Christ and Sin—disanalogies which have to do, systematically, with the disanalogies between God and Sin. On this point, Philip Clayton's emergence-informed doctrine of God is helpful. Clayton employs a modified version of Hartshorne's dipolar theism—in which God has both an antecedent and a consequent nature. On Clayton's account, God's antecedent nature describes God as the Ground or Source of all things; God's consequent nature describes God as the "infinitely Related One."[43] Clayton encourages us to understand the consequent nature of God in emergent terms: "God can be introduced as that spiritual identity, presence, and agency that we come to know out of the physical world (the universe) taken as a whole."[44] Clayton is insistent, however, that we supplement this emergentist, panentheistic understanding of God with a robust account of God's antecedent nature as eternal Ground. I take it that one way of describing the disanalogy between the Body of Sin and the Body of Christ would be to say that Sin, as a counterfeit deity, has only an emergent, consequent nature.[45] The tyrant Sin only exists to the extent to which sinful humanity underwrites its being by participating in the complex systems on which the tyrant supervenes. So, while God is invested in the integrity of God's creation, Sin has no investment in the creation, and certainly no investment in the individual identity of each human creation.[46] Human persons are, for Sin, mere instruments, for Sin is invested only in the unfolding of the world that gives rise to its being, not at all in the being of the creation—or the identities of creatures—as such.[47] God adopts a fundamentally different posture toward the human creature:

> To speak, then, of the sovereignty of God in the life of free women and men is equivalent to saying that they have taken the true position that corresponds to them as human beings on the earth. Their position is not as beings inferior to God, but simply as God's creatures summoned to live worthily, to give life to all, to defend it, and to enjoy it in communion with others. The sovereignty of God coincides with the realization of the human being. The sovereignty of the idol coincides with dehumanization.[48]

Sin's dominion yields dehumanization; God's dominion yields realization of the human subject. How Tamez refrains from citing Rom 5:17, I do not know. What she describes is nothing other than the restoration of Adamic dominion to redeemed humanity. Indeed, as I argued in Chapter 5, "reigning in life" is one of the crucial goods that participation in Christ's body delivers that the Body of Sin is unable to deliver.

Finally, I return to Tertullian's "*Unde malum, et quare?*"[49] While the focus of this project has been on Sin rather than on "evil" more generally, I take it that the emergentist account of Sin I have offered might fruitfully be compared to various ontologies of evil put forward in the Christian theological tradition. There is something "slippery" about this ontology of Sin that seems appropriate to its subject. Both Karl Barth's description of sin as the "impossible possibility," and his account of *Das Nichtige* that menaces the human subject, seem to embody this same slipperiness, and might be refined by or offer refinement to the emergentist ontology of Sin I have described. Comparison with Augustine's account of evil as privation would presumably be similarly fruitful.

On its own terms, I take it that the emergentist ontology of Sin that I have offered has much to recommend it on purely systematic grounds. First and most importantly, this ontology of Sin places Sin decidedly on the creation side of the creator-creation divide—as it ought to be. Sin emerges from the convoluted networks of transgression formed by human creatures. Sin, therefore—even as a "cosmic power"—is decidedly "this-worldly." I frame this in terms of the creator-creation divide in order to mitigate what might otherwise seem like a major strike against the emergent account: namely, that Sin (and, by extension, other forms of spiritual evil, if the ontology of Sin I have offered were extended) can seem on this account to be rather "tame." This seems especially problematic when one thinks in terms of a natural-supernatural distinction. In this model, one expects a cosmic power like Sin to fall on God's side—the supernatural side—of the divide, rather than on the natural, human side. Indeed, if we were dividing up the world between "natural" and "supernatural" entities, this might make sense. But it is not clear to me that this is a useful taxonomic division. As an Enlightenment category intelligible only against the backdrop of scientific naturalism, "supernatural" is a category foreign to the Bible. Indeed, the categories "natural" and "supernatural" as they are regularly deployed in post-Enlightenment Christian theology are usually a hindrance rather than a help. The ontology of Sin I have offered highlights Sin's taxonomic alignment along a division much more significant for Christian theology: the divide between Creator and creation.

It is tempting to imagine extending this sort of ontology to another more obviously "supernatural" entity: Satan. The existence and reign of this figure, too, is hard to account for in a world created good by God. The theodicy problems Satan raises are analogous to the problems raised by Paul's account of Sin. Understanding Satan as a real person, emergent from complex systems of human transgression, and tempting us to further transgression through their exercise of marginal control by setting the boundaries of our moral cognition, might allow us to locate Satan's power and authority in human freedom. Is it possible that Satan, in fact, is a person emergent from human evil? One might be inclined to object based on the synthetic, biblical, theological account of Satan as Edenic tempter.[50] But we might make more progress if we treat the story of any "original" (in the temporal sense) sinful act as heuristic. That is, we may want to suggest that the only account we can offer of sinning is one in which we are "always already" under the thumb of a cosmic power that itself/himself/herself has emerged from our sinning. In that case, then, the dynamics I have offered here might also describe Satan's emergence, being, personhood, and dominion. In fact, once we start down this road, we might be inclined to go one step further and suggest that Satan and Sin share not just an ontology—a formal account of their being—but in fact might actually be the same entity. Indeed, while these figures have their own cultural histories, it is not clear to me that they may not, in fact, refer to the same realities, the same "actual state of affairs." Clearly, the labels "Sin" and "Satan" have significantly different connotations—and one would not want to flatten biblical or theological texts by equating the two. But it is possible that, constructively, one might want to say that they refer to the same personal entity who really does menace the human agent.[51]

Confronting Youth Violence: A Personal Story and Modest Ecumenical Hope

New Haven, Connecticut has been my home now for more than fifteen years. For nearly a decade, I have had the privilege of first planting and now pastoring— along with my wife and many others—a fledgling church community here in the heart of the city. Like many post-industrial cities across the United States, New Haven struggles with its fair share of typically "urban" problems. Chief among them, perhaps, has been the city's perennial struggle with youth violence. When the weather gets warm, the streets get "hot"—with young people shooting and sometimes killing one another. Each slaying seems to contribute to several more, committed in response and retaliation.

It is a reality that puts the issue of youth violence at the top of any pastor's list of priorities. Yet, I have noticed something interesting about the ways leaders from different theological backgrounds respond to the same crisis.[52] Ask an evangelical pastor what ought be done, and you will hear about the need to impact the individual lives of these young people. Change one heart at a time—save one soul at a time—and eventually the violence will subside. But ask a liberal pastor (mainline Protestant or Catholic) the same question, and the answer is very different. Focusing on the individual means ignoring a whole host of systemic factors that are the real culprits. If you want to stem the tide of youth violence in the city, you need to address the cycles of poverty and the unjust, racist systems in which these youths are trapped. Typically, a Pentecostal pastor has yet a third solution: "Show me where the stronghold of the Spirit of Violence is in this community. Let's go there; let's cast it out. Then there will be peace on the streets of the city."

Each of these pastors struggles with how to respond to a real, material problem in the city. By now, the schema I have used to describe their range of responses is familiar. More or less, I think we can see these various Christian theological traditions rendering an account of youth violence at only one of the following levels: individual (my stereotyped "evangelical"), social (my stereotyped "liberal"); or mythological (my stereotyped "Pentecostal"). Granted, these examples are straw men. Many pastors are self-aware enough of their own location within the diversity of global Christianity to understand that the sort of knee-jerk biases I have described do not capture the full picture of s/Sin's operation in the world—nor, therefore, of a robust Christian response. There are ecumenical instincts to bridge these divides. But even these instincts operate from a basic understanding that these differences exist—at least in terms of points of emphasis and priorities.

Beyond a sort of generous intellectual/theological humility, my hunch is that even these more self-aware, ecumenical pastors would have a hard time articulating precisely how each of these traditional Christian interventions against s/Sin—in terms of personal discipleship, social action, and deliverance ministry—could possibly be effective all at once. How would one intervention relate to another? How might social action accomplish the overthrow of a demonic power? How might demonic deliverance—or social action, for that matter—materially alter the psychology of the individual disciple? Doubtless, there is much that remains to be said, but my sense is that an emergent account of Sin offers a framework within which well-theorized answers to these sorts of questions might be addressed. Within such a framework, the state of the individual exists in a network of social relations that themselves function as the (quite material) body of the "spiritual" entities that exercise "spiritual" power over social structures and, through them, the individuals within them.[53] So, causation between various Christian interventions against Sin could be theorized along the lines of "upward" and "downward" causation.[54]

Personal discipleship would have "upward-causation effects" on the social structures in which the individual is embedded and, indeed, on the mythological entities that emerge from these social structures. Effective social action would have "upward-causation effects" on the mythological entities that emerge from the social structures reformed by such action, and also downward-causation effects on the personal entities embedded within the social structures addressed. Deliverance ministry would have downward-causation effects on the social structures in which the mythological entities addressed supervene and, further, on the individuals within these social structures, who constitute the social bodies of these emergent entities. In this sense, emergentism might become a framework within which to theorize the relationships between mutually reinforcing practices of resistance against Sin—practices which have long coexisted within the Church.

Only this sort of multilevel resistance is appropriate to Sin's well-integrated, multilevel dominion. It is the integrated practice of a community awaiting the fulfillment of the promise that "the God of peace will soon crush Satan under your feet" (Rom 16:20).

NOTES

INTRODUCTION

1. "A Network of Possibilities," http://www.business.att.com/enterprise/online_campaign/network.

2. For the perspective of an economist, see George A. Akerlof and Robert J. Shiller, *Animal Spirits: How Human Psychology Drives the Economy, and Why it Matters for Global Capitalism* (Princeton, NJ: Princeton University Press, 2009). Admittedly, Akerlof and Shiller's revival of John Maynard Keynes's "animal spirits" is more or less completely reducible to the psychology of individual human agents, but the language is nonetheless vivid and suggestive. (Keynes's original landmark work was John Maynard Keynes, *The General Theory of Interest, Employment and Money* [London: Macmillan, 1936].) For the perspective of a comedian, consider Stephen Colbert: "The market is fine . . . We are the ones who are not functioning properly . . . the free market . . . requires faith. It is a lot like believing in another all-powerful being—God. The market is all around us. . . . It guides us with an invisible hand. . . . Like God, if we have faith in it, the free market is the answer to all our problems—but if we doubt it, it will withhold its precious gifts . . . Some out there, folks, are going to say that this financial meltdown shows the market is fallible—that it is, in fact, not God . . . It does not mean that the market is not God. It means that the market is just a dangerous and destructive god" (Stephen Colbert, "Ye of Little Faith," *The Colbert Report* [2008]). For a theologian's perspective, see Harvey Cox, "The Market as God: Living in the New Dispensation," *Atlantic Monthly* 283, no. 3 (1999): 18–23. Modern mythological discourse about the Market is taken up again in the conclusion of the project.

3. "most of the work on personified Sin in Romans concerns whether one should define personified *s*in in an anthropological sense, that which people do, or *S*in in a mythological sense, under whom people are enslaved" (Joseph R. Dodson, *The "Powers" of Personification: Rhetorical Purpose in the Book of Wisdom and the Letter to the Romans* [Berlin: Walter de Gruyter, 2008], 20).

CHAPTER 1

1. In scholarship on Romans 5–8, the Greek noun ἁμαρτία is rendered variously: as "Sin" (with a capital "S"), as "sin" (with a lower-case "s"), or simply as ἁμαρτία or some transliteration thereof. For my own text I will adopt the convention obliquely suggested by Beverly Gaventa when she explains that, "in Romans in particular, sin is Sin—not a lower-case transgression ... but an upper-case Power that enslaves humankind and stands over against God" (Beverly Roberts Gaventa, "The Cosmic Power of Sin in Paul's Letter to the Romans: Toward a Widescreen Edition," *Interpretation* [2004]: 231). That is, while conceding that precision may not be possible in practice (especially when trying to describe the views of other scholars), I will use "Sin" when what is meant is a suprahuman power, "sin" when what is meant is a concrete action (or aggregate of actions), and ἁμαρτία when the meaning is meant to be left open. I will also occasionally use the neologism "s/Sin" when the contested meaning is especially foregrounded.

2. Rom 5:12, 20 (twice), 21; 6:12, 14; 7:8, 9, 11, 17, 20.

3. Jon Whitman, *Allegory: The Dynamics of an Ancient and Medieval Technique* (Cambridge, MA: Harvard University Press, 1987), 271–72 (emphasis original).

4. Whitman, *Allegory*, 272, citing Howard Rollin Patch, *The Goddess Fortuna in Mediaeval Literature* (Cambridge, MA: Harvard University Press, 1927), 16.

5. The circular argumentation would go as follows: Ἁμαρτία in Paul does not have "a basis in fact" for Paul because Paul's treatment of ἁμαρτία is mere literary personification. We know that Paul's treatment of ἁμαρτία is a case of literary personification because ἁμαρτία does not have "a basis in fact" for Paul.

6. Rudolf Karl Bultmann, *The New Testament and Mythology and Other Basic Writings*, trans. Schubert M. Ogden (Philadelphia: Fortress Press, 1984), 1–2.

7. Bultmann, *New Testament and Mythology*, 3–4.

8. Origen, *Philocalia*, 4.3.4.

9. Bultmann, *New Testament and Mythology*, 11.

10. "Thus, negatively, demythologizing is criticism of the mythical world picture insofar as it conceals the real intention of myth. Positively, demythologizing is existentialist interpretation, in that it seeks to make clear the intention of myth to talk about human existence" (Bultmann, *New Testament and Mythology*, 99).

11. Bultmann, *New Testament and Mythology*, 11.

12. Rudolf Karl Bultmann, *Theology of the New Testament*, trans. Kendrick Grobel (New York: Scribner, 1951), I, 244.

13. Bultmann, *Theology*, I, 245.

14. Bultmann, *Theology*, I, 245.

15. Bultmann, *Theology*, 251.

16. Bultmann, *Theology*, 251.

17. Bultmann, *Theology*, I, 253 (emphasis original). Compare Bultmann's description of "man's situation as an enslavement to powers for whose dominion he nevertheless is himself responsible" (Bultmann, *Theology*, I, 257).

18. Bultmann, *Theology*, I, 257.

19. Bultmann, *Theology*, I, 258–59.

20. Bultmann, *Theology*, I, 258.

21. Bultmann, *Theology*, I, 257–58.

22. Bultmann, *New Testament and Mythology*, 4.

23. Troels Engberg-Pedersen, *Paul and the Stoics* (Louisville, KY: Westminster John Knox Press, 2000), 17.

24. E. P. Sanders, *Paul and Palestinian Judaism: A Comparison of Patterns of Religion* (Philadelphia: Fortress Press, 1977), 522.

25. The key difference between the Fortuna example and Bultmann's struggle to make sense of ἁμαρτία has to do with constructions of cultural continuity. While the continuity for the medieval writers was simply the character Fortuna, more or less orphaned from her original literary home, Bultmann as a Lutheran, Christian theologian needs to stand in continuity with not just Paul's character, "Sin," but rather Paul's entire text, which is living and breathing, in his ecclesial context. This means that not just the character, Sin, but also the network of relationships and significations implied through Paul's (admittedly mythological) rhetoric need to find some explanation in Bultmann's appropriation in theology. It is this need for continuity that forces him to constrain Paul's meaning with Bultmann's own sense of what is "the actual state of affairs."

26. James J. Paxson, *The Poetics of Personification* (New York: Cambridge University Press, 1994), 7.

27. William Henry Temple Gairdner and John R. Mott, *Echoes From Edinburgh, 1910* (New York: F. H. Revell Company, 1910).

28. Bultmann, *New Testament and Mythology*, 42 (emphasis mine).

29. E. E. Evans-Pritchard, *Theories of Primitive Religion* (Oxford: Clarendon Press, 1965), 105–06.

30. E.g., John V. Taylor, *The Primal Vision: Christian Presence Amid African Religion* (Philadelphia: Fortress Press, 1963); Andrew F. Walls, *The Missionary Movement in Christian History: Studies in the Transmission of Faith* (Maryknoll, NY: Orbis Books, 1996). For the language of "primal" rather than "primitive' or "animist," see: Harold Turner, "The Primal Religions of the World and Their Study," in *Australian Essays in World Religions*, ed. Victor C. Hayes (Bedford Park, Australia: Australian Association for the Study of Religions, 1977).

31. Gillian M. Bediako, *Primal Religion and the Bible: William Robertson Smith and His Heritage* (Sheffield, UK: Sheffield Academic Press, 1997), 15.

32. The comment of Andrew Walls, in reflecting on his experience in living in Sierra Leone in the 1950s, is particularly striking on this point: "I still remember the force with which one day the realization struck me that I, while happily pontificating on that patchwork quilt of diverse fragments that constitutes second-century Christian literature, was actually living in a second-century church" (Walls, *Missionary Movement*, xiii). Walls, of course, is positing too facile a correlation between twentieth-century sub-Saharan Africa and the ancient Greco-Roman

context, one that may give the impression that in order to gain insight into ourselves "back then," we simply have to look at "them" "over there"—a general principle with which Walls would certainly disagree. For a more sophisticated theoretical discussion of the affinities between contemporary African and ancient Mediterranean conceptions of spiritual powers, see Albert Kabiro wa Gatumu, *The Pauline Concept of Supernatural Powers: A Reading From the African Worldview* (Colorado Springs, CO: Paternoster, 2008).

33. As an example from outside the missiological school, in chapter 5 we will examine, in some detail, Barrie Reynolds's description of a group of Rhodesians in the 1950s devoted to delivering their countrymen from *bindele* (European spirits), a colonial-era extension of a traditional notion of *mahamba* (possession by ancestral spirits). The *bindele* represent nothing less than the "demon of Colonialism," which John Dominic Crossan can't help but find illuminating of the exorcism of (the Roman) Legion(s) in Mark 5:1–16. See Barrie Reynolds, *Magic, Divination, and Witchcraft Among the Barrettes of Northern Rhodesia* (London: Chatto & Windus, 1963), 133; John Dominic Crossan, *The Historical Jesus: The Life of a Mediterranean Jewish Peasant* (San Francisco: Harper, 1991), 313–18.

34. For example, David J. Southall, *Rediscovering Righteousness in Romans: Personified Dikaiosynē Within Metaphoric and Narratorial Settings* (Tübingen, Germany: Mohr Siebeck, 2008), 59–60.

35. S. N. Eisenstadt, "Multiple Modernities," *Daedalus* (2000): 1–29; Jean Comaroff, "Missionaries and Mechanical Clocks: An Essay on Religion and History in South Africa," *The Journal of Religion* 71, no. 1 (1991): 1–17.

36. A 1958 *Mad Magazine* comic depicts the Lone Ranger surrounded by Indian adversaries, asking his Indian sidekick, Tonto, "What are we going to do?" to which Tonto replies, "What do you mean . . . WE?" (Joe Orlando, "TV Scenes We'd Like to See," *Mad Magazine* 1, no. 38 [1958]: 42). And indeed, in the style of the comic, we might imagine Bultmann and Engberg-Pedersen, surrounded by a throng of ancient biblical authors and their nefarious mythological "world pictures," turning to a typical "modern," twenty-first-century Christian for aid (a sidekick who, given current demographical trends, would be a sub-Saharan African), only to have the "modern" friend reply, "what do you mean, 'we'?" Beverly Gaventa has raised similar questions about how the word "we" is used to constrain the range of admissible interpretations of Paul on this point, particularly with respect to the work of Troels Engberg-Pedersen. See Gaventa, "Cosmic Power," 238.

37. Ernst Käsemann, *Commentary on Romans*, trans. Geoffrey William Bromiley (Grand Rapids, MI: Eerdmans, 1980), 150.

38. Käsemann, *Romans*, 147.

39. Martinus C. de Boer, *The Defeat of Death: Apocalyptic Eschatology in 1 Corinthians 15 and Romans 5* (Sheffield, UK: JSOT Press, 1988), 28, quoting, last of all, Käsemann, *Romans*, 176.

40. Käsemann, *Romans*, 150.

41. Käsemann, *Romans*, 198.

42. "Yet it [Sin] is not thought of like Death in Rom 5:12ff, that is, as a ruler of this age, but rather as a very personal tyrant" (Martin Dibelius, *Die Geisterwelt Im Glauben Des Paulus* [Göttingen, Germany: Vandenhoeck & Ruprecht, 1909], 120, translation mine).

43. Dibelius, *Geisterwelt*, 122, translation mine.

44. Käsemann, *Romans*, 198.

45. Käsemann, *Romans*, 150.

46. Southall, *Rediscovering Righteousness*, 99.

47. Southall gives much weight to Bultmann's comment (cited above) that "this language stamps *flesh and sin as powers to which man has fallen victim* and against which he is powerless," and is hesitant to put him as far to the extreme as someone like Bruce Kaye. Southall, *Rediscovering Righteousness*, 104–05, n.126. Most of his discussion centers around Bruce Norman Kaye, *The Argument of Romans: With Special Reference to Chapter 6* (Austin, TX: Schola Press, 1979).

48. For Southall's discussion, see Southall, pp. 99–102. Most influential of these would be Gaventa, "Cosmic Power," Timo Laato, *Paul and Judaism: An Anthropological Approach* (Atlanta, GA: Scholars Press, 1995), 75, whom Southall rightly categorizes as more extreme than Käsemann, and Johan Christiaan Beker, *Paul the Apostle: The Triumph of God in Life and Thought* (Philadelphia: Fortress Press, 1980), 189–90, 214. One might expect to include Walter Wink in the list of scholars to stand with Käsemann, interested as Wink is in reformulating Bultmann's demythologization project and in affirming the reality of what he calls "the Powers." However, Wink distinguishes "sin, law, and death" in Paul from these Powers, arguing that while Paul certainly shares a Jewish apocalyptic worldview, populated with "angels, gods, spirits, demons and devils . . . Paul has already taken key steps toward 'demythologizing' or at least depersonalizing it by means of the categories of sin, law, and death" (Walter Wink, *Naming the Powers* [Philadelphia: Fortress, 1984]), 104. On the point of Paul perhaps engaging in his own demythologization, Wink is followed by James D. G. Dunn, *The Theology of Paul the Apostle* (Grand Rapids, MI: Eerdmans, 1997), 110.

49. For Southall's complete inventory, see, Southall, p. 97, n. 92. The most important of these would be James D. G. Dunn, *Romans 1–8*, vol. 38a, Word Biblical Commentary (Dallas, TX: Word Books, 1988), 146, 272, 287, 335–37, 378–81; Dunn, *Theology of Paul*, 96, 110–13; C. K. Barrett, *A Commentary on the Epistle to the Romans* (New York: Harper, 1957), 128, 134, 142–4; N T. Wright, *The Letter to the Romans: Introduction, Commentary, and Reflections*, vol. X, The New Interpreter's Bible (Nashville, TN: Abingdon, 2002), 457, 525, 530. Wright may best fit in Southall's second category: "'Sin' takes on a malevolent life of its own, exercising power over persons and communities. It is almost as though by 'sin' Paul is referring to what in some other parts of the Bible is meant by 'Satan'" (457). We might also add here the intriguing mediating position of Emma Wasserman,

who argues that, while any personal language is figurative, sin really does exercise agency. Wasserman describes Paul as using sin "to stand in for the irrational passions and appetites that operate as an evil counter-ruler within the soul" in various Hellenistic philosophical (primarily Platonic) descriptions. See Emma Wasserman, "Paul Among the Philosophers: The Case of Sin in Romans 6–8," *Journal for the Study of the New Testament* 30, no. 4 (2008): 388. For Wasserman, Paul's language is figurative because she takes the philosophers' language to be figurative. For my part, I wonder if Paul's apocalyptic world view might not give him cause to deploy the philosophers' discourse with more vivid, literal intentions, as I argue he does with the language of moral psychology, in chapters 4 and 5.

50. Käsemann, *Romans*, 149.

51. Käsemann, *Romans*, 149.

52. Christine Gudorf, "Liberation Theology's Use of Scripture: A Response to First World Critics," *Interpretation* 41, no. 1 (1987): 5–18.

53. Emblematic both in its focus on the gospels and its non-Western methodology: Ernesto Cardenal, *The Gospel in Solentiname* (Maryknoll, NY: Orbis Books, 1976). For a discussion of Paul's reputation in liberationist circles: Neil Elliott, *Liberating Paul: The Justice of God and the Politics of the Apostle* (Maryknoll, NY: Orbis Books, 1994), esp. 75–82.

54. This debate has been well-documented by the Lutheran theologian Derek Nelson:Derek R. Nelson, *What's Wrong With Sin: Sin in Individual and Social Perspective From Schleiermacher to Theologies of Liberation* (New York: T & T Clark, 2009), 92–101.

55. Óscar Arnulfo Romero, *Voice of the Voiceless: The Four Pastoral Letters and Other Statements*, trans. Michael J. Walsh (Maryknoll, NY: Orbis Books, 1985), 183. "No es por ello pura rutina que repitamos una vez más la existencia de estructuras de pecado en nuestro país. Son pecado porque producen los frutos del pecado: la muerte de los salvadoreños, la muerte rápida de la represión o la muerte lenta, pero no menos real, de la opresión estructural" (Óscar Arnulfo Romero, *La Voz de Los Sin Voz: La Palabra Viva de Monseñor Oscar Arnulfo Romero* [San Salvador, El Salvador: UCA Editores, 1980], 189).

56. While most modern English translations obscure the intertextual resonance for "los frutos del pecado" (the fruits of sin, following the Gk. καρπὸν), the resonance in Spanish is quite clear: "¿Qué frutos cosechasteis entonces de aquellas cosas que al presente os avergüenzan? Pues su fin es la muerte. Pero al presente, libres del pecado y esclavos de Dios, fructificáis para la santidad; y el fin, la vida eterna. Pues el salario del pecado es la muerte; pero el don gratuito de Dios, la vida eterna en Cristo Jesús Señor nuestro." (Rom 6:21–23)

57. Elsa Tamez, "A Latin American Rereading of Romans 7," in *Translating the New Testament: Text, Translation, Theology*, ed. Stanley E. Porter and Mark J. Boda (Grand Rapids, MI: Eerdmans, 2009), 301.

58. Tamez, "Latin American Rereading," 297.

59. Tamez, "Latin American Rereading," 297.

60. Tamez, "Latin American Rereading," 301, 297.

61. José Ignacio González Faus, "Sin," in *Systematic Theology: Perspectives From Liberation Theology: Readings From Mysterium Liberationis*, ed. Jon Sobrino and Ignacio Ellacuría (Maryknoll, NY: Orbis Books, 1996), 198 (emphasis original).

62. International Theological Commission, "Declaration on Human Development and Christian Salvation" in Nelson, *What's Wrong With Sin*, 92.

63. *Liberatis Nuntius*, IV.35 in Nelson, *What's Wrong With Sin*, 95.

64. Or, at the very least, they must be consequences "more" so. Ratzinger does not provide a theoretical framework for his apparent sliding scale of cause and consequence.

65. Juan Luis Segundo, *Evolution and Guilt* (Maryknoll, NY: Orbis Books, 1974), 72–73.

66. Nelson, who in many ways share's the Vatican's concerns, describes the problem with attributing agency to social sin: "Yet in all these various ways, the danger of exculpation looms large" (Nelson, *What's Wrong With Sin*, 97).

67. Nelson, *What's Wrong With Sin*, 101.

68. Leonardo. Boff, *Liberating Grace* (Maryknoll, NY: Orbis Books, 1979), 141–42.

69. Wink's understanding of "The Powers" (which do not, for him, include Sin) is relevant here. Indeed, Wink's work was born, as he describes it, out of a shocking encounter with "the everyday crush of oppression" in Latin America (Wink, *Naming the Powers*, ix). While critical of what he sees as a liberationist tendency to reduce the Powers "almost entirely to social structures," he shares their instincts vis-à-vis the evil of social structures: "The heavenly powers are not mere projections that mystify the real power relations. They are, quite the contrary, the real interiority of earthly institutions, systems and forces" (Wink, *Naming the Powers*, 6, 135). Sharing, as he does, this basic liberationist instinct, it is noteworthy that he also shares the idea that the key to understanding the reality of these social structures lies in a coordinate understanding of ourselves: "Is this not also the way we experience our own selves? For centuries philosophers and science sought in vain to locate the 'seat of the soul' in some physical organ. Today almost everyone agrees that no such organ exists but that the soul or self is the active awareness of the entire living body itself. And yet this 'withinness' is experienced as more than simply the sum of its parts . . . In an odd way, we seem to experience our selves as 'outside' or 'above' or 'transcendent' to our bodies, even though the self is clearly the interiority of all that flesh. But this is one of the ways interiority is known . . . We experience the self as distant from or outside the body in precisely the same way that we experience the Powers generally" (Wink, *Naming the Powers*, 144). Of course, even as there is a formal similarity, Wink and Boff also differ in important ways. Wink's conception of the self is about "interiority," whereas Boff is about "sociality," just as for Wink the powers are the "interiority of earthly institutions," whereas for Boff sin is primarily "social sin."

70. Boff, *Liberating Grace*, 141–42. While we are certainly working within a theological framework here, it is worth noting that such a radical decentering of the individual sounds quite at home within a Pauline—or indeed, any ancient Mediterranean—context.

71. Jerome Murphy-O'Connor, *Becoming Human Together: The Pastoral Anthropology of St. Paul*, 2d ed. (Wilmington, DE: M. Glazier, 1982), 92, 97.

72. Murphy-O'Connor, *Becoming Human*, 96–97.

73. Murphy-O'Connor, *Becoming Human*, 98–105.

74. Murphy-O'Connor, *Becoming Human*, 101.

75. Nelson quotes Chopp: "Sin results in suffering, the suffering of creation groaning in travail, the suffering of children without any hope. Sin manifests and embraces suffering, the suffering of lost identity, the suffering of freedom without a future, and the suffering of a future without freedom. Sin extracts its price as the victimization of the poor, the suffering of the tortured, the dispossession of the homeless. These are the victims of sin not because of moral inferiority or human depravity, but because they bear the brunt and carry the special burden of the world's sin. In the retrieval of this symbol, sin's arena is human praxis and its primary realization is massive global injustice" (Rebecca S. Chopp, *The Praxis of Suffering: An Interpretation of Liberation and Political Theologies* [Maryknoll, NY: Orbis Books, 1986], 105).

76. Nelson, *What's Wrong With Sin*, 113.

77. Language of "higher" and "lower" levels of analysis will be introduced with more precision in the next chapter. For now, let it suffice to say that there is nothing "spooky" intended. That is, I am *not* making a claim like the one Wink makes when he comments that "we speak of heaven as 'up' because it does have its own unique spatial quality at the symbolic level" (Wink, *Naming the Powers*, 144). Rather, "lower" levels of analysis here are taken to be levels more fundamental: for example, physics involves a lower, more fundamental, level of analysis than does chemistry; chemistry involves a lower level of analysis than does biology, and so forth.

78. Indeed, in Christian Smith's critical-realist account of personhood, causal agency plays an almost determinative role. See Christian Smith, *What is a Person?: Rethinking Humanity, Social Life, and the Moral Good From the Person Up* (Chicago: University of Chicago Press, 2011), 14–15.

79. In fact, at several points, we have seen interpreters' needs to marginalize Paul's apparent position in order to protect their own ontologies. Bultmann and Murphy-O'Connor, in fact, each resort to name-calling in order to foreclose upon vividly mythological readings of Paul. Bultmann's marginalizing of "certain unstable minds" has been discussed. Murphy-O'Connor's invocation of the minds of "simple people" earlier seems to function in a similar way. I admit, upon my first reading of Murphy-O'Connor, to being unable to keep from bursting out: "simple people like Paul?!"

There are, of course, those who are convinced they can know Paul's intentions by reading "behind the text," as Tamez says. Engberg-Pedersen and Emma Wasserman, for example, do so through philosophical constructions of Paul that allow them to use the technical writings of elite philosophical schools to construct what Paul could or could not have taken to have been the "actual state of affairs" when it came to personification of abstractions. Of course, ancient philosophy can be a great help as we try to construct Paul in his ancient environment. In chapters 4 and 5, I will suggest that Paul's personalist language—when understood as referring to social bodies rather than abstractions—fits quite nicely within a pluralist ancient philosophical environment. But I think it is important that we remember that Paul is not an elite Hellenistic philosopher (I do not take him to have had a philosophical education), but rather a religious teacher using philosophical ideas as suit his rhetorical purposes. Paul may deploy the discourses of ancient philosophy in ways that fundamentally shift the realm of what might possibly the "actual state of affairs." For example, for Paul—though not for most Hellenistic philosophers—the world is full of angels, demons, powers, and principalities. When Paul deploys ancient philosophical discourses—and I think he does—he transfers these discourses into a very different cosmic imaginary. Citing ancient philosophical common senses about what could or could not possibly be the "actual state of affairs" cannot help us set boundaries on the Pauline realm of the real.

80. Hans-Georg Gadamer, *Truth and Method*, trans. Joel Weinsheimer and Donald G. Marshall, 2d rev. ed. (New York: Continuum, 2003), 294–95, n. 224.

CHAPTER 2

1. This terminology corresponds with Bultmann's, but is intended without his Modernist bias. This project could rightly be described as one of "re-mythologization." The "mythological" level is formally introduced and defined at the end of the next chapter.

2. Admittedly, this is a modest concept of ontology, but philosophical modesty will be a hallmark of this chapter. We will find at multiple turns that philosophical arguments of various kinds can be left unresolved, while still providing the framework we need to move our particular conversation forward. If we wanted to retain a much more robust meaning for the term "ontology," we might instead have to concede that such a robust concept may be beyond the reach of the kinds of concepts with which scholars of religion must concern themselves. (Indeed, the research reviewed in the next two chapters would suggest that the list of excluded concepts might have to include that of intentions, the human person—even the integrated biological organism.) Some other term, like "functional ontology." would then have to be introduced, and the argument would proceed in the same direction that it has with this much more modest definition of ontology.

3. For the danger of certain sorts of intentional concepts in biological explanation, see the discussion of homunculi in Terrence W. Deacon, *Incomplete Nature: How Mind Emerged From Matter* (New York: Norton, 2011), 46–56.

4. In a series of lunches at Yale during the 2010–11 academic year on the topic of emergence, the many biologists gathered were able to chuckle about these arguments and the ways that pit one sub-discipline against another.

5. Philip Clayton adopts the term "trans-ordinal" from C. D. Broad. See Philip Clayton and Paul Davies, eds., *The Re-Emergence of Emergence: The Emergentist Hypothesis From Science to Religion* (Oxford: Oxford University Press, 2006), 9. In philosophy of science, "trans-ordinal" designates what applies across multiple scientific disciplines, an multiple levels of abstraction and analysis. For a detailed discussion of levels and ontology, see Claus Emmeche, et al., "Explaining Emergence: Towards an Ontology of Levels," *Journal for General Philosophy of Science* 28, no. 1 (1997): 83–117.

6. Establishing the plausibility of my reading of Paul will have to do with the plausibility of the emergence paradigm, so I am going to describe emergence in some detail. Readers quite familiar with—and more or less persuaded by—this framework may want to skip to chapter 3, where I make more novel (or at least, more idiosyncratic) interventions within the emergence frame.

7. As will become clear in some of the conversation that follows, I am using the word "supervenience" in a slightly idiosyncratic way. More detail is available later in the chapter. For now, let it suffice to say that I mean simply to describe one side of emergence's generative dialectic: the fact that emergents "sit on top of" lower-level entities, properties, or processes. This is the side of the dialectic which Christian Smith calls simply "emergence." See Smith, *What is a Person?*, 40.

8. Emergence, as the discussion to come will amply demonstrate, is a contested theory. My instinct is that emergence, in its many rival versions (as described in the pages that follow), contains important insights that are quite valuable in solving the sorts of problems presented by Paul's description of s/Sin in Romans. However, as a (trans-ordinal) scientific theory, emergence is falsifiable. It may turn out not to be true. If one or two wrinkles change, my sense is that much of what I say about s/Sin will be largely unchanged. But more substantial changes—or, indeed, the falsification of the theory—would mean that my account of s/Sin would have to change—and this is perhaps as it ought to be. Doing theology (I mean to include biblical studies in that category) in dialogue with science—especially alongside the cutting edge of scientific reflection—means making theology vulnerable to scientific advance. But if we want to do theology that makes normative claims about the world as it actually is, then dialogue with science is necessary, and we must assume the risks that such dialogue entails. (Indeed, if the argument of the last chapter is accepted, engaging critically with our best understanding of "the actual state of affairs" is often a necessary component even of "bare exegesis.") In this context, intellectual courage is a theological virtue.

9. Timothy O'Connor and Yu Wong Hong, "Emergent Properties," *The Stanford Encyclopedia of Philosophy*, http://plato.stanford.edu/archives/spr2009/entries/properties-emergent (emphasis mine).

10. For a celebration of the interdisciplinary nature of the concept, see Clayton and Davies, *Re-Emergence of Emergence*.

11. Alexander Bird, "Causal Exclusion and Evolved Emergent Properties," in *Revitalizing Causality: Realism About Causality in Philosophy and Social Science*, ed. Ruth Groff (New York: Routledge, 2008), 163–64.

12. R. O. Prum, et al., "Coherent Light Scattering By Blue Feather Barbs," *Nature* 396, no. 6706 (1998): 28–29. "Color," it turns out, is also quite significantly an issue of perception, such that the color "blue" may have to be theorized as emerging from the interference patterns of the scattered light *and* the perceptual faculty of the observer.

13. Robert Wilson describes this as "the *superorganism* tradition in evolutionary biology," which holds that "in certain groups of living things—in particular, in colonies of *Hymenoptera*—it is the group rather than the individual organism that lives in those groups, that functions as an integrated unit, having many of the properties that individual organisms possess in other species. Individual bees, ants, and wasps function more like organs or (parts of) bodily systems in those species" (Robert A. Wilson, *Boundaries of the Mind: The Individual in the Fragile Sciences* [Cambridge: Cambridge University Press, 2004], 268). The superorganism tradition will be of special relevance in the next chapter.

14. Edward O. Wilson, *The Social Conquest of Earth* (New York: Liveright, 2012).

15. The search for the so-called "grandmother cell"—that is, the individual neuron that codes a particular psychological unit, in this case, the memory of one's grandmother—has to this point been in vain. More complex and distributed methods of conceptual encoding seem to be employed in the brain. Charles G. Gross, "Genealogy of the 'Grandmother Cell'," *The Neuroscientist* 8, no. 5 (2002): 512–18.

16. John R. Searle, *Philosophy in a New Century: Selected Essays* (Cambridge: Cambridge University Press, 2008), 124. See also Deacon, *Incomplete Nature*, 28.

17. Philip Clayton, *Adventures in the Spirit: God, World, Divine Action* (Minneapolis: Fortress Press, 2008), 66.

18. Though of course, we do well to remember that the more ambitious meta-theory is always drawing on the basic kinds of questions about the relationships of parts and wholes that we asked earlier, in our examples of property emergence.

19. Italian scientist, physician, and Nobel Laureate Camillo Golgi is considered by many to be the father of modern neuroscience. Paolo Mazzarello, *Golgi: A Biography of the Founder of Modern Neuroscience*, trans. Aldo Badiani and Henry A. Buchtel (Oxford: Oxford University Press, 2010).

20. Indeed, no less an authority than Louis Pasteur declared his continued support of vitalism as late as 1860. Paul S. Cohen and Stephen M. Cohen, "Wöhler's Synthesis of Urea: How Do the Textbooks Report it?," *Journal of Chemical Education* 73, no. 9 (1996): 884. Vitalism in biology persisted at least as late as L. R. Wheeler's 1939 work (L. R. Wheeler, *Vitalism: Its History and Validity* [London: H. F. & G. Witherby Ltd., 1939]).

21. This does not mean that the theory has surrendered its influence on philosophy of science, especially philosophy of biology. Vitalism has had something of a productive afterlife as a discredited theory, serving as a signifier of what remains to be explained by some other mechanism than a vital substance. Consider Foucault's assessment: "if the 'scientificization' process is done by bringing to light physical

and chemical mechanisms . . . it has on the other hand, been able to develop only insofar as the problem of the specificity of life and of the threshold it marks among all natural beings was continually thrown back as a challenge. This does not mean that 'vitalism' . . . is true . . . It simply means that it has had and undoubtedly still has an essential role as an 'indicator' in the history of biology" (Michel Foucault, "Introduction," in *The Normal and the Pathological*, ed. G. Canguilhem [New York: Zone Books, 1989], 18, cited inMonica Greco, "On the Vitality of Vitalism," *Theory, Culture & Society* 22, no. 1 [2005)]: 17).

22. John Searle's rejection of various dualisms and "trialisms" is typical: "It is a kind of mystification to suppose that because we can write poems and develop scientific theories, somehow or other these inhabit a separate realm and are not part of the one real world we all live in" (John R. Searle, *Freedom and Neurobiology: Reflections on Free Will, Language, and Political Power* [New York: Columbia University Press, 2007], 22).

23. Though, as we will see in the account of chemistry given by emergentist philosophers of chemistry, the philosophical significance of this unification is still disputed, precisely in terms of whether or not physical chemistry amounts to a *reduction* of chemistry to physics.

24. So dualisms are "disjunctive trans-ordinal theories."

25. The relationships among these levels may well be more complex than a simple layering; there are also, in many cases, important sub-levels that could be added to give a more complete picture of the complexity of the world as it actually is.

26. While this synchronic relationship is a matter of "causation" for a reductionist, it is not necessarily so for an emergentist, who might well be inclined, at the very least, to distinguish between the various causes invoked in the description of a complex system. Emmeche et al., for example, argue that this synchronic "causation" is hardly the same type of "cause" generally invoked in scientific description: "Very often the idea of a temporal succession in the creation of new levels is spontaneously interpreted so as to imply a causal process. This idea leads to a metaphysical mistake which is evident when one considers objects in which several levels coexist at the same time: the idea that the lower levels cause the higher levels to exist. Of course this is true in a common-sense use of the word 'cause' but not in the standard scientific way of using it: if the higher level consists of units of the lower level, then they exist simultaneously. There is no temporal, causal process going on 'creating' the higher level out of the lower one, and no reductionist saying so has ever been able to show a cause running from the lower towards the higher level" (Emmeche et al., "Explaining Emergence: Towards an Ontology of Levels," 93).

27. P. M. Churchland, "Eliminative Materialism and the Propositional Attitudes," *The Journal of Philosophy* 78, no. 2 (1981), 67.

28. It would seem that one would not want to call such a thing a "belief," since the content of the belief is that beliefs are an illusory category.

29. The Churchlands, cited above, would be among those who support such a position. But reading such work, we must ask: who is it that has come to understand that "I" am merely a useful fiction?

30. Philosopher Jaegwon Kim enumerates several reasons for wanting to save mental causation at the beginning of his book, which ultimately argue for a physical reduction that is compatible with mental causation. See Jaegwon Kim, *Physicalism, or Something Near Enough* (Princeton, NJ: Princeton University Press, 2008), 9–10, 159–60. I will return to Kim's theory later in the chapter.

31. Deacon, *Incomplete Nature*, 28.

32. Searle, *Freedom and Neurobiology: Reflections on Free Will, Language, and Political Power*, 26. It should be noted that Searle's Scylla is "materialism," rather than strict reductionism, though strict reductionism, as I've described it, shares much in common with Searle's materialism.

33. Robert Van Gulick, "Reduction, Emergence, and Other Recent Options on the Mind/Body Problem: A Philosophic Overview," *Journal of Consciousness Studies* 8, nos. 9–10 (2001), 26. See also Deacon, *Incomplete Nature*, 174. In part, the term "emergence" has taken on such an expansive range of use because it is so useful for addressing many questions and concerns of contemporary science. For comparison, the New Testament scholar might think of the fate of the term "apocalyptic" in the study of ancient Christianity and Judaism in the second half of the twentieth century.

34. For complaints about the lack of a consistent meaning of emergence in various different accounts, see Peter A. Corning, "The Re-Emergence of 'Emergence': A Venerable Concept in Search of a Theory," *Complexity* 7, no. 6 (2002): 18–30; R. Keith Sawyer, "Emergence in Sociology: Contemporary Philosophy of Mind and Some Implications for Sociological Theory," *The American Journal of Sociology* 107, no. 3 (2001): 551–85; Jaegwon Kim, "Emergence: Core Ideas and Issues," *Synthese* 151, no. 3 (2006): 547–59.

35. George Henry Lewes, *Problems of Life and Mind* (London: Trübner & Co., 1877). Water's chemical properties (its transparency, its index of refraction, its freezing and boiling points, its adherence to certain physical laws) were, at least at that time, impossible to explain on the basis of considering it a compound of hydrogen and oxygen. As we will consider further, whether or not chemical properties are completely reducible to physical laws is still debated. Philosophers, as a rule, assume contemporary complete reduction of chemistry into physics via quantum mechanics, though some contemporary chemists are not so convinced. One might contrast Sawyer, "Emergence in Sociology," 560 and Joseph E. Earley, "How Philosophy of Mind Needs Philosophy of Chemistry," *HYLE* 14, no. 1 (2008): 1–26.

36. Samuel Alexander, *Space, Time, and Deity: The Gifford Lectures At Glasgow, 1916–1918* (London: Macmillan, 1920).

37. Intra-ordinal laws operate at a single order (e.g., the laws within psychology or the laws within Newtonian mechanics), while trans-ordinal laws operate across these

orders and describe how higher-level properties emerge from lower-level properties (e.g., laws that would govern how the human mind emerges from the biology of the brain). See C. D. Broad, *The Mind and Its Place in Nature* (New York: Harcourt, Brace & Co., 1925).

38. While the discussion that follows largely depends on Sperry, the basic principles of emergence first reappear largely in their contemporary form in Polanyi's 1962 Terry lectures: see Michael Polanyi, *The Tacit Dimension* (New York: Doubleday, 1967). Polanyi's discussion of boundary conditions will be of particular import in the next chapter.

39. Roger Wolcott Sperry, "A Modified Concept of Consciousness," *Psychological Review* 76, no. 6 (1969), 532–33.

40. Sperry's use of the term "supervene" was not followed by later emergentists, who retain the term but deploy in a different way (described later in the chapter). What Sperry seems to be describing here later emergentists call "downward causation."

41. Sperry, "Modified Concept," 533–34.

42. Sperry, "Modified Concept," 534.

43. For example, William Hasker, *The Emergent Self* (Ithaca: Cornell University Press, 1999); Smith, *What is a Person?*

44. Sawyer, "Emergence in Sociology," 555–56. The term "supervenience" is almost as notoriously slippery as the term "emergence." Originally, the term was coined by moral philosophers as a way of describing the relationship between two sets of properties (R. M. Hare, *The Language of Morals* [Oxford: Clarendon Press, 1952]; G. E. Moore, *Philosophical Studies* [New York: Harcourt, 1922]). Philosophers of science then took up the term as a way of describing the relationships between sets of entities, properties, and processes at two adjacent levels of scale and complexity. This gives rise to the language of "supervenience bases"—those lower-level entities, properties, and processes upon which emergents depend ontologically. This is the way I mean to use the term (and the way I take Sawyer to employ it here). That is, "supervenience" describes the way that higher-level entities, properties, and processes "sit on top of" the lower-level entities, properties, and processes from which they emerge. Only later, in the work of Jaegwon Kim, did the term "supervenience" come to refer precisely to an alternative to emergence. (So, e.g., Smith, *What is a Person?*, 31–32, which cites Kim.) I persist in using supervenience in the more generic sense of describing a relationship between higher- and lower-level properties precisely because I take this relationship (not entirely unlike Kim describes it) to be one crucial component of a robust account of emergence—an account which, as we will see below, Kim does not endorse. As noted, Sperry's earlier use of the word "supervene," which seems to mean "exercise downward causation upon" is idiosyncratic to him—and nearly the opposite of how I will use the word. For examples of the sort of usage of the terminology I take to be standard, see Graham MacDonald and Cynthia MacDonald, *Emergence in Mind* (Oxford: Oxford University Press, 2010), 145–46; Emmeche et al., "Explaining Emergence: Towards an Ontology

of Levels," 93–94; Timothy O'Connor and John Ross Churchill, "Nonreductive Physicalism or Emergent Dualism? The Argument From Mental Causation," in *The Waning of Materialism*, ed. Robert C. Koons and George Bealer (Oxford: Oxford University Press, 2010), 261–79.

45. There is further differentiation here between those, on the one hand, who understand emergents to be unexplainable in principle—that is, such emergents cannot now and never will be explainable at the lower level—and those, on the other hand, who understand emergents merely to be unexplainable by science as we have it now, but hold out hope that further research will ultimately vindicate the reductionist program.

46. Philip Clayton argues on the basis of the necessity of invoking biological entities in biological explanations that such entities ought to be construed as real. Clayton, *Adventures*, 90.

47. Mario Augusto Bunge, *Emergence and Convergence: Qualitative Novelty and the Unity of Knowledge* (Buffalo: University of Toronto Press, 2003), 21 in Poe Yu-ze Wan, "Emergence a la Systems Theory: Epistemological Totalausschluss or Ontological Novelty?," *Philosophy of the Social Sciences* 41, no. 2 (2011): 185. Compare a similar passage earlier in Bunge's corpus: "explained novelty is no less novel than unexplained novelty, and predicted novelty is no less novel than unpredicted (or perhaps even unpredictable) novelty: the concept of emergence is *ontological*, not *epistemological*." Martin Mahner and Mario Augusto Bunge, *Foundations of Biophilosophy* (New York: Springer, 1997), 29. In addition to Bunge, see also the comments of social theorist Dave Elder-Vass regarding what he calls "the redescription principle": "This is the principle that if we explain a causal power in terms of (i) the parts of an entity *H*; plus (ii) the relations between those parts that pertain only when they are organised into the form of an *H; then* because we have explained the power in terms of a combination—the parts and relations—that exists only when an *H* exists, we have not eliminated *H* from our explanation. The entities that are *H*'s parts would not have this causal power if they were not organised into an *H*, hence it is a causal power of *H* and not of the parts. The *lower level* account of *H*'s powers merely *redescribes* the whole, which remains implicit in the explanation. In other words 'upper and lower level accounts refer to the same thing, as a whole and as a set of configured interacting parts' (Wimsatt, 2006, p. 450) and hence a causal explanation which invokes the set of configured interacting parts implicitly invokes the same ontological structure as one that invokes the whole." See Dave Elder-Vass, "For Emergence: Refining Archer's Account of Social Structure," *Journal for the Theory of Social Behaviour* 37, no. 1 (2007), 30–31.

48. Dave Elder-Vass, "Luhmann and Emergentism: Competing Paradigms for Social Systems Theory?," *Philosophy of the Social Sciences* 37, no. 4 (2007): 415 in Wan, "Emergence a la Systems Theory: Epistemological Totalausschluss or Ontological Novelty?", 187.

49. "Emergence is the idea that a whole can have properties (or powers) that are not possessed by its parts—or, to put it more rigorously, properties that would not be possessed by its parts if they were not organized as a group into the form of this particular kind of whole" (Elder-Vass, "For Emergence: Refining Archer's Account of Social Structure," 28, in Wan, "Emergence a la Systems Theory: Epistemological Totalausschluss or Ontological Novelty?", 187).

50. By "whole" here I do not mean necessarily the whole feather; macroscopic bits of the whole feather will still appear blue. It is at the microscopic (smaller than nano-scale) level at which I mean to say that the materials of which the feathers are composed will not appear blue.

51. An eliminativist reductionist would share prediction about the eventual epistemological reduction of psychology to neurobiology, but would argue that that eventuality gives us reason to reduce the mind and the mental ontologically as well. They are not real; they are merely epiphenomena of complex neurobiological systems which are themselves "really" just chemical systems, which are "really" just physical systems.

52. On the Humean view, "personification" falls apart as a distinct category from "person identification." Thus, on the Humean view, we would have no grounds on which to distinguish that which is useful to think of as a person (what we typically call personification) from that which actually is a person. This argument is made in full at the end of the next chapter.

53. These emergent frameworks may develop and be oriented toward their own teleologies, as described in James W. Haag, et al., "The Emergence of Self," in *In Search of Self: Interdisciplinary Perspectives on Personhood*, ed. J. Wentzel Van Huyssteen and Erik P. Wiebe (Grand Rapids, MI: Eerdmans, 2011). This account will be engaged at length in the next chapter.

54. Earley, "How Philosophy of Mind Needs Philosophy of Chemistry," 16; Stuart A. Kauffman, *At Home in the Universe: The Search for Laws of Self-Organization and Complexity* (Oxford: Oxford University Press, 1995), 21.

55. Philip Clayton says that one way of understanding emergence as a whole is to say that "emergence is a theory about evolution . . . it's a theory about how the various scientific disciplines that study cosmic evolution are related to one another" (Clayton, *Adventures*, 65).

56. For a technical philosophical discussion of multiple species of downward causation, see: G. F. R. Ellis, "Top-Down Causation and Emergence: Some Comments on Mechanisms," *Interface Focus* 2, no. 1 (2012): 126–40.

57. However, it is useful to note that even philosophers who desire more modest emergence and worry about "spooky" emergence at the same time argue that downward causation is not necessarily problematic: "It is important to keep several different senses of the term 'emergence' distinct. Some philosophers and scientists use the term 'emergence' to describe properties of wholes that are not simple sums of the properties of components . . . Other philosophers and scientists use the term

'emergence' to mean that it is not possible to predict the behavior of a mechanism as a whole from what is known about the organization of its components. This is sometimes called 'epistemic emergence.' . . . However, one who insists that there is no explanation for a nonrelational property of the whole in terms of the properties of its component parts-plus-organization advocates a spooky form of emergence . . . The ability of organization to elicit novel causal powers (that is, nonaggregative behaviors and properties) is unmysterious both in scientific common sense and common sense proper . . . Appeal to strong or spooky emergence, on the other hand, justifiably arouses suspicion" (Carl F. Craver, *Explaining the Brain: Mechanisms and the Mosaic Unity of Neuroscience* [New York: Clarendon Press, 2007], 216–17).

58. For various scientific analyses of the causes of the motion of the bridge, see P. Dallard et al., "The London Millennium Footbridge," *Structural Engineer* (2001): 17–33; P. Dallard et al., "London Millennium Bridge: Pedestrian-Induced Lateral Vibration," *Journal of Bridge Engineering* (2001): 412–17; A. McRobie et al., "Section Model Tests on Human-Structure Lock-in," *Proceedings of the Institution of Civil Engineers: Bridge Engineering* 156 (2003): 71–79; Shun-ichi Nakamura, "Model for Lateral Excitation of Footbridges By Synchronous Walking," *Journal of Structural Engineering* 130, no. 1 (2004): 32–37; Steven H. Strogatz et al., "Crowd Synchrony on the Millennium Bridge," *Nature* 438, no. 3 (2005): 43–44.

59. Strogatz et al., "Crowd Synchrony on the Millennium Bridge."

60. Strogatz et al., "Crowd Synchrony on the Millennium Bridge." The analogy to the behavior of large groups of neurons—adapted here for reasons of the applicability of the mathematics involved—is, of course, intriguing for our purposes when in a moment we turn to the case of philosophy of mind.

61. For feedback loops in sociology, see Linnda R. Caporael and Reuben M. Baron, "Groups as the Mind's Natural Environment.," in *Evolutionary Social Psychology*, ed. J. A. Simpson and D. T. Kenrick (Hillsdale, NJ: Lawrence Erlbaum Associates, 1997), 324. Feedback loops between populations and the environments they help shape is the basic substance of population ecology. See A. A. Berryman, "On Principles, Laws and Theory in Population Ecology," *Oikos* 103, no. 3 (2003): 695–701. For a detailed discussion of both systems biology and sociology from an emergentist point of view, see later in this chapter.

62. Sperry, "Modified Concept," 534, 536.

63. Jaegwon Kim, *Mind in a Physical World: An Essay on the Mind-Body Problem and Mental Causation* (Cambridge, MA: MIT Press, 1998); Jaegwon Kim, *Philosophy of Mind* (Boulder, CO: Westview Press, 1996); Kim, "Emergence: Core Ideas and Issues." Kim takes the reductionism that seems inescapable from his argumentation to be necessary only if one wants to hold to physicalism; as we've seen, if one were willing to entertain mental dualism, there would be no such problem. As Loewer writes, "Kim argues that his and other versions of NRP [non-reductive physicalism] inevitably run aground on the problem of mental causation. If he is right about this, then philosophers true to their physicalism will have to swallow reductionism.

Those who find reductionism impossible to swallow will have to find a way of living without physicalism" (Barry Loewer, "Review: Mind in a Physical World," *The Journal of Philosophy* 98, no. 6 [2001]: 315).

64. Kim, "Emergence: Core Ideas and Issues," 557.

65. Kim, "Emergence: Core Ideas and Issues," 558.

66. Kim, "Emergence: Core Ideas and Issues," 558.

67. Polanyi, *The Tacit Dimension*, 38–39. Sperry invoked a very simple machine (a wheel) in making a similar argument: see Roger Wolcott Sperry, "Mind-Brain Interaction: Mentalism, Yes; Dualism, No," *Neuroscience* 5, no. 2 (1980): 195–206.

68. Polanyi, *The Tacit Dimension*, 40.

69. By "boundary condition," I take it that Polanyi means to evoke both the ordinary idea of boundaries, and a technical term from mathematics, where "boundary conditions" refer to sets of values and relations that are required to be satisfied in solving a set of differential equations.

70. Polanyi, *The Tacit Dimension*, 40.

71. The emergence of precisely such intrinsic teleologies (as opposed to extrinsic, *designed* teleologies) will be a focus of discussion in the next chapter.

72. Kim and I agree that "the emergence relation from P to M cannot properly be viewed as causal"—at least if by "causal" we mean (as one normally does in scientific discourse) "efficiently causal" (Kim, "Emergence: Core Ideas and Issues," 558). Emmeche et al., "Explaining Emergence: Towards an Ontology of Levels," 93–94 describes the emergence relation as one of material causation, but this is probably insufficient to the complex mereology involved. (That is, supervenience bases may not straightforwardly be the "material" out of which an emergent is "made." Emergence is precisely trying to describe a more complex relationship than the relationship between a whole and its material.)

73. Deacon, *Incomplete Nature*, 161.

74. While I will focus on J. E. Earley's 2008 article, see also Robert Findlay Hendry, "Ontological Reduction and Molecular Structure," *Studies in History and Philosophy of Science* 41, no. 2 (2010): 183–91; Robert Findlay Hendry, "Is There Downward Causation in Chemistry?," *Philosophy Of Chemistry* 242 (2006): 173–88. Hendry argues that if philosophers of mind were more engaged with contemporary discoveries in chemistry rather than an idealized and out-dated physics, "downward causation" would seem much more reasonable. For a more skeptical view, see Brian P. McLaughlin, "The Rise and Fall of British Emergentism," in *Emergence or Reduction? Essays on the Prospect of a Nonreductive Physicalism*, ed. Ansgar Beckerman et al. (Berlin: Walter de Gruyter, 1992). For a critical assessment of both Hendry and McLaughlin, see E. R. Scerri, "Top-Down Causation Regarding the Chemistry–Physics Interface: A Sceptical View," *Interface Focus* 2, no. 1 (2012): 20–25.

75. Earley, "How Philosophy of Mind Needs Philosophy of Chemistry," 5, 8, 9, and 14 (emphasis original).

76. Earley, "How Philosophy of Mind Needs Philosophy of Chemistry," 6. See also *Hendry, "Downward Causation," 182–83,* in which the discussion hinges on the distinction between resultant and configurational Hamiltonians in quantum chemical explanations of molecular bonding.

77. Noble, "A Theory of Biological Relativity," 59. See also Denis Noble, *The Music of Life: Biology Beyond the Genome* (New York: Oxford University Press, 2006), 42–54.

78. Noble, "A Theory of Biological Relativity," 59. It is intriguing that Noble, like the chemists Hendry and Earley above, locates downward causation mathematically, in the boundary conditions required to solve differential equations. (It is furthermore worth noting, as we did above, that the same sorts of differential equations that describe the biological systems with which Noble is dealing, were also used by engineers modeling the feedback loops in the case of the Millennium Bridge.) This is consistent with our sense that downward causation is exerted through constraint on the "environment" in which the "system" is realized—and the self-similarity of such systems is simply a result of the way that at subsequent scales, one level's "system" becomes the lower level's "environment" and vice versa. Michael Polanyi, as far back as 1968, suggested that boundary conditions in differential equations are the mathematical site of downward causation. See Michael Polanyi, "Life's Irreducible Structure," *Science* 160 (1968): 1308–12.

79. Noble, "A Theory of Biological Relativity," 55. Indeed, he insists, "all of this is fundamental, and, even, fairly obvious to integrative physiologists" (58).

80. P. C. W. Davies, "The Epigenome and Top-Down Causation," *Interface Focus* 2, no. 1 (2012): 42.

81. J. Craig Venter, *A Life Decoded: My Genome, My Life* (New York: Viking, 2007), front matter in Denis Noble, "Biophysics and Systems Biology," *Philosophical Transactions of the Royal Society* 368 (2010): 1127.

82. Davies, "The Epigenome and Top-Down Causation," 43. For a concise overview of the history of epigenetics: R. Holliday, "Epigenetics: A Historical Overview," *Epigenetics* 1, no. 2 (2006): 76–80. Recently, E. O. Wilson has used epigenetic explanation to describe the interface between cultural and biological evolution (Wilson, *Social Conquest*, 239).

83. Denis Noble, "Genes and Causation," *Philosophical Transactions of the Royal Society A: Mathematical, Physical and Engineering Sciences* 366, no. 1878 (2008): 3006.

84. Davies, "The Epigenome and Top-Down Causation," 45.

85. Davies, "The Epigenome and Top-Down Causation," 45.

86. Davies, "The Epigenome and Top-Down Causation," 43.

87. If this bidirectional causation is an unavoidable feature of biological explanation at the micro-level with which biologists are increasingly coming to grips, it is only more clearly embraced in the case of larger-scale evolutionary and population biology. All of evolutionary biology functions only inasmuch as the environment (to which the population contribute) exhibits downward causation back on the

population, especially on the population's genes. Evolutionary biology is almost exclusively about these downward causes, these environmental pressures that cause (probabilistic) adaptive changes in population genetic distributions.

88. J. S. Coleman, "Social Theory, Social Research, and a Theory of Action," *American journal of Sociology* (1986): 1312.

89. Peter Berger and Thomas Luckmann, *The Social Construction of Reality: A Treatise in the Sociology of Knowledge* (Garden City, NY: Doubleday, 1966), 57–58 (emphasis original).

90. Peter Berger and Stanley Pullberg, "Reification and the Sociological Critique of Consciousness," *History and Theory* 4, no. 2 (1965): 202.

91. Dave Elder-Vass, "Top-Down Causation and Social Structures," *Interface Focus* 2, no. 1 (2012): 83. This division, of course, is somewhat simplistic. For a more detailed review of the variegated landscape of contemporary social theory, and emergentism's place within that landscape, see: R. Keith Sawyer, *Social Emergence: Societies as Complex Systems* (Cambridge: Cambridge University Press, 2005), 189–229.

92. Margaret S. Archer, *Realist Social Theory: The Morphogenetic Approach* (Cambridge: Cambridge University Press, 1995), 9. Elder-Vass concedes that Archer's emergent social theory has not always been successful in maintaining the supervenience pole of this generative dialectic in Elder-Vass, "For Emergence: Refining Archer's Account of Social Structure," 35.

93. Sawyer, *Social Emergence*, 213. Sawyer's statement here regarding the "positivist," "objectivist" character of the emergence paradigm is, presumably, part of his defense of it as "scientific." I take it that Archer's description of emergence as "realist" is a more accurate description. As I will show below, emergence thinking more naturally fits with a Foucauldian epistemology.

94. For our purposes, we need not choose sides between, say, Sawyer and Berger. This is another case in which the broad range of approaches to which emergence lends itself is an advantage. Sawyer's claim that social systems "are causal even when individuals have no knowledge of them," which seems to be the core of his disagreement with interpretivists, will be explored further in the case study of racism below.

95. Indeed, it seems to contain within it both the insights of the Vatican—namely, that "structures, whether they are good or bad, are the result of human actions" (*Liberatis Nuntius* IV.35)—and of Käsemann, who notes that the human agent is constituted by the powers (in Käsemann's case, cosmic powers) to which the agent is subject, such that "anthropology is the projection of cosmology" (Käsemann, *Romans*, 150).

96. G. F. R. Ellis et al., "Top-Down Causation: An Integrating Theme Within and Across the Sciences?," *Interface Focus* 2, no. 1 (2012): 2–3.

97. Physical reductionism works similarly, as briefly demonstrated earlier.

98. Ruth F. Benedict, *Race and Racism* (London: Routledge & Kegan Paul, 1945), 87 (emphasis added), in Eduardo Bonilla-Silva, "Rethinking Racism: Toward a Structural Interpretation," *American Sociological Review* 62, no. 3 (1997): 465.

99. Richard T. Schaefer, *Racial and Ethnic Groups*, 4th ed. (Glenview, IL: Scott Foresman/Little Brown Higher Education, 1990), 16 in Bonilla-Silva, "Rethinking Racism," 465.

100. For example, T. W. Allen, *The Invention of the White Race* (New York: Verso, 1994).

101. Michel Foucault, *The History of Sexuality, Vol. 1: An Introduction*, trans. Robert Hurley (New York: Vintage, 1990), 101; Stephen D. Moore, *Poststructuralism and the New Testament: Derrida and Foucault At the Foot of the Cross* (Minneapolis: Fortress Press, 1994), 87. Ta-Nehisi Coates describes this dynamic plainly when he notes that "race is the child of racism, not the father." See Ta-Nehisi Coates, *Between the World and Me* (New York: Spiegel & Grau, 2015), 7.

102. Michel Foucault, *The Archaeology of Knowledge*, trans. A. M. Sheridan Smith (New York: Pantheon Books, 1972), 23, 22.

103. Eduardo Bonilla-Silva, *Racism Without Racists: Color-Blind Racism and the Persistence of Racial Inequality in the United States*, 3d ed., (Lanham, MD: Rowman & Littlefield, 2010), 8–9 (quotations on p. 9).

104. Bonilla-Silva, "Rethinking Racism," 467, 469.

105. Bonilla-Silva, "Rethinking Racism," 474–75.

106. Bonilla-Silva's note regarding "relative autonomy" reveals the way in which emergent thinking about levels can creep toward ambitious ontological statements: "The notion of relative autonomy comes from the work of Poulantzas (1982) and implies that the ideological and political levels in a society are partially autonomous in relation to the economic level; that is, they are not merely expressions of the economic level." See Bonilla-Silva, "Rethinking Racism," 474, n. 19.

107. Bonilla-Silva, *Racism Without Racists*, 11.

108. Bonilla-Silva, "Rethinking Racism," 472–73.

109. For example, David R. Williams's 1999 study showed a higher incidence of and rate of fatality from a number of diseases (including heart disease, cancer, cerebrovascular disease, diabetes, HIV/AIDS) among minority racial groups, resulting in shorter life expectancy—even when controlling for socioeconomic factors—and a widening gap from 1950 to 1995. See David R. Williams, "Race, Socioeconomic Status, and Health the Added Effects of Racism and Discrimination," *Annals of the New York Academy of Sciences* 896 (1999): 173–88.

110. Bonilla-Silva, "Rethinking Racism," 474.

111. Studying the response only of white patients: Elizabeth A. Phelps et al., "Performance on Indirect Measures of Race Evaluation Predicts Amygdala Activation," *Journal of Cognitive Neuroscience* (2000): 729–38. Studying the response of both black and white patients: A. J. Hart et al., "Differential Response in the Human Amygdala to Racial Outgroup vs Ingroup Face Stimuli," *Neuroreport* 11, no. 11 (2000): 2351–55.

112. Phelps et al., "Performance on Indirect Measures of Race Evaluation Predicts Amygdala Activation," 729–30.

113. Joan Y. Chiao et al., "Cultural Specificity in Amygdala Response to Fear Faces," *Journal of Cognitive Neuroscience* 20 (2008), 2167.

114. M. D. Lieberman et al., "An fMRI Investigation of Race-Related Amygdala Activity in African-American and Caucasian-American Individuals," *Nature Neuroscience* 8, no. 6 (2005): 722.

115. Chiao et al., "Cultural Specificity in Amygdala Response to Fear Faces," 2171, 2167. Indeed, Paul Whalen, one of the contributors to Hart et al., speculated in 2000 that this research would require both "top-down" and "bottom-up" explanations. See David Berreby, "How, But Not Why, the Brain Distinguishes Race," *New York Times*, 2000.

116. I am not suggesting that racial majorities are to be forgiven for what is outside their control. Rather, my sense is that members of racial majorities have to see our culpability expanded, whether or not we espouse racist ideas. Participation in racialized systems itself entangles us in serious culpability and requires from us active resistance of structural racism.

117. Nelson, *What's Wrong With Sin*, 113. Nelson largely tries to occupy a mediating position on the importance of *structure* in describing sin; the cited passage may be something of an outlier in his thought.

118. Faus, "Sin," 198 (emphasis original).

119. Indeed, the Vatican's problem with emergentist liberationists also fits a type: the reductionist taking an emergentist to be a crypto-dualist.

120. This is not to downplay the other factors—political and theological—that, no doubt, impacted the Vatican's position. The liberationists were dangerous politically, and sinful social systems are hard to fit in a confessional so as to receive absolution. Nevertheless, the rhetoric, as we've seen, is modernist and reductionist.

121. Bultmann, *Theology*, I, 251.

122. Käsemann, *Romans*, 147.

123. Murphy-O'Connor, *Becoming Human*, 96–97.

CHAPTER 3

1. Rather than adopting some more or less arbitrary anthropology from the outset that would privilege one or the other of these terms as basic, this chapter will instead discuss each of these terms as it arises in the scholarship addressed. Doubtless, each of these terms overlaps with others, and together the constellation forms what it is we have in mind when we perform the sort of comparison implicit in distinguishing personification from person-identification. For an extensive account of this "constellation" that constitutes a human person, see Smith, *What is a Person?*, 25–116.

2. Nelson, *What's Wrong With Sin*, 113; Murphy-O'Connor, *Becoming Human*, 96–97.

3. Whitman, *Allegory*, 271–72.

4. Emile Durkheim, "Individual and Collective Representations," in *Sociology and Philosophy* (New York: Free Press, 1974), 25. Durkheim's analogy affirms emergentist philosophers' basic intuition that theories of emergence should apply equally

to any contiguous pair of levels of analysis. R. Keith Sawyer, "Nonreductive Individualism Part Ii—Social Causation," *Philosophy of the Social Sciences* 33, no. 2 (2003): 221.

5. Durkheim, Emile Durkheim, *Suicide*, trans. John A. Spaulding (Glencoe, IL: Free Press, 1951), 310 in R. Keith Sawyer, "Durkheim's Dilemma: Toward a Sociology of Emergence," *Sociological Theory* 20, no. 2 (2002): 232. I am not claiming here that Durkheim either was influenced by or had an historical influence on "Emergentists," though the similarities are striking, and Sawyer's work has explicated this affinity quite extensively.

6. Emile Durkheim, *The Rules of Sociological Method and Selected Texts on Sociology and Its Method* (London: Macmillan Press, 1982), 251–52.

7. I will argue that, while there are reasons to avoid this Humean position (on realist grounds), it is nevertheless compatible with the larger argument. A human person that is some composite of at least these two "useful fictions"—body and mind—levels the playing field for other, "fictive" would-be persons like Sin.

8. In pursuing these various levels of "selves," they follow the lead of Michael Polanyi, who described a "consolidation of the center" of the "individual that increases as we move from vegetable, to animal, and then finally to human life—where it finally "rises to the level of personhood." See Polanyi, *The Tacit Dimension*, 50.

9. Haag et al., "The Emergence of Self," 321. Note that while Haag et al. do not use language of personhood, it seems reasonable to suppose that we could map "person" onto this "self experienced by creatures with complex brains," which emerges from the "minimally selfy self" of the (merely) organismic self.

10. Haag et al., "The Emergence of Self," 328.

11. This is intended humorously. The statement employs a folk dualism to which I do not ascribe that would distinguish between the "you" and the body in which "you" wake up.

12. Here I mean that they appear "simple" inasmuch as we have commonsense intuitions that it would be easy to make a case for these entities having continuity over time. Over course, the difficulty arises precisely because such entities are not "simple" in the technical philosophical sense (they are not unities)—that is, they are at least aggregates if not (minimally) complex systems.

13. The instance of quantum phenomena reveals that—as in the case of Kim's critique of downward causation—if we were to lay aside our persistent Newtonian atomistic common senses, we would be forced to wrestle with the fact that all these concerns about identity and ontology apply just as much to entities at the most "fundamental" level as they do to systems at higher levels of complexity. That is, a "fundamental particle," conceived (as it must be from time to time) as a wave raises these same questions about the continuity of its identity. This is only made worse when one considers the smallest scales at which quantum theory suggests that particles are consistently coming into existence and then being annihilated. At this level, our materialism reveals itself to be less materialist than we first imagined. The reductionistic instinct cannot save us from

wrestling with these fundamental issues. The identity of such entities—even in a materialist framework—cannot be conceived in substantial terms. This has important consequences for well-worn arguments in philosophy of mind, for if even the body cannot be defined in substantive terms, the physicality leaks out of any attempt to solve the mind-body problem through "*physical* reduction." Chemist Joseph Earley wrestles with this lack of "simple" wholes and what it requires of a scientific conception of *physicality* in Earley, "How Philosophy of Mind Needs Philosophy of Chemistry," 8–9.

14. Because of this influx of energy, dissipative systems, though they represent the spontaneous appearance of order, do not violate the Second Law of thermodynamics—that the entropy, or the disorder, of an isolated system never decreases. The dissipative system itself is not isolated, and only creates order locally within the system, at the cost of the energy it absorbs, and returns to the larger environment.

15. Mark H. Bickhard, "Process and Emergence: Normative Function and Representation," *Axiomathes* 14 (2004): 121–55.

16. Haag et al. argue persuasively that Bickhard's language of "self" here is a simple function of English usage and does not smuggle in what he is attempting to describe. See Haag et al., "The Emergence of Self," 331.

17. Haag et al., "The Emergence of Self," 329.

18. Haag et al., "The Emergence of Self," 329. As we saw in the previous chapter, so we see here again that there are substantial resonances between emergent ontology and constructivist epistemology. There are also, it should be mentioned, significant resonances with Käsemann's anthropology, the human person constituting the cosmic reality, and that cosmic reality in turn constituting the human person.

19. Haag et al., "The Emergence of Self," 323 (emphasis original).

20. Polanyi, "Life's Irreducible Structure."

21. Haag et al., "The Emergence of Self," 324. Let the reader note that this means that a facile contrast between the mind as mere abstraction and the body as material— a standard feature of many modern descriptions of the mind-body problem—is therefore ruled out.

22. Haag et al., "The Emergence of Self," 325.

23. Deacon, *Incomplete Nature*; Kauffman, *At Home in the Universe*.

24. Immanuel Kant, *Critique of Judgement, Part Two: Critique of Teleological Judgement*, trans. James Creed Meredith (Oxford: Clarendon Press, 1952), 18 (marginal pagination, 371).

25. Kauffman, *At Home in the Universe*, 274.

26. Kauffman, *At Home in the Universe*, 274–75.

27. Kauffman, *At Home in the Universe*, 24.

28. Haag et al., "The Emergence of Self," 329–30.

29. Haag et al., "The Emergence of Self," 333–36, quoting 336.

30. Haag et al., "The Emergence of Self," 337.

31. Broad, *Mind and Its Place*; Sperry, "Modified Concept"; Philip Clayton, *Mind and Emergence: From Quantum to Consciousness* (New York: Oxford University Press, 2004).

32. Haag et al., "The Emergence of Self," 337.

33. Jennifer Ackerman, "The Ultimate Social Network," *Scientific American* 306, no. 6 (2012): 38.

34. An oft-cited source of the recent consensus around the endosymbiotic origin of eukaryotic cells is Lynn Margulis, *Origin of Eukaryotic Cells: Evidence and Research Implications for a Theory of the Origin and Evolution of Microbial, Plant, and Animal Cells on the Precambrian Earth* (New Haven, CT: Yale University Press, 1970). However, the basic idea is not so recent; Margulis herself cites a number of others (the earliest being Konstantin Mereschkowsky, "*Theorie der zwei Plasmaarten als Grundlage der Symbiogenesis, einer neuen Lehre von der Entstehung der Organismen,*" *Biologisches Centralblatt* 30 [1910]: 353–67) in one of her first articles on the topic: Lynn Sagan, "On the Origin of Mitosing Cells," *Journal of Theoretical Biology* 14, no. 3 (1967): 225–74.

35. Richard Dawkins, *The Selfish Gene*, 30th anniversary ed., (New York: Oxford University Press, 2006), 182.

36. The original article is Andy Clark and David Chalmers, "The Extended Mind," *Analysis* 58, no. 1 (1998): 7–19. Clark has defended and extended this theory in multiple publications: Andy Clark, "Intrinsic Content, Active Memory and the Extended Mind," *Analysis* 65, no. 1 (2005): 1–11; Andy Clark, "Memento's Revenge: The Extended Mind, Extended," in *The Extended Mind*, ed. Richard Menary (Cambridge, MA: MIT Press, 2006); Andy Clark, "Curing Cognitive Hiccups: A Defense of the Extended Mind," *Journal of Philosophy* 104 (2007): 163–92; Andy Clark, "Pressing the Flesh: A Tension in the Study of the Embodied, Embedded Mind?," *Philosophy and Phenomenological Research* 76, no. 1 (2008): 37–59. The idea is given a book-length treatment in Andy Clark, *Supersizing the Mind: Embodiment, Action, and Cognitive Extension* (New York: Oxford University Press, 2008). Extended Mind has garnered considerable support and, of course, detractors. For a summary of the debate, see: Richard Menary, ed., *The Extended Mind* (Cambridge, MA: MIT Press, 2010).

37. Mark Rowlands notes, "This view is not particularly new. James Gibson (1966; 1979) essentially defends it, and a position that is at least on nodding terms with the one described is found in A. Luria and L. Vygotsky ([1917] 1992). It has clear affinities with those of Martin Heidegger ([1927] 1962), Jean-Paul Sartre ([1943] 1957), M. Merleau-Ponty ([1943] 2002), and Ludwig Wittgenstein (1953)" (Mark Rowlands, "The Extended Mind," *Zygon* 44, no. 3 [2009]: 629).

38. Clark and Chalmers, "Extended Mind," 8.

39. Clark and Chalmers, "Extended Mind," 8.

40. Of course, what is extended here is not the mind as distinct from the body, but rather the "body-becoming-mind," as helpfully argued by Douglas Robinson,

Feeling Extended: Sociality as Extended Body-Becoming-Mind (Cambridge, MA: MIT Press, 2013).

41. David Kirsh and Paul Maglio, "On Distinguishing Epistemic From Pragmatic Action," *Cognitive Science* 18, no. 4 (1994): 513–49.

42. Clark and Chalmers, "Extended Mind," 8–9.

43. As a low-tech example, Clark points to an exchange between Richard Feynman and the historian of science Charles Weiner. Weiner, discovering Feynman's hand-written notes, called the notes "a record of [Feynman's] day-to-day work." Feynman objected to this characterization: " 'I actually did the work on the paper,' he said. 'Well,' Weiner said, 'the work was done in your head, but the record of it is still here.' 'No, it's not a record, not really. It's working. You have to work on paper and this is the paper. Okay?' " James Gleick, *Genius: The Life and Science of Richard Feynman* (New York: Pantheon Books, 1992), 409, in Clark, *Supersizing the Mind: Embodiment, Action, and Cognitive Extension*, xxv.

44. David Chalmers, "Foreword," in Clark, *Supersizing the Mind: Embodiment, Action, and Cognitive Extension*, ix.

45. This integration of self and the technology we use has not, of course, escaped the notice of smartphone marketing. Consider the striking campaign for Verizon Wireless's flagship 2012 phone. The spot shows an athletic young man strapped into a (medical?) chair with the new phone "plugged in" to him at the center of his sternum (reminiscent of Marvel Comics' Iron Man character). Animations of his DNA and neural networks "upgrading" follow. The tag line for the campaign: "Introducing Droid DNA by HTC. It's not an upgrade to your phone. It's an upgrade to your *self*." "Droid DNA 'Hyper Intelligence'," video, http://vimeo.com/56384500 (accessed 12/29/2012).

46. Mark Rowlands, "Consciousness, Broadly Construed," in *The Extended Mind*, ed. Richard Menary (Cambridge, MA: MIT Press, 2010).

47. Deborah Perron Tollefsen, "From Extended Mind to Collective Mind," *Cognitive Systems Research* (2006), 148. See also Georg Theiner, "From Extended Minds to Group Minds: Rethinking the Boundaries of the Mental" (PhD diss., Indiana University, 2008); Shaun Gallagher and Anthony Crisafi, "Mental Institutions," *Topoi* 28, no. 1 (2009): 45–51; Georg Theiner et al., "Recognizing Group Cognition," *Cognitive Systems Research* 11, no. 4 (2010): 378–95.

48. Tollefsen, "Extended Mind," 141–42, 142, 147–49.

49. Research on so-called "mirror neurons" suggests a neurological basis for this extension. See Giacomo Rizzolatti and Laila Craighero, "The Mirror-Neuron System," *Annual Review of Neuroscience* 27 (2004): 169–92.

50. Roger Wolcott Sperry, "Hemisphere Deconnection and Unity in Conscious Awareness," *American Psychologist* 23 (1968): 724.

51. Sperry, "Hemisphere Deconnection and Unity in Conscious Awareness," 724. Jill Taylor, "Jill Bolte Taylor's Stroke of Insight," *TED: Ideas Worth Spreading*,

February 2008, http://www.ted.com/index.php/talks/jill_bolte_taylor_s_pow-erful_stroke_of_insight.html.

52. In terms of these concerns, my sense is that Tollefsen's word, "encompass," is probably not the best, as it gives one the sense of this science-fiction-like melding of minds.

53. Tollefsen, "Extended Mind," 147.

54. "Eusocial" is used (or at least ought to be used; see comments at the end of the chapter) in this context without any ethical weight given to the "eu-" prefix. The sociality of the collective may be viewed either in terms of "altruism" or in terms of coercive constraint. In both cases the adjective "eusocial" still applies.

55. Gk., πολιτικά. Aristotle, *Historia Animalium*, 488a7.

56. Gk., ἡγεμών, βασιλεῖς τῶν μελιττῶν, and τὰ ἄναρχα, respectively. *Hist. Animal.*, 488a11, 623b9.

57. *Hist. Animal.*, 553b14-18. This is in harmony with Aristotle's political preference for oligarchy.

58. Jan Swammerdam, *The Book of Nature: Or, the History of Insects*, trans. Thomas Flloyd (London: C. G. Seyffert, 1758), 121.

59. W. M. Wheeler, "The Ant-Colony as an Organism," *Journal of Morphology* 22 (1912): 307–25.

60. Wheeler, "The Ant-Colony as an Organism," 308.

61. Wheeler, "The Ant-Colony as an Organism," 310. Wheeler adopts Ernst Haeckel's rather idiosyncratic, technical use of the term "person." Haeckel was particularly fascinated by the question of the givenness of the organismic unit. By "person," Haeckel means "the entire body," which Wheeler takes to be the paradigmatic case of the category "organism." Ernst Haeckel, *The Evolution of Man: A Popular Exposition of the Principal Points of Human Ontogeny and Phylogeny*, vol. 2 (New York: Appleton, 1879).

62. Wheeler, "The Ant-Colony as an Organism," 309.

63. Wheeler, "The Ant-Colony as an Organism," 324.

64. Wheeler, "The Ant-Colony as an Organism," 309.

65. Wilson, *Social Conquest*, 133 (emphasis mine). Of course, Wilson doesn't mean to say that eusociality *created* anything. It's simply that, when eusociality is in play, "superorganism" becomes a meaningful level of analysis, a useful vocabulary for analyzing a biological system. Nevertheless, following the logic of emergence, we could just as well turn that around. Eusociality absolutely created superorgan-isms, in the same sense that increasingly complex neurobiological systems created (and continue to create) subjective persons. What we see here again is that our ontology needs to allow for considerable flexibility in dealing with the categories that are meaningful at different levels of analysis.

66. Wilson, *Social Conquest*, 143–44.

67. This is, of course, a flagship example of "downward causation" in biology of the sort discussed by Denis Noble, and it exposes the "level" of the genome as an

incomplete "level" in the proper sense, because identical states at the genomic level can give rise to different states at the "higher," phenotypic level. Something more complex is going on.

68. Wilson, *Social Conquest*, 143.

69. Wilson, *Social Conquest*, 152, 186.

70. Wilson, *Social Conquest*, 146, 162.

71. G. C. Williams is regularly cited as the progenitor of the individualist orthodoxy that, in some circles, continues to hold sway: see G. C. Williams, *Adaptation and Natural Selection: A Critique of Some Current Evolutionary Thought* (Princeton, NJ: Princeton University Press, 1966). For a discussion of the history of group selection in evolutionary theory, see David Sloan Wilson and Elliott Sober, "Reintroducing Group Selection to the Human Behavioral Sciences," *Behavioral and Brain Sciences* 17 (1994): 585–654. E. O. Wilson's *Social Conquest of Earth* is perhaps the strongest recent case for multilevel selection in evolutionary biology.

72. Nowak and Highfield, *Supercooperators*, 82.

73. Charles Darwin, *The Descent of Man and Selection in Relation to Sex* (London: John Murray, 1871), 159–60.

74. Nowak and Highfield, *Supercooperators*, 138.

75. Nowak and Highfield, *Supercooperators*, 94.

76. Indeed, the complex interactions of individual- and group-level evolutionary forces can be modeled mathematically and yield the expected outcomes for eusocial superorganismic systems. See H. Kern Reeve and Bert Hölldobler, "The Emergence of a Superorganism Through Intergroup Competition," *Proceedings of the National Academy of Sciences* 104, no. 23 (2007): 9736–40.

77. Wilson, *Social Conquest*, 142.

78. Wilson, *Social Conquest*, 162, emphasis original.

79. Wilson, *Social Conquest*, 162–63. The ethical program here is not quite as simplistic as it might at first seem. Wilson is aware that group-beneficial "altruism" can manifest in destructive cycles like tribalism and ethnocentrism. See Wilson, *Social Conquest*, 60. Nevertheless, Wilson does want to map ethical categories onto this evolutionary dialectic—and in this he errs. For example, he is still quite willing to insist that "individual selection is responsible for much of what we call sin, while group selection is responsible for the greater part of virtue. Together they have created the conflict between the poorer and the better angels of our nature" (Wilson, *Social Conquest*, 241). I doubt very much that even this qualified generalization holds. The thesis of this book is, by and large, that the social is just as fallen as the individual—indeed, their fallenness is deeply intertwined.

80. Wilson, *Social Conquest*, 162.

81. Noble, "Biophysics and Systems Biology," 1131. On scale relativity theory more generally (and its application in the biological sciences), see Charles Auffray and Laurent Nottale, "Scale Relativity Theory and Integrative Systems

Biology: 1: Founding Principles and Scale Laws," *Progress in Biophysics and Molecular Biology* (2008): 79–114.

82. Wilson, *Social Conquest*, 52.

83. In defense of his use of the term "epigenetic" in this more extended sense, Wilson cites the definition of the term given by the U.S. National Institutes of Health: "changes in the regulation of gene activity and expression that are not dependent on gene sequence," including "both heritable changes in gene activity and expression (in the progeny of cells or individuals) and also stable, long-term alterations in the transcriptional potential of a cell that are not necessarily heritable" (Wilson, *Social Conquest*, 204).

84. Wilson, *Social Conquest*, 203. For an extended account of gene-culture coevolution, see Peter J. Richerson and Robert Boyd, *Not By Genes Alone: How Culture Transformed Human Evolution* (Chicago: University of Chicago Press, 2004), 191–236.

85. Wilson, *Social Conquest*, 198.

86. Wilson, *Social Conquest*, 203.

87. Wilson, *Social Conquest*, 211. This is a case of scientific evidence of Heideggerian epistemology: our linguistic categories (in this case, genetically hardwired!) constrain even what we "see." We are always already interpreting.

88. Wilson, *Social Conquest*, 224.

89. Wilson, *Social Conquest*, 229. For Tomasello's relevant work, see Michael Tomasello, *The Cultural Origins of Human Cognition* (Cambridge, MA: Harvard University Press, 1999); Michael Tomasello, *Constructing a Language: A Usage-Based Theory of Language Acquisition* (Cambridge, MA: Harvard University Press, 2005); Michael Tomasello et al., "Understanding and Sharing Intentions: The Origins of Cultural Cognition," *Behavioral and Brain Sciences* (2005); Michael Tomasello and Malinda Carpenter, "Shared Intentionality," *Developmental Science* 10, no. 1 (2007): 121–25.

90. In their important article on rehabilitating group-level selection in evolutionary biology, evolutionary biologist David Sloan Wilson and philosopher Elliott Sober write: "As the most facultative species on earth, humans have the behavioral potential to span the full continuum from organ to organism, depending on the situations we encounter and the social organizations that we build for ourselves. We often see ourselves as 'organs.' We sometimes identify ourselves primarily as members of a group and willingly make sacrifices for the welfare of our group. We long to be part of something larger than ourselves. We have a passion for building, maintaining, and abiding by fair social organizations." Wilson and Sober, "Reintroducing Group Selection to the Human Behavioral Sciences," 605. Wilson and Sober highlight Hutterite communities as examples of highly integrated human superorganisms.

91. I prefer the more neutrally descriptive "combinatorial" to the ethically freighted "cooperative."

92. John Maynard Smith and Eörs Szathmáry, *The Major Transitions in Evolution* (Oxford: Oxford University Press, 1997). For a more recent appraisal of this

important work, see John Maynard Smith and Eörs Szathmáry, *The Major Transitions in Evolution Revisited* (Cambridge, MA: MIT Press, 2011). Maynard Smith, for his part, continues to resist multilevel selection of the type E. O. Wilson, D. S. Wilson, and Nowak support.

93. David Sloan Wilson et al., "Multilevel Selection Theory and Major Evolutionary Transitions," *Current Directions in Psychological Science* 17, no. 1 (2008): 7.

94. Indeed, the individual human body can be conceived of as a multi-species super-organism, given how many of our basic physiological functions are carried out in concert with our bacterial symbiotes. On multi-species superorganisms, see David Sloan Wilson and Elliott Sober, "Reviving the Superorganism," *Journal of Theoretical Biology* 136 (1989): 349.

95. Wilson et al., "Multilevel Selection Theory and Major Evolutionary Transitions," 7.

96. "It is an interesting fact, worth the attention of social historians, that the concept of the group as an organism was widely accepted until the middle of the twentieth century, when it was rejected by various scientific disciplines. It is now making a comeback through the application of MLS [multi-level selection] thinking, providing a firm scientific foundation for the concept of groups as organisms—not as an axiomatic statement about all societies but as a possibility that is realized when certain conditions are met" (Wilson et al., "Multilevel Selection Theory and Major Evolutionary Transitions," 9).

97. D. S. Wilson et al., "Multilevel Selection Theory and Major Evolutionary Transitions," 7. E. O. Wilson never describes human social groups as "superorganisms," reserving this language for the social insects, given his explanation of social insect colonies as "extrasomatic extensions" of the queen. For E. O. Wilson, the dialectic of individual- and group-level selection in human evolution precludes this sort of social arrangement: "The victory can never be complete; the balance of selection pressures cannot move to either extreme. If individual selection were to dominate, societies would dissolve. If group selection were to dominate, human groups would come to resemble ant colonies" (E. O. Wilson, *Social Conquest*, 243). D. S. Wilson, for his part, insists that in all major transitions, the triumph of group-level selective forces is not complete. "Even multicellular organisms, which might seem like paradigms of internal harmony, contain a disturbing number of genes that spread at the expense of other genes in the same organism rather than for the good of the organism (cf. intragenomic conflict)" (D. S. Wilson et al., "Multilevel Selection Theory and Major Evolutionary Transitions," 7).

98. David Sloan Wilson, *Darwin's Cathedral: Evolution, Religion, and the Nature of Society* (Chicago: University of Chicago Press, 2003), 33.

99. Wilson et al., "Multilevel Selection Theory and Major Evolutionary Transitions," 8.

100. Durkheim, "Individual and Collective Representations," 25.

101. T. D. Seeley, *The Wisdom of the Hive: The Social Physiology of Honey Bee Colonies* (Cambridge, MA: Harvard University Press, 1995); T. D. Seeley, "Honey Bee

Colonies Are Group-Level Adaptive Units," *The American Naturalist* 150, no. S1 (1997): 22–41.

102. David Sloan Wilson, "Altruism and Organism: Disentangling the Themes of Multilevel Selection Theory," *The American Naturalist* 150, no. S1 (1997): S128–29.

103. Wilson, *Darwin's Cathedral*, 34. For the description of decision-making dynamics within bee colonies, Wilson cites T. D. Seeley and S. C. Buhrman, "Group Decision Making in Swarms of Honey Bees," *Behavioral Ecology and Sociobiology* 45, no. 1 (1999): 19–31. For the description of the neurological "best-of-n" algorithm, he cites John W. Payne et al., *The Adaptive Decision Maker* (Cambridge: Cambridge University Press, 1993).

104. H. H. T. Prins, *Ecology and Behaviour of the African Buffalo: Social Inequality and Decision Making* (London: Chapman & Hall, 1996).

105. Wilson, "Altruism and Organism," 132.

106. Wilson, "Altruism and Organism," 129.

107. For a review of the substantial group-mind literature from the viewpoint of emergence, see Georg Theiner and Timothy O'Connor, "The Emergence of Group Cognition," in *Emergence in Science and Philosophy*, ed. Antonella Corradini and Timothy O'Connor (New York: Routledge, 2009), 78–120.

108. Edwin Hutchins, *Cognition in the Wild* (Cambridge: MIT Press, 1995).

109. Clark and Chalmers make use of Hutchins's work in their original seminal article, as does Tollefsen in her expansion of their work. See also below: Karin Knorr Cetina, *Epistemic Cultures: How the Sciences Make Knowledge* (Cambridge, MA: Harvard University Press, 1999); Theiner et al., "Recognizing Group Cognition"; Theiner and O'Connor, "The Emergence of Group Cognition"; Theiner, "From Extended Minds to Group Minds." Others have used Hutchins's work in describing collective memory, web-based communities, and organizational behavior, respectively: Amanda J. Barnier et al., "A Conceptual and Empirical Framework for the Social Distribution of Cognition: The Case of Memory," *Cognitive Systems Research* 9 (2008): 33–51; Lee Li-Jen Chen and Brian R. Gaines, "A Cyberorganism Model for Awareness in Collaborative Communities on the Internet," *International Journal of Intelligent Systems* 12, no. 1 (1997): 31–56; Selin Kesebir, "The Superorganism Account of Human Sociality: How and When Human Groups Are Like Beehives," *Personality and Social Psychology Review* 16, no. 3 (2012): 233–61.

110. Philip Pettit, "Groups With Minds of Their Own," in *Socializing Metaphysics*, ed. Frederick F. Schmitt (Lanham, MD: Rowman & Littlefield, 2003), 167. Given the current political resonances of language of "institutional persons," it is perhaps worth noting that Pettit was writing before the *Citizens United* decision and, at any rate, is not arguing for granting rights to collectivities, but instead is arguing for an expansive sense of what can be demanded of them as rational interlocutors.

111. Pettit, "Groups With Minds of Their Own," 168–70.

112. Pettit, "Groups With Minds of Their Own," 168.

113. Pettit, "Groups With Minds of Their Own," 178.

114. Pettit, "Groups With Minds of Their Own," 185, citing Carol Anne Rovane, *The Bounds of Agency: An Essay in Revisionary Metaphysics* (Princeton, NJ: Princeton University Press, 1997); Philip Pettit and Michael Smith, "Freedom in Belief and Desire," *The Journal of Philosophy* (1996): 429–49.

115. Pettit, "Groups With Minds of Their Own," 191.

116. For a cautious review of this literature, see Ronald N. Giere and Barton Moffatt, "Distributed Cognition: Where the Cognitive and the Social Merge," *Social Studies of Science* 33, no. 2 (2003): 301–10.

117. Knorr Cetina, *Epistemic Cultures*, 4. The scare quotes around "superorganism"—which come fully equipped with a sternly worded disclaimer in Knorr Cetina's earlier work (Karin Knorr Cetina, "How Superorganisms Change: Consensus Formation and the Social Ontology of High-Energy Physics Experiments," *Social Studies of Science* 25, no. 1 [1995]: 119–47)—eventually disappear in *Epistemic Cultures* (e.g., p. 297). Knorr Cetina seems more convinced of the literalness of the superorganism language and of the reality of the experiment as a collective epistemic subject: "HEP experiments, as communitarian collaborations, are fictional in the sense that they are 'contradicted' by the forms of order centered on the individual subjects. But they are very real in the sense of the integrated functioning of these experiments, without which HEP could not produce results." Knorr Cetina, *Epistemic Cultures*, 250.

118. Knorr Cetina, *Epistemic Cultures*, 167–68.

119. Knorr Cetina, *Epistemic Cultures*, 178.

120. Knorr Cetina, *Epistemic Cultures*, 178–79.

121. On the policing of the genealogy of the superorganism as an emergent process of producing "the reasonable," see Knorr Cetina, "How Superorganisms Change: Consensus Formation and the Social Ontology of High-Energy Physics Experiments," 136. On proving significance, Knorr Cetina insists that "experiments, not just individual physicists, have a need to prove their worth through the production of results." Knorr Cetina, *Epistemic Cultures*, 168.

122. Knorr Cetina, *Epistemic Cultures*, 214–15.

123. Knorr Cetina, *Epistemic Cultures*, 202.

124. Pettit, "Groups With Minds of Their Own," 185–86.

125. Knorr Cetina, *Epistemic Cultures*, 163. Knorr Cetina explicitly distinguishes HEP experiments from "the corporate actor concept." Knorr Cetina, *Epistemic Cultures*, 294.

126. "Individuals can claim to know the conclusions of scientific inquiries because they know these results are reliably produced. This implies there will typically be a short period of time after members of a research group have reached consensus on a conclusion, and can thus each personally claim to know the conclusion, even though this result does not yet count as public scientific knowledge. Later, anyone knowing that the conclusion has been certified by accepted scientific

procedures can legitimately claim to know the conclusion" (see Ronald N. Giere, "Distributed Cognition Without Distributed Knowing," *Social Epistemology* 21, no. 3 [2007]: 318).

127. The distinction between "analogous" and "formally identical" is admittedly subtle. My point is to distinguish self-consciously "fictive" comparisons from their more credulous counterparts (along the lines of the distinction suggested by Whitman in chapter 1). This distinction will be called into question by the end of this chapter.

128. Theiner et al., "Recognizing Group Cognition," 392.

129. Gustave Le Bon, *The Crowd: A Study of the Popular Mind* (New York: Macmillan, 1897), v.

130. Le Bon, *The Crowd: A Study of the Popular Mind*, 2, in Wilson, *Boundaries of the Mind*, 271.

131. Wilson, *Boundaries of the Mind*, 271–72.

132. This is true of Knorr Cetina's work as well, save for a stray comparison to drug addiction that sounds more like Le Bon: "In the language Matza once used to describe marijuana users (1969: 130ff), these experts appeared engrossed in their project, entranced by the thing they were doing; they created the impression that they forgot themselves and their immediate environment. The drug, of course, is not marijuana, but the experiment; it is work that weighs more because it is embedded in and interlinked with the work of others" (Knorr Cetina, *Epistemic Cultures*, 170). Even in this case, it is not that the experiment's mind has taken over the expert's mind; it is simply that the individual researchers are engrossed in their work.

133. Wilson, "Altruism and Organism," 128.

134. Wilson, *Boundaries of the Mind*, 281.

135. Wilson, *Boundaries of the Mind*, 282.

136. Wilson, *Boundaries of the Mind*, 286, 301.

137. Compare Wilson's comments about groups having "full-blown minds": "That is clearly science fiction, not borderline science, in the league of Attack of the Killer Tomatoes rather than, say, the Gaia Hypothesis" (Wilson, *Boundaries of the Mind*, 290).

138. Robert Wilson uses the language of "multilevel," but in a rather different way. Wilson describes psychological properties in Le Bon's account of crowds as multilevel inasmuch as they are taken to be identical on both the level of the crowd, and the level of the individual. This is quite different from how an emergentist would use the term multilevel (or, indeed, how it is used by evolutionary biologists), who use the term precisely to describe accounts of complex systems that allow for related (through supervenience and downward causation), but quite distinct, processes at various levels. So multilevel evolutionary theory, for example, assumes precisely that selection pressures at the individual and group levels work at cross purposes to one another.

139. Furthermore, in light of Sperry's research, perhaps we could say that the group could literally be said to have a mind that the individuals do not, just as whole brains have a mind that the individual hemispheres do not. The individual hemispheres, apparently, do have minds. But they are separable from one another and, so far as we can tell, ought to be thought of as separate. The mind that emerges from the two hemispheres combined is not accessible to the hemispheres in isolation. The influence comes in the form of rather straightforward downward causation, rather than mind-meld.

140. Caporael and Baron, "Groups as the Mind's Natural Environment." In a somewhat confusing concession at the end of *Boundaries of the Mind*, Robert Wilson holds open the possibility of arguing along the lines that I am arguing here:

> "In the last few sections I have voiced a suspicion about general appeals—to the level at which selection occurs, or to the kinds of characteristics that we find in individuals—as the basis for defending the group mind hypothesis. But this, together with the overall deflationary message of Part Four, should not be taken to imply my skepticism about whether group minds exist. There can be no group-level focal cognitive processes and abilities without the activities of individuals, and in at least some cases those individuals are cognitive agents, agents with minds. In articulating a view of the mind, however, in which the social embeddedness of the individual makes a crucial difference to the kind of mind that individual has, I hope to have arrested the thought that the dependence relations here flow simply from 'higher levels' (the group, the social) to 'lower levels' (the individual, the cognitive). The minds that individuals have are already the minds of individuals in groups" (Wilson, *Boundaries of the Mind*, 305–06).

> If this is ultimately where Wilson wants to land, it seems we can summarize his contribution, in the terms of emergence, as merely insisting that we take good account of the bottom-up relationships with the system, not merely the top-down. This is surely correct, though one wonders whether this is really the side of the dialectic that needs shoring up, given the rampant atomistic individualism in much social theory.

141. Mary Douglas, *How Institutions Think* (Syracuse, NY: Syracuse University Press, 1986), 8.

142. Douglas, *How Institutions Think*, x.

143. Douglas, *How Institutions Think*, 92.

144. Emile Durkheim, *The Elementary Forms of the Religious Life*, trans. Joseph Ward Swain (New York: Free Press, 1915), 30, cited in Douglas, *How Institutions Think*, 12.

145. Ludwik Fleck, *Genesis and Development of a Scientific Fact* (Chicago: University of Chicago Press, 1979), 78.

146. Fleck, *Genesis and Development of a Scientific Fact*, 41.

147. Douglas, *How Institutions Think*, 13.

148. Haag et al., "The Emergence of Self," 337.

149. Fleck, *Genesis and Development of a Scientific Fact*, 41. I would only subscribe to Fleck's description of thought styles exerting "an absolutely compulsive force" if we understand that this force has a limited scope, such that this coercive regulation doesn't eliminate individual agency. That is, I take it that the reigning thought style does define categories and supply the structure within which individuals and groups do their thinking and arguing. But, within these constraints, these acts are indeed actors—perhaps even creative or, as I will discuss in the final chapter, subversive, actors.

150. For example: female male left right people king Douglas, *How Institutions Think*, 49. This of course has much in common with J. Louis Martyn's reading of στοιχεῖα τοῦ κόσμου ("elements of the cosmos") in Galatians; see J. Louis Martyn, *Galatians: A New Translation With Introduction and Commentary* (New York: Doubleday, 1997), 403–06.

151. Douglas, *How Institutions Think*, 63.

152. For an estimate of the number of neurons in the average human brain, see F. A. C. Azevedo et al., "Equal Numbers of Neuronal and Nonneuronal Cells Make the Human Brain an Isometrically Scaled-up Primate Brain," *The Journal of Comparative Neurology* 513, no. 5 (2009): 532–41.

153. Auffray and Nottale, "Scale Relativity Theory and Integrative Systems Biology: 1: Founding Principles and Scale Laws." That Paul ascribes agency to ἁμαρτία was apparent from the history of scholarship in chapter 1. That Paul describes ἁμαρτία as having a body (in Romans 6:6) will be argued extensively in chapter 4.

154. The surprising possibility we must leave open is whether there is some amount of "overlap" in these two network models. That is, it may be that the human individual person, constructed from the "bottom-up," may go "higher" than the level of the human individual who is taken to be the "atom" within the larger social structure. Extended mind, especially, suggests that there is this sort of overlap. So, "node" may be too precise. We may have to admit that it is not entirely clear at what level the human individual person exists, caught in this dialectical constitution "from above" and "from below." As a result, distinguishing individual agency from social agency may be impossible, unclear as it is where the "individual" ends and the "social" begins.

155. Durkheim, *Rules*, 251–52.

156. We might especially think of models of the individual agent that look to behavioral economics to describe this agent in terms of behavioral economics.

157. Elder-Vass, "Top-Down Causation and Social Structures," 89.

158. In this case, the only question would be how useful that fiction is. The persistence of mythological or apocalyptic readings of ἁμαρτία in Paul suggests that this fiction is quite useful in at least this case.

159. Daniel Clement Dennett, *Consciousness Explained* (Boston: Little, Brown and Co., 1991), 412–13.

160. Dennett, *Consciousness Explained*, 460.

161. Dennett gives us a typically exuberant, ambivalent answer. For him, human persons are "*magnificent* fictions, fictions anyone would be proud to have created" (Dennett, *Consciousness Explained*, 429).

162. Bruno Latour says it well: "Once you realize that scientific objects cannot be socially explained, then you realize too that the so-called weak objects, those that appear to be candidates for the accusation of antifetishism, were never mere projections on an empty screen either" (see Latour, "Why Has Critique Run out of Steam? From Matters of Fact to Matters of Concern" *Critical Inquiry* 30, no. 2 [2004]: 239).

163. Pettit, "Groups With Minds of Their Own," 182.

164. Tollefsen, "Extended Mind," 147.

165. Clayton, *Adventures*, 195–96.

166. Recall that "mythology" here is the analog to psychology.

167. I say "hypothesis" rather than "thesis" to highlight my intention to test this hypothesis exegetically in the next chapter.

168. Bultmann, *Theology*, I, 251.

169. Wilson, *Social Conquest*, 241.

170. Consider, for example, the equation of "cooperation" and "altruism" in the title of Nowak and Highfield's *Supercooperators: Altruism, Evolution and Why We Need Each Other to Succeed*. Sarah Coakley has commented on the way that Nowak "often talks carelessly as if cooperation were 'good' and defection 'bad.' But that is to commit the so-called 'naturalistic fallacy.' There is nothing intrinsically good about cooperating as such, and indeed cooperating human groups are—as Darwin himself saw—capable of inflicting destruction on other groups, or of being propelled by violent or (what we might want now to call) 'unethical' goals." See Sarah Coakley, "Cooperation, *alias* Altruism: Game Theory and Evolution Reconsidered" (Lecture 1 of "Sacrifice Regained: Evolution, Cooperation and God," The 2012 Gifford Lectures, Aberdeen University, 19 April, 2012), http://www.giffordlectures.org/lectures/sacrifice-regained-evolution-cooperation-and-god.

171. Wilson, *Social Conquest*, 259.

172. If Paul knew the category of "religion" at all, he might also have been quite happy to describe this as "religion" of a certain sort. As it is, Paul may already have dismissed this way of life as enslavement to "weak and beggarly elements [στοιχεῖα]," that is, enslavement to the founding analogies (Douglas's lists of opposites) of the κόσμος which is now coming to nothing (Gal. 4:9). For this reading of Galatians, see Martyn, *Galatians*, 393–406.

173. Certainly Pettit would argue for the "personhood" of the institutes, as Knorr Cetina has argued for understanding the experiment as a collective epistemic subject.

CHAPTER 4

1. Indeed, Emma Wasserman, in the conclusion of her study on ἁμαρτία in Romans 7, pinpoints precisely this problem: "Though apocalypticism may well turn out to be the 'mother of Pauline theology,' as Käsemann famously argued, the common view that

Paul inhabits a universe of warring cosmic hypostases needs to be subjected to more searching historical inquiry. An important first step in this project will be to develop criteria for distinguishing between the metaphorical and literal uses of language" (Emma Wasserman, *The Death of the Soul in Romans 7: Sin, Death, and the Law in Light of Hellenistic Moral Psychology*, vol. 256, Wissenschaftliche Untersuchungen Zum Neuen Testament [Tübingen, Germany: Mohr Siebeck, 2008], 147).

2. Gadamer, *Truth and Method*, 294–95, n. 224. This analysis is consonant with that of Jon Whitman, who argued that literary personification necessarily has to do with a self-conscious distance between the literary persona and the "actual state of affairs" as understood by the author. Whitman, *Allegory*, 271–72. Since the "actual state of affairs" in Paul's mind is exactly what is at issue, we can hardly use this as a criterion for answering the question. What we see happening in the history of scholarship is scholars, lacking esoteric insight into Paul's psychology, supplying their own sense of the "actual state of affairs."

3. If Krister Stendahl is right that much of what makes Romans incomprehensible to us is that we bring to it a totally foreign, modern notion of the self, then perhaps this is good news for our readiness to read Romans. See Krister Stendahl, "The Apostle Paul and the Introspective Conscience of the West," *The Harvard Theological Review* (1963): 199–215.

4. Deacon, *Incomplete Nature*, 470, 473.

5. Recall the definition of "mythological" described at the end of the previous chapter. I mean to use the word to refer to a real, emergent level of complexity which supervenes on the social, as the social does on the psychological, and so on. I use the term "mythological" in order to indicate that, to a large degree, this realm contains the sorts of entities Bultmann found it necessary to excise—chiefly, the cosmic power, Sin. I do not mean to import any of Bultmann's bias against taking the existence of such entities quite seriously. Quite the opposite, I mean to suggest that we can give an account of the emergence of such an entity—namely, Sin—that strongly suggests that its being is quite analogous to other entities we describe as "persons." (There are, of course, disanalogies between Sin's being and the being of human creatures that would be important theologically. On the "slippery" existence of Sin, see my comments in the concluding chapter.)

6. Troels Engberg-Pedersen, *Cosmology and Self in the Apostle Paul: The Material Spirit* (Oxford: Oxford University Press, 2010), 83. Hume's concept of "useful fictions" is an attempt to accommodate these reductionist instincts while still grounding some sort of realistic engagement with a world so obviously full of many more things than fundamental particles or whatever basic, low-level reality counts as "real" (e.g., "individuals" in reductionist social theory).

7. Hayden White, "The Historical Text as Literary Artifact," in *Tropics of Discourse: Essays in Cultural Criticism* (Baltimore: Johns Hopkins University Press, 1978).

8. Indeed, one of the influential works that provides some of this "ancient" background for Romans—in this chapter and the next—is John J. Winkler, *The*

Constraints of Desire: The Anthropology of Sex and Gender in Ancient Greece (New York: Routledge, 1990), a part of Routledge's "New Ancient World" series. The title of the series could hardly be a better expression of the dynamic at work. Indeed, as I will note below, Winkler's work (and much of the work of the Pauline scholars who follow him, e.g., Dale Martin and Stanley Stowers) would not have been possible before Michel Foucault—an avowed non-specialist in the ancient world—identified the root dynamic that Winkler and others explored at length. Michel Foucault, *The History of Sexuality, Vol. 2: The Use of Pleasure*, trans. Robert Hurley (New York: Vintage Books, 1990), 33–77. Much of my "historical" reading of Romans is situated in this "new ancient" world.

9. Stanley K. Stowers, *A Rereading of Romans: Justice, Jews, and Gentiles* (New Haven: Yale University Press, 1997), 122–25.

10. Seneca, *Ep.* 90.28.

11. Pseudo-Heraclitus, *Ep.* 4.10–15 in Harold W. Attridge, *First-Century Cynicism in the Epistles of Heraclitus* (Cambridge, MA: Scholars Press, 1976). The striking parallels to ancient Jewish invective originally led some (e.g., A. M. Denis, *Introduction Aux Pseudépigraphes Grecs D'Ancien Testament*, vol. 1, Pseudepigrapha Veteris Testamenti Graece [Leiden: Brill, 1970], 220–22.) to assume that at least two of these letters (*Ep.* 4 and 7) must be from a Jewish source. However, scholarly consensus has turned against this identification and instead views the whole corpus as Greco-Roman in origin. Attridge argues for a specifically *Cynic* background for these letters (13–23). See also the discussion in Stanley K. Stowers, "Paul's Four Discourses About Sin," in *Celebrating Paul: Festschrift in Honor of Jerome Murphy-O'Connor, O.P., and Joseph A. Fitzmyer, S.J.*, ed. Peter Spitaler, Catholic Biblical quarterly: Monograph series (Washington: Catholic Biblical Association of America, 2011), 112–13. Stowers also cites Heraclitus, *frg.* 5 and Xenophanes, *frg.* 11, 12, 14–16.

12. Seneca, *Ep.* 90.3. See also the role of *avaritia* in 90.38–39: "What race of men was ever more blest than that race? They enjoyed all nature in partnership. Nature sufficed for them, now the guardian, as before she was the parent, of all; and this her gift consisted of the assured possession by each man of the common resources. Why should I not even call that race the richest among mortals, since you could not find a poor person among them? But avarice [*avaritia*] broke in upon a condition so happily ordained, and, by its eagerness to lay something away and to turn it to its own private use, made all things the property of others, and reduced itself from boundless wealth to straitened need. It was avarice [*avaritia*] that introduced poverty and, by craving much, lost all. And so, although she now tries to make good her loss, although she adds one estate to another, evicting a neighbour either by buying him out or by wronging him, although she extends her country-seats to the size of provinces and defines ownership as meaning extensive travel through one's own property—in spite of all these efforts of hers no enlargement of our boundaries will bring us back to the

condition from which we have departed. When there is no more that we can do, we shall possess much; but we once possessed the whole world!"

13. Seneca, *Ep.* 90.6.

14. Stowers, "Paul's Four Discourses About Sin," 109.

15. Seneca, *Ep.* 90.46. This is how Stowers understands this passage. Stowers, "Paul's Four Discourses About Sin." In its original context, it is at least as easy to see the passage actually denegrating the moral value of the original pristine state, inasmuch as their "virtue" was mere innocence rather than a result of true wisdom. While this second reading leaves a weaker resonance with Paul, it still serves as evidence of ancient Greco-Roman reflection on the role of knowledge of sin in defining the nature of sinful behavior itself.

16. Stowers, "Paul's Four Discourses About Sin," 110.

17. Stowers identifies the letter's encoded audience as explicitly and exclusively Gentile—regardless of whether or not there were empirical readers who were Jewish. Stowers, *Rereading Romans*, 29–33. I am more inclined to see the audience as a mix of Jewish and Gentile members of Roman house churches. For example, while Stowers sees all of Romans 1:18–2:16 as addressed to a Gentile audience, I am inclined to say that the shift of person, from the third person to the second person in 2:1 indicates that the invective of Romans 1:18–32 has been a speech in character in which Paul is performing the role of Jewish stereotyper of Gentiles in their wickedness, hoping that his Jewish audience will get caught up in the act. One thinks of the modern comedy of Sacha Baron Cohen, for example his sketch "Throw the Jew Down the Well," in which, as the "Kazakh" character, Borat, Baron Cohen performs an antisemitic song in front of an American country western bar in order to expose the prejudice of his audience as they begin to sing along. In 2:1, then, Paul addresses the Jews in his audience regarding the judgment they hold against the Gentiles in their churches—judgment which they've just exercised through wholehearted approval of Paul's speech in character in 1:18–32. (Beverly Gaventa offers a similar description of the rhetoric of these passages—of Paul "springing a trap" on those "nodding their heads in smug agreement." Gaventa, "Cosmic Power," 233.) The key difference, of course, between Paul and Baron Cohen is that Paul really *does* believe the veracity of the decline narrative he tells about the Gentiles—he just thinks that the Jews in his audience ought not think they are morally superior (Rom 2:1–3).

18. I take it that the toleration of these consequences has to do with God's actually having given dominion and authority to human beings in creation (Gen 1:26, Ps 8:3–8). This dominion is constitutive of the human creature, to the extent that Gen 1:26 describes it as a gloss of what it means to have been made in the image of God. What humanity experiences in disobedience to God is that this dominion over the creation is transferrable; Sin exercises human dominion over the earth in place of humanity and against humanity's best interests. God refuses simply to negate Sin's

dominion by fiat because a) it is humanity's dominion and b) humanity's dominion is constitutive of human creatures. (Even if we live under Sin's parodic execution of our God-given dominion—suffering at the hands of a creature of our own making—we nevertheless continue to exercise this "dominion" in exercising real agency in underwriting Sin's dominion.) Rather, God's intervention in Christ's obedience (Rom 5:19) restores human dominion (Rom 5:17), both setting human beings free from the dominion of Sin and restoring Adamic dominion.

19. In Rom 1, the particular human beings in view are Gentiles, though it is clear that for Paul sinning is a universal human practice (Rom 3:9, 23).

20. Gaventa, "Cosmic Power," 233.

21. Dunn, *Romans 1–8*, 148. Dunn cites Sir 21:2, 27:10 and 1QH 1:27; 4:29–30 as ancient parallels for this idea of a sin as a cosmic power.

22. Gaventa, "Cosmic Power," 230.

23. See, for example, Dunn, *Romans 1–8*, 273, discussed below.

24. Käsemann, *Romans*, 148.

25. Robert Jewett, *Romans: A Commentary* (Minneapolis: Fortress Press, 2007), 413.

26. By "one's own creation," I mean to emphasize the sinners' participation in the systems from which Sin emerges—not that the sinner is in any sense personally or individually the cause of Sin's emergence.

27. This, of course, is an expression of Paul's mission: to bring about the obedience of faith among all the Gentiles. (1:5)

28. Stowers, "Paul's Four Discourses About Sin," 113.

29. Bultmann, *Theology*, I, 251.

30. Wink, *Naming the Powers*, 136.

31. Stowers, "Paul's Four Discourses About Sin," 114.

32. Deacon, *Incomplete Nature*, 470.

33. Anders Nygren, *Commentary on Romans*, trans. C. C. Rasmussen (Philadelphia: Fortress, 1949), 232–33.

34. Tannehill agrees with Nygren's sense that this locution should be taken in a collective sense, but suggests that it also somehow is identified with Christ's crucified body: "In v. 6 Paul wishes to make clear that this death has freed the believers from slavery to sin, but in explaining this he uses two short clauses which help us to understand how he conceived the death of the believer with Christ. In the one Paul speaks of the crucifixion of 'our old man' with Christ; in the other of the destruction of the 'body of sin.' These phrases do not refer to the 'old man' and 'body' of each individual, but to a collective entity which is destroyed in the death of Christ. This is made clear, first, by Rom. 7:4 and Col. 2:11 . . . this body is at the same time the body which died on the cross and a corporate body in which the believers were included. This body has a negative quality, for redemption takes place through its destruction" (Robert C. Tannehill, *Dying and Rising With Christ: A Study in Pauline Theology* [Berlin: Töpelmann, 1967], 24). I concur with Tannehill's instinct to read this in a collective sense. Inasmuch as the Body of Sin is crucified *with* Christ—if in some sense these two bodies are identified on the cross—we may have

a way of beginning to make sense of 2 Cor 5:21: "For our sake he made him to be Sin [ἁμαρτίαν ἐποίησεν] who knew no sin."

35. Dale B. Martin, *The Corinthian Body* (New Haven, CT: Yale University Press, 1995); Michelle V. Lee, *Paul, the Stoics, and the Body of Christ* (Cambridge: Cambridge University Press, 2006).

36. A. A. Long, *Soul and Body in Stoicism* (Berkeley: Center for Hermeneutical Studies, 1980), 3.

37. "πᾶν γὰρ τὸ ποιοῦν σῶμά ἐστι." Diogenes Laertius, *Vit. phil.* 7.56.

38. "Quod facit, corpus est." Seneca, *Ep.* 106.4.

39. Seneca, *Ep.* 106.4–6. Here and below I have slightly adapted the LCL translation to make it a bit more literal, for example, translating "*corpora sint*" as "are bodies" rather than "are corporeal."

40. Seneca, *Ep.* 106.9–10.

41. On Stoic materialism, see Engberg-Pedersen, *Cosmology and Self*, 19–22.

42. Lee, *Paul, the Stoics, and the Body of Christ*, 50. Lee cites Achilles, *Isagoge 14* (SVF 2.368) and Alexander of Aphrodisias, *Mixt.* 216.14–16.

43. Lee, *Paul, the Stoics, and the Body of Christ*, 46.

44. Diogenes Laertius, *Vit. Phil.* 7:139.

45. Engberg-Pedersen distinguishes three Stoic discourses: the physicalist, the cognitive, and the personalistic (describing super-human personal entities) and suggests that "there is no intrinsic constrast between those ways of speaking. Just to give one example, it is widely acknowledged that the Stoics identified God (Zeus) with 'fate'. But of fate they gave an account that was distinctly physical, indeed, fate is the essence, namely, the causal sequence—of the physical world as the Stoics understood this. In addition to identifying fate (physical discourse) with Zeus (personal discourse), they also ascribed 'providence' (that is cognitive discourse) to Zeus, taking it that God's providence was operative *through* fate, which they even called 'the *mind* of God'" (Engberg-Pedersen, *Cosmology and Self*, 81).

46. Lee, *Paul, the Stoics, and the Body of Christ*, 44.

47. Plato, *Tim.*, 30b.

48. Plato, *Tim.*, 69c. See also 36e.

49. Martin, *Corinthian Body*, 16.

50. Seneca, *Ep.* 95.51–53.

51. Seneca, *Otio*, 4.1.

52. Martin, *Corinthian Body*, 38. See also Margaret M. Mitchell, *Paul and the Rhetoric of Reconciliation: An Exegetical Investigation of the Language and Composition of 1 Corinthians* (Louisville, KY: Westminster John Knox Press, 1993), 60–64. The fable of Menenius Agrippa is perhaps the best known example of the *homonoia* genre (Livy, *Hist.* 2.32; Epictetus 2.10.4–5; Dionysius of Halicarnasus, *Ant. Rom.*, 6.83–86).

53. Seneca, *De Clem.*, 1.3.5–1.4.1.

54. Isocrates, *Panathenaicus*, 138. See also *Areopagiticus*, 14. Both are cited by Michelle Lee and discussed in Lee, *Paul, the Stoics, and the Body of Christ*, 41.

55. Wilson, *Social Conquest*, 186.

56. Seneca, *De Clem.*, 1.5.1 in Lee, *Paul, the Stoics, and the Body of Christ*, 37.

57. David E. Hahm, *The Origins of Stoic Cosmology* (Columbus: Ohio State University Press, 1977), 211 in Lee, *Paul, the Stoics, and the Body of Christ*, 48 n.7.

58. Lee, *Paul, the Stoics, and the Body of Christ*, 93.

59. Lee, *Paul, the Stoics, and the Body of Christ*, 88.

60. Martin, *Corinthian Body*, 17–18.

61. Martin, *Corinthian Body*, 21.

62. In part, this correspondence results from the Stoic commitment to non-reductive materialism—their insistence on corporeal explanations combined with a realist approach to psychology—of which emergentism is a modern species.

63. Though, note also the use of the phrase "τοῦ σώματος τοῦ Χριστοῦ" in Rom 7:4, discussed below.

64. This passage also raises the intriguing possibility that the collective body to be redeemed might be a cosmic body that includes the creation itself.

65. I have addressed this dynamic in more detail in Matthew Croasmun, "'Real Participation': The Body of Christ and the Body of Sin in Evolutionary Perspective," in *"In Christ" in Paul: Explorations in Paul's Theology of Union and Participation*, ed. Michael J. Thate, et al., WUNT (Tübingen, Germany: Mohr Siebeck, 2014).

66. Jewett, *Romans*, 744.

67. James D. G. Dunn, *Romans 9–16*, vol. 38b, Word Biblical Commentary (Dallas: Word Books, 1988), 722.

68. Käsemann, *Romans*, 339.

69. We might also imagine this in terms of Bourdieu's *habitus* as does Engberg-Pedersen (Engberg-Pedersen, *Cosmology and Self*, 141–42).

70. Recall that it was in wrestling with how best to describe the "psychosomatic unity" of entities emergent at Durkheim's "social" level that led us to introduce the technical definition of the "mythological" level at the end of the previous chapter. We agreed that we would describe superorganismic selves as "social bodies," while describing the subjective selves that emerge from these bodies as "mythological persons."

71. As noted above, Tannehill offers some support for this reading, arguing that both of these terms, "Body of Sin" and "our old self," are corporate entities (Tannehill, *Dying and Rising*, 29).

72. Smyth §998 describes the "distributive singular," but notes that it is rare with concrete substantives like σῶμα.

73. Gaventa, "Cosmic Power," 234.

74. The use of τοῖς μέλεσιν ἡμῶν in Rom 7:5 is a liminal case, the pivot point around which Paul makes the turn from the macrocosm to the microcosm.

75. I take the καὶ in 6:13 as epexegetical or explicative. See also Rom 6:19–20: "For just as you once presented your members [τὰ μέλη ὑμῶν] as slaves to impurity and to greater and greater iniquity, so now present your members [τὰ μέλη ὑμῶν] as

slaves to righteousness for sanctification. When you were slaves of sin [ὅτε γὰρ δοῦλοι ἦτε τῆς ἁμαρτίας], you were free in regard to righteousness." As in 6:13, Paul switches seamlessly from "your members" to "you." For ὅπλα as "weapons" in this verse, see Jewett, *Romans*, 410.

76. Douglas, *How Institutions Think*, 13.
77. Engberg-Pedersen, *Cosmology and Self*, 142.
78. Martyn, *Galatians*, 393–406.
79. Douglas, *How Institutions Think*, 53.
80. Seneca, *Ep.* 90.40.
81. Seneca, *Ep.* 90.44.
82. To some degree, Troels Engberg-Pedersen's entire project in *Cosmology and Self* is a (largely successful) attempt to demonstrate this possibility.
83. Compare the use of καταργέω in 1 Cor. 6:13, 13:8, 13:10, 15:24, 15:26.
84. Here, I simply mean to use the term "apocalyptic" in the sense of having to do with a "turning-of-the-ages," rather than with any specific relationship to the ancient literary genre, "apocalyptic." My sense is that, especially in Pauline studies through the work of J. Louis Martyn, these two senses of "apocalyptic" (the genre and the theological sensibility) are no more than homonymous.
85. Käsemann, *Romans*, 150.
86. Seneca, *Otio*, 4.1.
87. Käsemann, *Romans*, 176.
88. Tannehill, *Dying and Rising*, 19.
89. 1QS 3:20–23.
90. This presumably has to do with Christ's status as Son, who is to "be the firstborn within a large family" (Rom 8:29).
91. Tannehill cites additional parallels in the *Testaments of the Twelve Patriarchs*: Rebeun 4:11; Issachar 7:7; Dan 4:7; Asher 1:3–8, 6:5; Benjamin 3:3; Judah 20:1–2. One might also map this language onto the Rabbinic language of the good and evil *yetzer*, about which see, for example, Ishay Rosen-Zvi, *Demonic Desires: "Yetzer Hara" and the Problem of Evil in Late Antiquity* (University of Pennsylvania Press, 2011).
92. Note again the use of the plural possessive, ὑμῶν, with the singular concrete noun, σαρκὸς. About the apologetic comment generally, Tannehill notes, "It is not easy to explain what is both slavery and freedom at the same time" (Tannehill, *Dying and Rising*, 17).
93. Wilson, *Social Conquest*, 259. We noted before that what Wilson described as "religion" Paul would much more likely describe as Sin and, indeed, the Body of Sin Paul describes has precisely this contour.
94. Elsa Tamez, *The Amnesty of Grace: Justification By Faith From a Latin American Perspective* (Nashville, TN: Abingdon Press, 1993), 145.
95. For discussion of αἰῶνες, see Rom 12:2, 1 Cor 1:20, 2:6, 2:8, 3:18, 10:11, 2 Cor 4:4, Gal 1:4. For new creation, see 2 Cor 5:17, Gal 6:15. For discussion of "this world," see 1 Cor 3:19, 5:10, 7:31.

96. Whether this is good Stoic philosophy is no matter; Paul wasn't a Stoic. He is seeing what he can get away with from the scraps of philosophy he has heard in the *agora* for the sake of his apostolic mission to the Gentiles.

97. Stowers, "Paul's Four Discourses About Sin," 103–04. Stowers here is expanding the case he made briefly in *A Rereading of Romans*, 180: "If one goes with a psychological or a demonological meaning, then how does one reconcile this with Paul's seeming supposition of human freedom and his discussion of 'sin as transgression'?"

98. Jewett, *Romans*, 376. I take it that while "choices of evil deeds" in the abstract are inevitable in the context of Sin's dominion, we can still imagine individual choices as conditioned but free. Recall that the working hypothesis is that Sin's dominion functions through downward causation—understood as setting boundary conditions—that is, establishing what is *likely* (Haag et al., "The Emergence of Self," 337).

99. Rom 5:12, 14, 17, 21; 6:16, 21, 23; 7:5, 10, 13, 24; 8:2, 6.

100. Franz J. Hinkelammert, *The Ideological Weapons of Death: A Theological Critique of Capitalism*, trans. Phillip Berryman (Maryknoll, NY: Orbis Books, 1986), 135.

101. Romero, *Voice of the Voiceless*, 183. While we ought not allow this experience of literal death shift from the center of a working definition of sin, we might expand it to include all that works against the abundant, flourishing life of human beings and the creation as a whole. (In this sense, it is not possible to give a definition of sin without first articulating a vision of the flourishing of the creation—including, in particular, the flourishing human life.)

102. Isocrates, *Panathenaicus*, 138.

103. Here I understand "members" as multivalent, signifying both the activity of Sin's passions throughout the social body and also within the bodies of constituents, a first step toward the microcosm-macrocosm correspondence that will dominate much of Rom 7.

104. Martinus C. de Boer, "Paul's Mythologizing Program in Romans 5–8," in *Apocalyptic Paul: Cosmos and Anthropos in Romans 5–8*, ed. Beverly Gaventa (Waco, TX: Baylor University Press, 2013); Susan R. Garrett, *No Ordinary Angel: Celestial Spirits and Christian Claims About Jesus* (New Haven, CT: Yale University Press, 2008), 119.

105. Franz J. Hinkelammert, *La Fe de Abraham y el Edipo Occidental*, 2. ampliada ed., (San José, Costa Rica: Editorial DEI, 1991), 28 (all translations mine). The original: "El texto habla del pecado, pero no se trata de la transgresión de alguna ley. Está en la ley, actúa a través de la ley, usa la ley. En la ley cumplida actúa el pecado. Ahora, San Pablo habla de una ley y de mandamientos institucionalizados en estructuras. Es ley vigente, que es la otra cara de una estructura. El pecado opera a través de la estructura y su ley vigente, y no a través de la transgresión de la ley. Este pecado es un ser sustantivado, del cual la ley deriva su propia existencia y que está presente en esta ley. Es un pecado estructural."

106. Hinkelammert, *Fe de Abraham*, 28. "El cumplimiento de la ley" (literally, "the fulfillment of the law") is a technical term for "law enforcement" (i.e., the police). So, for Hinkelammert, it is a straightforward exegetical matter that policing leads to death.

107. Josh Sanburn, "All the Ways Darren Wilson Described Being Afraid of Michael Brown," *Time*, November 25, 2014, http://time.com/3605346/darren-wilson-michael-brown-demon.

108. Chia, et al., "Cultural Specificity in Amygdala Response to Fear Faces"; Hart et al., "Differential Response in the Human Amygdala to Racial Outgroup vs Ingroup Face Stimuli"; Lieberman et al., "An fMRI Investigation of Race-Related Amygdala Activity in African-American and Caucasian-American Individuals"; Phelps et al., "Performance on Indirect Measures of Race Evaluation Predicts Amygdala Activation."

109. For a discussion of fear in self-defense cases: Cynthia Lee, "Making Race Salient: Trayvon Martin and Implicit Bias in a Not Yet Post-Racial Society," *North Carolina Law Review* 91 (2013): 1580–85. For racial bias in the use of deadly force, see, for example: Joshua Correll et al., "The Police Officer's Dilemma: Using Ethnicity to Disambiguate Potentially Threatening Individuals," *Journal of Personality and Social Psychology* 83, no. 6 (2002): 1314–29.

110. "Seventy-three percent of Floridians who killed a Black person faced no penalty under Florida's Stand Your Ground law compared to fifty-nine percent of those who killed a White person" (Lee, "Making Race Salient," 1567).

111. It is here we see Sin operating as a collective person of the type Pettit described. The cognition that generates the conclusion "black lives matter less" follows takes roughly the form of the judicial paradox Pettit analyzes in which a court issues an opinion at odds with the conclusions of each member of the court. Pettit, "Groups With Minds of Their Own," 178. The fact is, however, that once Sin thinks this thought and thinks it persistently, one of the effects is that this thought's inevitability—if not its justice—becomes intuitive for those who participate in the racist culture.

112. Hinkelammert, *Ideological Weapons of Death*, 135.

113. Tamez, *Amnesty of Grace*, 142.

114. I take it that the two ἵνα clauses express divine providential intentions, not the intentions of Sin.

115. Tamez, *Amnesty of Grace*, 142, citing Hinkelammert, *Fe de Abraham*, 28–29.

116. Hinkelammert, *Fe de Abraham*, 28–29. The original: "Es pecador sin ninguna transgresión de la ley. Es pecador al identificarse con el pecado estructural. Por supuesto, es él el pecador, no la estructura. Pero lo es al someterse al pecado, que actúa a través de la estructura. Se hace esclavo del pecado. . . Esa, por lo menos, es la enseñanza de San Pablo."

117. So Stowers, *Rereading Romans*, 42–82, discussed below.

118. I take it that the much-discussed "ἐγώ" of Rom 7 is simply the self under the dominion of Sin.

119. Hinkelammert, *Fe de Abraham*, 28–29. Hinkelammert distinguishes in the original between "el pecado" and "los pecados," which I have rendered here as "Sin" and "sins," following my own rough convention for rendering ἁμαρτία as s/Sin, sin, or Sin. Hinkelammert's original: "hay pecados en el sentido de transgresiones de alguna ley, y hay pecado, un ser que mata por el propio cumplimiento de la ley. . . Pero este pecado tiene una gran diferencia con los pecados. Los pecados son transgresiones, y quien las comete, tiene conciencia del hecho de que está transgrediendo una norma ética. El pecado es distinto. La ética lo confirma, pide que se lo cometa. Tiene que hacerlo, porque cualquier ética pide cumplimiento y orienta la conciencia del pecado hacia las transgresiones. Para la ética normativa solamente existen pecados, el pecado como pecado estructural no existe. Como se ubica en el interior de la ética y de su cumplimiento, ésta no puede denunciarlo. Exclusivamente puede denunciar transgresiones. Por eso, el pecado consistente en la identificación con el pecado estructural, se comete necesariamente sin conciencia del pecado. Su propio carácter lleva a la eliminación de la conciencia del pecado. Este pecado se comete con buena conciencia; es decir, con la conciencia de cumplir con las exigencias éticas." Compare Walter Rauschenbusch: "If a group practises evil, it will excuse or idealize it, and resent any private judgment which condemns it. Evil then becomes part of the standards of morality sanctioned by the authority of society. This confuses the moral judgement of the individual. The faculty of inhibition goes wrong. The magnetic pole itself shifts and the compass-needle of conscience swings to S.E." (Walter Rauschenbusch, *A Theology for the Social Gospel* (New York: The MacMillan Company, 1917), 62).

120. Fleck, *Genesis and Development of a Scientific Fact*, 41.

121. Wasserman, for example, suggests that this is a key reason to take Paul's language as figurative: the tyranny of s/Sin is exercised internally rather than internally. This internal domination is, as she notes, explained quite well by the moral psychological paradigm that she and Stowers advance. In Hellenistic philosophy, she notes, "The monstrous ruler of the appetites emerges as if to answer the question 'if reason is not in control, who or what is?' Yet, no scholar of ancient philosophy would argue that Plato actually views this bodyguard as external to the person, as it clearly represents the appetites" (Wasserman, *Death of the Soul*, 69–70). The emergence paradigm suggests that this external power emerges from dynamics within the individual and exercises downward causation back upon the individual. We do not need to choose between describing this force as "internal" or "external"—a dynamic which helps Paul harmonize what he has gleaned from popular philosophy with his apocalyptic cosmology. Similarly, we need not choose between the emergent account and the most compelling features of the "moral psychological" reading offered by Stowers and Wasserman. The

dominion of Sin emerges from and recursively reenforces a disordered moral psychology.

122. Chiao et al., "Cultural Specificity in Amygdala Response to Fear Faces"; Hart et al., "Differential Response in the Human Amygdala to Racial Outgroup vs Ingroup Face Stimuli"; Lieberman et al., "An fMRI Investigation of Race-Related Amygdala Activity in African-American and Caucasian-American Individuals"; Phelps et al., "Performance on Indirect Measures of Race Evaluation Predicts Amygdala Activation."

123. Stowers, *Rereading Romans*, 42–82. This ideology will be discussed at length in the next chapter.

124. Aristotle, *Nic. Ethics*, 1150b20.

125. Euripides, *Medea*, 1077–80 in Stowers, *Rereading Romans*, 260.

126. Epictetus, *Diss.*, 2.26.1 in Stowers, *Rereading Romans*, 262.

127. Of course, our modern conceptions of the mind-body relation make it hard to cleanly divide the flesh and the members—if we understand them as synonymous with the body—from the mind. Instead, my practice in this reading is to read the flesh and members as the material interfaces with the broader Body of Sin. In many respects, this is a struggle that ancient Stoics, as ontological monists, faced in appropriating popular dualist Platonic ideas of moral psychology (Stowers, *Rereading Romans*, 262).

128. Plato, *Laws*, 875c. The natural connection between νοῦς and πνεῦμα is a commonplace in ancient philosophical cosmological reflection in which νοῦς is materially composed of πνεῦμα. (Though see Martin, *Corinthian Body*, 96–102.)

129. Hinkelammert, *Ideological Weapons of Death*, 137, going on to cite Rom 6:11–14.

130. Douglas, *How Institutions Think*, 113.

131. Douglas, *How Institutions Think*, 124. See further discussion below.

132. David L. Smith provides a schematic of five distinct theories of the transmission of sin: realism, federalism, example, social transmission, and biological transmission.David L. Smith, *With Willful Intent: A Theology of Sin* (Wheaton, IL: BridgePoint, 1994), 367. My discussion will be limited to biological and social transmission (though "biological transmission" in the sense I will discuss it seems also to include what Smith calls "realism").

133. Jesse Couenhoven, *Stricken By Sin, Cured By Christ: Agency, Necessity, and Culpability in Augustinian Theology* (New York: Oxford University Press, 2013), 43–44.

134. Smith, *Willful Intent*, 369.

135. Daryl P. Domning, *Original Selfishness: Original Sin and Evil in the Light of Evolution* (Hampshire, UK: Ashgate, 2006), 118, 149.

136. For example, for Donald Campbell, it is sociocultural evolution toward urban living that ultimately means that "urban humankind . . . approaches the social insects in self-sacrificial altruism" (Donald T. Campbell, "On the Conflicts

Between Biological and Social Evolution and Between Psychology and Moral Tradition," *Zygon* 11, no. 3 [1976], 188).

137. Couenhoven, *Stricken By Sin*, 44 cites *Contra Julian* VI.25.82, *Contra Julian Opus Imperfectum* III.62, 65, VI.21, 23.

138. Friedrich Schleiermacher, *The Christian Faith* (London: T & T Clark, 1999), §71, 2.

139. Albrecht Ritschl, *The Christian Doctrine of Justification and Reconciliation: The Positive Development of the Doctrine*, vol. III (Edinburgh: T & T Clark, 1900), 338–44. For analysis of Ritschl's critique and expansion of Schleiermacher, see Nelson, *What's Wrong With Sin*, 29–36.

140. "The kingdom of sin, however, is a substitute for the hypothesis of original sin which gives due prominence to everything that the notion of original sin was rightly enough meant to embrace" (Ritschl, *Justification and Reconciliation*, 344).

141. Ritschl, *Justification and Reconciliation*, 348.

142. Monika Hellwig in Domning, *Original Selfishness*, 16.

143. Wilson, *Social Conquest*, 193.

144. Deacon, *Incomplete Nature*, 470.

145. This suggestion will be explored in more depth in the Conclusions.

146. Stowers, "Paul's Four Discourses About Sin," 106.

147. Douglas, *How Institutions Think*, 124.

148. Douglas, *How Institutions Think*, 124.

CHAPTER 5

1. Stowers, *Rereading Romans*, 42–82.

2. Crucial to this comparison is the claim that both Roma and Hamartia may be understood as ideologically (not simply grammatically) feminine. (Of course, just about every Greek *polis* was represented by a female deity.)

3. Foucault, *Use of Pleasure*, 65.

4. Plato, *Laws*, 626a, c–e. John Madison Cooper and D. S. Hutchinson, eds., *Plato: Complete Works,* trans. Trevor J. Saunders (Indianapolis, IN: Hackett Publishing Company, 1997).

5. Winkler, *Constraints of Desire*, 49–50. Just how to conceive of this battle against oneself provided a challenge to various philosophical schools' anthropologies, and they solved it in different ways. The Platonic solution was to concede that the various locutions involved indicated that, indeed, the self was divided into a "better" and "worse" part (*Rep.*, 431a). Stoics, on the other hand, even in talking about self-mastery, stressed the unity of the mind. Stowers points to Chrysippus's interpretation of the *Medea*: "this passion is not a sort of foreign power, which wrests dominion from the mind; it is Medea's mind, which in unhealthy agitation chooses the bad" (Stowers, *Rereading Romans*, 262). As I have noted already, this distinction between the "self" and "other" is not necessarily the most meaningful

distinction in the ancient world inasmuch as the self is constituted for the ancients in social terms and the body has a highly porous boundary. Precisely the discourse of warring powers within the self (e.g., ἐπιθυμία and νοῦς) should be an indication of the difficulty of importing a modern, atomistic self into these discussions. There are reasons to imagine that Paul especially was open—precisely on the grounds of his "porous" anthropology—to ideas of the invasion of the self. See Martin, *Corinthian Body*, 17–18.

6. Xenophon, *Mem.*, 1.3.11.
7. Xenophon, *Mem.*, 1.3.14.
8. Stowers, *Rereading Romans*, 45, quoting Winkler, *Constraints of Desire*, 50.
9. Winkler, *Constraints of Desire*, 50.
10. Thomas Walter Laqueur, *Making Sex: Body and Gender From the Greeks to Freud* (Cambridge, MA: Harvard University Press, 1990).
11. Stephen D. Moore, "Metonymies of Empire: Sexual Humiliation and Gender Masquerade in the Book of Revelation," in *Postcolonial Interventions: Essays in Honor of R. S. Sugirtharajah*, ed. Tat-Siong Benny Liew (Sheffield, UK: Sheffield Phoenix Press, 2010), 86.
12. Laqueur, *Making Sex*, 62.
13. Diana M. Swancutt, "'The Disease of Effemination': The Charge of Effeminacy and the Verdict of God (Romans 1:18–2:16)," in *New Testament Masculinities*, ed. Stephen D. Moore and Janice Capel Anderson, New Testament Masculinities (Atlanta: Society of Biblical Lit, 2003). See detailed discussion below.
14. Stowers, *Rereading Romans*, 53. "Dio" here refers to Dio Cassius, *Hist. Rom.* 50.28.3.
15. Stowers, *Rereading Romans*, 53.
16. Craig A. Williams, *Roman Homosexuality: Ideologies of Masculinity in Classical Antiquity* (New York: Oxford University Press, 1999), 141.
17. Williams, *Roman Homosexuality*, 137.
18. Aristotle, *Nicomachean Ethics*, 1150b.
19. Stowers, *Rereading Romans*, 52–56.
20. Cicero, *Tusc.* 2.47–48. Translation from Williams, *Roman Homosexuality*, 133–34.
21. Cicero, *Tusc.* 2.53, 55. Translation from Williams, *Roman Homosexuality*, 135.
22. Stowers, *Rereading Romans*, 122–25.
23. Philo, *Opif.* 165. Translation from Thomas H. Tobin, "The Jewish Context of Rom 5:12–14," *Studia Philonica Annual* 13 (2001), 164. Philo professes his consent to the generic, gendered, ancient ideology of the passions and the necessity of *imperium* over the passions in *De Vita Mosis* I.26: "For these passions are the causes of all good and of all evil; of good when they submit to the authority of dominant reason [ἡγεμόνι λόγῳ], and of evil when they break out of bounds and scorn all government and restraint."
24. Wayne A. Meeks, "The Image of the Androgyne: Some Uses of a Symbol in Earliest Christianity," *History of Religions* 13, no. 3 (1974): 165–208.

25. Laqueur, *Making Sex*, 25–26. On the possibility of physical transformation, see Pseudo-Aristotle, *Problemata* 4.26, which suggests that it is possible for an effeminate man to become a woman (γυνὴ γὰρ ἂν ἐγένετο) through effeminating practices. For the possibility of the masculinization of women's bodies through gender-transgressive practices, see Swancutt's discussion of the *tribas* below.

26. Laqueur, *Making Sex*, 35.

27. Williams, *Roman Homosexuality*, 142. See also Laqueur, *Making Sex*, 59.

28. David M. Halperin, *One Hundred Years of Homosexuality: And Other Essays on Greek Love* (New York: Routledge, 1990), 29.

29. Philo, *Spec.* 3.37–41 in Swancutt, "Disease of Effemination," 177–78. See additional discussion below.

30. Halperin, *One Hundred Years of Homosexuality*, 133; Swancutt, "Disease of Effemination," 182–92.

31. Clement, *Paed.* 2.10 in Swancutt, "Disease of Effemination," 186.

32. While it is true that Philo in some ways anticipates the philosophical return to Platonism, his conception of νοῦς was still primarily Stoic (and, therefore, somatic and material). Engberg-Pedersen, *Cosmology and Self*, 20.

33. Indeed, as Halperin argues, in the ancient world "the social body precedes the [individual] sexual body" (Halperin, *One Hundred Years of Homosexuality*, 38).

34. e.g., NRSV, NIV, NASB, and NJB.

35. "Nature" here, as it does for Paul, refers not to what is inevitable (as the modern concept of "natural law" might incline us to imagine), but rather what is ideal—and, therefore, is so often under threat.

36. We see this gendered framework again at work in Rom 16:18. If this passage is, as Jewett suggests, part of a non-Pauline interpolation (which, if it is, I take it would be vv.17–19, not 17–20a; the image of the God of peace crushing Satan under their feet seems quite within the world of the Pauline imagination), then we would have to admit that the interpolator does a good job at resuming the gendered, stereotypical self-mastery language, contrasting κυρίος with κοιλία. See Jewett, *Romans*, 986–88.

37. Milton, too, describes Sin as having a female body: "The one seem'd Woman to the waste, and fair/ But ended foul in many a scaly fould/ Voluminous and vast, a Serpent arm'd/ With mortal sting" (*Paradise Lost*, 2.650–53). Regarding the monstrous "scaly folds," see the discussion of "gender monsters" below.

38. As we will see below, the dominant ideology had terms precisely for these impossibilities, these "gender monsters." Of particular importance will be the case of the *tribas*. Diana M. Swancutt, "Still Before Sexuality: 'Greek' Androgyny, the Roman Imperial Politics of Masculinity, and the Roman Invention of the Tribas," in *Mapping Gender in Ancient Religious Discourses*, ed. Todd Penner and Caroline Vander Stichelle (Boston: Brill, 2007), 11–61.

39. Ronald Mellor, Θεα Ρωμη: *The Worship of the Goddess Roma in the Greek World* (Göttingen: Vandenhoeck & Ruprecht, 1975), 16.

40. Mellor, Θεα Ρωμη, 16.

41. The assumption here seems to be that an object of religious devotion would not be so reducible, but, rather, would operate on what I have called the mythological level.

42. Mellor, Θεα Ρωμη, 25.

43. S. R. F. Price, *Rituals and Power: The Roman Imperial Cult in Asia Minor* (Cambridge: Cambridge University Press, 1984), 247.

44. James Knight, "Was Roma the Scarlet Harlot? The Worship of the Goddess," in *Religious Rivalries and the Struggle for Success in Sardis and Smyrna*, ed. Richard S. Ascough (Waterloo, ON: Wilfrid Laurier University Press, 2005), 113, quoting Price, *Rituals and Power*, 9.

45. Whitman, *Allegory*, 271–72.

46. Price, *Rituals and Power*, 40–43.

47. *Forschungen in Ephesos*. Vol. III (Vienna: Österreichishes Archäologisches Institut, 1923), 27–28.

48. Mellor, Θεα Ρωμη, 26.

49. Mellor, Θεα Ρωμη, 22–23. Later, Mellor argues that "Roma existed solely as a divine embodiment of the Romans themselves" (199).

50. Mellor, Θεα Ρωμη, 26, 195.

51. Mellor, Θεα Ρωμη, 196.

52. Mellor argues that Roma Aeterna is "no longer a deification of the Roman people; she is now a symbolic embodiment of the capital of the Empire and of the Empire itself." Mellor, Θεα Ρωμη, 202. My sense is that the simple removal of the word "symbolic" from Mellor's sentence would suggest that Roma's transformation is hardly so drastic and, moreover, would explain her persistence into the Middle Ages and the Renaissance.

53. Mellor, Θεα Ρωμη, 199.

54. Seneca, *De Clem.*, 1.3.5-1.4.1. See discussion in previous chapter.

55. Mellor, Θεα Ρωμη, 195.

56. Moore, "Metonymies of Empire," 74. The structural feature of this power as both external and yet somehow intimately near sounds quite similar to the way Paul describes *Hamartia*.

57. In the previous chapter, we noted this sort of awkward alternation and juxtaposition of singular and plural in Romans when Paul refers to emergent entities.

58. Adela Yarbro Collins, *Mark: A Commentary* (Minneapolis: Fortress Press, 2007), 269. Collins is doubtful that this story originally had a political meaning, largely because she takes Mark to have no anti-imperial rhetoric elsewhere.

59. Crossan, *Historical Jesus*, 313–18.

60. Crossan, *Historical Jesus*, 315.

61. Reynolds, *Magic*, 133.

62. Crossan, *Historical Jesus*, 315.

63. Paul W. Hollenbach, "Jesus, Demoniacs, and Public Authorities: A Socio-Historical Study," *Journal of the American Academy of Religion* 49, no. 4 (1981): 575. A 2014 *New York Times* article discusses a similar dynamic in a rash of possessions by

ancestral spirits in Cambodian garment factories: see Julia Wallace, "Workers of the World, Faint!" *New York Times*, 2014, SR4.

64. Fanon, after all, notes that Frenchmen as well as Algerians experienced mental illness in the context of the Algerian Revolution (Frantz Fanon, *The Wretched of the Earth* [New York: Grove Press, 1968], 277).

65. Moore, "Metonymies of Empire," 74. While Crossan's methodology demands that he leave the exorcism of Legion out of his construction of the historical Jesus (because of its limited attestation), his vivid placement of the narrative—even more, precisely the possession and exorcism themselves—within a probable ancient imperial context suggests that it can be interpreted productively within the context of the life of the historical Jesus—if "only for general background" (Crossan, *Historical Jesus*, 314).

66. It would be possible, of course, to see Legion's being sent into swine in Mark 5:13 as a moment in which Legion slides off the gender spectrum entirely. As Butler notes, "those bodily figures who do not fit into either gender fall outside the human, indeed, constitute the domain of the dehumanized and the abject against which the human itself is constituted" (Judith Butler, *Gender Trouble: Feminism and the Subversion of Identity* [New York: Routledge, 1999], 142). See Moore's comments regarding the gendered significance of the abundance of beasts in Revelation in Moore, "Metonymies of Empire," 92.

67. Paul Rehak and John G. Younger, *Imperium and Cosmos: Augustus and the Northern Campus Martius* (Madison: University of Wisconsin Press, 2006), 113.

68. Moore, "Metonymies of Empire," 75.

69. Moore and Mellor each discuss the hymn: Moore, "Metonymies of Empire," 78–79; Mellor, *Θεα Ρωμη*, 121–24. Also worth consulting isAndrew Erskine, "Rome in the Greek World: The Significance of a Name," in *The Greek World*, ed. Anton Powell (New York: Routledge, 1995), 368–69. I am using Erskine's translation.

70. Erskine mistakenly translates "λαῶν" as "men."

71. For *imperium* as the heart of Roman ideology of masculinity, see Williams, *Roman Homosexuality*, 137.

72. Moore, "Metonymies of Empire," 76–77. Like the Greek ἀνδρεία, we might translate *virtus* rather too woodenly, in line with its etymology as "manliness."

73. Cornelius Clarkson Vermeule, *The Goddess Roma in the Art of the Roman Empire* (London: Spink, 1959), 71.

74. Williams, *Roman Homosexuality*, 134.

75. Moore, "Metonymies of Empire," 85.

76. Moore, "Metonymies of Empire," 84.

77. Moore, "Metonymies of Empire," 80.

78. Moore, "Metonymies of Empire," 85.

79. Moore, "Metonymies of Empire," 86.

80. Moore, "Metonymies of Empire," 89.

81. *On Chronic Diseases* 4.9.132, translation from Bernadette J. Brooten, *Love Between Women: Early Christian Responses to Female Homoeroticism* (Chicago: University of Chicago Press, 1996), 150. This text survives only in a fifth-century Latin translation/adaptation by Caelius; thus, various authors will refer to the same work as either Soranus's or Caelius's. I am referring to the work as Soranus because, with Brooten, I take the features of the text that are salient for our purposes to go back to the time of Soranus. For discussion of this passage, see Halperin, *One Hundred Years of Homosexuality*, 21–24, and Brooten, *Love Between Women*, 150–62. This text is rather late for our purposes. Diana Swancutt has gathered the material from our period, however, to show the currency of the category, *tribas*, in the first century (Swancutt, "Still Before Sexuality").

82. "The actions of the mollis and the tribade were thus unnatural not because they violated natural heterosexuality but because they played out—literally embodied—radical, culturally unacceptable reversals of power and prestige" (Laqueur, *Making Sex*, 53). The classification of the *tribas* together with the *mollis* in Soranus does not indicate that the salient feature of both figures is their homoerotic "orientation." Rather, as David Halperin has demonstrated, "if such men and women are classified alike, it is either because they are both held to reverse their proper sex-roles and to adopt the sexual styles, postures, and modes of copulation conventionally associated with the opposite sex or because they are both held to alternate between the personal characteristics and sexual practices proper, respectively, to men and to women" (Halperin, *One Hundred Years of Homosexuality*, 24).

83. "The gender trouble with the tribas is not that she is a homoerotic woman, or even a woman who commits sexually deviant sex acts, but that h/e's penetrating others, a viril(izing) act, while not being a *vir*" (Swancutt, "Still Before Sexuality," 43).

84. Swancutt, "Still Before Sexuality," 12.

85. Seneca, *Controversies*, 1.2.22–23. See discussion in Swancutt, "Still Before Sexuality," 51–53.

86. "The figure of the tribas reflected Roman anxieties of empire" (Swancutt, "Still Before Sexuality," 13).

87. "During the first century CE, male oversight over women's economic activity lessened, first because of the Julian legislation exempting women who had borne the proper number of children from tutelage and afterward through the emperor Claudius' removal of automatic guardianship by paternal kin in cases of intestacy (Gai. Inst. 1.157, 171). It is likely that affluent women took advantage of their increased financial freedom, a development that might have been perceived as threatening" (Marilyn B. Skinner, *Sexuality in Greek and Roman Culture* [Malden, MA: Blackwell, 2005], 253).

88. Seneca, *Ep. 95*, 20–21. Translation adapted from Gummere. Compare Seneca's description—especially the description of hyper-masculine wrestling, overeating, overdrinking, and carousing—to Martial's portrayal of the *tribas*, Philaenis: "*Tribas*

Philaenis buggers boys, and fierce with a husband's erection, penetrates eleven girls a day. She also plays with the harpastum high-girt, gets yellow with sand, and with effortless arm rotates weights that would tax an athlete. Muddy from the crumbly wrestling floor, she takes a beating from the blows of an oiled trainer. She does not dine or lie down for dinner before she has vomited six pints of neat wine, to which she thinks she can decently return when she has eaten sixteen collops. When after all this she gets down to sex, she does not fellate men (she thinks it not virile enough), but rather devours girls' middles" (*Epigram* 7.67 in Swancutt, "Still Before Sexuality," 40).

89. Seneca does not use the word *tribas*, but the penetrative sexual activity he describes is paradigmatic of this figure. Ancient opinion varied on the proper way to identify the sexual anatomy of one who could perpetrate this "most impossible variety of unchastity." Caelius's *Gynecology* suggests that such women are "affected by the lust/erection [*tentigo*] (typical) of men" and therefore "take on a similar desire." Soranus, therefore, provides for a surgical correction for this "uncouth size . . . present in certain clitorises" through cliterectomy (Caelius Aurelianus *Gynaecia*, 2.112, translation in Brooten, *Love Between Women*, 164). Brooten notes that the word *tentigo* might best be translated as "erection," given its basic meaning of "swelling" or "stiffness." It is only by metaphorical extension that the word comes to mean "lust." It is therefore quite possible that what Caelius has in mind is precisely what Swancutt suggests below: namely, that these women have acquired male genitalia to match their masculine sexual appetites.

90. Swancutt, "Still Before Sexuality," 21.

91. "Natural" in ancient discourse regularly entails "proper" or "ideal," but not "universal," and certainly not "inevitable." That which is ideally natural nevertheless is something to be achieved.

92. Swancutt, "Still Before Sexuality," 12.

93. Valerius Maixmus, 9.1.ext.7 in Williams, *Roman Homosexuality*, 137.

94. "The conceptual anomaly inherent in this situation (men submitting to women's dominion) is directly embodied in Valerius' language, through the oxymoronic *delicato imperio*: if *imperium* is masculine it is normally anything but *delicatum*. Thus a *delicatum imperium* is a self-contradictory impossibility, and these men are depicted as gender deviants: an *effeminatior multitudo* whose claim to the title *viri* is disputed" (Williams, *Roman Homosexuality*, 137).

95. Consider Hor. *Epod.* 9:12–14; Serv. *ad Aen.* 8.696; Plutarch, *Life of Antony*, 60.1.

96. Thus, Suetonius, even in the midst of a moralistic tirade agains Nero's sexual misconduct, allows himself to be distracted from the charge of incest in order to note the danger of his mother, Agrippina, through sexual congress with the emperor, gaining too much power (Suetonius, *Life of Nero*, 28.2.). In doing so, Suetonius echoes Tiberius's own censure of Agrippina the Elder's ambitions

as being far too masculine, as reported by Tacitus (Tacitus, *Annals*, 6.25 cited in Williams, *Roman Homosexuality*, 320: "*aequi impatiens, dominandi avida, virilibus curis feminarum vitia exuerat*"; 12.7: "*adductum et quasi virile servitium*").

97. Cato's line is preserved in Plutarch, *Cato Maior*, 8.4. Translation in Williams, *Roman Homosexuality*, 137.

98. Swancutt, "Still Before Sexuality," 55. Whether or not such people existed is not important for Swancutt's argument, nor is it relevant for mine. The point is to demonstrate that this is a "live" category in first-century gender ideology.

99. The reliefs at Aphrodisias were not the only ancient representations of conquered peoples. R. R. R. Smith lists at least five other known *gentes devictae*. R. R. R. Smith, "Simulacra Gentium: The Ethne From the Sebasteion At Aphrodisias," *The Journal of Roman Studies* 78 (1988): 71–72. While Smith notes that not all of the images at Aphrodisias are as explicit in their depiction of the *capta* theme apparent in other Roman triumphal art (presumably as part of the political rhetoric of the temple as a whole—a colonial attempt to "write oneself into" the imperial ideology), the images nevertheless retain "at least overtones of conquest and capture." Smith, "Simulacra Gentium," 57. Smith does not pay special attention to the gender ideology of such depictions, which, I argue, make these "overtones" much more prominent. As evidence of the prominence of the emasculating stigma for ancient colonial peoples, we might note that the reliefs do not include the Aphrodisians themselves. Even in the somewhat tamed form—these ἔθνη are not the graphically abject figures of some other triumphal art—the Aphrodisian sponsors of the reliefs would not have wanted to imagine themselves as among the conquered peoples, emasculated by hypermasculine Roman *imperium*.

100. Jonathan L. Reed, *The Harpercollins Visual Guide to the New Testament: What Archaeology Reveals About the First Christians*, 1st ed. (New York: HarperOne, 2007), 117.

101. The fact that these sorts of depictions of nations developed, according to Smith, from the Roman practice of triumph, in which "conquered foreigners were paraded in chains" only further serves to concretize the bodies involved (Smith, "Simulacra Gentium," 71). Ideologically, of course, the individual bodies paraded were no less feminine than the collectively emasculated social body of which they were members.

102. Smith, "Simulacra Gentium," 77.

103. Joyce Reynolds, "New Evidence for the Imperial Cult in Julio-Claudian Aphrodisias in Dem Gedächtnis Von Hans-Georg Pflaum," *Zeitschrift für Papyrologie und Epigraphik Bonn* 43 (1981): 323.

104. In this way the *tribas* embodies a radically different androgyny than is imagined, for example, in Gal 3:28 (or assumed in Philo's interpretation of Genesis 1–3). These texts imagine an original, ideal (and therefore, in ancient eyes, *masculine*)

androgyny. Rather, the *tribas* and the *mollis* partake in a hyper-feminine androgyny, which Swancutt properly identifies (again, on the terms of ancient ideology) as "monstrous." This feminine androgyny would be marked by an over-indulgence of desire. In the case of the *tribas*, we have a "woman," driven by untamed desire, to assume the (unnatural) penetrative role. In the case of the *mollis*, we have a "man," driven by untamed desire, to assume the (unnatural) passive role.

105. I address the issue of whether or not Paul is making any direct politic critiques through his rhetoric in a note below.

106. Swancutt, "Disease of Effemination," 179.

107. Clement, *Paed.* 2.10 in Swancutt, "Disease of Effemination," 186.

108. Chrysostom, *Homilies on Romans,* 4.1, 3 in Swancutt, "Disease of Effemination," 191.

109. This is the consequence of the ideological complex that we have been examining: moral (self-)discipline, high social status, political *imperium*, penetrative sexual practice, and rational psychology must (ideologically) correspond with the status *vir*. Anything else indicates that one is lacking in *virtus,* and therefore makes one less than *vir*, and begins a cascade of gender transformation in all other aspects. Effeminate sexual practice could cause irrational feminine psychology, but irrational feminine psychology could just as well cause effeminate sexual practice. Submitting to the *imperium* of another was ideologically equivalent to being sexually passive, and could be evidence of such passivity or an eventual inevitable consequence of such passivity. This is what leads Brooten to ask, regarding Pseudo-Aristotle's *Problemata* 4.26, when it describes the possibility of a sexually passive man "becoming a woman": "Does 'woman' here mean a human being who is penetrated?" (Brooten, *Love Between Women,* 149). The answer must be "yes," and the consequences are far-reaching: "woman" (just as "man") in this ideology has a set of necessary correspondences, such that any one gendered identifier is taken to indicate the presence (or eventual appearance) of all others. What we see in the case of Hamartia in Romans is an account of this sort of gender deviance, and the resulting cascade of consequences at the individual, social, and mythological levels.

110. Swancutt, "Disease of Effemination," 204. Philo, *Opif.* 165 (see discussion above). This effeminate mind has the power to alter the physiology of the body: "Pederasty is now a matter of boasting not only to penetrators but also to the passives, who habituate themselves to endure the disease of effemination . . . and leave no ember of their male sex-nature to smolder. Mark how conspicuously they braid and adorn the hair of their heads, and how they scrub and paint their faces with cosmetics and pigments and the like, and smother themselves with fragrant unguents (for of all such embellishments, used by all who deck themselves out to wear a comely appearance, fragrance is the most seductive); in fact their contrivance to transform, by scrupulous refinement, the male nature to the female

does not raise a blush. These persons are rightly judged worthy of death by those who obey the law, which ordains that the androgyne who debased the currency of nature should perish unavenged, suffering not to live for a day or even an hour, as a disgrace to himself, his household, his homeland, and the whole of humanity" (Philo, *Spec.* 3.37–41 in Swancutt, "Disease of Effemination," 177–78). Philo's language about the deservedness of the law's assignment of capital punishment for this physiologically-transformative gender-deviance (is Lev 20:13 in view?) mirrors closely Paul's language in Rom 1:32 (though in Romans, there is a larger litany of sins in view).

111. Swancutt, "Disease of Effemination," 175.

112. Jonathan Walters, "Invading the Roman Body: Manliness and Impenetrability in Roman Thought," in *Roman Sexualities*, ed. Judith P. Hallett and Marilyn B. Skinner (Princeton, NJ: Princeton University Press, 1997), 39–40.

113. My assumption is that Romans assumes a male audience—that is, that the "encoded audience" is male, while presumably the original "empirical audience" included women. On the categories, "encoded audience" and "empirical audience," see Stowers, *Rereading Romans*, 21–22.

114. The dynamic of a power at once internal and foreign aligns with the way Crossan described the colonial "schizophrenic" experience of "a power admittedly greater than oneself, admittedly 'inside' oneself, but that one declares to be evil and therefore beyond any collusion or cooperation" (Crossan, *Historical Jesus*, 313–14). It also resonates with Moore's description of Roma: "a power that was at once irresistible and external to the city, emanating from a place far distant from it, yet extending deep within it." Moore, "Metonymies of Empire," 74.

115. Neil Elliott, *The Arrogance of Nations: Reading Romans in the Shadow of Empire* (Minneapolis: Fortress Press, 2008), 60–81.

116. Suetonius, *Claudius*, 33 in Elliott, *Arrogance of Nations*, 65.

117. Suetonius, *Calilgula*, 36.Translation from Suetonius, *Lives of the Caesars*, trans. Catharine Edwards (New York: Oxford University Press, 2000).

118. Philo, *Legatio ad Gaium*, 111 (Yonge's translation).

119. Philo, *Leg.*, 14.

120. Elliott also cites similar passages in Tacitus (*Ann.* 13.20); see Elliott, *Arrogance of Nations*, 82. The similarity between Suetonius's description of Gaius and Paul's description of Gentile moral decline in Rom 1:18–32 is enough for Elliott to conclude that "Paul intends his hearers to recognize definite allusions to none other than the Caesars themselves" (Elliott, *Arrogance of Nations*, 79). Rather than being distracted—as both Elliott and various opponents of "empire criticism" would have us be—by concerns about authorial intent, I take it that we would be better served simply to acknowledge the ways imperial ideology functions as a totalizing discourse. (For one recent assessment of "empire criticism" that seems to be distracted precisely by questions of historical certainty regarding authorial

intent, see Scot McKnight and Joseph B. Modica, eds., *Jesus is Lord, Caesar is Not: Evaluating Empire in New Testament Studies* [Downers Grove, IL: InterVarsity Press, 2013].)

Our discussion of the social basis of cognition is quite useful here. Imperialism so takes over the thought world of a culture that all cognitive resources are connected to its networks of meaning-making. Nothing can be said that does not speak of empire. (Again, whether it does so "intentionally" or "unintentionally" is relatively unimportant.) Indeed, in terms of sociolinguistic cognition, this might be the definition of empire.

Therefore, whatever Paul was to say about Hamartia was always going to be "political" in this sense—regardless of his intentions. Whatever Paul was going to say about Hamartia was likewise going to be "gendered," given the degree to which Roman imperial discourse was deeply gendered. What Paul did in Romans, in his description of Hamartia, was to paint her (whether intentionally or unintentionally, who can know?) in terms of a tribadic, feminine, and effeminating imperium that struck at the core of gendered Roman imperial ideology. The character of Hamartia's rule—intemperate in its quest for domination, spilling over into intemperance more generally—is that of the intemperate, effeminate Roman emperors of Suetonius and Philo. Her feminine-yet-imperial identity has the contour of that of the goddess Roma, read as *tribas*. Her dominion has a form that can be read off the structure of the cosmos as Paul experienced it, defined as it was by Roman imperial ideology, aspiration, and insecurity. Paul's solution to this dominion will inevitably have political implications—whether we take Paul's solution to be subversively revolutionary or ultimately conventional (see discussion in the conclusion of this chapter). This is simply what it meant to say anything of significance in his time and place.

121. Tamez, *Amnesty of Grace*, 142. I am not making a claim here about the authorial intention of Paul (see note above).

122. This is the inversion of the language Seneca uses to describe the *tribades,* who have "put off their womanly nature." In Rom 13:14, the hearers are told to "put on the [masculine] Lord Jesus Christ" precisely in order no longer to "make provision for the flesh, to gratify its [feminine] desires."

123. Douglas, *How Institutions Think*, 124. (See extended discussion in chapter 4.)

124. Cic., *Tusc.*, 2.47. For context, see more detailed discussion above.

125. Within this context, Paul's mission "to bring about the obedience of faith among all the gentiles" (1:5, cf. 15:18, 16:26) is a shockingly brash description of a mission of conquest of the Israelite messiah-king, Jesus—not just to rule, but to capture slaves. The gentiles are to be conquered subjects of this Davidic king, slaves suffering the fate of the barbarian peoples of the reliefs at Aphrodisias and countless images of triumph art that one finds in imperial propaganda. Bringing about "obedience" is a straightforward term of domination. It is this vision of divine mission and conquest that Jewett argues sets the stage for Paul's description of

those who become members of Christ's Body as "supervictors" (8:37) (Jewett, *Romans*, 548–49).

126. J. E. Lendon, *Empire of Honour: The Art of Government in the Roman World* (New York: Oxford University Press, 1997), 20.

127. Lendon, *Empire of Honour*, 20–21. On the social problem posed by placing a demand for obedience, Lendon cites Cicero *ad Fam.* 13.26.3: "That you might be able to do that with the less hesitation, I have secured a despatch to you from the consul M. Lepidus, not conveying any order—for that I did not think consonant with your position—but to a certain extent and in a manner commendatory."

128. Lendon, *Empire of Honour*, 21.

129. Dio Cassius, *Roman History*, 4.17.

130. Martin, *Corinthian Body*, 42–43.

131. Cic., *Tusc.*, 2.47. Cicero illustrates this macrocosm-microcosm correspondence when he describes the *imperium* of reason by means of analogy to "the way a master gives orders to his slave, or a commander to his soldier, or a father to his son."

132. This verse may establish the paradigm by which "δεδικαίωται ἀπὸ τῆς ἁμαρτίας" (Rom 6:7) becomes the opposite of "δουλεύειν ἡμᾶς τῇ ἁμαρτίᾳ" (Rom 6:6)—a pairing which otherwise seems more than a bit opaque.

133. Walters, "Invading the Roman Body," 39.

134. Diana M. Swancutt, "Sexing the Pauline Body of Christ: Scriptural Sex in the Context of the American Christian Culture War," in *Toward a Theology of Eros: Transfiguring Passion At the Limits of Discipline*, ed. Virginia Burrus and Catherine Keller (New York: Fordham University Press, 2006), 84.

135. To understand the contrast with dominant ideology, it is crucial here to remember that the believers' obedience is conceived mimetically. Obedience to the gods would have been more or less easily assimilated into the dominant ideology. Imitation of an obedient god—even, or especially, of a king given divine honors—would not have been so easily assimilated.

136. Jewett, *Romans*, 410.

137. Whether this thought was ever present in Paul's mind, no one can know.

138. Moore, "Metonymies of Empire," 90.

139. Price, *Rituals and Power*, 247.

140. Butler, *Gender Trouble*, 185.

141. Moore, *Poststructuralism and the New Testament: Derrida and Foucault At the Foot of the Cross*, 28–38, 48. Moore helpfully compiles citations for Derrida, Paul de Man, J. Hillis Miller, Barbara Johnson, and Shoshana Felman articulating this shared deconstructive insight.

142. From the point of view of deconstruction, "the actual state of affairs" would qualify as a "text" just as well as any literary interpretation of that state.

143. Douglas, *How Institutions Think*, 111–28.

144. Hinkelammert, *Fe de Abraham*, 29.

145. Of course, I have not even begun to speculate about the ways in which our own— or, more to the point, my own—interpretation of Paul's account of Sin partici- pates in and reinscribes the invisible sins of our own cultural moment. My only hope can be that this work will prove insignificant enough not to merit such a critique—or should it receive such treatment, that this critique will serve the larger Body of Christ in the struggle against the dominion of Sin. In any case, what is clear is this: if we are to describe Sin in ways that contribute to the actual liberation of enslaved individuals and social structures, it will take nothing less than the work of God's Spirit (8:1–2).

146. Butler, *Gender Trouble*, 185, 175.

147. Ultimately, the ambivalence of Paul's engagement with this ideological com- plex may be encapsulated in the smallest of exegetical challenges: how ought we understand ὑπερνικῶμεν—"we have hyper-conquered"—in Rom 8:37? It is pos- sible to understand this in straightforwardly militaristic terms, as does Jewett, we he translates "we are supervictors" (Jewett, *Romans*, 548–49). In this reading, Paul would have fallen into precisely the trap which, according to Moore, the Seer fell. In critiquing the dominant ideology, Paul merely reinscribes it. Christ's obe- dience may have taken him to the cross. And those who are members of his body may, in mimetic obedience, have been co-crucified. But, ultimately, what results is simply a divinely supercharged conquering power. Paul has merely claimed for Christ and his social Body a superior degree of (nevertheless Roman) imperium. The "proof is in the pudding" for those who go with this reading—that is, in centuries of imperialistic Christianity following the conversion of Constantine. Moore notes the ironic role that Roma plays in this saga: "As *Roma Aeterna* she remained the primary symbol of the Roman Empire even after the Constantinian turning point and the movement of effective government to Constantinople. She was adopted by Christianity and survived through the Middle Ages and into the Renaissance, becoming the emblem of European civilization [Christendom] itself" (Moore, "Metonymies of Empire," 93).

On the other hand, what if we took "we have hyper-conquered" to mean some- thing like "we have conquered conquering"? What if this was, in fact, the great victory assured for the members of the Body of Christ? Indeed, the imperium secured in 5:17 does have a striking absence of an object: "those who receive the abundance of grace and the free gift of righteousness will exercise dominion in life through the one man, Jesus Christ." Exercise dominion over whom? Hamartia's dominion (exercised through death) has a clear object: her subjects (5:14, 6:16). But the dominion secured through mimetic obedient co-crucifixion is of a fun- damentally different character.

148. Jewett provides a summary of dizzying variety of interpretations of this pericope in modern scholarship. Jewett, *Romans*, 785–90. See note above regarding the irrelevance of authorial intention when it comes to assessing the relationship of Paul's text to Roman imperial ideology.

149. Gadamer, *Truth and Method*, 265–71.

150. Stephen D. Moore, *God's Gym: Divine Male Bodies of the Bible* (New York: Routledge, 1996), 108–17.

151. Butler, *Gender Trouble*, 185.

CONCLUSIONS

1. Whitman, *Allegory*, 271–72.

2. De Boer correctly identifies theological anthropology as the heart of the dispute between Bultmann and Käsemann. See de Boer, *Defeat of Death*, 28.

3. Murphy-O'Connor, *Becoming Human*, 96–97.

4. Haag et al., "The Emergence of Self."

5. Pettit, "Groups With Minds of Their Own"; Knorr Cetina, *Epistemic Cultures*.

6. Douglas, *How Institutions Think*, 49.

7. "This is the network. It's more than advanced technology. It's a living, breathing intelligence … It's teaching inventory to learn, allowing content to run faster and helping co-workers work better together … Machines have a voice … Money works smarter … Medical history is brought to life" ("A Network of Possibilities," *AT&T Enterprise Business*, 2011, http://www.business.att.com/enterprise/online_campaign/network/.)

8. Recall what David Chalmers had to say about the ways technology increasingly becomes incorporated into the minds of subjects, who then become increasingly dependent on its use, in David Chalmers, "Foreword," in Clark, *Supersizing the Mind: Embodiment, Action, and Cognitive Extension*, ix. This dynamic of interacting with a power both internal and external to us has become a recognizable feature of interacting with what I have called a "mythological person."

9. One might think of distributed systems like reCAPTCHA, through which difficult to decipher words from scanned books are digitized by harnessing a vast distributed "community" of individuals simply trying to prove that they are, in fact, real human users of a website (https://en.wikipedia.org/wiki/ReCAPTCHA). Individual words are deciphered by multiple users all across the globe until a consensus emerges. No single user ever sees the word in context. No single user necessarily has to give the right answer. But an intelligent consensus emerges from the complex of millions of users and the software rubrics for synthesizing these inputs. The Network also facilitates distributed computational models that more or less bypass users entirely, and simply harness the computing power of the various processors connected to it (e.g., SETI@home, Folding@home).

10. For two examples that use emergence to theorize the "global brain," see Gottfried Mayer-Kress and Cathleen Barczys, "The Global Brain as an Emergent Structure From the Worldwide Computing Network, and Its Implications for Modeling," *The Information Society* 11, no. 1 (1995): 1–27; Francis Heylighen, "The Global Superorganism: An Evolutionary-Cybernetic Model of the Emerging Network Society," *Journal of Social and Evolutionary Systems* (2002): 57–117. For a history of the concept of the "global brain," see Francis Heylighen, "Conceptions of a

Global Brain: An Historical Review," in *Evolution: Cosmic, Biological, and Social*, ed. Leonid Grinin et al. (Volgograd, Russia: Uchitel Publishing House, 2011).

11. This case study appeared in chapter 2 and considered the research of: Chiao et al., "Cultural Specificity in Amygdala Response to Fear Faces"; Hart et al., "Differential Response in the Human Amygdala to Racial Outgroup vs Ingroup Face Stimuli"; Lieberman et al., "An fMRI Investigation of Race-Related Amygdala Activity in African-American and Caucasian-American Individuals"; Phelps et al., "Performance on Indirect Measures of Race Evaluation Predicts Amygdala Activation."

12. Harvey Cox shares the following anecdote: "A few years ago a friend advised me that if I wanted to know what was going on in the real world, I should read the business pages. Although my lifelong interest has been in the study of religion, I am always willing to expand my horizons; so I took the advice, vaguely fearful that I would have to cope with a new and baffling vocabulary. Instead I was surprised to discover that most of the concepts I ran across were quite familiar . . . Behind descriptions of market reforms, monetary policy, and the convolutions of the Dow, I gradually made out the pieces of a grand narrative about the inner meaning of human history, why things had gone wrong, and how to put them right. Theologians call these myths of origin, legends of the fall, and doctrines of sin and redemption" (Cox, "Market as God," 18).

13. Anthony Mirhaydari, "Is the Market Overvalued?" *CBS News*, February 28, 2014, http://www.cbsnews.com/news/is-the-market-overvalued.

14. Alexandra Twin, "Dow's Biggest 2-Day Run Since '87," *CNN Money*, November 24, 2008, http://money.cnn.com/2008/11/24/markets/markets_newyork/index.htm.

15. Cox, "Market as God," 18. Cox's reference to "Saint Paul" is obscure. He may be referring to 2 Cor 4:18, 5:7, or Rom 8:24. Or he may be referring to Heb 11:1, with an ancient assumption of Pauline authorship of Hebrews.

16. Cox, "Market as God," 22.

17. Prins, *Ecology and Behaviour of the African Buffalo: Social Inequality and Decision Making*.

18. John Coates, *The Hour Between Dog and Wolf: Risk-Taking, Gut Feelings and the Biology of Boom and Bust* (London: HarperCollins, 2012), 29.

19. Keynes, *The General Theory of Interest, Employment and Money*, 12, VII.

20. Akerlof and Shiller, *Animal Spirits*, 3–4.

21. Akerlof and Shiller, *Animal Spirits*, 164.

22. Akerlof and Shiller, *Animal Spirits*, 160.

23. Akerlof and Shiller, *Animal Spirits*, 140.

24. Coates, *The Hour Between Dog and Wolf*, 6.

25. Coates, *The Hour Between Dog and Wolf*, 248.

26. Coates, *The Hour Between Dog and Wolf*, 4.

27. Coates, *The Hour Between Dog and Wolf,* 23.

28. Coates, *The Hour Between Dog and Wolf,* 27.

29. Coates, *The Hour Between Dog and Wolf,* 24.

30. Coates, *The Hour Between Dog and Wolf,* 6.

31. Knorr Cetina, *Epistemic Cultures,* 178. See my answer to Ronald N. Giere's critique of Knorr Cetina's account of distributed knowing in chapter 3 above.

32. Coates, *The Hour Between Dog and Wolf,* 248.

33. Coates, *The Hour Between Dog and Wolf,* 251.

34. Coates, *The Hour Between Dog and Wolf,* 254.

35. Akerlof and Shiller, *Animal Spirits,* 176. One gets a similar sense when considering Akerlof and Shiller's suggestions for "taming the beast" (146).

36. Wink, *Naming the Powers,* 137.

37. Douglas, *How Institutions Think,* 188.

38. Douglas, *How Institutions Think,* 81–90.

39. Douglas, *How Institutions Think,* 124.

40. Hinkelammert, *Fe de Abraham,* 29.

41. Louis Martyn's description of the crucifixion of a cosmos built on a set of (roughly Pythagorean) elements (στοιχεῖα) represents an important way of placing such a concept in Paul's historical environment. See Martyn, *Galatians,* 393–406.

42. I take it that here, Paul and Judith Butler are struggling with similarly dire diagnoses of the scope of the coercive power of oppressive regimes of thought.

43. "For present purposes, dipolarity need mean nothing more than that God is related to the world in two modes: as its eternal Ground, the source of all its possibilities, and as the Infinitely Related One, the One who internalizes and unifies all experiences within the world, bathes them in infinite love, and transmits them back to other experiencers in the form of the divine lure . . . both Ground and Responder" (Clayton, *Adventures,* 180).

44. Clayton, *Adventures,* 146. This understanding of the God-world relation is reminiscent of Samuel Alexander's description which Clayton cites but also critiques. See Alexander, *Space, Time, and Deity: The Gifford Lectures At Glasgow, 1916–1918.* One might also compare Pierre Teilhard de Chardin, *The Phenomenon of Man,* trans. Bernard Wall and Julian Huxley (New York: Harper Torchbooks, 1959).

45. Harvey Cox's description of the Market (above) takes the form of a malformed process conception of God.

46. This provides theological confirmation of E. O. Wilson's intuition that a human superorganism of the ant colony type would necessarily be less-than-human. Wilson contrasts "authentically cooperating individuals, as in human societies" with "robotic extensions of the mother's genome, as in eusocial insects" (Wilson, *Social Conquest,* 162). I would suggest that Sin wills to build for itself an entomological superorganism composed of human agents who function as mere "robotic

extensions" of Sin's tyrannical will, while Christ aims to form a Body that fundamentally underwrites the creaturely integrity of the individual believer.

47. Comparing the Sin-world relation and the God-world relation has particular relevance to Paul, given the way he conceives of these two bodies—the Body of Sin and the Body of Christ—precisely as two worlds, two ages, two creations.

48. Tamez, *Amnesty of Grace*, 145.

49. Tertullian, *De Praescriptione Haereticorum*, 7. This line served as the epigraph for chapter 1.

50. For an overview of the development of Satan in biblical theology, see Garrett, *No Ordinary Angel*, 112–26.

51. Susan Garrett points out just how similar are the roles and functions of Paul's Sin and the ancient concept of Satan. See Garrett, *No Ordinary Angel*, 119, 125.

52. The following are, of course, gross over-generalizations, but I take it that the tensions in practical ministry priorities they describe are quite real.

53. I use scare quotes for "spiritual" because it is not yet clear to me how, exactly, one might render an account of the "spiritual" along emergent terms in such a way that it would make sense to apply such a term both to entities like Sin and also to the Holy Spirit. My hunch is that "spiritual," on an emergent account, has to do with the dynamic that we have seen on several occasions now: interacting with a power that is at once fundamentally external and other to us, and yet also experienced as quite profoundly internal to us, inseparable from us, because the boundaries of the self overlap with this larger reality—because we are "within" this power. There would be, of course, important disanalogies to observe between the ways Sin and the Holy Spirit exhibit this most general quality of being "spiritual." My initial remarks above regarding the relationship between an emergent ontology of Sin and a dipolar doctrine of God presumably point in the direction of the sorts of disanalogies that would hold on this account.

54. One prediction of such a model of Christian intervention against Sin would be that interventions that apparently take place at both the individual and mythological levels (e.g., a personal exorcism) would necessarily have effects at the social level. This would be more or less as Crossan predicts.

REFERENCES

Ackerman, Jennifer. "The Ultimate Social Network." *Scientific American* 306, no. 6 (2012): 36–43.

Akerlof, George A., and Robert J. Shiller. *Animal Spirits: How Human Psychology Drives the Economy, and Why it Matters for Global Capitalism*. Princeton, NJ: Princeton University Press, 2009.

Alexander, Samuel. *Space, Time, and Deity: The Gifford Lectures At Glasgow, 1916–1918*. London: Macmillan, 1920.

Allen, T. W. *The Invention of the White Race*. New York: Verso, 1994.

Archer, Margaret S. *Realist Social Theory: The Morphogenetic Approach*. Cambridge: Cambridge University Press, 1995.

Attridge, Harold W. *First-Century Cynicism in the Epistles of Heraclitus*. Cambridge, MA: Scholars Press, 1976.

Auffray, Charles, and Laurent Nottale. "Scale Relativity Theory and Integrative Systems Biology: 1: Founding Principles and Scale Laws." *Progress in Biophysics and Molecular Biology* (2008): 79–114.

Azevedo, F. A. C., L. R. B. Carvalho, L. T. Grinberg, J. M. Farfel, R. E. L. Ferretti, R. E. P. Leite, R. Lent, and S. Herculano-Houzel. "Equal Numbers of Neuronal and Nonneuronal Cells Make the Human Brain an Isometrically Scaled-up Primate Brain." *The Journal of Comparative Neurology* 513, no. 5 (2009): 532–41.

Barnier, Amanda J., John Sutton, Cella B. Harris, and Robert A. Wilson. "A Conceptual and Empirical Framework for the Social Distribution of Cognition: The Case of Memory." *Cognitive Systems Research* 9 (2008): 33–51.

Barrett, C. K. *A Commentary on the Epistle to the Romans*. New York: Harper, 1957.

Bediako, Gillian M. *Primal Religion and the Bible: William Robertson Smith and His Heritage*. Sheffield, UK: Sheffield Academic Press, 1997.

Beker, Johan Christiaan. *Paul the Apostle: The Triumph of God in Life and Thought*. Philadelphia: Fortress Press, 1980.

Benedict, Ruth F. *Race and Racism*. London: Routledge & Kegan Paul, 1945.

Berger, Peter, and Thomas Luckmann. *The Social Construction of Reality: A Treatise in the Sociology of Knowledge*. Garden City, NY: Doubleday, 1966.

Berger, Peter, and Stanley Pullberg. "Reification and the Sociological Critique of Consciousness." *History and Theory* 4, no. 2 (1965): 196–211.

Berreby, David. "How, But Not Why, the Brain Distinguishes Race." *New York Times*, September 5, 2000.

Berryman, A. A. "On Principles, Laws and Theory in Population Ecology." *Oikos* 103, no. 3 (2003): 695–701.

Bickhard, Mark H. "Process and Emergence: Normative Function and Representation." *Axiomathes* 14 (2004): 121–55.

Bird, Alexander. "Causal Exclusion and Evolved Emergent Properties." In *Revitalizing Causality: Realism About Causality in Philosophy and Social Science*, edited by Ruth Groff, 163–78. New York: Routledge, 2008.

Boff, Leonardo. *Liberating Grace*. Maryknoll, NY: Orbis Books, 1979.

Bonilla-Silva, Eduardo. "Rethinking Racism: Toward a Structural Interpretation." *American Sociological Review* 62, no. 3 (1997): 465–80.

Bonilla-Silva, Eduardo. *Racism Without Racists: Color-Blind Racism and the Persistence of Racial Inequality in the United States*. 3d ed. Lanham, MD: Rowman & Littlefield, 2010.

Broad, C. D. *The Mind and Its Place in Nature*. New York: Harcourt, Brace & Co., 1925.

Brooten, Bernadette J. *Love Between Women: Early Christian Responses to Female Homoeroticism*. Chicago: University of Chicago Press, 1996.

Bultmann, Rudolf Karl. *Theology of the New Testament*. Translated by Kendrick Grobel. New York: Scribner, 1951.

Bultmann, Rudolf Karl. *The New Testament and Mythology and Other Basic Writings*. Translated by Schubert M. Ogden. Philadelphia: Fortress Press, 1984.

Bunge, Mario Augusto. *Emergence and Convergence: Qualitative Novelty and the Unity of Knowledge*. Buffalo: University of Toronto Press, 2003.

Butler, Judith. *Gender Trouble: Feminism and the Subversion of Identity*. New York: Routledge, 1999.

Campbell, Donald T. "On the Conflicts Between Biological and Social Evolution and Between Psychology and Moral Tradition." *Zygon* 11, no. 3 (1976): 167–208.

Caporael, Linnda R., and Reuben M. Baron. "Groups as the Mind's Natural Environment." In *Evolutionary Social Psychology*, edited by J. A. Simpson, and D. T. Kenrick, 317–44. Hillsdale, NJ: Lawrence Erlbaum Associates, 1997.

Cardenal, Ernesto. *The Gospel in Solentiname*. Maryknoll, NY: Orbis Books, 1976.

Chen, Lee Li-Jen, and Brian R. Gaines. "A Cyberorganism Model for Awareness in Collaborative Communities on the Internet." *International Journal of Intelligent Systems* 12, no. 1 (1997): 31–56.

Chiao, Joan Y., Tetsuya Iidaka, Heather L. Gordon, Junpei Nogawa, Moshe Bar, Elissa Aminoff, Norihiro Sadato, and Nalini Ambady. "Cultural Specificity in Amygdala Response to Fear Faces." *Journal of Cognitive Neuroscience* 20 (2008): 2167–74.

Chopp, Rebecca S. *The Praxis of Suffering: An Interpretation of Liberation and Political Theologies*. Maryknoll, NY: Orbis Books, 1986.

Churchland, P. M. "Eliminative Materialism and the Propositional Attitudes." *The Journal of Philosophy* 78, no. 2 (1981): 67–90.

Clark, Andy. "Intrinsic Content, Active Memory and the Extended Mind." *Analysis* 65, no. 1 (2005): 1–11.

Clark, Andy. "Memento's Revenge: The Extended Mind, Extended." In *The Extended Mind*, edited by Richard Menary, 43–66. Cambridge, MA: MIT Press, 2006.

Clark, Andy. "Curing Cognitive Hiccups: A Defense of the Extended Mind." *Journal of Philosophy* 104 (2007): 163–92.

Clark, Andy. "Pressing the Flesh: A Tension in the Study of the Embodied, Embedded Mind?" *Philosophy and Phenomenological Research* 76, no. 1 (2008): 37–59.

Clark, Andy. *Supersizing the Mind: Embodiment, Action, and Cognitive Extension*. New York: Oxford University Press, 2008.

Clark, Andy, and David Chalmers. "The Extended Mind." *Analysis* 58, no. 1 (1998): 7–19.

Clayton, Philip. *Mind and Emergence: From Quantum to Consciousness*. New York: Oxford University Press, 2004.

Clayton, Philip. *Adventures in the Spirit: God, World, Divine Action*. Minneapolis: Fortress Press, 2008.

Clayton, Philip, and Paul Davies, eds. *The Re-Emergence of Emergence: The Emergentist Hypothesis from Science to Religion*. Oxford: Oxford University Press, 2006.

Coakley, Sarah. "Cooperation, *alias* Altruism: Game Theory and Evolution Reconsidered." Lecture 1 of "Sacrifice Regained: Evolution, Cooperation and God," The 2012 Gifford Lectures, Aberdeen University, April 19, 2012, http://www.giffordlectures.org/lectures/sacrifice-regained-evolution-cooperation-and-god.

Coates, John. *The Hour Between Dog and Wolf: Risk-Taking, Gut Feelings and the Biology of Boom and Bust*. London: HarperCollins, 2012.

Coates, Ta-Nehisi. *Between the World and Me*. New York: Spiegel & Grau, 2015.

Cohen, Paul S., and Stephen M. Cohen. "Wöhler's Synthesis of Urea: How Do the Textbooks Report it?" *Journal of Chemical Education* 73, no. 9 (1996): 883–86.

Colbert, Stephen. "Ye of Little Faith." *The Colbert Report* (September 29, 2008).

Coleman, J. S. "Social Theory, Social Research, and a Theory of Action." *American Journal of Sociology* (1986): 1309–35.

Collins, Adela Yarbro. *Mark: A Commentary*. Minneapolis: Fortress Press, 2007.

Comaroff, Jean. "Missionaries and Mechanical Clocks: An Essay on Religion and History in South Africa." *The Journal of Religion* 71, no. 1 (1991): 1–17.

Cooper, John Madison, and D. S. Hutchinson. *Plato: Complete Works*. Indianapolis: Hackett Publishing Company, 1997.

Corning, Peter A. "The Re-Emergence of 'Emergence': A Venerable Concept in Search of a Theory." *Complexity* 7, no. 6 (2002): 18–30.

Correll, Joshua, Bernadette Park, and Bernd Wittenbrink. "The Police Officer's Dilemma: Using Ethnicity to Disambiguate Potentially Threatening Individuals." *Journal of Personality and Social Psychology* 83, no. 6 (2002): 1314–29.

Couenhoven, Jesse. *Stricken By Sin, Cured By Christ: Agency, Necessity, and Culpability in Augustinian Theology*. New York: Oxford University Press, 2013.

Cox, Harvey. "The Market as God: Living in the New Dispensation." *Atlantic Monthly* 283, no. 3 (1999): 18–23.

Craver, Carl F. *Explaining the Brain: Mechanisms and the Mosaic Unity of Neuroscience*. New York: Clarendon Press, 2007.

Croasmun, Matthew. "'Real Participation': The Body of Christ and the Body of Sin in Evolutionary Perspective." In *"In Christ" in Paul: Explorations in Paul's Theology of Union and Participation*, edited by Michael J. Thate, Kevin J. Vanhoozer, and Constantine R. Campbell, 127–56. Tübingen: Mohr Siebeck, 2014.

Crossan, John Dominic. *The Historical Jesus: The Life of a Mediterranean Jewish Peasant*. San Francisco: Harper, 1991.

Dallard, P., A. J. Fitzpatrick, A. Flint, and S. Le Bourva. "The London Millennium Footbridge." *Structural Engineer* 79, no. 22 (2001): 17–33.

Dallard, P., T. Fitzpatrick, A. Flint, and A. Low. "London Millennium Bridge: Pedestrian-Induced Lateral Vibration." *Journal of Bridge Engineering* (2001): 412–17.

Darwin, Charles. *The Descent of Man and Selection in Relation to Sex*. London: John Murray, 1871.

Davies, P. C. W. "The Epigenome and Top-Down Causation." *Interface Focus* 2, no. 1 (2012): 42–48.

Dawkins, Richard. *The Selfish Gene*. 30th Anniversary ed. New York: Oxford University Press, 2006.

de Boer, Martinus C. *The Defeat of Death: Apocalyptic Eschatology in 1 Corinthians 15 and Romans 5*. Sheffield, England: JSOT Press, 1988.

de Boer, Martinus C. "Paul's Mythologizing Program in Romans 5–8." In *Apocalyptic Paul: Cosmos and Anthropos in Romans 5-8*, edited by Beverly Gaventa, 1–20. Waco: Baylor University Press, 2013.

Deacon, Terrence W. *Incomplete Nature: How Mind Emerged From Matter*. New York: Norton, 2011.

Denis, A. M. *Introduction Aux Pseudépigraphes Grecs D'Ancien Testament*. Vol. 1, *Pseudepigrapha Veteris Testamenti Graece*. Leiden: Brill, 1970.

Dennett, Daniel Clement. *Consciousness Explained*. Boston: Little, Brown and Co., 1991.

Dibelius, Martin. *Die Geisterwelt Im Glauben Des Paulus*. Göttingen: Vandenhoeck & Ruprecht, 1909.

Dodson, Joseph R. *The "Powers" of Personification: Rhetorical Purpose in the Book of Wisdom and the Letter to the Romans*. Berlin: Walter de Gruyter, 2008.

Domning, Daryl P. *Original Selfishness: Original Sin and Evil in the Light of Evolution*. Hampshire, UK: Ashgate, 2006.

Douglas, Mary. *How Institutions Think*. Syracuse: Syracuse University Press, 1986.

Dunn, James D. G. *Romans 1–8*. Vol. 38a, *Word Biblical Commentary*. Dallas: Word Books, 1988.

Dunn, James D. G. *Romans 9–16*. Vol. 38b, *Word Biblical Commentary*. Dallas: Word Books, 1988.

Dunn, James D. G. *The Theology of Paul the Apostle*. Grand Rapids, MI: Eerdmans, 1997.

Durkheim, Emile. *The Elementary Forms of the Religious Life*. Translated by Joseph Ward Swain. New York: Free Press, 1915.

Durkheim, Emile. *Suicide*. Translated by John A. Spaulding. Glencoe, IL: Free Press, 1951.

Durkheim, Emile. "Individual and Collective Representations." In *Sociology and Philosophy*, 1–34. New York: Free Press, 1974.

Durkheim, Emile. *The Rules of Sociological Method and Selected Texts on Sociology and Its Method*. London: Macmillan Press, 1982.

Earley, Joseph E. "How Philosophy of Mind Needs Philosophy of Chemistry." *HYLE* 14, no. 1 (2008): 1–26.

Eisenstadt, S. N. "Multiple Modernities." *Daedalus* (2000): 1–29.

Elder-Vass, Dave. "For Emergence: Refining Archer's Account of Social Structure." *Journal for the Theory of Social Behaviour* 37, no. 1 (2007): 25–44.

Elder-Vass, Dave. "Luhmann and Emergentism: Competing Paradigms for Social Systems Theory?" *Philosophy of the Social Sciences* 37, no. 4 (2007): 408–32.

Elder-Vass, Dave. "Top-Down Causation and Social Structures." *Interface Focus* 2, no. 1 (2012): 82–90.

Elliott, Neil. *Liberating Paul: The Justice of God and the Politics of the Apostle*. Maryknoll, NY: Orbis Books, 1994.

Elliott, Neil. *The Arrogance of Nations: Reading Romans in the Shadow of Empire*. Minneapolis: Fortress Press, 2008.

Ellis, G. F. R. "Top-Down Causation and Emergence: Some Comments on Mechanisms." *Interface Focus* 2, no. 1 (2012): 126–40.

Ellis, G. F. R., Denis Noble, and Timothy O'Connor. "Top-Down Causation: An Integrating Theme Within and Across the Sciences?" *Interface Focus* 2, no. 1 (2012): 1–3.

Emmeche, Claus, Simo Køppe, and Frederik Stjernfelt. "Explaining Emergence: Towards an Ontology of Levels." *Journal for General Philosophy of Science* 28, no. 1 (1997): 83–117.

Engberg-Pedersen, Troels. *Paul and the Stoics*. Louisville, KY: Westminster John Knox Press, 2000.

Engberg-Pedersen, Troels. *Cosmology and Self in the Apostle Paul: The Material Spirit*. Oxford: Oxford University Press, 2010.

Erskine, Andrew. "Rome in the Greek World: The Significance of a Name." In *The Greek World*, edited by Anton Powell, 368–85. New York: Routledge, 1995.

Evans-Pritchard, E. E. *Theories of Primitive Religion*. Oxford: Clarendon Press, 1965.

Fanon, Frantz. *The Wretched of the Earth*. New York: Grove Press, 1968.

Faus, José Ignacio González. "Sin." In *Systematic Theology: Perspectives From Liberation Theology: Readings From Mysterium Liberationis*, edited by Jon Sobrino, and Ignacio Ellacuría, 194–204. Maryknoll, NY: Orbis Books, 1996.

Fleck, Ludwik. *Genesis and Development of a Scientific Fact*. Chicago: University of Chicago Press, 1979.

Foucault, Michel. *The Archaeology of Knowledge*. Translated by A. M. Sheridan Smith. New York: Pantheon Books, 1972.

Foucault, Michel. "Introduction." In *The Normal and the Pathological*, edited by G. Canguilhem, 7–24. New York: Zone Books, 1989.

Foucault, Michel. *The History of Sexuality, Vol. 1: An Introduction*. Translated by Robert Hurley. New York: Vintage, 1990.

Foucault, Michel. *The History of Sexuality, Vol. 2: The Use of Pleasure*. Translated by Robert Hurley. New York: Vintage Books, 1990.

Gadamer, Hans-Georg. *Truth and Method*. Translated by Joel Weinsheimer and Donald G. Marshall. 2d rev. ed. New York: Continuum, 2003.

Gairdner, William Henry Temple, and John R. Mott. *Echoes From Edinburgh, 1910*. New York: F. H. Revell Company, 1910.

Gallagher, Shaun, and Anthony Crisafi. "Mental Institutions." *Topoi* 28, no. 1 (2009): 45–51.

Garrett, Susan R. *No Ordinary Angel: Celestial Spirits and Christian Claims About Jesus*. New Haven, CT: Yale University Press, 2008.

Gaventa, Beverly Roberts. "The Cosmic Power of Sin in Paul's Letter to the Romans: Toward a Widescreen Edition." *Interpretation* (2004): 229–40.

Giere, Ronald N. "Distributed Cognition Without Distributed Knowing." *Social Epistemology* 21, no. 3 (2007): 313–20.

Giere, Ronald N., and Barton Moffatt. "Distributed Cognition: Where the Cognitive and the Social Merge." *Social Studies of Science* 33, no. 2 (2003): 301–10.

Gleick, James. *Genius: The Life and Science of Richard Feynman*. New York: Pantheon Books, 1992.

Greco, Monica. "On the Vitality of Vitalism." *Theory, Culture & Society* 22, no. 1 (2005): 15–27.

Gross, Charles G. "Genealogy of the 'Grandmother Cell.'" *The Neuroscientist* 8, no. 5 (2002): 512–18.

Gudorf, Christine. "Liberation Theology's Use of Scripture: A Response to First World Critics." *Interpretation* 41, no. 1 (1987): 5–18.

Haag, James W., Terrence W. Deacon, and Jay Ogilvy. "The Emergence of Self." In *In Search of Self: Interdisciplinary Perspectives on Personhood*, edited by J. Wentzel Van Huyssteen, and Erik P. Wiebe, 319–37. Grand Rapids, MI: Eerdmans, 2011.

Haeckel, Ernst. *The Evolution of Man: A Popular Exposition of the Principal Points of Human Ontogeny and Phylogeny*. Vol. 2. New York: Appleton, 1879.

Hahm, David E. *The Origins of Stoic Cosmology*. Columbus: Ohio State University Press, 1977.

Halperin, David M. *One Hundred Years of Homosexuality: And Other Essays on Greek Love*. New York: Routledge, 1990.

Hare, R. M. *The Language of Morals*. Oxford: Clarendon Press, 1952.

Hart, A. J., P. J. Whalen, L. M. Shin, S. C. McInerney, H. Fischer, and S. L. Rauch. "Differential Response in the Human Amygdala to Racial Outgroup vs Ingroup Face Stimuli." *Neuroreport* 11, no. 11 (2000): 2351–55.

Hasker, William. *The Emergent Self*. Ithaca, NY: Cornell University Press, 1999.

Hendry, Robert Findlay. "Is There Downward Causation in Chemistry?" *Philosophy Of Chemistry* 242 (2006): 173–88.

Hendry, Robert Findlay. "Ontological Reduction and Molecular Structure." *Studies in History and Philosophy of Science* 41, no. 2 (2010): 183–91.

Heylighen, Francis. "The Global Superorganism: An Evolutionary-Cybernetic Model of the Emerging Network Society." *Journal of Social and Evolutionary Systems* (2002): 57–117.

Heylighen, Francis. "Conceptions of a Global Brain: An Historical Review." In *Evolution: Cosmic, Biological, and Social*, edited by Leonid Grinin, Robert L. Carneiro, Andrey V. Korotayev, and Fred Spier, 274–89. Volgograd, Russia: Uchitel Publishing House, 2011.

Hinkelammert, Franz J. *The Ideological Weapons of Death: A Theological Critique of Capitalism*. Translated by Phillip Berryman. Maryknoll, NY: Orbis Books, 1986.

Hinkelammert, Franz J. *La Fe de Abraham y el Edipo Occidental*. 2d ampliada ed. San José, Costa Rica: Editorial DEI, 1991.

Hollenbach, Paul W. "Jesus, Demoniacs, and Public Authorities: A Socio-Historical Study." *Journal of the American Academy of Religion* 49, no. 4 (1981): 567–88.

Holliday, R. "Epigenetics: A Historical Overview." *Epigenetics* 1, no. 2 (2006): 76–80.

Hutchins, Edwin. *Cognition in the Wild*. Cambridge, MA: MIT Press, 1995.

Jewett, Robert. *Romans: A Commentary*. Minneapolis: Fortress Press, 2007.

Kant, Immanuel. *Critique of Judgement, Part Two: Critique of Teleological Judgement*. Translated by James Creed Meredith. Oxford: Clarendon Press, 1952.

Käsemann, Ernst. *Commentary on Romans*. Translated by Geoffrey William Bromiley. Grand Rapids, MI: Eerdmans, 1980.

Kauffman, Stuart A. *At Home in the Universe: The Search for Laws of Self-Organization and Complexity*. Oxford: Oxford University Press, 1995.

Kaye, Bruce Norman. *The Argument of Romans: With Special Reference to Chapter 6*. Austin, TX: Schola Press, 1979.

Kesebir, Selin. "The Superorganism Account of Human Sociality: How and When Human Groups Are Like Beehives." *Personality and Social Psychology Review* 16, no. 3 (2012): 233–61.

Keynes, John Maynard. *The General Theory of Interest, Employment and Money*. London: Macmillan, 1936.

Kim, Jaegwon. *Philosophy of Mind*. Boulder, CO: Westview Press, 1996.

Kim, Jaegwon. *Mind in a Physical World: An Essay on the Mind-Body Problem and Mental Causation*. Cambridge, MA: MIT Press, 1998.

Kim, Jaegwon. "Emergence: Core Ideas and Issues." *Synthese* 151, no. 3 (2006): 547–59.

Kim, Jaegwon. *Physicalism, or Something Near Enough*. Princeton, NJ: Princeton University Press, 2008.

Kirsh, David, and Paul Maglio. "On Distinguishing Epistemic From Pragmatic Action." *Cognitive Science* 18, no. 4 (1994): 513–49.

Knight, James. "Was Roma the Scarlet Harlot? The Worship of the Goddess." In *Religious Rivalries and the Struggle for Success in Sardis and Smyrna*, edited by Richard S. Ascough, 107–16. Waterloo, ON: Wilfrid Laurier University Press, 2005.

Knorr Cetina, Karin. "How Superorganisms Change: Consensus Formation and the Social Ontology of High-Energy Physics Experiments." *Social Studies of Science* 25, no. 1 (1995): 119–47.

Knorr Cetina, Karin. *Epistemic Cultures: How the Sciences Make Knowledge*. Cambridge, MA: Harvard University Press, 1999.

Laato, Timo. *Paul and Judaism: An Anthropological Approach*. Atlanta, GA: Scholars Press, 1995.

Laqueur, Thomas Walter. *Making Sex: Body and Gender From the Greeks to Freud*. Cambridge, MA: Harvard University Press, 1990.

Latour, Bruno. "Why Has Critique Run Out of Steam? From Matters of Fact to Matters of Concern." *Critical Inquiry* 30, no. 2 (2004): 225–48.

Le Bon, Gustave. *The Crowd: A Study of the Popular Mind*. New York: Macmillian, 1897.

Lee, Cynthia. "Making Race Salient: Trayvon Martin and Implicit Bias in a Not Yet Post-Racial Society." *North Carolina Law Review* 91 (2013): 1555–612.

Lee, Michelle V. *Paul, the Stoics, and the Body of Christ*. Cambridge: Cambridge University Press, 2006.

Lendon, J. E. *Empire of Honour: The Art of Government in the Roman World*. New York: Oxford University Press, 1997.

Lewes, George Henry. *Problems of Life and Mind*. London: Trübner & Co., 1877.

Lieberman, M. D., A. Hariri, J. M. Jarcho, N. I. Eisenberger, and S. Y. Bookheimer. "An fMRI Investigation of Race-Related Amygdala Activity in African-American and Caucasian-American Individuals." *Nature Neuroscience* 8, no. 6 (2005): 720–22.

Loewer, Barry. "Review: Mind in a Physical World." *The Journal of Philosophy* 98, no. 6 (2001): 315–24.

Long, A. A. *Soul and Body in Stoicism*. Berkeley, CA: Center for Hermeneutical Studies, 1980.

MacDonald, Graham, and Cynthia MacDonald. *Emergence in Mind*. Oxford: Oxford University Press, 2010.

Mahner, Martin, and Mario Augusto Bunge. *Foundations of Biophilosophy*. New York: Springer, 1997.

Margulis, Lynn. *Origin of Eukaryotic Cells: Evidence and Research Implications for a Theory of the Origin and Evolution of Microbial, Plant, and Animal Cells on the Precambrian Earth*. New Haven, CT: Yale University Press, 1970.

Martin, Dale B. *The Corinthian Body*. New Haven, CT: Yale University Press, 1995.

Martyn, J. Louis. *Galatians: A New Translation With Introduction and Commentary*. New York: Doubleday, 1997.

Mayer-Kress, Gottfried, and Cathleen Barczys. "The Global Brain as an Emergent Structure From the Worldwide Computing Network, and Its Implications for Modeling." *The Information Society* 11, no. 1 (1995): 1–27.

Mazzarello, Paolo. *Golgi: A Biography of the Founder of Modern Neuroscience*. Translated by Aldo Badiani and Henry A. Buchtel. Oxford: Oxford University Press, 2010.

McKnight, Scot, and Joseph B. Modica, eds. *Jesus is Lord, Caesar is Not: Evaluating Empire in New Testament Studies*. Downers Grove, IL: InterVarsity Press, 2013.

McLaughlin, Brian P. "The Rise and Fall of British Emergentism." In *Emergence or Reduction? Essays on the Prospect of a Nonreductive Physicalism*, edited by Ansgar Beckerman, Hans Flohr, and Jaegwon Kim, 49–93. Berlin: Walter de Gruyter, 1992.

McRobie, A., G. Morgenthal, J. Lasenby, and M. Ringer. "Section Model Tests on Human-Structure Lock-in." *Proceedings of the Institution of Civil Engineers: Bridge Engineering* 156 (2003): 71–79.

Meeks, Wayne A. "The Image of the Androgyne: Some Uses of a Symbol in Earliest Christianity." *History of Religions* 13, no. 3 (1974): 165–208.

Mellor, Ronald. Θεα Ρωμη: *The Worship of the Goddess Roma in the Greek World*. Göttingen: Vandenhoeck & Ruprecht, 1975.

Menary, Richard, (ed.) *The Extended Mind*. Cambridge, MA: MIT Press, 2010.

Mirhaydari, Anthony. "Is the Market Overvalued?" *CBS News*, February 28, 2014, http://www.cbsnews.com/news/is-the-market-overvalued.

Mitchell, Margaret M. *Paul and the Rhetoric of Reconciliation: An Exegetical Investigation of the Language and Composition of 1 Corinthians*. Louisville, KY: Westminster John Knox Press, 1993.

Moore, G. E. *Philosophical Studies*. New York: Harcourt, 1922.

Moore, Stephen D. *God's Gym: Divine Male Bodies of the Bible*. New York: Routledge, 1996.

Moore, Stephen D. *Poststructural-Ism and the New Testament: Derrida and Foucault At the Foot of the Cross*. Minneapolis: Fortress Press, 1994.

Moore, Stephen D. "Metonymies of Empire: Sexual Humiliation and Gender Masquerade in the Book of Revelation." In *Postcolonial Interventions: Essays in Honor of R. S. Sugirtharajah*, edited by Tat-Siong Benny Liew, 71–97. Sheffield, UK: Sheffield Phoenix Press, 2010.

Murphy-O'Connor, Jerome. *Becoming Human Together: The Pastoral Anthropology of St. Paul*. 2d ed. Wilmington, DE: M. Glazier, 1982.

Nakamura, Shun-ichi. "Model for Lateral Excitation of Footbridges By Synchronous Walking." *Journal of Structural Engineering* 130, no. 1 (2004): 32–37.

Nelson, Derek R. *What's Wrong With Sin: Sin in Individual and Social Perspective From Schleiermacher to Theologies of Liberation*. New York: T & T Clark, 2009.

Noble, Denis. *The Music of Life: Biology Beyond the Genome*. New York: Oxford University Press, 2006.

Noble, Denis. "Genes and Causation." *Philosophical Transactions of the Royal Society A: Mathematical, Physical and Engineering Sciences* 366, no. 1878 (2008): 3001–15.

Noble, Denis. "Biophysics and Systems Biology." *Philosophical Transactions of the Royal Society* 368 (2010): 1125–39.

Noble, Denis. "A Theory of Biological Relativity: No Privileged Level of Causation." *Interface Focus* 2, no. 1 (2012): 55–64.

Nowak, Martin A., and Roger Highfield. *Supercooperators: Altruism, Evolution and Why We Need Each Other to Succeed*. New York: Free Press, 2011.

Nygren, Anders. *Commentary on Romans*. Translated by C. C. Rasmussen. Philadelphia: Fortress, 1949.

O'Connor, Timothy, and John Ross Churchill. "Nonreductive Physicalism or Emergent Dualism? The Argument From Mental Causation." In *The Waning of Materialism*, edited by Robert C. Koons, and George Bealer, 261–79. Oxford: Oxford University Press, 2010.

O'Connor, Timothy, and Hong, Yu Wong. "Emergent Properties." *Stanford Encyclopedia of Philosophy*, http://plato.stanford.edu/archives/spr2009/entries/properties-emergent.

Orlando, Joe. "TV Scenes We'd Like to See." *Mad Magazine* 1, no. 38 (1958): 42.

Patch, Howard Rollin. *The Goddess Fortuna in Mediaeval Literature*. Cambridge, MA: Harvard University Press, 1927.

Paxson, James J. *The Poetics of Personification*. New York: Cambridge University Press, 1994.

Payne, John W., James R. Bettman, and Eric J. Johnson. *The Adaptive Decision Maker*. Cambridge: Cambridge University Press, 1993.

Pettit, Philip. "Groups With Minds of Their Own." In *Socializing Metaphysics*, edited by Frederick F. Schmitt, 167–93. Lanham, MD: Rowman & Littlefield, 2003.

Pettit, Philip, and Michael Smith. "Freedom in Belief and Desire." *The Journal of Philosophy* (1996): 429–49.

Phelps, Elizabeth A., Kevin J. O'Connor, William A. Cunningham, E. Sumie Funayama, J. Christopher Gatenby, John C. Gore, and Mahzarin R. Banaji. "Performance on Indirect Measures of Race Evaluation Predicts Amygdala Activation." *Journal of Cognitive Neuroscience* (2000): 729–38.

Polanyi, Michael. *The Tacit Dimension*. New York: Doubleday, 1967.

Polanyi, Michael. "Life's Irreducible Structure." *Science* 160 (1968): 1308–12.

Price, S. R. F. *Rituals and Power: The Roman Imperial Cult in Asia Minor*. Cambridge: Cambridge University Press, 1984.

Prins, H. H. T. *Ecology and Behaviour of the African Buffalo: Social Inequality and Decision Making*. London: Chapman & Hall, 1996.

Prum, R. O., R. H. Torres, S. Williamson, and J. Dyck. "Coherent Light Scattering By Blue Feather Barbs." *Nature* 396, no. 6706 (1998): 28–29.

Rauschenbusch, Walter. *A Theology for the Social Gospel*. New York: The MacMillan Company, 1917.

Reed, Jonathan L. *The Harpercollins Visual Guide to the New Testament: What Archaeology Reveals About the First Christians*. 1st ed. New York: HarperOne, 2007.

Reeve, H. Kern, and Bert Hölldobler. "The Emergence of a Superorganism Through Intergroup Competition." *Proceedings of the National Academy of Sciences* 104, no. 23 (2007): 9736–40.

Rehak, Paul, and John G. Younger. *Imperium and Cosmos: Augustus and the Northern Campus Martius*. Madison: University of Wisconsin Press, 2006.

Reynolds, Barrie. *Magic, Divination, and Witchcraft Among the Barotse of Northern Rhodesia*. London: Chatto & Windus, 1963.

Reynolds, Joyce. "New Evidence for the Imperial Cult in Julio-Claudian Aphrodisias." *Zeitschrift für Papyrologie und Epigraphik Bonn* 43 (1981): 317–27.

Richerson, Peter J., and Robert Boyd. *Not By Genes Alone: How Culture Transformed Human Evolution*. Chicago: University of Chicago Press, 2004.

Ritschl, Albrecht. *The Christian Doctrine of Justification and Reconciliation: The Positive Development of the Doctrine*. Vol. III. Edinburgh: T & T Clark, 1900.

Rizzolatti, Giacomo, and Laila Craighero. "The Mirror-Neuron System." *Annual Review of Neuroscience* 27 (2004): 169–92.

Robinson, Douglas. *Feeling Extended: Sociality as Extended Body-Becoming-Mind*. Cambridge, MA: MIT Press, 2013.

Romero, Óscar Arnulfo. *La Voz de Los Sin Voz: La Palabra Viva de Monseñor Oscar Arnulfo Romero*. San Salvador, El Salvador: UCA Editores, 1980.

Romero, Óscar Arnulfo. *Voice of the Voiceless: The Four Pastoral Letters and Other Statements*. Translated by Michael J. Walsh. Maryknoll, NY: Orbis Books, 1985.

Rosen-Zvi, Ishay. *Demonic Desires: "Yetzer Hara" and the Problem of Evil in Late Antiquity*. Philadelphia: University of Pennsylvania Press, 2011.

Rovane, Carol Anne. *The Bounds of Agency: An Essay in Revisionary Metaphysics*. Princeton, NJ: Princeton University Press, 1997.

Rowlands, Mark. "The Extended Mind." *Zygon* 44, no. 3 (2009): 628–41.

Rowlands, Mark. "Consciousness, Broadly Construed." In *The Extended Mind*, edited by Richard Menary, 271–94. Cambridge, MA: MIT Press, 2010.

Sagan, Lynn. "On the Origin of Mitosing Cells." *Journal of Theoretical Biology* 14, no. 3 (1967): 225–74.

Sanburn, Josh. "All the Ways Darren Wilson Described Being Afraid of Michael Brown." *Time*, November 25, 2014. http://time.com/3605346/darren-wilson-michael-brown-demon.

Sanders, E. P. *Paul and Palestinian Judaism: A Comparison of Patterns of Religion*. Philadelphia: Fortress Press, 1977.

Sawyer, R. Keith. "Emergence in Sociology: Contemporary Philosophy of Mind and Some Implications for Sociological Theory." *The American Journal of Sociology* 107, no. 3 (2001): 551–85.

Sawyer, R. Keith. "Durkheim's Dilemma: Toward a Sociology of Emergence." *Sociological Theory* 20, no. 2 (2002): 227–47.

Sawyer, R. Keith. "Nonreductive Individualism Part Ii—Social Causation." *Philosophy of the Social Sciences* 33, no. 2 (2003): 203–24.

Sawyer, R. Keith. *Social Emergence: Societies as Complex Systems.* Cambridge: Cambridge University Press, 2005.

Sayers, Dorothy L. *Clouds of Witness.* New York: Harper & Row, 1955.

Scerri, E. R. "Top-Down Causation Regarding the Chemistry-Physics Interface: A Sceptical View." *Interface Focus* 2, no. 1 (2012): 20–25.

Schaefer, Richard T. *Racial and Ethnic Groups.* 4th ed. Glenview, IL: Scott Foresman/ Little Brown Higher Education, 1990.

Schleiermacher, Friedrich. *The Christian Faith.* Edited by H.R. Mackintosh, and J.S. Stewart. London: T & T Clark, 1999.

Searle, John R. *Freedom and Neurobiology: Reflections on Free Will, Language, and Political Power.* New York: Columbia University Press, 2007.

Searle, John R. *Philosophy in a New Century: Selected Essays.* Cambridge: Cambridge University Press, 2008.

Seeley, T. D. *The Wisdom of the Hive: The Social Physiology of Honey Bee Colonies.* Cambridge, MA: Harvard University Press, 1995.

Seeley, T. D. "Honey Bee Colonies Are Group-Level Adaptive Units." *The American Naturalist* 150, no. S1 (1997): 22–41.

Seeley, T. D., and S. C. Buhrman. "Group Decision Making in Swarms of Honey Bees." *Behavioral Ecology and Sociobiology* 45, no. 1 (1999): 19–31.

Segundo, Juan Luis. *Evolution and Guilt.* Maryknoll, NY: Orbis Books, 1974.

Skinner, Marilyn B. *Sexuality in Greek and Roman Culture.* Malden, MA: Blackwell, 2005.

Smith, Christian. *What is a Person?: Rethinking Humanity, Social Life, and the Moral Good From the Person Up.* Chicago: University of Chicago Press, 2011.

Smith, David L. *With Willful Intent: A Theology of Sin.* Wheaton, IL: BridgePoint, 1994.

Smith, John Maynard, and Eörs Szathmáry. *The Major Transitions in Evolution Revisited.* Cambridge, MA: MIT Press, 2011.

Smith, John Maynard, and Eörs Szathmáry. *The Major Transitions in Evolution.* Oxford: Oxford University Press, 1997.

Smith, R. R. R. "Simulacra Gentium: The Ethne From the Sebasteion At Aphrodisias." *The Journal of Roman Studies* 78 (1988): 50–77.

Southall, David J. *Rediscovering Righteousness in Romans: Personified Dikaiosynē Within Metaphoric and Narratorial Settings.* Tübingen, Germany: Mohr Siebeck, 2008.

Sperry, Roger Wolcott. "Hemisphere Deconnection and Unity in Conscious Awareness." *American Psychologist* 23 (1968): 723–33.

Sperry, Roger Wolcott. "A Modified Concept of Consciousness." *Psychological Review* 76, no. 6 (1969): 532–36.

Sperry, Roger Wolcott. "Mind-Brain Interaction: Mentalism, Yes; Dualism, No." *Neuroscience* 5, no. 2 (1980): 195–206.

Stendahl, Krister. "The Apostle Paul and the Introspective Conscience of the West." *The Harvard Theological Review* (1963): 199–215.

Stowers, Stanley K. *A Rereading of Romans: Justice, Jews, and Gentiles*. New Haven, CT: Yale University Press, 1997.

Stowers, Stanley K. "Paul's Four Discourses About Sin." In *Celebrating Paul: Festschrift in Honor of Jerome Murphy-O'Connor, O.P., and Joseph A. Fitzmyer, S.J*, edited by Peter Spitaler, 100–27. Washington, DC: Catholic Biblical Association of America, 2011.

Strogatz, Steven H., Daniel M. Abrams, Allan McRobie, Bruno Eckhardt, and Edward Ott. "Crowd Synchrony on the Millennium Bridge." *Nature* 438, no. 3 (2005): 43–44.

Suetonius. *Lives of the Caesars*. Translated by Catharine. Edwards. New York: Oxford University Press, 2000.

Swammerdam, Jan. *The Book of Nature: Or, the History of Insects*. Translated by Thomas Flloyd. London: C. G. Seyffert, 1758.

Swancutt, Diana M. "'The Disease of Effemination': The Charge of Effeminacy and the Verdict of God (Romans 1:18–2:16)." In *New Testament Masculinities*, edited by Stephen D. Moore and Janice Capel Anderson, 169–210. Atlanta, GA: Society of Biblical Lit, 2003.

Swancutt, Diana M. "Sexing the Pauline Body of Christ: Scriptural Sex in the Context of the American Christian Culture War." In *Toward a Theology of Eros: Transfiguring Passion At the Limits of Discipline*, edited by Virginia Burrus, and Catherine Keller, 65–98. New York: Fordham University Press, 2006.

Swancutt, Diana M. "Still Before Sexuality: 'Greek' Androgyny, the Roman Imperial Politics of Masculinity, and the Roman Invention of the Tribas." In *Mapping Gender in Ancient Religious Discourses*, edited by Todd Penner and Caroline Vander Stichele, 11–61. Boston: Brill, 2007.

Tamez, Elsa. *The Amnesty of Grace: Justification By Faith From a Latin American Perspective*. Nashville, TN: Abingdon Press, 1993.

Tamez, Elsa. "A Latin American Rereading of Romans 7." In *Translating the New Testament: Text, Translation, Theology*, edited by Stanley E. Porter and Mark J. Boda, 290–304. Grand Rapids, MI: Eerdmans, 2009.

Tannehill, Robert C. *Dying and Rising With Christ: A Study in Pauline Theology*. Berlin: Töpelmann, 1967.

Taylor, Jill. "Jill Bolte Taylor's Stroke of Insight." *TED: Ideas Worth Spreading*, February 2008, http://www.ted.com/index.php/talks/jill_bolte_taylor_s_powerful_stroke_of_insight.html.

Taylor, John V. *The Primal Vision: Christian Presence Amid African Religion*. Philadelphia: Fortress Press, 1963.

Teilhard de Chardin, Pierre. *The Phenomenon of Man*. Translated by Bernard Wall and Julian Huxley. New York: Harper Torchbooks, 1959.

Theiner, Georg. "From Extended Minds to Group Minds: Rethinking the Boundaries of the Mental." PhD diss., Indiana University, 2008.

Theiner, Georg, Colin Allen, and Robert L. Goldstone. "Recognizing Group Cognition." *Cognitive Systems Research* 11, no. 4 (2010): 378–95.

Theiner, Georg, and Timothy O'Connor. "The Emergence of Group Cognition." In *Emergence in Science and Philosophy*, edited by Antonella Corradini and Timothy O'Connor, 78–119. New York: Routledge, 2009.

Tobin, Thomas H. "The Jewish Context of Rom 5:12–14." *Studia Philonica Annual* 13 (2001): 159–75.

Tollefsen, Deborah Perron. "From Extended Mind to Collective Mind." *Cognitive Systems Research* (2006): 140–50.

Tomasello, Michael. *The Cultural Origins of Human Cognition*. Cambridge, MA: Harvard University Press, 1999.

Tomasello, Michael. *Constructing a Language: A Usage-Based Theory of Language Acquisition*. Cambridge, MA: Harvard University Press, 2005.

Tomasello, Michael, and Malinda Carpenter. "Shared Intentionality." *Developmental Science* 10, no. 1 (2007): 121–25.

Tomasello, Michael, Malinda Carpenter, Josep Call, Tanya Behne, and Henrike Moll. "Understanding and Sharing Intentions: The Origins of Cultural Cognition." *Behavioral and Brain Sciences* 28 (2005): 675–735.

Turner, Harold. "The Primal Religions of the World and Their Study." In *Australian Essays in World Religions*, edited by Victor C. Hayes, 27–37. Bedford Park, Australia: Australian Association for the Study of Religions, 1977.

Twin, Alexandra. "Dow's Biggest 2-Day Run Since '87." *CNN Money*, November 24, 2008, http://money.cnn.com/2008/11/24/markets/markets_newyork/index.htm.

Van Gulick, Robert. "Reduction, Emergence, and Other Recent Options on the Mind/Body Problem: A Philosophic Overview." *Journal of Consciousness Studies* 8, nos. 9–10 (2001): 1–34.

Venter, J. Craig. *A Life Decoded: My Genome, My Life*. New York: Viking, 2007.

Vermeule, Cornelius Clarkson. *The Goddess Roma in the Art of the Roman Empire*. London: Spink, 1959.

wa Gatumu, Albert Kabiro. *The Pauline Concept of Supernatural Powers: A Reading From the African Worldview*. Colorado Springs, CO: Paternoster, 2008.

Wallace, Julia. "Workers of the World, Faint!" *New York Times*, 2014, SR4.

Walls, Andrew F. *The Missionary Movement in Christian History: Studies in the Transmission of Faith*. Maryknoll, NY: Orbis Books, 1996.

Walters, Jonathan. "Invading the Roman Body: Manliness and Impenetrability in Roman Thought." In *Roman Sexualities*, edited by Judith P. Hallett, and Marilyn B. Skinner, 29–43. Princeton, NJ: Princeton University Press, 1997.

Wan, Poe Yu-ze. "Emergence à la Systems Theory: Epistemological Totalausschluss or Ontological Novelty?" *Philosophy of the Social Sciences* 41, no. 2 (2011): 178–210.

Wasserman, Emma. *The Death of the Soul in Romans 7: Sin, Death, and the Law in Light of Hellenistic Moral Psychology*. Vol. 256, *Wissenschaftliche Untersuchungen Zum Neuen Testament*. Tübingen, Germany: Mohr Siebeck, 2008.

Wasserman, Emma. "Paul Among the Philosophers: The Case of Sin in Romans 6–8." *Journal for the Study of the New Testament* 30, no. 4 (2008): 387–415.

Wheeler, L. R. *Vitalism: Its History and Validity*. London: H. F. & G. Witherby Ltd, 1939.

Wheeler, W. M. "The Ant-Colony as an Organism." *Journal of Morphology* 22 (1912): 307–25.

White, Hayden. "The Historical Text as Literary Artifact." In *Tropics of Discourse: Essays in Cultural Criticism*, 81–100. Baltimore: Johns Hopkins University Press, 1978.

Whitman, Jon. *Allegory: The Dynamics of an Ancient and Medieval Technique*. Cambridge, MA: Harvard University Press, 1987.

Williams, Craig A. *Roman Homosexuality: Ideologies of Masculinity in Classical Antiquity*. New York: Oxford University Press, 1999.

Williams, David R. "Race, Socioeconomic Status, and Health the Added Effects of Racism and Discrimination." *Annals of the New York Academy of Sciences* 896 (1999): 173–88.

Williams, G. C. *Adaptation and Natural Selection: A Critique of Some Current Evolutionary Thought*. Princeton, NJ: Princeton University Press, 1966.

Wilson, David Sloan. "Altruism and Organism: Disentangling the Themes of Multilevel Selection Theory." *The American Naturalist* 150, no. S1 (1997): S122–33.

Wilson, David Sloan. *Darwin's Cathedral: Evolution, Religion, and the Nature of Society*. Chicago: University of Chicago Press, 2003.

Wilson, David Sloan, and Elliott Sober. "Reviving the Superorganism." *Journal of Theoretical Biology* 136 (1989): 337–56.

Wilson, David Sloan, and Elliott Sober. "Reintroducing Group Selection to the Human Behavioral Sciences." *Behavioral and Brain Sciences* 17 (1994): 585–654.

Wilson, David Sloan, Mark Van Vugt, and Rick O'Gorman. "Multilevel Selection Theory and Major Evolutionary Transitions." *Current Directions in Psychological Science* 17, no. 1 (2008): 6–9.

Wilson, Edward O. *The Social Conquest of Earth*. New York: Liveright, 2012.

Wilson, Robert A. *Boundaries of the Mind: The Individual in the Fragile Sciences*. Cambridge: Cambridge University Press, 2004.

Wimsatt, William C. "Reductionism and Its Heuristics: Making Methodological Reductionism Honest." *Synthese* 151, no. 3 (2006): 445–75.

Wink, Walter. *Naming the Powers*. Philadelphia: Fortress, 1984.

Winkler, John J. *The Constraints of Desire: The Anthropology of Sex and Gender in Ancient Greece*. New York: Routledge, 1990.

Wright, N. T. *The Letter to the Romans: Introduction, Commentary, and Reflections*. Vol. X. *The New Interpreter's Bible*. Nashville, TN: Abingdon, 2002.

INDEX

Note: 'figures are indicated by an italic "f" following the page/paragraph number.'

Printed in the USA/Agawam, MA
August 6, 2018

680099.009